Emergent Forms

Emergent Forms

*Origins and Early Development
of Human Action and Perception*

EUGENE C. GOLDFIELD
Children's Hospital, Boston

New York   Oxford
OXFORD UNIVERSITY PRESS
1995

For Peter H. Wolff, M.D.

Oxford University Press

Oxford   New York   Toronto
Delhi   Bombay   Calcutta   Madras   Karachi
Kuala Lumpur   Singapore   Hong Kong   Tokyo
Nairobi   Dar es Salaam   Cape Town
Melbourne   Auckland   Madrid

and associated companies in
Berlin   Ibadan

Library of Congress Cataloging-in-Publication Data
Goldfield, Eugene Curtis.
Emergent forms: origins and early development of human action and perception
Eugene C. Goldfield.
p.   cm.   Includes bibliographical references and index.
ISBN 0-19-506589-1   ISBN 0-19-509502-2 (pbk.)
1. Motor ability in infants. 2. Intentionalism. I. Title.
BF720.M69G65   1995
155.42'223—dc20   94-18639

9 8 7 6 5 4 3 2 1

Printed in the United States of America
on acid-free paper

PREFACE

This is a book that addresses the processes by which humans discover how to use the body to perform different functions. For example, young infants may use the hands to grasp an object, bring food to the mouth, or support the body while prone during locomotion. What functions of the brain have evolved that are able to transform a body part like the hand into a variety of special-purpose tools, such as a grabber or lifter? The book adopts a functionalist, developmental, and dynamic systems framework for examining this question (see, e.g., Goldfield, 1989, 1993). At the heart of this approach is the idea that humans begin life with an aggregate of degrees of freedom (neurons, muscles, bones, etc.) that become assembled into a variety of specialized means of action in different task settings. The central theme throughout the book is that human action systems continue a biological strategy evident in the earliest multicellular animals: *a sharing of limited resources among populations of microscopic entities with specialized functions.* In particular, I argue that the ontogeny of human action may be governed by the dynamics of energy sharing between populations of neurons and skeleto-muscular elements under task constraints.

Each particular action system is a functional class of behavior which has evolved in the human species and continues to develop during ontogeny in response to particular environmental pressures (Pick, 1989; Reed, 1982). These classes of behavior include orientation, eating and drinking, locomotion, investigation, manipulation, emotional expression, and communication. So, for example, the availability of particular nutrients and metabolites (resources) in the context of human evolutionary history resulted in the evolution both of an orienting system to find these nutrients and an appetitive system (mouth, digestive tract, and organized sucking and swallowing) that is prepared to ingest them. Ontogeny continues the assembly of action systems at a shorter time scale (an individual lifetime), and perception regulates the assembly of action systems at the microgenetic time scale of seconds. One goal of the book, therefore, is to understand *how actions organized in real time and embedded within evolutionary and ontogenetic time scales make use of available resources.*

How do action systems develop? Each action system consists of microscopic component degrees of freedom (e.g., neurons, muscles, skeletal links and joints) that aggregate (self-organize) into stable "preferred" modes under certain conditions and not others. A particular dynamic of component degrees of freedom assembles *only when they can be used together to achieve a common goal.* For example, as prone infants attempt to approach a toy placed at a distance, the efforts of reaching, kicking, and balancing the body above the surface result in the coordination of these different functional acts into a locomotor pattern. It is the intention to approach the object that binds together the component degrees of freedom. Another objective of the book, then, is to explore *how action systems develop by assembling whatever means are available at a particular point in time to perform specific goal-directed activities.*

The book also adopts an ecological approach to action and its development: the idea that behavioral order emerges from the competitive and cooperative relationship between the various components of the action system, including the environment. Competition and cooperation occur in changing habitats, such as the uterus and the social environment provided by the adult. A third goal of the book, therefore, is to understand *how the ontogeny of action fits within the changing habitats of the early development of humans.* Extending the work of the Gibsons (e.g., J. J. Gibson, 1966, 1979; E. J. Gibson, 1982, 1988) with concepts from developmental psychobiology (e.g., Hall & Oppenheim, 1987) is central to this task.

The perspective offered here is distinctive from "motor" theories because of its emphasis on the cooperativity between the brain and body. Motor approaches assume that the brain "commands" the muscles (see, e.g., Kupferman & Weiss, 1978). The lessons of the Russian physiologist Bernstein (1967), however, imply that the brain is designed to adapt to the dynamics of the body (e.g., the forces generated during movement) and to changes in dynamics with growth. Thus, besides self-organization, action systems develop by a process of *selecting parameters that fit the assembled components to the task.* So, for example, the brain appears to have evolved to transform the body into a variety of special-purpose "devices," a collection of simple biological "machines" (e.g., the bones as levers and the muscles as adjustable springs) by setting parameters that fit the resources of the body to the task. As infants explore the body during spontaneous activity, different parameter settings of muscular "springs" may be used for obtaining particular resources. A fourth goal, therefore, is to examine *how active exploration allows the child to regulate the properties of the body, conceived as biophysical devices, so that these devices are suitably adapted to a particular task.*

Another implication of Bernstein's work on dynamics concerns the processes by which functional acts form cooperative arrangements under certain conditions, disassemble, and then reassemble to form new "alliances." Studies of organizational transitions during quadrupedal gait (e.g., Hoyt & Taylor, 1981) and adult coordination (Kelso & Tuller, 1985) indicate that such transitions occur at critical values of some parameter (e.g., velocity). The phenomenon of coordination and the transitions between organized behavioral states have recently been the focus of a "dynamic-systems" approach in development, using the tools of qualitative geometry to describe the conditions under which systems remain stable or enter new patterns (e.g., Goldfield, 1993; Smith & Thelen, 1993; Thelen & Smith, 1994; Wolff, 1993). During the development of action in humans, there are abrupt transitions to new stable states—for example, in the sleep–wake patterns of newborns, in bimanual activity, and in locomotion. A fifth goal of this book, therefore, is *to examine the emergence of novel forms of behavior.*

The book is organized into four parts: Part I examines the ecological and dynamic foundations of the present approach and issues in the development of action. The chapters of Part II present concepts from the study of self-organizing systems, the biological origins of cooperativity (assembly), and contemporary views on selection (tuning) as background for a developmental theory of human action systems. Each of the chapters in Part III focuses on the development of a particular action system—orienting, locomoting, etc.—using the ideas developed in the first two parts as a framework. Then, in Part IV, I consider applications and implications—for example, the use of an action–systems approach to aid the clinician in the assessment and treatment of "motor" disturbances.

Boston, Massachusetts   E.C.G.
April 1994

ACKNOWLEDGMENTS

Some of the research reported here was supported by National Research Service Award 1F32MH 09056 from the National Institute of Mental Health, and grant R01HD 31139 from the National Institute of Child Health and Human Development.

My sincerest thanks to the following individuals who made important contributions to this book at different points in its gestation and birth: Michael Turvey and Bob Shaw at the Center for the Ecological Study of Perceiving and Acting, University of Connecticut, for introducing me to the ideas of Gibson and Bernstein, and for their inspiration as professors; Elliot Saltzman at Haskins Laboratories for his deep insights into dynamics and for his generosity in sharing ideas; Bruce Kay and Bill Warren at Brown University for helping me to apply dynamics to infant development; George Michel at dePauw University for his particular slant on postural development in infants; Esther Thelen at Indiana University, for inviting me to share my ideas on dynamics and development at a number of forums over the years; Herb Pick at the University of Minnesota for his encouragement and his insights into action systems; and Ed Reed at Franklin and Marshall College for helping me to put Darwin in an ecological and developmental perspective, and for taking the time to read the manuscript with a critical eye. Thanks also to Sherri Gardner at Children's Hospital for compiling the author index, and to Joan Bossert at Oxford University Press for her patience and good cheer. Finally, this book could not have been written without the love and support of my wife, Beverly, and my daughter Anna. My love and thanks to them for understanding all those times when I had to sit at the computer and couldn't come out to play.

CONTENTS

11. The Performatory Action System: Manual Activity

PART IV   CONCLUSION

Part I
Dynamic and Ecological Foundations

The motor activity of organisms is of enormous biological significance – it is practically the only way in which the organism not only interacts with the surrounding environment, but also actively operates on this environment, altering it with respect to particular results.

Nikolai Bernstein, 1967, p. 343

As is clear in the quotation from Bernstein's classic book, *The coordination and regulation of movements*, action is a fundamental part of adaptive life. But what is action, and how are actions performed? With the advent of the cognitive revolution of the 1960s, the study of action fell into the background and became simply "output" in a flowchart of information processing. Emerging from eddies of more recent currents of thought in the 1990s, the freshly minted field of cognitive science is beginning to appreciate action in the fundamental sense recognized by Bernstein (see, e.g., Jordan & Rosenbaum, 1989). The chapters of this part offer the dynamic and ecological foundations of the book from the fields of physical biology (see, e.g., Jeka & Kelso, 1989; Kelso, Ding, & Schoner, 1993; Turvey, 1990; Yates, 1987) and ecological psychology (e.g., Kugler & Turvey, 1987; Shaw, Turvey, & Mace, 1982).

The ecological approach of the Gibsons. Reed (1988a) traces the history of the ecological study of perception through a biography of James J. Gibson, its originator. Other volumes (e.g., Lombardo, 1987), including collected writings (e.g., Reed & Jones, 1982), provide an historical perspective on J. J. Gibson's work, as well as a chronicle of the contributions of Eleanor J. Gibson in her studies of human development (see her collected writings; E. J. Gibson, 1991). J. J. Gibson considered himself a functionalist, in the tradition of William James, E. B. Holt, Edward Tolman, and Leonard Troland, and also acknowledged the work of the Gestalt psychologists, especially Kurt Koffka. These two influences are apparent in the goals of an ecological research program which Gibson outlined in his last book, *The ecological approach to visual*

1

perception: (1) to describe the environment at the level of ecology, (2) to describe the information available for perception (ecological optics), and (3) to describe the extraction of invariants as the basis for perception (J. J. Gibson, 1979).

Gibson referred to his research program as *ecological* because it assumed a mutuality between animal and environment—that is, a proper analysis of the environment is one scaled to the size and masses of the animals that populate it. To capture the notion of an environment scaled to the size of an animal, Gibson proposed that the environment consisted of a nesting of "forms within forms both up and down the scale of size" (p. 9). However, Gibson was careful in distinguishing the idea of nesting from a hierarchy of atomistic elements, and proposed subordinate and superordinate units.

A second, and equally radical, way that Gibson attempted to scale the environment to the properties of animals was his proposal that while a particular composition and layout of the environment was invariant for all living creatures on the planet, its "values" and "meanings" were scaled to the size, form, and capabilities of different living forms. These meanings or "affordances" are "what it offers the animal, what it provides or furnishes, either for good or ill" (p. 127). For example, a surface that is horizontal, flat, extended, and rigid affords support for the postural requirements of only certain body morphologies and certain sizes.

Gibson also offered important insights into how perceptual systems adapt to the layout of the environment, and proposed five perceptual systems, each with a particular function or mode of attention (see Table I.1). He argued that each of these perceptual systems was able to detect properties of the environment through a process of active exploration, which was investigated intensively in developmental work by Eleanor Gibson (see, e.g., E. J. Gibson, 1969, 1982, 1988), which will be discussed in detail in Chapter 3.

Table I.1. The perceptual systems

Perceptual System	Organ Involved	Activity	Obtained Information
Basic orienting	Vestibular organs; mechanoreceptors	Body equilibrium	Direction of gravity (unstable equilibrium)
Auditory	Cochlear organs with middle ear and auricle	Orienting to sounds	Nature and location of vibratory events
Haptic	Skin, joints, muscles	Active touch	Object shapes; material states
Taste-smell	Nasal-oral cavity	Sniffing, savoring	Volatile sources; nutritive and biochemical values
Visual	Eyes, head, and body	Accommodation, fixation, convergence, exploration	Variables of optic structure

Source: After J. J. Gibson, 1966.

Gibson proposed that in addition to exploratory activity, animals used the perceptual systems to guide performatory activity, such as locomotion, eating, etc. However, he left it as a challenge to his students and colleagues to specify in greater detail how environmental properties guided performatory activity, and there have been several attempts to do so, including one based on the work of Nikolai Bernstein and D'Arcy Thompson (see, e.g., Turvey, 1990; Turvey, Fitch, & Tuller, 1982), and one based more broadly on Darwinian thought in biology (Reed, 1985). Because Bernstein constitutes a significant foundation for the work of this book, I consider him briefly here, and in greater detail in later chapters.

Bernstein. It is fitting in this era of renewed Russian–American cooperation that we look to the work of a Russian physiologist, Nikolai Bernstein (1967; and see Whiting, 1984). In much the same way that Gibson worked to rid psychology of the idea that the foundation of perception was "sensation," Bernstein objected to the reflex arc as the basis for movement. He assumed instead that "the reflex is not an element of action but just elementary action" (Gelfand, Gurfinkel, Fomin, & Tsetlin, 1971), and saw the appropriate domain as "the setting and realization of behaviorally significant goals" (Boylls & Greene, 1984).

Turvey (1977; Turvey, Shaw, & Mace, 1978) offers one starting point for using Bernstein's insights as a means of solving the Gibsonian puzzle of perceptually guided action. With regard to coordination, in Turvey's early work, he and his colleagues introduced the concept of coordinative structure, "a group of muscles often spanning several joints that is constrained to act as a unit." Collecting muscles in this way was offered as a solution to Bernstein's degrees-of-freedom problem—that is, how to functionally collect the large number of degrees of freedom of the skeletomuscular articulators so that an animal has to merely select a "ballpark" of possible organizations of the articulators, and not the state of each articulator.

In keeping with Bernstein's distinction between coordination and regulation, Turvey (1978) proposes a separate process of tuning by which coordinative structures are "tailored" to current contingencies within the "ballpark." It is in the regulatory process of tuning that Bernstein and Gibson meet.

Newer theoretical work with Kugler and Kelso (e.g., Kugler, Kelso, & Turvey, 1980, 1982) developed the dynamic aspects of coordinative structures by identifying them as *dissipative*—that is, as "metabolic processes that degrade more free energy than the drift toward equilibrium" (Kugler et al., 1980, p. 17). The most recent work (see, e.g., Turvey, 1988, 1990, which is discussed in detail in Chapter 2) treats the problem of coordination with respect to lawful relations among variables at a macroscopic scale. In these later models of the perceptual guidance of action, tuning is understood with respect to the use of the indefinite nesting of optical structure. This analysis is as yet in its infancy, but at its heart is understanding how to translate Gibson's ideas about the nesting of optical structure into concepts from qualitative geometry (e.g., Abraham & Shaw, 1987; Mandelbrot, 1982; Warren, 1988b).

Reed (1982) has adopted a different tack in approaching Gibson's challenge to understand the role of perception in action, one which takes as a starting point Bernstein's "physiology of activity" and the idea that

> the animal is in continual disequilibrium with its environment, requiring not that it react to stimuli, but rather that it act all the time and that it constantly evaluate its actions with respect to ever-changing current conditions, while at the same time modulate its activities so as to meet its needs and goals within the environment. Bernstein's evaluator function is performed by *perceptual systems* which actively explore stimulation and his modulation function is accomplished by *action systems* which construct, coordinate, and adjust the animal's movements, so as to perform adaptively in its environment. (Reed, 1982, p. 109)

J. J. Gibson (1966) offered a list of performatory systems parallel to the exploratory functions of his perceptual systems, and Reed (1982) has elaborated on these with reference to the environmental resources and cycles of activity that gain resources from a particular habitat. Reed calls these *action systems*, and his taxonomy of action systems (see Table I.2) is used in this book to organize the content of chapters in Part III.

Reed (1982) proposes that action systems are specific functional collections of *postures* and *movements*, and he categorizes each action system on the basis of the environmental properties or *resources* that it enables the animal to exploit. This follows both from Darwin's claim that functional differences in animals are the result of selective pressures owing to competition for environmental resources, and from Gibson's demonstration that, in different

Table I.2. The action systems

Action System	Activity	Achieved Goals
Basic orienting	Control posture	Maintain head, torso upright
Locomotion	Approach, avoidance, steering	Change body position relative to surface layout
Appetition	Ingest foodstuffs	Satisfy hunger, thirst
Performatory	Reach for, hold, and explore objects	Bring objects close to body for inspection by mouth, hands
Expressive	Facial expressions	Regulate own arousal, energy expenditure, and control behavior of others

Source: Modified from Reed, 1982.

animals, different types of organs evolved to detect the same kind of information. For example, Gibson (1966) shows how various kinds of eyes evolved independently, but that all of them belong to the functional category "visual system," because it is this system alone which exploits a single kind of resource, the information available in light.

In his theory of information pickup, J. J. Gibson (1966, 1979) argues that because of the nested nature of information, the process of perceptual activity is necessarily cyclical.

Reed (1982) carries this argument further. He makes a compelling case against arbitrary separation of afferent and efferent activity, and offers instead a cyclical process of activity under mixed control. It is for this reason that Reed (1982, 1988a) often refers to action systems as modes, or functionally organized perception–action cycles of activity.

CHAPTER 1

FUNDAMENTAL ISSUES AND PERSPECTIVES IN THE DEVELOPMENT OF ACTION

> The perspectives of action as being (a) dynamic, (b) relational, (c) multidimensional, and (d) multileveled are, I think, obvious—but much more work is needed in fleshing out the deeper implications of these perspectives. An especially fascinating theme, in this context, is how underlying control systems (however and at whatever level we define them) can exhibit a necessary dynamic balance between tendencies toward interaction and self-organization.
>
> Fentress, 1990, p. 4

In this chapter, I examine the balance between self-organization and interaction, because these two processes are central to a theory that explains the development of action systems. The issues central to this discussion include: (1) the relation between spontaneous activity (synonymous with self-organization and order) and regulation, (2) the regulatory roles of perceptual input, (3) the nesting of local cycles of activity within more macroscopic temporal cyles, and (4) the emergence of novel forms, or innovations. After examining each of these issues we turn to several developmental perspectives as background for the developmental model offered here. Before addressing developmental concerns, I turn to a broader issue in the "motor control" literature—namely, the distinction between "motor" and "action."

THE MOTOR–ACTION CONTROVERSY

Motor system versus action system. In the traditional information processing perspective within cognitive science, the use of the term "motor system" refers to the brain and spinal cord as they perform computations on current and previously stored information and generate sets of instructions or commands that are translated into muscle activations and the generation of forces that lead to displacements (movements). Ghez (1985), for example,

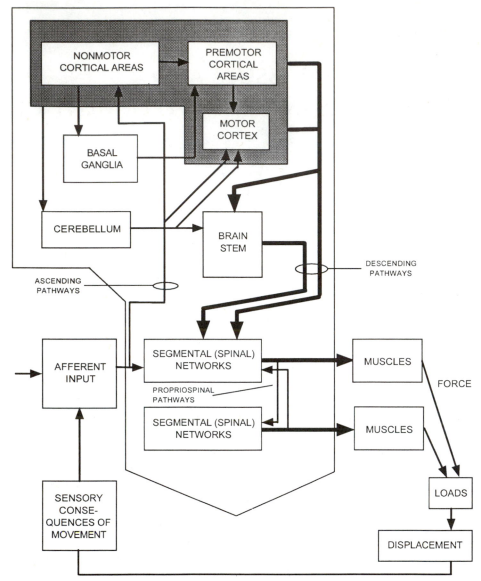

Figure 1.1. Components of the motor system. Arrows denote strong influences. Crossing of pathways is not indicated and the thalamus has been omitted for clarity. (Adapted from Ghez, 1985. Copyright © 1986 by Elsevier Press, Inc. Reprinted by permission.)

schematizes the major components of the motor system as a hierarchy of components (see Fig. 1.1).

Conspicuously absent in this diagram is any indication of what the actor is doing. The end effector is simply conceived as a muscle performing some work. To what tasks do the forces generated relate? What functional organization of the muscles are required for particular tasks? Studying action must certainly include an attempt to understand the role of brain and muscle (see Chapter 5), but also implicates the body and the task (cf. J. J. Gibson, 1979). In the approach of this book, the subject matter of interest is the functional organization of the body as it performs specific tasks relative to the surfaces and media of the environment. Actions are made possible by action systems, which Pick (1989) describes as follows:

> These are considered to be very general functional classes of behavior that have evolved in diverse species in response to common environmental pressures. Such general activities as orienting behavior, communicative behavior, consummatory behavior, reproductive behavior, locomotion, object manipulation, and so on, exemplify action systems. (p. 868)

The difference between the motor systems approach captured in Fig. 1.1 and the one to be developed in these pages constitutes what Beek and Meijer (1988) call the "motor-action controversy," and is outlined in Table 1.1. A fundamental distinction between these two views is in the way they treat the relation between dynamics and information. In the motor view, the role of information is to adjust or correct movement relative to some internalized standard. While it is recognized that some movement may be "open loop" (i.e., there is no mechanism for detecting the changes due to the system's generated response; Stelmach & Requin, 1980), a large class of movements is believed to be "closed loop" (e.g., Adams, 1984; Schmidt, 1988; see also Fig. 1.2), error sensitive, and error corrective. There is a reference of correctness in which feedback from the system's response is compared with the reference to determine the degree of error. The system then operates to eliminate error.

Table 1.1. Distinctions between the "motor" and "action" perspectives

Motor Systems	Action Systems
Perception is indirect; i.e., meaning is added to sensations via inferences and comparisons on the basis of internal representations	Perception is direct; i.e., information is specific to its source by virtue of active pickup by the observer. The same information has many potential meanings
Coordination and control of the large number of degrees of freedom of the motor apparatus is realized by commands from an *a priori* existing program	Coordination and control are localized in the organism-environment system as a whole. The CNS has evolved to harness degrees of freedom in order to minimize responsibility in control
Motor learning involves association of sensory and central information with motor responses	Learning involves modification of parameters as a consequence of exploration of a perception–action workspace
During development, invariant reflexes and hardwired central programs become organized into a hierarchical control system	During development, flexibly assembled task-specific devices (functions) are distilled out of an aggregate of degrees of freedom

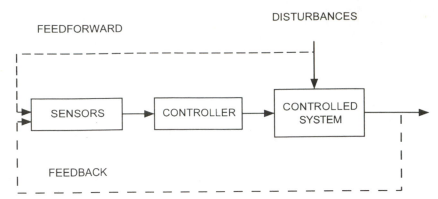

Figure 1.2. Open- versus closed-loop control. In open -loop (feedforward) control, no sensory guidance is used for agonist or antagonist muscle commands. In feedforward mode, regulation is based on sensed disturbances. In feedback, regulation is based on the sensed effects that disturbances have on the regulated variables. (Adapted from Brooks, 1986. Copyright © 1986 by Oxford University Press, Inc. Reprinted by permission.)

Figure 1.3 portrays in schematic form the contrasting action perspective adopted here with reference to how information is used by an animal adapting to the demands of changing ecological niches. Here, information is not a quantity to be stored, but rather is a relation among properties distributed over animal and environment (Ghiselin, 1981; Reed, 1982; Kugler & Turvey, 1987);

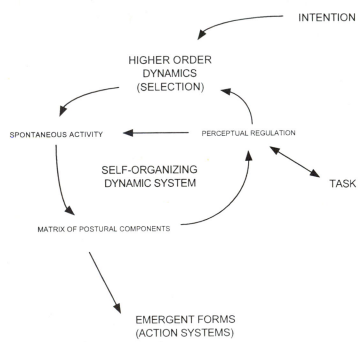

Figure 1.3. The processes involved in the emergence of action systems.

not a reference for correcting movement error, but a supportive medium for the process of selecting a particular functional relation from a population of functions (cf. Saltzman & Munhall, 1992). And finally, control systems are not organized into fixed cybernetic loops of feedback and feedforward, but rather are "softly assembled" perception–action cycles characterized by changing patterns of neural and biomechanical resonance. Much of this contrasting terminology needs to be unpacked, and that is the goal of later chapters in the first part of the book.

Contrasting assumptions. Returning to Table 1.1, several other issues highlight the distinction between the motor and action views. These issues relate to the historical and philosophical origins of these perspectives, and I will argue throughout this book that the study of development (both comparative development and human ontogeny) provides unique opportunities for testing the assumptions of the action perspective with respect to these issues. Toward that end, the chapters in Part II are organized with these issues in mind, for example, by considering how a particular action system evolves in an *ecological context*, how the earliest functional capabilities of humans *adapt to the task demands of our culture*, and how an initial collection of dynamic systems is transformed via ontogenetic experience into a collection of functionally adapted action systems.

The distinction between the motor and action views is no more clearly articulated than with respect to the question of the relation between an animal and its environment (Schmidt, 1988; Turvey & Shaw, 1978). The motor view adopts two assumptions of *indirect perception*. Namely, the senses are provided with an impoverished description of the world, and animals and their environment are treated as independent entities (Michaels & Carello, 1981)

According to Gibson's thesis of direct perception (J. J. Gibson, 1966, 1979; Michaels & Carello, 1981), by contrast, (1) specification of the nature of objects, places, and events is directly available to an animal, and (2) as it actively explores the environment, an animal's structure and function influence the selection of information so that it is useful for achieving particular goals. In other words, *by virtue of the evolutionary history of mobility of animals on our planet, there can be no logical distinction between animal and environment*. Moreover, it is because of these two assumptions that action theorists pursue the kinds of questions that distinguish their research programs from those adopting the motor view, for example, how perceived information is scaled to the size and form of the perceiver (see, e.g., Warren, 1988a); and how actors use body-generated optical flow to guide their locomotion (J. J. Gibson, 1979; Lee & Young, 1986). Information, then, is defined in terms of both the animal and the environment (Turvey, 1988).

Units. A second issue that contrasts the motor and action views concerns the nature of units underlying coordinated activity (Kelso & Tuller, 1981; Turvey, Fitch, & Tuller, 1982). The motor view, as represented by Gallistel (1980), asserts that there are three elementary units of behavior: the reflex, the oscillator, and the servomechanism. A variety of processes (including inhibition and chaining) are used to organize these elements into a hierarchically structured motor system.

The conclusion that distinctly different kinds of observable behavior (reflexive, rhythmic, and coordinated movements) must have unique physio-logical units generating them is based on Gallistel's review of the elegant research of Sherrington, von Holst, and Weiss, respectively. For example, he notes that in the scratch and stepping reflexes studied by Sherrington, the timing of the response is independent of the timing of the stimulus and, thus, must be autonomous of the stimulus. Gallistel then turns to the work of von Holst, who discovered that rhythmic fin movements in fish seemed to be generated autonomously and, thus, embraces the assumption that such rhythms reflect a "neural metronome," a unit distinct from the reflex. He similarly discusses the work of Weiss to explain how movements become coordinated. Weiss performed experiments in which he reversed a salaman-der's front limbs so that they pointed backward rather than forward, having the effect of propelling the salamander backward. Weiss's conclusion was that units controlling the front and hind limbs were constrained by some central program to produce a particular pattern of stepping by the four limbs.

On the basis of his review of these classic works, Gallistel proposes higher level units that potentiate (increase the potential for action) some lower units and depotentiate others. However, by turning briefly to early human development, we encounter reasons to suspect that units with isolated functions do not capture the richness of infant behavior. For example, it is often difficult to classify an infant's behavior as either reflexive or rhythmic. Neonatal sucking may be elicited, but also appears spontaneously; newborns will grasp an object placed in their fingers, but will also move their fingers spontaneously at the sight of an object; they will orient the head to the side on which their cheek is stroked, but will also actively orient to a sound on one side. Must we, therefore, assume that under different circumstances the same behavior is controlled by different units?

In the chapters that follow, I will argue, as do Fentress (e.g, 1984), Reed (1982), and Woolridge (1975), that behavior is *dynamic, relational, and multileveled*, and that the idea of "units as pieces" does not adequately capture this richness. Instead, I adopt the view that *distinct actions are composed of continuous changes in co-occurring individual dimensions.* Fentress (1984) articulates this beautifully as follows:

the relative movements of limb segments plus their combined action can be traced, yielding a picture rather like a complex musical score, where it is the blending of the different parts that provides the overall orchestral cohesion. (p. 106)

A related issue concerns the extent to which we may attribute observable changes in behavior to developmental changes in the brain and spinal cord. A classical perspective on the role of the brain in locomotor activity comes from the work of McGraw (1945):

> Developmental changes in overt behavior are associated with advancement in cortical maturation. Cortical maturation is reflected in behavior by the suppression or diminution of certain activities and by the emergence and integration of other neuromuscular performances ... Development tends to proceed in a cephalocaudal direction. (p. 12)

McGraw's view reflects a traditional strategy in the study of the relation between brain and behavior following from the work of Coghill (1929) and Conel (1929): correlating features of anatomy with observable changes in behavior. A problem with this approach is that it assumes that behavior directly reflects brain growth, unmediated by any other growth-related changes in the body. Contemporary with Gesell and McGraw (but most likely unknown by them), the Soviet physiologist Bernstein was making it clear in his work with adult humans that a given innervational state does not have a fixed movement consequence. There are anatomical, mechanical, and physiological sources of indeterminacy (Bernstein, 1984).

Bernstein's message about the significance of sources of indeterminacy is only now being actively incorporated into developmental theory. During development, not only are there different movement consequences from the same muscle activation, but also, different muscle activations result in the same movement consequences, depending on the effects of gravity and passive torque on limb mass.

Two brief examples from the work of Thelen and her colleagues on infant kicking demonstrate the problem of indeterminacy for a theory of the development of action. Thelen and Fischer (1982) demonstrated that the rapid deposition of fat relative to muscle during the first 8 weeks of life rather than the appearance of a new neuromotor function was responsible for the so-called "disappearing" stepping reflex. As the mass of the body increased, the same muscle activation had different movement consequences: resistance of mass on the muscle resulted in no kick despite a muscle activation. Schneider, Zernicke, Ulrich, Jensen, and Thelen (1990) studied limb intersegmental dynamics in kicking by supine three-month-olds and found that muscle torques were used in a context sensitive fashion: muscle torques were adjusted to produce a net torque that reversed the kicking motion and produced a smooth trajectory, despite considerable heterogeneity in the movement context of each kick.

What, then, is the role of the brain in the development of action systems? Stated succinctly here, and elaborated in Chapter 5, *the nervous system controls only to the extent that it complements the force field generated by the body* (cf. Kelso & Saltzman, 1982). Such a view not only requires a study of the sources of indeterminacy in development of action, it also rejects the methodology of correlating an observable change in behavior with changes in some variable of brain growth (e.g., myelin deposition, synaptogenesis, etc.; see, e.g., Goldfield, 1990). Correlating behavior with a change in brain growth is a kind of reductionism in which observable behavior is treated as a thing reducible to its elemental properties (e.g., nerve tracts). It is clear from studies of neonatal behavioral state (Prechtl, 1974; Wolff, 1987) that novel properties of behavioral organization appear that cannot be predicted from knowledge of the component physiological processes alone.

The alternative approach discussed in Chapter 7, owing to recent advances in dynamic systems (Kugler & Turvey, 1987; Smith & Thelen, 1993), opts for a different kind of reductionism: a reductionism to a minimum set of laws that holds for functional systems of neurons as well as of muscles and joints. It will be argued in these chapters that behavior of large and complex aggregates, regardless of their particular structural embodiment, follows the same laws (see, e.g., Kelso & Kay, 1987).

The relation between order and regulation. While order (coordination) is the process by which a system's free variables are constrained to act as a single functional unit, control (regulation) is the process by which values are assigned to that behavioral unit (Davis, 1986). Following von Holst's lead, coordination is often identified with central processes, and regulation with peripheral ones (Brooks, 1986; Gallistel, 1980). However, as Reed (1982) and Fentress (1990) observe, rather than being dichotomized, central–peripheral function must be organized into a relational framework that accounts for the context- conditioned variability demonstrated by Bernstein. That is, a model of central–peripheral organization must allow central signals to be modulated by ongoing sensory activity.

Fentress (1990) offers an insightful analysis of the problem of how the systems underlying action exhibit a "necessarily dynamic balance between tendencies toward interaction and self-organization" (p. 4). He proposes that the way to address the central–peripheral distinction is to examine the same basic parameters of action and examine the balance of central and peripheral mediation under different expressive contexts. Fentress (1990) demonstrates that the "degree to which integrated actions are guided by sensory events can change as a function of such factors as speed and stereotypy of expression" (p. 10). For example, in studies of mouse grooming, sudden loads added to the slow and flexible phases of activity interrupted grooming, but during rapid and stereotyped phases, the same perturbations are not disruptive. Fentress explains this finding relative to the functional importance of the activity for the animal.

Reed (1982, 1985, 1988b) comes to a similar conclusion about the importance of the study of function for understanding the relation between central coordination and peripheral regulation, and proposes that action systems must be categorized by function. For Reed, this means that they should be defined in terms of environmental properties that impose selection pressures. Given the arguments of Fentress and Reed, and the considerations of the motor–action controversy already delineated, I adopt a functional approach in this book in order to understand the relation between order and regulation in the development of action systems during human ontogeny.

Another manifestation of the relation between order and regulation is the dimension of spontaneous versus responsive forms of early movement. This is evident in Preyer's early (1885) analysis of chick embryos in which he observed that spontaneous forms of behavior occurred before elicited behaviors. Similarly, Coghill (1929) reported detailed observations of the salamander *Amblystoma* during its earliest development. He demonstrated that each of the distinct stages of behavior (e.g., coiling or S-flexure) could be correlated with specific anatomical changes in the nervous system, and that such changes occurred even when sensory input was prevented (by immersing the animal in an anesthetic). On the basis of this work, Coghill not only emphasized the spontaneous nature of the first forms of activity, but also proposed a theory about how coordination (order) proceeded developmentally:

> Behavior develops from the beginning through the progressive expansion of a perfectly integrated total pattern and the individuation within it of partial patterns which acquire various degrees of discreteness. (quoted in Carmichael, 1970, p. 458)

The primacy of spontaneity over perceptually regulated behavior in early development has been confirmed in the elegant experimental work of Hamburger, Wenger, and Oppenheim (1966), who found that even when the entire dorsal half of the chick lumbosacral spinal cord was removed at 2 to 2.5 days (thus eliminating sensory feedback), spontaneous movements continued to develop normally (see Fig. 1.4). More recently, Coghill's theory has been couched in the terminology of neural pattern generation. Bekoff (1981, p. 135), for example, suggests that:

> (1) at least in anamniotes (fish and amphibians), the neural pattern generating circuitry for coordinated limb movements is activated obligatorily with the pattern generator(s) for the trunk movements of swimming at early developmental stages and (2) that only at later stages of development can the limb pattern generating circuitry be turned on and off separately.

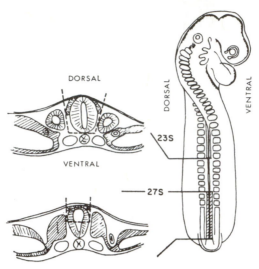

Figure 1.4. To determine whether the early movements of the chick embryo are truly spontaneous (without the necessity for sensory initiation or maintenance), chick embryos were deafferented at the leg level at around 40 h of development. The microsurgery involved (*a*) removing the dorsal (sensory) side of the spinal cord at the leg level (below the level of 27S in the diagram) and (*b*) creating a complete gap at the thoracic level (between 23S and 27S to prevent impulses from higher levels from reaching the lower limb segments). The non-deafferented control group merely had the latter operation, so that the sensory innervation of their legs was intact. (From Hamburger et al., 1966. Copyright © 1966 by the *Journal of Experimental Zoology*. Reprinted by permission.)

Given the consensus of a primacy of spontaneous activity, and that coordination in complex behaviors develops from a trunk-dominated pattern to one that integrates the activity of the limbs, might perceptual input play some role in the latter, and if so, what kind of role? This has been a fundamental question in recent work in developmental psychobiology (see, e.g., Hall & Oppenheim, 1987; Oppenheim & Haverkamp, 1986; Smotherman & Robinson, 1988).

Owing to the early influence of Coghill (1929), the field of developmental psychobiology has focused on the relation between early and later forms of behavior that accomplish the same function. An example of this view is the following by Hall and Oppenheim (1987): "the behavior exhibited by developing animals reflects a balance between meeting the needs of the moment and preparing for later life."

This view captures three possible roles for an earlier behavior in the ontogeny of a later behavior which serves the same function. First, the behavior may be an *ontogenetic adaptation*: it may serve some immediate adaptive role for the developing individual (Oppenheim, 1981). For example, spontaneous movements in vertebrate embryos appear to regulate prenatal musculoskeletal development (Oppenheim, Pitman, Gray, & Maderdrut, 1978; Drachman &

Coulombre, 1962), and postnatal suckling is used for appetition by infant mammals (although it is absent in the adults of most species; Blass, Fillion, Rochat, Hoffneiger, & Metzger 1979). Second, the observed behavior may serve as an ontogenetic adaptation, but may also *persist* in such a way that it is exploited during later periods for new capabilities:

> Novel ontogenetic adaptations may create special evolutionary opportunities by shifting development towards new capabilities and niches. Expressed in another manner, evolution can proceed by adding new characteristics to the end of a developmental sequence, by altering the relative rates of development of different characteristics, or by inserting new characteristics early in the developmental sequence. (Hall & Oppenheim, 1987, p. 119)

Third, the behavior may be an "anticipatory function" (Carmichael, 1970), in which, prior to its actual use for survival, a behavior becomes functional and so exposes the animal to sensory input that is essential for the normal later expression of the function (see Fig. 1.5).

In Chapter 7 of this book, I apply the distinction between ontogenetic adaptations and anticipations in addressing the relation between the spontaneous movements of infants and the assembly of action systems. Behaviors, such as arm waving or kicking, not only serve an adaptive function during the

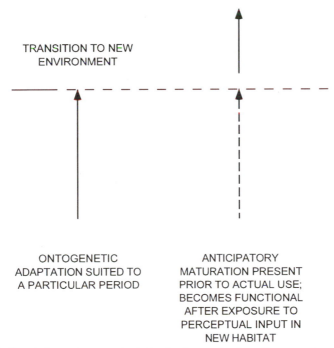

Figure 1.5. Coexisting processes in behavioral organization. Ontogenetic adaptations and anticipatory behaviors may co-exist until the latter becomes better suited to a changing environment. At that point, the anticipatory behavior becomes dominant.

period in which they are observed, they also reveal perceptual information to
the infant that may be a kind of "workspace" for the selection of acts *useful* in
achieving a particular goal.

The possible regulatory roles of perceptual input. Given the appreciation in developmental psychobiology of the primacy of the spontaneity of
action in prenatal life, Gottlieb (1983) offers three possible ways that
perceptual input may act during embryogenesis to influence postnatal behavior:

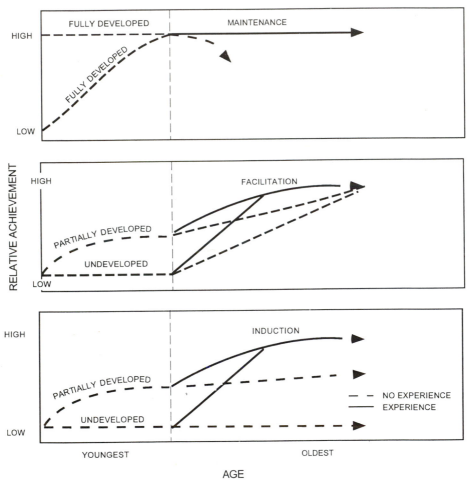

Figure 1.6. Three ways in which experience can contribute to species-typical development.
Maintenance preserves already-developed achievements. Facilitation acts as a temporal regulator
of achievements which will be reached even without normally occurring experience. Induction
is a process in which experience is essential if a particular structure or function is to be fully
achieved. The vertical line indicates when experience first occurs. The curves to the left of the
vertical refer to stages of maturation of the system prior to experience. (Adapted from Gottlieb,
1983. Copyright © 1983 by John Wiley and Sons, Inc. Reprinted by permission.)

maintenance, facilitation, and induction (see Fig. 1.6). Maintenance preserves already developed achievements, as is illustrated when sensory deprivation results in atrophy of sensory neural tissue. *Facilitation* acts as a temporal regulator of developmental events which are achieved even under conditions of sensory deprivation, but accelerated when appropriate sensory stimulation occurs. And finally, *induction* is a process that completely determines whether or not a developmental achievement will manifest itself later in development.

These three processes have offered a useful framework for understanding the possible regulatory roles of perception in the transition from prenatal to postnatal life, and may have implications for other developmental periods of transition. Gottlieb (1981), for example, has shown that prenatal auditory experience in ducks influences postnatal behavior. In posthatch mallard ducklings, there is normally a specific responsiveness to the repetition rate of the maternal call. He found, however, that when he devocalized duckling embryos *in ovo*, this selective responsiveness is lost postnatally, and the ducklings respond equally well to the calls of other species. Here, prenatal experience may selectively tune the duck's auditory system so that it has a particular threshold to certain variables (such as repetition rate) useful in postnatal interactions with conspecifics.

Gottlieb's findings may be instructive for understanding the relation between early spontaneous activities during human infancy, and the gradual development of action systems. Consider, for example, the spontaneous activities of young infants that seem to occur at specific times, just prior to the onset of a new skill. For example, just prior to articulating their first words, infants spontaneously utter long repetitive sequences of babbling (Kent, 1992; Kent, Mitchell, & Sancier, 1991; Koopmans-van Beinum & van der Stelt, 1986). The period of heightened spontaneous activity just prior to a new skill may be a time when infants are exploring the perceptual consequences of their own goal-directed acts in order to select those dynamics that are useful for the task at hand. The challenge, of course, for a theory of the development of action systems is to specify precisely how this happens.

The temporally distributed nature of regulation. I propose in this book that phylogenetic (species-specific) modes of regulation (e.g., the earliest organized patterns of orienting, feeding in altricial animals), ontogenetic patterns of exploratory and performatory acts, and microgenetic perception-action cycles are all regulatory processes which operate in parallel during goal-directed activity (Gould, 1977, 1980; Johnston & Turvey, 1980; Reed, 1985). Following Sommerhoff (1969), Johnston and Turvey relate phylogenesis, learning, and coordination of perception and action via the concept of back-reference period, a kind of operation lag of the three regulatory processes, with respect to a particular adaptive response. At issue are environmental properties to which an animal responds (constraints on the variability of response), the adaptive response itself, and its back-reference period. Consider, for example, the escape of an animal from a predator. At the evolutionary time scale of eons, locomotion has become a useful adaptation to substrates for locomotion (ground, water, etc.), while at the time scale of learning (several days to a few years), the learning of a route of travel has become a useful adaptation to the particular locations of food, water, and shelter. And at the briefest back-reference period of seconds, perception is used to guide acts of avoidance relative to the appearance of a predator. A fundamental question, though, is how to relate these three scales of time.

Phylogenetic regulation, as it is manifest in the embryogenesis of an individual (e.g., the first organized mouthing of the human fetus), regulates the assembly of ordered systems by introducing the selective pressures operating throughout the history of all life on our planet. Phylogenetic regulation brings to bear these selective pressures at a drastically accelerated rate during embryogenesis of each new member of the species (cf. Gould, 1977). The ordered systems assembled under phylogenetic regulation (cells and their extracellular matrix) serve as a constraint on ontogenetic activities so that they are compatible with species-specific goals (cf. Edelman, 1987). Two character-istics distinguish phylogenetic and ontogenetic regulation. Ontogeny imposes constraints that have existed for a shorter period of life's history—namely, the history of a species—and it influences behavior beyond the period of embryogenesis of an individual i.e., throughout postnatal life. Finally, microgenesis, or learning, is a regulatory process that attunes behavior to the present moment and, indeed, anticipates future events.

Emergentism: stages and stage transitions. What is the process underlying observable stage-like patterns as well as transitions between stages in motor behavior during human ontogeny? Posture and movement undergoing developmental change exhibit considerable variability as well as periods in which there are rapid reorganizations. For example, an infant observed crawling one day may stand the next. Motor theorists have typically attributed such transitions or "stages" (Roberton, 1982) to linear growth of the behavior as it comes under a new "executive" influence, previously independent of the behavior in question. So, for example, McGraw (1945) attributes new stages of locomotor behavior to new cortical inhibitions of subcortical centers; Bruner (1971) suggests that new motor skills result as a consequence of a freeing of attentional capacity; and both Piaget (1954) and Fischer (1980) promote the view that abrupt stage transitions in motor behavior are a consequence of constructing new sensorimotor systems that come to control older ones.

By assuming linearity in growth, these motor theorists must all rely on the introduction of an *extrinsic* influence—inhibition, attention, or representa-tion—as an executive in a hierarchical control system in order to account for abrupt transitions. Action theorists, by contrast, assume that nonlinearities are *intrinsic* to growth at the outset, and that these nonlinearities are the source of variability, order, and abrupt reorganization. This assumption allows the action theorist to eschew a growth process that requires control by an outside agency to account for abrupt transitions, and leads to a model of action that is execution-driven rather than executive-driven (Turvey, 1988).

A challenge for a theory of development of action systems, then, is to address how developmental change in these execution-driven dynamic systems results in ordered forms of behavior and how such systems allow for regulation of ordered forms.

DEVELOPMENTAL PERSPECTIVES ON THE NATURE OF ACTION

Ethological perspectives: Fentress and Wolff. I next consider the work of two scientists who have adopted an ethological approach to observations of complex behaviors: John Fentress, who has focused on animals, and Peter Wolff, who has studied neonatal human behavior. The research of both has strong links to the insights of the great neurobiologist Paul Weiss (e.g., 1941) who was an early investigator of the hierarchical structuring of action. Weiss had proposed that there was a central state underlying observable behavior, and that this state could be characterized as a kind of "score" (akin to music). The central score has the following properties:

1. The score is stable relative to the functional requirements of a particular motor act.
2. The score combines with other scores at different levels of the system, and the totality is a "motor repertoire."
3. The scores are "discrete entities with no intergradations."
4. The scores develop by a process of self-differentiation, and not all of them develop at the same time.

Moreover, the central state was part of a hierarchy of functional levels which in increasing complexity includes: the neuron, the muscle, the muscle complex, the organ (spanning several joints), the organ system used for performing a functional act (e.g., locomotion), and, at the highest level, all of the acts "put into the service of the animal as a whole under the control of the sensory apparatus."

Fentress (1990; Fentress & MacLeod, 1986) reiterates the idea of central activation in his "center–surround" model for order and regulation. The model has much in common with the autocatalytic process proposed by Meinhardt (1984) for pattern formation (and see Chapter 5). The Fentress model is particularly instructive because it attempts to address the specificity or boundaries of action. For example, how are the acts involved in grooming related to locomotor acts? Fentress proposes that action control systems have an excitatory core and an inhibitory surround. The core strengthens with increased activation, while the surround expands.

Fentress addresses the hierarchical ordering of action in a temporal fashion, as Weiss did with the notion of scores of action. Consider, for example, his work on grooming in mice. Golani and Fentress (1985) have adapted a geometric notation system from dance choreography (Eshkol & Wachman, 1958) to address questions about the relation between behaviors in mouse grooming. They use movement notation to interpret how body movements are related to each other during performance of a functional activity. By applying a polar coordinate system, it is possible to plot the position of a given segment from the perspective of other segments.

Fentress (1989; Fentress & McLeod, 1986) describes three complementary "streams" of grooming behavior: forepaw to face contacts, forelimb trajectories, and limb segment kinematics. In the earliest phase of grooming (4 to 5 postnatal days), all three are poorly coordinated. Between postnatal days 4 and 7, there is a loss of variety in the movements seen earlier, and after day 8, consistent contact pathways can now be accomplished by a wide variety of individual movement combinations (see Fig. 1.7). Movements take on "a rich and flowing appearance, with the head, body, and forelimbs contributing to the production of contact pathways" (Fentress & McLeod, 1986).

Peter Wolff's work on temporal patterns in human neonatal behavior pursues the same two themes as the animal studies of Fentress: central activation and the nesting of streams of behavior. In one line of studies, Wolff explicitly searched for central activation in behavioral rhythms such as sucking (e.g., Wolff, 1968) and crying (Wolff, 1969), as well as magnet effects (cf. von Holst, 1973) in these central activations (e.g., in sucking and respiration; Dreier, Wolff, Cross, & Cochran, 1979). These studies have supported the idea that early behavioral rhythms were endogenously generated, and that when observed within the context of the streams of activity in other bodily systems (e.g., sleep–wake patterns), it is apparent that these rhythms became organized into functional patterns useful for social interaction.

Wolff gave the name *behavioral state* to his characterization of nested streams of behavior (Wolff, 1966, 1987, 1993; see also Table 1.2). While other investigators have used the concept of behavioral state descriptively (see, e.g., Thoman, 1990), Wolff has consistently argued that behavioral states are more than just descriptions of behavior: they are the emergent properties of a complex system. There are only a limited number of behavioral states that are realized from the very large number of possible organizations of the degrees of freedom of this complex system, because of the dynamic nature of the system:

> Behavioral states are the a posteriori consequences of spontaneous interactions among many fluctuating subsystems ... the dynamic stability and critical

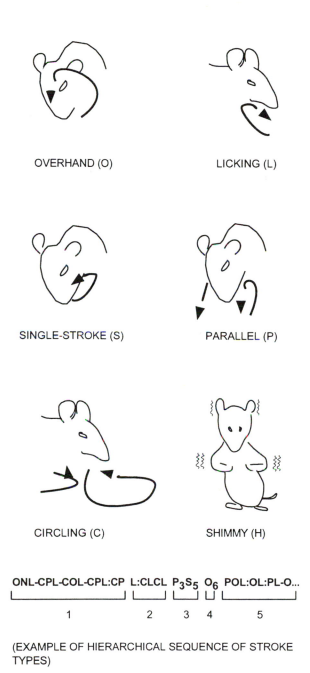

OVERHAND (O)

LICKING (L)

SINGLE-STROKE (S)

PARALLEL (P)

CIRCLING (C)

SHIMMY (H)

ONL-CPL-COL-CPL:CP L:CLCL P_3S_5 O_6 POL:OL:PL-O...

1   2   3 4   5

(EXAMPLE OF HIERARCHICAL SEQUENCE OF STROKE TYPES)

Figure 1.7. Streams of behavior in mouse facial grooming. The letters represent a grooming series, and refer to stroke types. The numbers beneath the brackets refer to "higher-order" groupings of these strokes. (Adapted from Fentress & McLeod, 1986. Copyright © 1986 by Plenum Press, Inc. Reprinted by permission.)

Table 1.2. Neonatal behavioral states

Behavioral State	Description
State 1 (Regular, synchronous, non-REM sleep)	(a) stable rhythm, high amplitude, and low frequency of breathing, (b) firm closure of the eyelids, (c) absence of vocalizations, and (d) absence of general movements
State 2 (Irregular, paradoxical, or REM sleep)	(a) irregular respirations of higher mean frequency and more variable amplitudes than in state 1, (b) intermittent movements of the limbs, mouth, trunk, and head, (c) closed eyes, and (d) absence of vocalizations
State 3 (Quiet alertness)	(a) the infant's eyes are open and make intermittent conjugate movements, (b) the limbs and trunk are at rest except for occasional smooth movements, (c) respirations are more regular than in state 2, and (d) vocalizations are minimal or absent
State 4 (Waking activity)	(a) the eyes are open, (b) the limbs and trunk make intermittent general movements, (c) respirations are irregular and more rapid than in state 3, and (d) the infant makes occasional "fussy" vocalizations
State 5 (Cry)	(a) cry vocalizations, (b) eyes are open or pinched shut, (c) limbs and trunk are active, and (d) respirations are variable

Source: After Wolff, 1993.

instability of states can be studied experimentally at a macroscopic level to demarcate the boundaries between adjacent states. (Wolff, 1993, p. 192)

Development as a self-organizing system. While Fentress (1989) has used the center–surround model to understand the dynamic properties of a combination of observable variables, Thelen (1989a) extends the synergetics of Haken (1983) in order to examine the dynamics and development of behavior as a self-organizing system. The stability of a self-organizing system may be illustrated with a tool from dynamic systems theory: the state space. The *state space* is a graphical means of displaying on the same axes the behavior of collections of trajectories. Of particular interest are sets of trajectories that stay within equilibrium regions of the phase space. These are called *attractors* (Abraham & Shaw, 1987; see Table 1.3).

Table 1.3. What is an attractor?

1. An attractor is a region of state space (the set of all states that may be reached by a system, together with the paths for doing so) where trajectories come to rest.
2. An attractor can be a point, cycle, or area of state space.
3. A physical system can have one or more attractors, and it is the number and layout of these attractors that influence the system.
4. Each attractor exerts a force on the system by means of a potential difference. The trajectory followed by the system is determined by the net sum of the forces exerted by the various attractors.
5. The configuration of attractors has a critical influence on the behavior of the system. A change in the layout of attractors leads to new competition between attractors and results in a shift to different modes.

Source: After Kugler and Turvey, 1987; Thompson and Stewart, 1986.

A distinctive property of attractors is their stability despite external perturbation; despite different starting conditions, trajectories will settle into orbits with distinctive shapes (see Fig. 1.8). With a point attractor, for example, the system is attracted to one point, and then remains at that point. A limit cycle attractor is a closed oscillation maintained by a competition between forces (Newell, Kugler, van Emmerik, & McDonald, 1989). The torus attractor emerges when two or more limit cycles are weakly coupled: it exhibits multiple stability because of a competition between the attractors in which neither attractor is able to assume complete dominance. And finally, a chaotic attractor exhibits folding and stretching that gives it the property of locally diverging and globally folding back (Newell et al., 1989). Each attractor has characteristic dynamics and dimensionality, and there are specific techniques for identifying attractors in behavior (see, e.g., Robertson, Cohen, & Mayer-Kress, 1993; see Table 1.4).

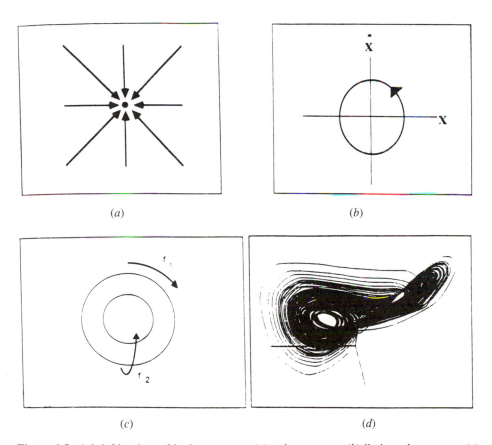

Figure 1.8. A brief bestiary of basic attractors: (*a*) point attractor, (*b*) limit-cycle attractor, (*c*) torus attractor, and (*d*) a Lorenz attractor (an example of a strange or chaotic attractor). (From Newell, Kugler, van Emmerik, & McDonald, 1989. Copyright © 1989 by Elsevier Science Publishers, Inc. Reprinted by permission.)

Table 1.4. Techniques for identifying attractors

---

1. *Construct a state space* (where the coordinate axes are the state variables). The state of the system at any given time is represented as a position in this state space, and the temporal evolution of the system is represented as a trajectory in state space. The collection of trajectories followed by the dynamic system is its phase portrait.
2. *Find an attractor in state space.* This addresses the question of whether, in a potentially high-degree-of-freedom system, there is a relatively low-dimensional attractor on which the system's trajectories lie. Evidence for an attractor may be found by (a) manipulating initial conditions (where a trajectory begins) and determining whether distant trajectories converge, and (b) examining the way trajectories, when deflected by an experimental perturbation, return to the original phase portrait.
3. *Characterize the attractor by measuring its dimensionality.* Dimensionality is a measure of geometric complexity. So, for example, a limit cycle has a dimensionality of 1, a torus attractor has a dimensionality of 2, and chaotic attractors have non-integer dimensionality. Techniques for assessing dimensionality include the Kolgomorov capacity, and the correlation dimension.
4. *Measure the rate of convergence and divergence of trajectories.* If a chaotic attractor is present, a dynamic "diagnostic" is the exponential divergence of nearby trajectories. Measure divergence by the use of Lyapunov exponents.

Source: After Kay, Sultzman, and Kelso, 1991; Robertson, Cohen, and Mayer-Kress, 1993.

Thelen uses attractor dynamics to attempt to explain familiar developmental phenomena. She proposes that both action and the process of development

1. Are a compression of the high-dimensional nature of dynamic systems, and this compression can be described by a collective variable.
2. Emerge as a function of the cooperation of the many subsystems in a task context, with no subsystem having logical priority in the assembly of the behavior.
3. Exhibit stable or "preferred" behavioral configurations that are determined by organismic status and task context.
4. Undergo organizational change governed by a series of stabilizing and destabilizing attractors.
5. May be reorganized as the result of the influence of one or a few control parameters that can, themselves, change over time.

The first proposition addresses the degrees-of-freedom problem raised by Bernstein (and discussed in Chapter 2): how the large number of elements comprising complex systems can generate patterns that have fewer dimensions than the original elements. Thelen proposes that under certain conditions of thermodynamic nonequilibrium, patterns form because the elements may self-organize. When the elements of a dynamic system are viewed as component processes, each may develop in parallel and at a different rate. For this reason, "some elements of functional actions may be in place long before the performance but may not be manifest until the slowest component allows the system to dynamically assemble into a new form (the *rate-limiting* component)" (Thelen, 1989a, pp. 90–91). Because the organization of components is conceptualized as heterarchical rather than hierarchical, no single component

Table 1.5. A strategy for studying development from a dynamical systems perspective

1. Identify the collective variable of interest.
2. Characterize the behavioral attractor states.
3. Describe the dynamic trajectory of the collective variable.
4. Identify points of transition (characterized by loss of stability).
5. Exploit the instabilities at transitions to identify potential control parameters.
6. Manipulate the putative control parameters to generate phase transitions experimentally.

Source: After Thelen and Ulrich, 1991.

has a logical priority in driving the system into a new organizational state. As component processes change, either in a continuous or punctate fashion, a new "landscape" of behavioral potentialities emerges. A particular strength of this approach is that these propositions imply a specific methodology (see Table 1.5).

An ecological perspective: The embedding of rhythms within more macroscopic temporal cycles. Ecology is a discipline allied with ethology and, in many ways, complementary to it. According to Alberts and Cramer (1988), ecological perspectives focus on specific environmental features and organismic characteristics, as well as the functional relations between the two. Another distinctive aspect of an ecological approach is *task description* (Johnston, 1981; Miller, 1988) which involves detailed observational and quantitative analyses of animals in their species-typical habitats.

Developmental approaches within an ecological perspective identify the changing relation between a *habitat* (an animal's immediate environment) and a niche ("making a living" in a habitat). For example, there is a succession of habitats during the development of the Norway rat including (a) the uterus, (b) the mother's body, (c) the huddle (a pile of siblings in the nest), and (d) the coterie or social group. The way in which the rat negotiates the use of resources in each of these habitats constitutes an ontogenetic progression of niches (Alberts & Cramer, 1988). The challenge for developmental theory is to understand how the animal's self-organizing behavior (the niche) is regulated by the supportive network of the habitat. The key to the relationship between self-organization and regulation appears to be the embedding and control of temporal patterns of behavior.

The approach of this book: Coalitions of dynamic systems. The present approach includes a theoretical statement about structure, function, and development. It is a functional approach in the sense of Anokhin (1935, 1940) and Luria (1980). *Action* is based upon a "complex dynamic constellation of connections, situated at different levels of the nervous system, that, in the performance of the adaptive task, may be changed with the task itself remaining unchanged" (Luria, 1980, p. 22). Action systems, as they are described here, are functional systems that have three properties noted by Luria: (1) they are complex in composition, (2) they are plastic in the variability of their elements, and (3) they exhibit dynamic autoregulation.

In this book, it is proposed that there are two fundamental processes involved in the developmental transformation of spontaneous activity into a task-specific action pattern: assembly of a system with low-dimensional dynamics, and tuning of the system via perceptual exploration to refine the movement. Assembly is a process of self-organization that establishes a temporary relationship among the components of the musculoskeletal system, transforming it into a task-specific device, such as a kicker, walker, or shaker (Bingham, 1988; Saltzman & Kelso, 1987). Once assembled, the parameters of this dynamic system can be tuned by the infant in order to adapt the movement to particular conditions.

The present approach also emphasizes the organization of behavior in space-time. Following the usage of Farmer (1990) and Saltzman and Munhall (1992), I adopt three levels in discussing the coalitional organization of action systems in this book: state, parameter, and graph dynamics, respectively (see Table 1.6). These three levels are distinguished mainly by the time scale at which their variables change. At the highest level of graph dynamics, the actor must assemble a task-specific device from the many

Table 1.6. State, parameter, and graph dynamics

Type of Dynamics	Definition	Example
State	Processes in "real time" that directly shape patterns of motion in a dynamic system's state variables (dynamics of coordinative structures); *i.e., the variables to be assembled* (a system's architecture and its parameter set)	Angular positions and velocities at the elbow and shoulder joints vary throughout the act of lifting a cup to the lips in a manner specific to the task
Parameter	The processes that directly govern motion patterns in a dynamic system's parameters; operates at a longer time scale	A constant parameter (e.g., stiffness or equilibrium position) that represents the spatial position of the target constrains the evolution of the system's state variables (angular positions and velocities) in reaching; frequency parameter is constant for sustained rhythmic oscillations
Graph	The processes that directly influence the assembly of a system's actual architecture, its size, composition, and connectivity. A process of selecting and combining those subcomponents that can contribute successfully to accomplishing the task at hand	The architecture of a system may grow or shrink in size due to graph dynamic processes analogous to call birth or death

Source: After Saltzman and Imunhall, 1992.

components of the action system—abstractly, a function for a dynamic system (see Chapter 2). At an intermediate level, the actor must set the parameters on the function to yield a class of movements adapted to the task (see chapter 3). And finally, when performing the task, the actor must let the dynamic system "run" or evolve through a series of states to achieve a stable movement pattern.

To illustrate these three levels, consider the set of all possible limb configurations in a high-dimensional *state space*, in this case "joint space," whose dimensions are the 100 degrees of freedom of the joints, with each joint in the space representing a posture and a trajectory through the space representing a movement (see Fig. 1.9). At the highest level of analysis, a particular musculo-skeletal organization is a specific relationship among the system's many degrees of freedom. However, a description of the system at this level of detail would be inordinately complex. Rather than describing all the microscopic degrees of freedom of an organized system, we can provide a simplifying macroscopic description of its behavior in terms of a *function* for a dynamic system. The function expresses the system's low-dimensional dynamics, characterized by the preferred states or attractors toward which the system tends (Fig. 1.9(c)).

At an intermediate level of analysis, we can evaluate the effects of varying the *parameters* of this function, such as the mass, stiffness, damping, and forcing frequency of a mass-spring, on the behavior of the system. This can be represented as exploration of "parameter space," whose dimensions are the system parameters and some measure of the behavior such as a cost function (Fig. 1.9(b)). A surface in parameter space would then reflect the consequences of various parameter settings, with a minimum in the surface indexing an appropriate combination of parameter values for the task. Parameter tuning via exploration adjusts movement to the local conditions of the task.

At the lowest level, once parameter values are set, we can consider how the *state* of the system evolves over time from various initial conditions. The states of a mass-spring system, for example, are the possible positions and velocities of the mass, represented by points in the phase plane; for the action system, they may be a subset of limb positions and velocities. These stable movement patterns feed back on the other two, for the properties of the resulting behavior may be used to evaluate the global function and tune its parameters.

An example of the specification of functions in graph dynamics is the relationship of functionally organized movement patterns in different states of sleep and wakefulness, or behavioral states (Wolff, 1987, 1993), as discussed earlier. Behavioral states are defined as higher-order relations among the different subsystems of the body. Each behavioral state ensures that the neonate is prepared to act adaptively in the environment. At the same time, temporal components nested within behavioral states (e.g., behavioral rhythms such as

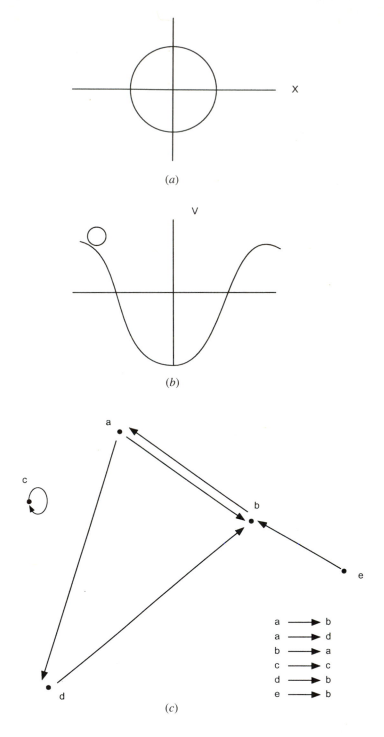

Figure 1.9. A schematic diagram of three levels of dynamics: (*a*) state dynamics, (*b*) parameter dynamics, and (*c*) graph dynamics.

sucking) retain sufficient variability so that they may be tuned to local conditions. So, for example, sucking is evident in some behavioral states and not others. Behavioral states become increasingly differentiated during development (e.g., waking states become evident) at the same time that cooperative patterns become better coordinated with each other.

I propose here that each action system is a bounded collection of functions, or emergent forms. The particular form that emerges may be illustrated by analogy to a physical system, the vortex patterns emerging in fluids constrained within a two-walled cylinder (Turvey & Fitzpatrick, 1993; see Fig. 1.10). The analogy is based upon the abstract similarity between the degrees of freedom of the body and the atomisms of the liquid. Action systems are emergent forms analogous to the eddies that form in liquid as it flows, hence the title of the book. However, while in a physical system the conduit is a material structure, in a biological system, the conduit may be an energy field (e.g., the nervous system or a perceptual field). In other words, the channeling

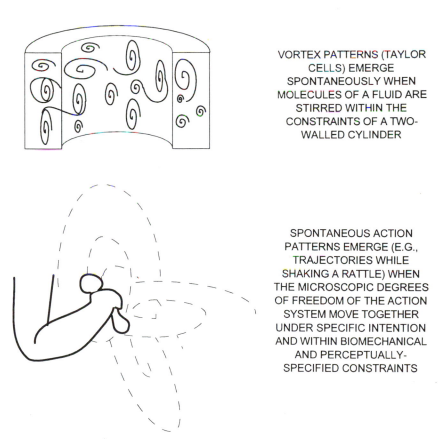

VORTEX PATTERNS (TAYLOR CELLS) EMERGE SPONTANEOUSLY WHEN MOLECULES OF A FLUID ARE STIRRED WITHIN THE CONSTRAINTS OF A TWO-WALLED CYLINDER

SPONTANEOUS ACTION PATTERNS EMERGE (E.G., TRAJECTORIES WHILE SHAKING A RATTLE) WHEN THE MICROSCOPIC DEGREES OF FREEDOM OF THE ACTION SYSTEM MOVE TOGETHER UNDER SPECIFIC INTENTION AND WITHIN BIOMECHANICAL AND PERCEPTUALLY-SPECIFIED CONSTRAINTS

Figure 1.10. Constraints on complex (high-dimensional, nonlinear) physical and biological sytems results in pattern formation.

of energy flows into stable forms may be achieved by softly assembled "virtual" conduits (Kugler & Turvey, 1987).

I emphasize here that these self-organizing forms, or functions, generate only *approximate* movements for performing the various adaptive tasks facing the actor. The *actual* movements that are useful for performing the task must be selected by means of perceptual exploration of the dynamics. Each action system is the product of both evolutionary "tinkering" and ontogeny in the sense that it is an assembly of variables from different parts of a complex system (Saltzman & Kelso, 1987; Saltzman & Munhall, 1989; Turvey, Schmidt, Rosenblum, & Kugler, 1988). The effectors may be thought of as "machines" in the body (Wells, 1971), capable of doing different kinds of work (see chapter 5). The same body part may be transformed into different kinds of machine: the hand as a "grabber" or a "pointer," the leg as a "kicker" or a "lifter" (Turvey, Shaw, Reed, & Mace, 1981). Thus, a family of actions may be functionally equivalent (e.g., writing the letter A with a pen held in the hand, mouth, or foot), because the same dynamic regime is assembled, but the components from which it is assembled are different. A challenge for a developmental theory of action is how humans discover that a particular kind of dynamic regime may be assembled from different body subsystems in order to perform different kinds of work (e.g., point attractor dynamics coupled to the arm and hand for reaching).

Exploration of task dynamics occurs at all three levels of analysis: graph, parameter, and state. In the course of learning a task, the infant actor experiments with different combinations of musculoskeletal components, in effect adopting different functions over the degrees of freedom of the action system, and explores the attractor layout that emerges. The infant also explores parameter space, identifying the configuration of parameters that is most appropriate for a given task. Within a particular parameter setting, the actor lets the state of the system evolve to an attractor, yielding a stable movement pattern. Thus, the theory would predict that when an infant learns a task, the large-scale variability in movement trajectories would be reduced as the infant becomes sensitive to the task dynamics, locates an attractor, and tunes the parameters.

In highlighting the processes of assembly and perceptual exploration, I adopt the distinction made in developmental psychobiology between *onto-genetic adaptations*, or behaviors with an adaptive advantage at a particular period in development (Oppenheim, 1981; Hofer, 1988), and *anticipations*, the patterns of behavior which "emerge early to provide a period in which a pattern may be modified and perfected before it is needed in a functional context" (Smotherman & Robinson, 1988, p. 26). In this book, however, I take this distinction one step further with respect to the development of action. I assert that the earliest spontaneous actions of the infant (sucking, arm waving, kicking) may serve as ontogenetic adaptations for the assembly of action systems. Moreover, I propose that it is a competition between ontogenetic adaptations and perceptually regulated postural acts that creates new cooperative emergent forms—functionally adapted action systems—during ontogeny. For example, rhythmic arm waving becomes useful for reaching when visually controlled postural adjustments of the body become embedded within a temporal structure. In other words, each emergent action system may be an embedding of perceptually regulated postural adjustments within a temporal pattern.

CHAPTER 2

FROM BERNSTEIN AND VON HOLST TO DYNAMIC SYSTEMS

The secret of coordination lies not only in not wasting superfluous force on extinguishing reactive phenomena but, on the contrary, in employing the latter in such a way as to employ active muscle forces only in the capacity of complementary forces

Nikolai Bernstein, 1967, p. 218

Complexity. In this last decade of the twentieth century, scientists in many fields have sensed the inadequacy of the kind of linear, reductionist thinking that was introduced by Newtonian physics. The problem that has led to this dissatisfaction is how to describe and understand the order which emerges in complex systems of all kinds—physical, biological, psychological, social, and economic. New coalitions of scientists crossing disciplinary boundaries have begun to address complexity with new tools from mathematics and new insights from physics and biology (Gleick, 1989; Waldrop, 1992). In this chapter, I examine a similar evolution of ideas about complexity in attempts to understand how human nervous systems accomplish coordination in action systems. I do so by highlighting the work of Nikolai Bernstein and attempts by students of Bernstein to use ideas from dynamic systems to explain how behavioral order emerges from the interplay of multiple components.

ROUND 1 OF BERNSTEIN-INSPIRED WORK

Coordination. In Chapter 1, I briefly introduced Bernstein's recognition of the complexity involved in the production of action, including the degrees-of-freedom (df) problem and the problem of indeterminacy or context-conditioned variability. Turvey (1990) summarizes the core issues and basic principles of organization relevant to Bernstein's work up until 1980, and I elaborate here upon some of these. I begin with the gathering together of degrees of freedom (df) into macroscopic functional units (see Table 2.1).

34

Table 2.1. Bernstein's problem: Round 1

Bernstein's Themes	Description
Distributed construction of movements	The kinematic (spatiotemporal) details of any coordinated state are contributed gradually, by many subsystems working together
Indefiniteness of action plans	The "plan" for a coordinated act is probably defined functionally in an abstract manner, i.e., with reference to relations among properties that are relatively few in number, realizable in all body segments, and capable of generating many different motions
Local expediencies	The subsystems that compose a biological movement system are relatively autonomous; each related to the medium of surrounding subsystems by a local expedient, minimal interacion (see text)
Separation of activation and tuning	When a subsystem is active, a "ballpark" of states (family of functions) is established. In order to produce a variant suityed to current circumstances, the activated subsystems must by "tuned"
Executive ignorance and equivalence classes	Due to distributed control, executive knowledge is only approximate, referring to *classes* of tunings and subsystems (lower-level processes) that are equivalent because they can be used to achieve the same purpose
Reduction of df by coordinative structures	A group of muscles spanning several joints, and capable of contracting independently of each other can become functionally linked so as to behave as a single task-specific unit. All coordinative structures participating in a task adjust to local perturbation so as to maintain the task goal
Spring model of control	Ballistic movements are put to considerable use, and are achieved by setting the muscle linkage to behave like a spring whose equilibrium position is the intended position. By varying spring damping and stiffness, movement patterns can be repetitive or discrete
Special-purpose solutions to real-world complexity	The generality of biological action systems is the result of task-specific solutions gathered into a coherent style of organization
Complementarity of action and environmental context	Coordination must be understood with respect to environmental variables which reduce the dimensionality of the variables to be controlled
Simultaneous organization of afference and efference	Inflow must be organized in ways suited to outflow

Source: After Turvey, 1990.

Turvey (1990) notes that the challenge of degrees of freedom arises from the very large number of components to be coordinated. For example, with the human body conceptualized as an aggregate of just hinge joints like the elbow (which underestimates its complexity), it would comprise about 100 mechanical degrees of freedom. If each of these is characterized by two states, position and velocity, then to describe the body would require a state space of 200 dimensions. Bernstein proposed that the solution to the degrees of freedom problem lies in *linking the degrees of freedom in such a way that they change relative to each other and preserve the relationship of muscles relative to each other.* He gives the name *synergy* to units that have components which automatically adjust to each other, and in order to further emphasize their flexible assembly Turvey and his students refer to these synergies as *coordinative structures*. Coordinative structures are defined as "a group of muscles often spanning several joints that is constrained to act as a single functional unit" (Tuller, Turvey, & Fitch, 1982, p. 253) or "an assemblage of many microcomponents . . . assembled temporarily and flexibly, so that a single microcomponent may participate in many different coordinative structures on different occasions" (Kay, 1988, p. 344) or "a preservation of internal relations among muscles and kinematic components that is stable across scalar changes in such parameters as rate and force" (Kelso, Tuller, Vatikiotis-Bateson, & Fowler, 1984).

There is now a body of evidence for coordinative structures in a variety of action systems—for example, speech (Kelso et al., 1984), the performatory system (Kelso, Southard, & Goodman, 1979), and basic orienting (Arutyunyan, Gurfinkel, & Mirsky, 1969). In the latter, for example, when a skilled marksman sights a target, the wrist and shoulder joints are constrained to act as a single unit such that any horizontal oscillation in the wrist is matched by an equal and opposite oscillation in the shoulder. It is important to note that coordinative structures, while allowing a variety of *movements*, allow only one kind of *action*. Aiming actions accomplish the function of pointing an extremity (an action) while allowing a range of movements which all accomplish that function.

Equations of constraint. Given that the microcomponents to be controlled are a collection of variables, it is possible to think of a coordinative structure more abstractly as an equation of constraint. The equation of constraint is an abstract tool for conceptualizing the way that elements (components of body subsystems, including neural networks, muscles, joints, and tendinous elements) become coupled into macroscopic functional units. Consider Fig. 2.1, an illustration (from Saltzman, 1979) of how equations of constraint reduce the degrees of freedom of components so they are controllable and, at the same time, continue to provide the kind of flexibility required for a context-sensitive system. The system in question is graphed as two points in a plane. Each point in this Cartesian coordinate space has two df (a total of four df). If the points are connected by a line of fixed length, L, the number of degrees of freedom is reduced to three, because the line provides an equation of constraint as follows:

$$(x_1 - x_2)^2 + (y_1 - y_2)^2 = L^2$$

in which a specification of any three variables determines the fourth. In general, the number of degrees of freedom is $(D_n - c)$, where D is the number of dimensions (two in this example), n is the number of elements (also two), and c is the number of equations of constraint linking the elements.

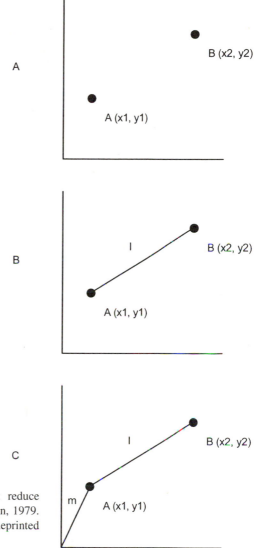

Figure 2.1. How equations of constraint reduce degrees of freedom. (Adapted from Saltzman, 1979. Copyright © 1979 by Academic Press, Inc. Reprinted by permission.)

Tuller et al. (1982) demonstrate how equations of constraint may be operative in the step cycle of an animal. Their important insight is that *when muscles are constrained to act as a functional unit, these muscle groups must compensate immediately in a way that preserves the task-specific relationship of the muscles within the collection.* Consider the task of locomotion, where the body must maintain a certain orientation to the ground plane while at the same time maneuvering through a cluttered environment. The step cycle (see Fig. 2.2) must insure that some muscle groups are used to move the body forward, while others are used to compensate for such movement so that the body

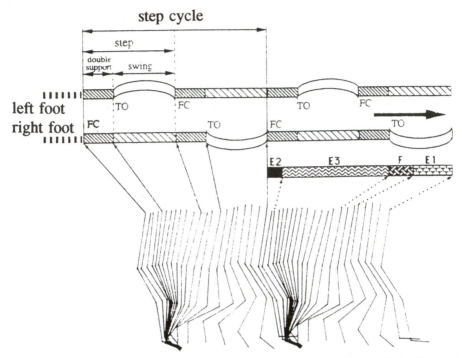

Figure 2.2. Gait cycle and stick diagram of a child walking. The right side of the diagram is a step cycle defined from the flexion–extension of the knee: phase E2 from FC to deep knee flexion (DKF); E3 from DKF to TO; F from TO to DKF, E1 from DKF to FC. (From Bril & Breniere, 1991. Copyright © 1991 by North-Holland Press. Reprinted by permission.)

maintains orientation to the ground plane. The phases of the step cycle are organized so that *body weight is transferred in particular ways at particular times.*

Coordinative structures and postural precedence. A critical point here is that the *task* serves as a macroscopic organizational structure which constrains all of the participating elements so that *even if only a local one is perturbed, they all immediately compensate.* This compensation is similar to a phenomenon discussed by Reed, postural precedence effects. Reed (1988a) reviews several experiments which support the idea that "a voluntary movement of a body member is preceded by postural muscle adjustments in the service of body stability (p. 54). So, for example, Belen'kii, Gurfinkel and Pal'tsev (1967) found that there are adjustments in the thigh muscles which act as body support *in advance of* a standing person raising an arm. Similarly, in a paradigm in which standing subjects use their thumbs to pull repeatedly on a stiff wire attached to a torque motor, when the wire is abruptly pulled by the motor, postural adjustments in the shoulder muscle *preceded* displacements of the elbow (Marsden, Merton, & Morton, 1981, 1983). Thus, postural adjustments prior to limb movements are highly functionally specific, even though they occur with very short latencies.

Reed (1988a) offers a model for the relation between maintaining posture and movement that is quite congenial to the idea proposed in this book that articulator components are assembled into "special purpose devices." He proposes that maintaining posture is a basic mode, a basic orienting system. Because the body is in a constant state of disequilibrium with respect to gravity and support surfaces, posture should be defined as the activity of keeping the body oriented to the environment.

On this view, basic orienting is the primary context for movements, in the sense that

> a movement is a functionally nested change from one posture to another. By "functionally nested" I mean that, in addition to serving its own function (whatever that might be) a movement must not be dysfunctional with respect to ongoing postures. (Reed, 1988b, p. 61)

Reed further proposes that actions, which are made up of continually changing postural adjustments and movements, are organized into separate streams of activity that constantly overlap. This idea is similar to that of Fentress (1984; Fentress & McLeod, 1986) and is discussed in chapter 1. Reed has used observations of adults in clinical settings who are "re-learning" skills of everyday living to examine (1) the way in which various streams of activity are nested into unified acts and (2) how each stream of activity is kept separately nested, "cycling in parallel." In learning to pour from a pitcher, for example, Reed demonstrates that there is always a preparatory period which functions to enable the nesting of nested streams of activity, including orienting the body toward the cup which is to receive the liquid, adjust their seated posture and the position of the objects.

Modes of action (action systems) and basic acts. Reed relates postures and movements to the structure of the environment by considering the functional utility of different environmental resources for particular animals. He suggests that those nestings of posture and movement which have been selected during evolution constitute a small set (dozens perhaps) of characteristic modes (eating, locomoting), and organized means for acting within these modes (action systems). Reed also emphasizes that the nesting of movements into postures requires perceptual regulation. This raises the question of the nature of the task variables that are complementary to those of the action system, the problem of perception–action coupling (Warren, 1988a,b).

Perception–action coupling. During the "first round" of Bernstein-inspired research, the problem of perception–action coupling was placed in a Gibsonian context (see Chapter 3). In particular, there has been much research on the question of how the properties of the action system may be a natural standard for scaling the properties of the environment to a goal-directed act. Warren (1988a,b), for example, has been pursuing an analysis which attempts to identify *critical points* in the fit between actor and environment at which a particular action breaks down, and *optimal points* at which the action is most efficient or comfortable.

He uses dimensionless ratios, called *pi numbers*, to construct a natural standard for intrinsically measuring the relation between an intended act and the properties of the environment which support that act. Consider the act of stair-climbing. The ratio of riser height (R) with respect to the climber's leg length (L), for example, yields a pi ratio of the fit of the climber to the stairs. As riser height varies with leg length, there should be, in this analysis, an optimal point at which the energy expenditure required to climb through a vertical distance is minimum. Moreover, there should also be a critical point at which it becomes impossible to climb up the stairs by means of bipedal stepping, and at which a quadrupedal hands and knees gait is required. Warren (1984, 1988a,b) reports that when both short and tall subjects made judgments about which of several sets of stairs were "climbable", the critical point is a constant function of the ratio of R and L (0.88). This value is identical to the one predicted by a biomechanical model of maximal leg flexion. Optimal riser height (measured by oxygen consumption during climbing) was found to be constant for short and tall subjects when plotted as a function of R/L.

Summary of round 1. While this "first round" of Bernstein-inspired research focused on how action systems might take advantage of the availability of large numbers of degrees of freedom, and the relationship of affordances to action, the "second round" has turned to the insights of dynamic systems in the context of physical biology and ecological psychology. It has sought new tools for examining the fundamental question of order as emergent from many subsidiary processes. Before turning to the newer work, though, I must first prepare the way for the reader by examining the work of von Holst. His concept of magnet effect (see the quote opening this chapter) foreshadowed some of the ideas about attractor dynamics that are at the heart of the "second round" of Bernstein-inspired research on problems of order and regulation.

A PRELUDE TO ROUND 2

von Holst. Following the pioneering work of Graham Brown (1914), the German physiologist von Holst performed a series of experiments on insects

Table 2.2. Three macroscopic "order" phenomena discovered by von Holst

Phenomenon	Description (in Fish)	Examples from Human Infants
Superposition	One fin's oscillation sometimes shows up as a second periodicity in the oscillation of another fin	Superposition of sucking rhythm on respiration (Dreier, Wolff, Cross & Cochran, 1979)
Magnet effect	Each fin oscillation tries to draw the other fin(s) to its characteristic period (the one it exhibits when oscillating alone), so that they settle on a cooperative tempo	Coupling of suck and swallow in nutritive sucking (Wolff, 1973)
Maintenance tendency	Each oscillator tries to maintain its identity when participating in a coupling, as indexed by fluctuations around the mean cooperative period	Coupling of chest and abdomen during respiration in different states (Goldman, Pagani, Trang, & Praud, 1993; Curzi-Dascalova & Plassart, 1978)

and fish that studied questions about the nature of coordination. He discovered three fundamental principles: *superposition*, an additive combination of the output of two oscillators running at different frequencies; *the magnet effect*, in which two oscillations may maintain a common tempo and a fixed difference in momentary phase; and *maintenance tendency* (see Table 2.2).

On the basis of these studies von Holst drew some conclusions about the nature of coordination. These are summarized by Jeka and Kelso (1989) as follows:

1. Only a certain proportion of the extremely wide range of behavioral forms is actually realized. The ones observed are distinguished from others by their greater stability.
2. This stability is expressed in the fact that with smooth or gradual alteration of internal or external conditions, periodic forms maintain themselves until a critical limiting condition is reached. Transference to another equilibrium relationship occurs—usually abruptly—which is then maintained over a particular range of conditions.
3. The stability that characterizes the periodic forms as a whole does not apply to individual temporal subdivisions, in which disequilibrium states are more likely to occur.
4. There is a general tendency towards transference to equilibrium states of ever-increasing stability.

ROUND 2: MODELING BEHAVIOR ON DYNAMIC SYSTEMS

The work of von Holst suggested the possibility of a dynamic basis for order and regulation. But this promissory note could not be realized until new analytical tools were applied to the study of behavior. Toward this end, students of Bernstein began to model systems that generate order as *dynamic systems*, that is, they assumed that the motor apparatus behaves in a manner qualitatively similar to a physical system (Jeka & Kelso, 1989; Kelso, Ding, & Schoner, 1992; Kelso & Kay, 1987; Kugler & Turvey, 1987; Turvey, 1988). Let us consider how physical law is relevant to the study of action.

Energy dissipation and structure formation. Contemporary physicists studying complex systems such as chemical reactions (Prigogine (1980; Glansdorff & Prigogine, 1971; Prigogine & Stengers, 1984) began to identify some startling properties when these systems were far from equilibrium. While at equilibrium or near equilibrium molecules mix together homogeneously. However, in far-from-equilibrium systems, this is not the case:

> Far-from-equilibrium, new types of structure may originate spontaneously. In far-from-equilibrium conditions, we may have transformation from disorder, from thermal chaos, into order. New dynamic states of matter may originate, states that reflect the interaction of a given system with its surroundings. We have called these new structures dissipative structures to emphasize the constructive role of dissipative processes in their formation. (Prigogine & Stengers, 1984, p. 12)

Biologists quickly recognized the implication of Prigogine's work for the question of why the natural world is ordered the way it is (see, e.g., Brooks & Wiley, 1986; Wicken, 1987). Prigogine demonstrated that increasing complexity and organization accompanied entropy production in systems far from equilibrium. While living systems are *open systems* because they exchange energy and matter with their surround, they also "maintain their identity while undergoing such changes ... they are nonequilibrium systems and not totally open systems. Rather they have some definite boundaries or individual characteristics" (Brooks & Wiley, 1986, p. 36). Brooks and Wiley suggest that the fundamental interaction between one stochastic and one determinate factor in the relation between genetic and epigenetic processes is both the basis for an individual's identity and for the production of metabolic pathways.

Are there other examples of collective behavior of biological systems which exhibit this tendency to form structure when kinetics is constrained by a patterned field? The self-organizing behavior of a large population (on the order of 5 million) of social insects illustrates what happens when a self-organizing system is able to tap internally generated energy supplies relative to the information specified in perceptual gradients. The system self-organizes into macroscopic modes (modes of nest-building activity, see Fig. 2.3) and transforms energy into work. The flying insects have evolved a perceptual coupling to the macroscopic layout of pheromones (an attractor) deposited by the motion of the insects:

> The insects relate to the pheromone field through a perceptual coupling that circularly maps kinematic descriptions of the pheromone field into the insect's

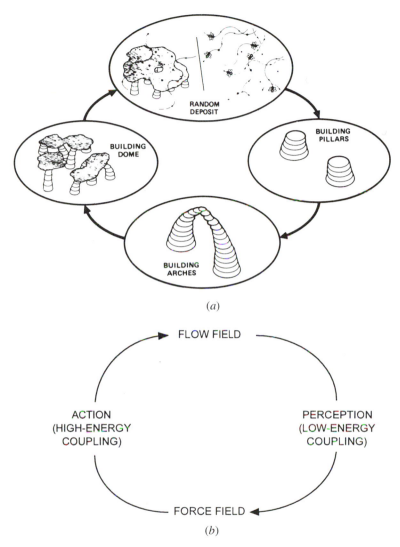

(a)

FLOW FIELD

ACTION
(HIGH-ENERGY
COUPLING)

PERCEPTION
(LOW-ENERGY
COUPLING)

FORCE FIELD

(b)

Figure 2.3. (a) Self-organizing ring of nest-building modes. The modes of nest building follow a circular causality of flows and forces. In the random deposit mode, the earliest deposits of waste are not chemotactically guided by pheromones. In building pillars, the insects are more likely to make pheromone-laden deposits at a pheromone-laden spot, and pillars begin to form. In building arches, two pillars which are built sufficiently close have pheromone diffusion fields which interact. The result is a saddlepoint midway between the two pillars, which introduces a bias toward depositing waste between the two pillars. Building a dome occurs when the arch is complete, because the saddlepoint is annihalated and new attractors and saddlepoints emerge. (b) A perception-action cycle. (From Kugler & Turvey, 1987. Copyright © 1987 by Lawrence Erlbaum Associates, Inc. Reprinted by permission.)

nervous system, and back into the world of kinetics through the insect's actuators. The perceptual coupling links the insects to the pheromone field only in regions of the building site where the pheromone concentration exceeds a critical activation threshold for their perceptual system. (Kugler, Shaw, Vincente, & Kinsella-Shaw, 1989/1990, p. 13)

In a *tour de force*, Kugler and Turvey (1987) present an analysis of modes of termite nest-building activity to illustrate how a new morphology of existing components arises as a consequence of the use of a diffusive flowfield to guide the forces generated by animals enveloped in that flowfield.

In building their nest, the behavior of African termites consists of four distinct phases:

1. *Random deposit*, in which pheromone-laden building materials are carried into a site and deposited *randomly*, until there emerge *preferred* sites that number far fewer than the original number of deposits.
2. *Formation of pillars*, in which, as a consequence of following pheromone gradients to sites of highest concentration (cf. definition of an attractor as a concentration of a conserved quantity), the material buildup at a particular site begins to take the shape of a pillar,
3. *Interaction of diffusion fields*, in which two pillars, which are sufficiently close to each other so that the pheromone gradients overlap at a point midway between them (cf. the concept of saddlepoint in a dynamic system), are joined together so that they form a single structure.
4. *Formation of a domed roof*, in which the concentration of pheromones at the midpoint of the arch results in formation of a roof which, in turn, is the site of random deposits that are the basis for beginning a new cycle. The termite nest is, thus, a product of the gradient-guided activities of a collection of insects. It persists and, indeed, becomes the home for future generations of insects.

Action systems and collective behavior. The activity of the perceptual and action systems of humans may also be construed as kinetic processes which are constrained by the enveloping patterned array described by Gibson (see Chapter 3). But how does the patterned array become instantiated in receptive fields so that efferent neural flow may be constrained? In the work of Kugler and Turvey (1987) as well as Turvey's more recent work (e.g., Burton & Turvey, 1990; Solomon, Turvey, & Burton, 1989) the haptic field is proposed as a model of how receptive fields might be organized in a way which constrains action. They draw a strong analogy between the example given above of individual insects being collectively organized when guided by an informational gradient and the way in which each "atomism" in a neural field (an individual microregion of tissue, each served by a mechanoreceptor) is connected. In their model of a "haptic cube," local muscle/tendon stress/strain distortions are propagated globally via the nervous system.

Let us, then, return to Bernstein's degrees-of-freedom problem with the tutorial on energy transactions at microscopic and macroscopic scales in mind.

Assembly as a reduction of dimensionality. Kay (1988) offers a framework for addressing the df problem which is based upon the process by which energy loss at the level of microscopic components in a nonconservative system results in reduction of degrees of freedom at the level of observed behavior. Consider the example of a damped mass-spring system (see Fig. 2.4), a block attached to a vertical support via a spring, riding on a rough surface. This system may be characterized by two degrees of freedom, since its equation of motion ($mx = -k(x - x_0) - bx$) requires two coordinates, position and velocity, to describe the evolution of the system at any time. Because of friction, the block always comes to rest, and when position and velocity are plotted against each other by means of a phase-plane diagram, the system's final behavior is a point with a mathematically zero dimension. Thus, the friction makes the damped mass-spring a nonconservative process: it generates overall energy loss in the system.

Kay considers human action systems as abstractly similar to physical devices such as the mass-spring system, in the sense that the behavior of an actor may be described in terms of the same equation of motion as the behavior of the mass-spring. He proposes two-constraint processes by which energy flow in action systems results in a reduction of dimensionality (see Fig. 2.5).

Resource dynamics. Bingham (1988) proposes that the degrees of freedom of action systems are dependent upon the energy flows in the nonconservative dynamics (resource dynamics) of the microcomponents of the body: bones, tendons, ligaments, nerves, blood, and blood vessels. For Bingham, understanding the process of assembly of these components into functional macroscopic systems (what he calls task-specific devices, TSDs) involves working backward from the dynamics of the TSD in specific contexts to infer the particular resource dynamics used. As he acknowledges, this is a very difficult problem, since the resource dynamics are nonlinear.

Consider a specific example of this approach. Bingham begins by distinguishing four systems which comprise the dynamic resources (see Fig. 2.6): the link-segment, musculotendon, circulatory, and nervous systems, respectively. Each of these has distinctive nonlinearities. One might not ordinarily suppose that constraints imposed at the ankles would influence performance at the wrists, but such influences might be mediated by the circulatory system. Bingham, Schmidt, Turvey, and Rosenblum (1991) specifically examined the influence of tonic activity at the ankles on coordination at the wrists as a way of inferring the participation of nonlinearities in circulatory and nervous system resource dynamics on

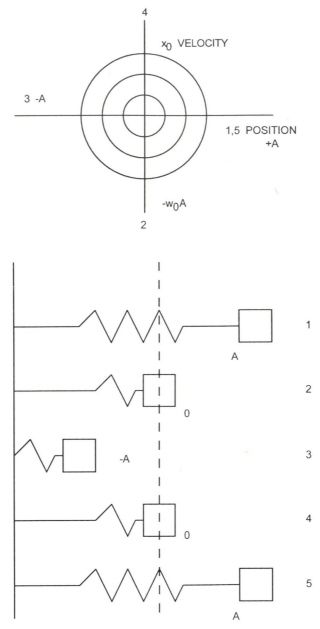

Figure 2.4. Phase portrait of the family of orbits (all possible trajectories) of an *mk* system. This is plotted on the phase-plane (position versus velocity). The family of orbits depends upon initial conditions (the energy put into the system, e.g., different masses). For fixed parameters, the size of the trajectory, but not the shape, changes.

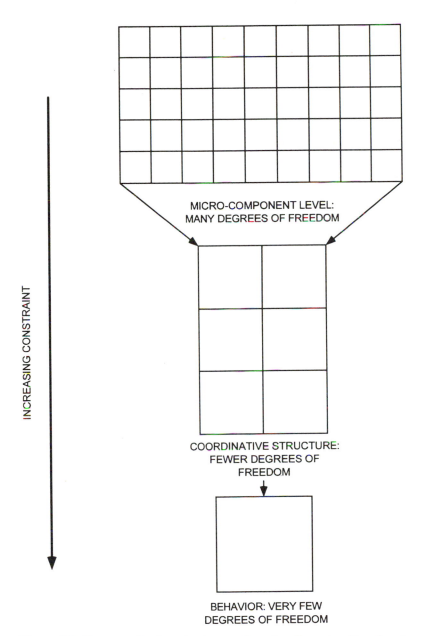

Figure 2.5. How coordinative structures reduce the dimensionality of a dynamic system. (Adapted from Kay, 1988. Copyright © 1988 by Elsevier Science Publishers, Inc. Reprinted by permission.)

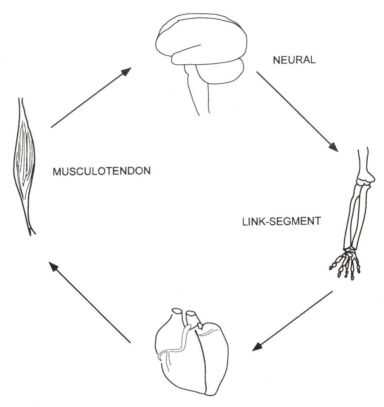

Figure 2.6. Four component subsystems comprising the action system.

behavior in a wrist-pendulum task. Of interest was whether experimental increases in tonic activity in one part of the body (the ankles) might influence wrist dynamics via circulatory resource dynamics.

The principal finding of the study was that when tonic activity at the ankle was increased, stiffness at the wrists also increased, in proportion to the wrist's inertial load. In evaluating this finding, Bingham and his colleagues worked backwards from the dynamics of the wrist to presumed circulatory dynamics. So, for example, they hypothesized that muscle activity at the ankle increased global blood pressure (this was later confirmed in a separate study), which changed the properties of the muscle so that there was increased power output in proportion to inertial load.

Modeling cooperativity. A hallmark of the second round of Bernstein-inspired research was Kugler, Kelso, and Turvey's (1980) proposal that coordinative structures were instances of dynamic regimes, systems that evolve over time and behave in a qualitatively similar way to a physical system. In this revision of the ecological approach to the study of coordination (see, e.g., Schmidt & Turvey, 1989), the microstructural resources of a single limb during locomotion were modeled by a mass-spring pendular system in a gravitational field with a linear spring attached (Turvey, et al., 1988).

Research done within the framework of task dynamics specifically begins with a rationale for selecting an equation of motion to model the dynamic system, and then conducts experiments aimed at identifying the values of parameters in the equations of motion. The rationale is based upon the abstract similarity between the body as a mechanical system and physical systems such as masses attached to springs. In the classical physical sense, dynamics is the study of how the forces in a system evolve over time to produce motions. Recently, the notion of dynamics has been expanded to include situations in which forces and motions are abstract concepts which do not require physical interpretation (e.g., Abraham & Shaw, 1987). Forces and motions then simply express relationships among variables of interest. The resulting abstract dynamics is a general science of how systems evolve over time, regardless of how the notions of force and motion are interpreted. In particular, abstract dynamics offers a theory of how low-dimensional behavior can be assembled from high-dimensional systems.

The starting point for the assembly of low-dimensional behavior is energy flow through a system (Kugler & Turvey, 1988; Morowitz, 1978). Systems through which there is energy flow are termed nonconservative, while those in which there is no energy flow are called conservative. There are three reasons why nonconservative models are being adopted in the study of biology and behavior: (1) they are more biologically realistic than conservative systems, since biological systems are open systems in which there are energy exchanges between the system and the environment, (2) energy flow induces stability, a hallmark of biological systems, and, most relevant to the present discussion (3) energy flow in nonconservative systems induces low-dimensional behavior from higher-dimensional components, i.e., during the time-evolution of a nonconservative system, degrees of freedom are being "dissipated out" (Kugler & Turvey, 1987).

We can illustrate these last two points with respect to two models of rhythmic, or oscillatory, behavior. The first, a simple conservative oscillator is the ideal undamped mass-spring:

$$m\dot{x} + k\ddot{x} = 0$$

where m = mass, k = spring stiffness, and $\dot{x}$ and $\ddot{x}$ are the position and acceleration, respectively, of the mass. This is a second-order system, meaning that it has two fundamental coordinates or components (position and velocity). The only energy exchanges that occur in this system occur within the system itself, between the mass and the spring. When the mass is perturbed away from its rest position ($x = 0$), the spring delivers a restoring force to bring the mass back to the rest position. However, since there are no losses in the system (that is, no flow of energy to the environment), the mass does not stop at the rest position, but goes through it and then oscillates around it.

Relevant to the second point above, this system exhibits one and only one stability: its frequency of oscillation is constant for constant m and k. However, the oscillation amplitude is unstable; if the mass is perturbed again, a new amplitude almost always results. Moreover (and see the third point above), the time-evolution of the system induces no reduction of degrees of freedom from the number of components to the observed behavior: the system starts out as a second-order system, i.e., having two dynamically relevant states (position and velocity), and the system's behavior is two-dimensional. Position and velocity must be known in order to know what its amplitude will be, because of the amplitude instability. On the phase-plane, which plots position versus velocity, the possible behaviors of the system fill up the entire two-dimensional plot.

An example of a nonconservative oscillator is the van der Pol oscillator (van der Pol, 1926; see Jordan & Smith, 1977). In its most abstract form, it may be described by a second order equation:

$$m\ddot{x} - a\dot{x} + bx^2\dot{x} + kx = 0$$

where m, k, $\dot{x}$, and $\ddot{x}$ are the same as for the ideal mass-spring, but where x is the velocity of the mass and a and b are coefficients on two nonconservative terms. These two terms introduce energy flow to the system: the first term (with coefficient a) always delivers energy to the mass, and the second term (with coefficient b) always takes energy away from the mass. A physical instantiation of the van der Pol oscillator is a simple mass-spring system: a mass attached at one end to a support (e.g., the ceiling) and at the other end to a freely moving mass.

The energy flow that thus occurs during the evolution of the oscillation of the van der Pol induces our above two phenomena. First, the amplitude of the oscillation is now stable in the face of perturbations. The van der Pol oscillator also exhibits other kinds of stability, including a stable relationship between two of its observables (frequency and amplitude) and a type of temporal stability (phase resetting) (see Kay, Saltzman, & Kelso, 1991). These are all due to the presence of energy flow. Second, the degrees of freedom are reduced during system evolution from the two original ones (again, position and velocity) to one. After an initial startup (transient) period, if one knows the position or velocity alone, one can predict the system behavior for all time. On the phase plane, the steady-state (post-transient) behavior occupies a very limited portion of the plot: a single cyclic trajectory, or limit cycle. Mathematically, this limit cycle is a one-dimensional object. Thus, two degrees of freedom have been reduced to one during the transient evolution of the system from an arbitrary starting point not on the limit cycle.

Abstract dynamics is, thus, a framework for describing systems that evolve over time. Dynamic models of nonconservative systems in particular allow us to investigate how high-dimensional, multicomponent systems evolve to produce low-dimensional behavior, and can be used to investigate behaviors more complex than simple rhythms.

Building a dynamic model: Methodology. How does one go about generating a dynamic model of some interesting behavior? The first step is to decide how complex a model is needed, by characterizing the complexity of the observed behavior. For nonconservative systems, the number of degrees of freedom at the component level must exceed the degrees of freedom at the behavioral level, because the degrees of freedom are reduced by the energy flow through the system. So, a first step is to characterize the complexity of the behavior of interest (Kay, 1988). This sets a lower limit on the complexity of the model.

One example of this kind of methodology is a study with adults by Kay, Kelso, Saltzman, and Schoner (1987). Their subjects performed wrist motions at various required frequencies, and the amplitude of motion was observed over several steady-state cycles, in which the subjects did not overtly change what they were doing. The resultant frequency–amplitude function had a particular form that was closely approximated by a particular nonconservative limit-cycle oscillator. Thus, a pattern of coordination was characterized by low-dimensional collective variables (an equation of motion).

A second example of the modeling methodology is the work by Haken, Kelso, and Bunz (1985) on relative phase of the rhythmic movement of the left and right finger. In earlier work, Kelso (1981, 1984) had subjects rhythmically move their index fingers or hands so that homologous muscle activation was either in phase or alternating. At a certain critical frequency, switching occurs spontaneously from the anti-phase to in-phase mode, but not in the reverse direction. Thus, while there are two stable patterns for low-frequency oscillation, only one pattern remains as frequency is scaled beyond a certain region. Here, relative phase is an order parameter or collective variable because it characterizes all observed coordinative patterns, has simple dynamics, and changes abruptly at the transition.

Haken et al. (1985) were able to model four properties of this system: the stationary states of 0 and 180 degrees, the bistability of the patterns, 2 pi periodicity, and the symmetry of the left and right hands. Their model is a potential, V, that combines two cosine functions:

$$V = -a \cos\phi - b \cos2\phi$$

where a and b are control parameters. The behavior generated by this model is depicted in Fig. 2.7. As b/a decreases from 1.00, the ball illustrates the systems's transition from out-of-phase to in-phase ($b/a = 0$).

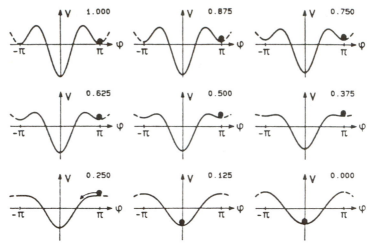

Figure 2.7. The consequence of a changing potential landscape. The potential V/a changes as values of b/a are varied. The numbers refer to the ratio b/a. (From Haken, Kelso, & Bunz, 1985. Copyright © 1985 by Springer-Verlag Publishers. Reprinted by permission.)

The model also makes certain predictions about the stability of the system close to transition points. As the system approaches a critical point, there may be an accompanying increase in fluctuations around the mean state of the collective variable (phase). The switch to a new pattern is accompanied by a marked decrease in fluctuations. The loss of stability is believed to be the chief mechanism that effects a change of pattern: fluctuations drive the system away from its present state. This is precisely what Kelso and Scholz (1985) and Kelso, Scholz, and Schoner (1986) found when they observed actual behavior. A second prediction is critical slowing down: when a system is close to a transition point, it reacts more slowly to external perturbation than when it is far away from the critical point. For both enhancement of fluctuations and critical slowing down, new states evolve without specific influences from the outside.

Relevance of the modeling approach for understanding development of action systems. In Chapter 1, I introduced the idea that the transformation of spontaneous activity into a task-specific action pattern involves the processes of assembly and tuning. The various equations of motion presented above may constitute a veritable bestiary of dynamic systems with characteristic attractors, on which global musculoskeletal functions may be modeled. How are such functions assembled?

I suggest here that spontaneous activity in the context of task constraints results in the formation of stable action patterns, akin to morphogenesis in biological systems or pattern formation in physical systems (Haken, 1983;

Murray, 1989; and see Chapter 5). The high-dimensional solution space is restricted by task constraints—the intrinsic dynamics of a system of pendular limbs and spring-like muscles, and the physical properties of the environmental context. These define a virtual layout of attractors that yield specific classes of movement, such as the class of point-attractor or limit-cycle behaviors. The actor must then explore this layout to locate an attractor—sometimes randomly as in the global flailing often exhibited by infants, or in more directed ways, such as probing the space with an existing repertoire of skills or reflexes. The notion is that the discovery of a low-dimensional attractor serves to index an appropriate configuration of the action system's components. In Haken's (1983) terms, the emergence of an attractor from the interplay of the system's many degrees of freedom reciprocally acts to "enslave" those degrees of freedom and assemble an appropriate class of movements. This implies that one of the functions of spontaneous activity in infancy is to explore possible organizations by allowing the free interplay of components and becoming sensitive to the attractors that emerge.

There are two possible advantages to operating at an attractor for a given task. First, it is often noted that preferred movements are energetically efficient. Indeed, there is a large literature showing that, for actions as various as walking or using a bicycle pump, actors freely adopt "optimal" movement patterns that require minimum energy expenditure within the constraints of the task (Holt, Hamill, & Andres, 1990; Hoyt & Taylor, 1981; Corlett & Mahaveda, 1970; Ralston, 1976; Turvey, et al., 1988). On this interpretation, the dynamics can be described in terms of a potential landscape (see above) with hills (maxima) representing high energy cost and valleys (minima) representing attractors with low energy cost. Such landscapes can be defined at the function, parameter, and state levels of analysis (see Chapter 1). Minima in function space correspond to global attractors or musculoskeletal organizations for a given task. Minima in parameter space correspond to efficient parameter configurations. And with fixed parameters, the attractor toward which the system evolves is also a minimum energy state.

Once infants discover the attractor in function space, they may systematically evaluate the effects of varying the parameters of this function, such as mass, stiffness, damping, and forcing frequency of a mass-spring, on the behavior of the system. This can be represented as an exploration of "parameter space." A surface in parameter space would then reflect the consequences of various parameter settings, with a minimum in the surface indexing an appropriate combination of parameter values for the task. Some parameters are often fixed by the task constraints, but others may be modulated by parameter tuning which adjusts movement to local conditions of the task. The developing infant thus becomes sensitive to minima in parameter space and uses them to configure the parameters for a given task. An example of this is presented in Chapter 7 when I evaluate the proposition that infants explore the dynamics of their own movement in order to adjust leg stiffness to task constraints (bouncing while supported by a spring).

Most parameter changes are benign in that they do not qualitatively affect the system's behavior, and the system is considered "structurally stable" under such changes. But for nonlinear systems, certain parameter changes can alter the system's behavior qualitatively, giving rise to a different number, type, or layout of attractors. At such critical points, the system is said to "bifurcate" or, in physical terms, undergo a phase transition. Exploring the parameter range assesses the structural stability of a particular organization and may be critical in learning to control transitions from one mode of behavior to another.

Note.   The sections of this chapter from pp. 49 to 54 were written in collaboration with Bruce Kay and Bill Warren. I am, of course, responsible for any errors which remain. E.C.G.

CHAPTER 3

ECOLOGICAL FOUNDATIONS

> The world of physical reality does not consist of meaningful things. The world of ecological reality, as I have been trying to describe it, does.
>
> J. J. Gibson, 1979, p. 33

At the heart of Gibson's vision of ecological reality is the idea that the fundamental unit of analysis for studying the regulatory function of perception in the organization of action is the relation between animal and environment. To know something about one requires an understanding of the other. In his three books, Gibson (1950, 1966, 1979) was primarily concerned with (1) describing the energy flow that bathes our planet and the patterning of that energy flow by the terrestrial media, substances, and surfaces, and (2) describing functionally specific perceptual systems (e.g., for seeing, listening, etc.) evolved as a consequence of using the same kinds of patterning (e.g., gradients) of different kinds of energy (e.g., electromagnetic, gravitational, etc.).

More recent work (e.g., Kugler & Turvey, 1987; Reed, 1985, 1988b; Warren, 1988a) extends Gibson and provides a second focus for an ecological study of the animal environment relation: the study of how macroscopic functional organizations of living tissue have evolved to exploit patterned energy in guiding their functional activities. These two foci are the basis for the first sections on Gibson.

GIBSON: AMBIENT ARRAY, PATTERNED FLOW, AND PERCEPTUAL SYSTEM

The ambient optic array. The perceiving and acting of animals occurs via energy flow at an ecological scale of analysis, i.e., one that is intermediate between the energy flows at the geological and biological cellular scales, respectively (see Fig. 3.1, and cf. Shaw & Kinsella-Shaw, 1988). At all three time scales, the systems in question are open with respect to the exchange of materials across boundaries (e.g., the earth's atmosphere, an animal's epithelial

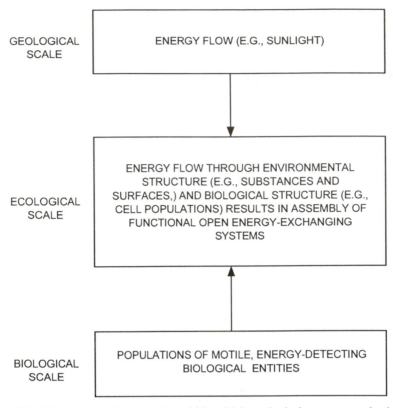

Figure 3.1. The ecological time scale, within which ecological systems evolved on earth, consists of relatively short-lived, but complex organisms.

and receptor surfaces, and the membrane of a cell), and so are subject to the laws of flow, or thermodynamics (Kugler & Turvey, 1987). The flow, or exchange of energy across boundaries is, thus, the basis for an ecological definition of information.

Gibson recognized early in his work on perception the fundamental relation between energetic particles and the "energy reflecting" fields that envelop them. It is upon this relation that Gibson builds his theory of direct perception, i.e., that perceptual information is an alternative description of (i.e., is specific to) the fields that envelop the forces produced by interacting substances. According to Gibson (1979), the central concept of his program of ecological optics is the *ambient optic array* at a point of observation. Gibson defines the array as a sphere which envelops an animal and which can be divided into a nested hierarchy of solid angles all having a common apex:

> The components of the array are the visual angles from the mountains, canyons, trees, and leaves (actually, what are called solid angles in geometry). ... Every solid angle, no matter how small, has form in the sense that its cross-section has

a form ... Solid angles can fill up a sphere in the way that sectors fill up a circle ... The surface of the sphere whose center is the common apex of all the solid angles can be thought of as a kind of transparent film or shell, but it should not be thought of as a picture. (p. 68)

The array is ambient in the sense that it is structured, i.e., caused to have discontinuities within it by (1) the physical inclinations of the faces and facets of surfaces, (2) the reflectance of substances, and (3) the chromatic reflectance of substances. Each position within the array can *potentially* be occupied by an animal. At a particular point of observation, there is a unique array. As an animal moves through the optic array, each point of observation is linked into a trajectory. On the one hand, this trajectory specifies the specific displacement being made by the animal as it locomotes through the environment, and on the other specifies the unique successive overlapping samples of the array which are picked up by the animal's perceptual systems during the specific displacement (see Tables 3.1 and 3.2).

An illustration of how the optic array, a field, envelops the displacement of an animal and is specific to each kind of displacement can be seen in Fig. 3.2, from Gibson (1966). It depicts the flow of the optic array surrounding a bird during its locomotion (i.e., flight) through the medium of air above the ground plane. When the bird flies in a straight line, there is a flow of the structure of the field past the head relative to a moving point of observation (see text below). From the bird's point of observation, the center of outflow specifies approach and direction of approach, and with each change in direction, there is a shift in the center of outflow. Gibson proposed that fields are distinguished by animals on the basis of the relative density of their structure, or gradients, and that such gradients are revealed to an animal during its displacement within the optic array.

Table 3.1. The optic array and the process of information pickup

Concept	Definition
Ambient optic array	A nested hierarchy of (visual) solid angles all having a common apex. The array is ambient in the sense that it is structured, i.e., caused to have borders within it by (1) the physical inclinations of the faces and facets of surfaces, and (2) the reflectance (including spectral) of substances
Point of observation	A position in the medium that can potentially be occupied by an animal. For every fixed point of observation, there is a unique optic array
Successive sampling	Successive overlapping samples of the ambient optic array are picked up by an observer during head movements (a moving point of observation, or path). The field of view of each eye in the head is a sliding sample of the array as the head turns, gaining structure at the leading edge, and losing structure at the trailing edge

Source: After J. J. Gibson, 1966, 1979.

Table 3.2. The specificity between action and information

Action	Information Specific to Action
A. Invariants of locomotion	
1. Motion	Flow (reflections from particles of the terrain streaming past the head relative to a moving point of observation)
2. Stasis	Non-flow
3. Approach to	Outflow (magnification of flow)
4. Retreat from	Inflow (minification of flow)
5. Direction of locomotion	Center of outflow
6. Change in direction	Shift in center of outflow
B. Affordances for locomotion	
1. Obstacle	A rigid object, attached or detached, which affords collision
2. Opening	An aperture, hole, or gap in a surface; affords passage
3. Brink	A drop-off in the ground (e.g., a step or the edge of a perch) affords falling off of

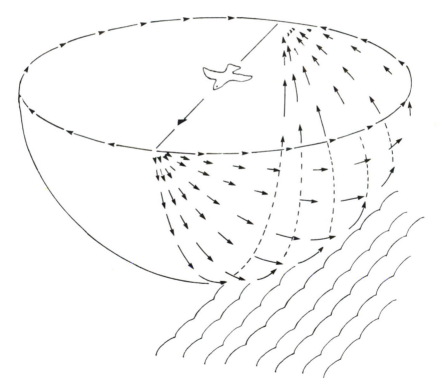

Figure 3.2. The flow of the optic array during locomotion in a terrestrial environment. When a bird moves parallel to the earth, the texture of the lower hemisphere of the optic array flows under its eyes. The flow consists of focuses of expansion (ahead) and contraction (behind). The greatest velocity of backward flow corresponds to the nearest bit of the earth and the other velocities decrease outward from this perpendicularly in all directions, vanishing at the horizon. The vectors in the diagram represent angular velocities. (From J. J. Gibson, 1986 (originally published 1979). Copyright © 1986 by Lawrence Erlbaum Associates. Reprinted by permission.)

58

Gibson's ecological description of the patterning of the array into gradients is really a geometric taxonomy of the patterning of the array by the substances and surfaces of our world. He offers an ecology of surface layout (see Tables 3.3a, 3.3b, and 3.3c) that progressively assembles a world of surface topologies, attachments, openings, enclosures, embeddings and overlaps. His theory offers a taxonomy of events that characterize the ecology of

Table 3.3(a). The ecology of surface layout: Some examples of an applied geometry

Term	Definition
Substance	Solids and liquids that vary in composition, and in resistance to change
Surface	A substance with a characteristic texture, reflectance, and layout
Layout	The persisting arrangement of surfaces relative to one another and to the ground
Ground	A reference surface for all other surfaces, usually perpendicular to the force of gravity
Horizon	The margin between earth and sky
Edge	A junction of two surfaces that make a convex dihedral angle
Corner	A junction of two surfaces that make a concave dihedral angle
Occluding edge	An edge that both separates and connects the hidden and unhidden surface, both divides and unites them
Detached object	A substance with a surface that is topologically closed and capable of displacement
Attached object	A layout of surfaces less than completely surrounded by the medium; usually continuous with the substance of another surface
Partial enclosure	A layout of surfaces that only partly encloses the medium
Enclosure	A layout of surfaces that surrounds the medium to some degree
Hollow object	An object that is also an enclosure (an object from the outside, but an enclosure from the inside)

Source: After J. J. Gibson, 1979.

Table 3.3(b). Ecological laws of surfaces

1. All persisting substances have surfaces, and all surfaces have a layout.
2. Any surface has resistance to deformation, depending on the viscosity of the substance.
3. Any surface has resistance to disintegration, depending on the cohesion of the substance.
4. Any surface has a characteristic texture, depending upon the composition of the substance. It generally has both a layout texture and a pigment texture.
5. Any surface has a characteristic shape, or large-scale layout.
6. A surface may be strongly or weakly illuminated, in light or in shade.
7. An illuminated surface may absorb either much or little of the illumination falling on it.
8. A surface has a charactistic reflectance, depending on the substance.
9. A surface has a characteristic distribution of the reflectance rations of the different wavelengths of light, depending upon the substance (color).

Source: After J. J. Gibson, 1979.

Table 3.3(c). Rules for the visual control of locomotion

Functional Activity	Rule
Standing	Keep the feet in contact with a surface of support; keep the boundaries of the field of view oriented with the implicit horizon
Starting	To startm make the array flow
Stopping	To stop, cancel the flow
Going back	To go back, make the flow reverse
Turning	To turn, shift the center of outflow from one patch in the optic array to another
Steering	To steer, keep the center of outflow outside the patches of the array that specify barriers, obstacles, and brinks, and within a patch that specifies an opening
Approaching	To approach, magnify a patch in the array
Entering enclosures	To enter an enclosure, magnify the angle of its opening to 180 degrees and open the vista. Make sure that there is gain of structure inside the contour and not loss outside, or else collide with obstacle
Keeping a safe distance	To prevent an injurious encounter, keep the optical structure of the surface from magnifying to the degree that specifies an encounter
Fleeing	To flee, so move as to minify the dangerous form and to make the surrounding optic array flow inward
Predating (chasing for the purpose of eating)	To predate, move as to magnify the succulent form by making the surrounding array flow outward until it reaches the proper angular size for capturing

Source: After J. J. Gibson, 1979.

our planet (see Fig. 3.3), such as those that distinguish living from inanimate things in motion (translation, looming, zooming, radial flow, perspective transformation), interactions between things (e.g., deformation, accretion–deletion, common fate, occlusion), events unique to living things (growth/decay, biological motion) and changes of state (e.g., melting of a solid into a liquid, construction and destruction).

In providing a geometrical description of material forms that would be useful for animals which have evolved into different forms of living tissue, Gibson was faced with a conundrum: how could a patterning of the array by substances and surfaces and by events be perceived in a way that would specify activities *common* to all animals, and at the same time specify for a particular animal the *user-specific* meanings of things in the environment? In other words, what guides the flight of a bird, the dance of a bee, and the gait of a human as each forages for food and, at the same time, specifies for each that a material form is edible?

For Gibson, the underlying link between all animals on the planet is their *mobility*: a particular relation between surfaces is perceived as invariant (unchanging over transformations resulting from motion) because animals with different forms and different kinds of receptors can reveal the same information

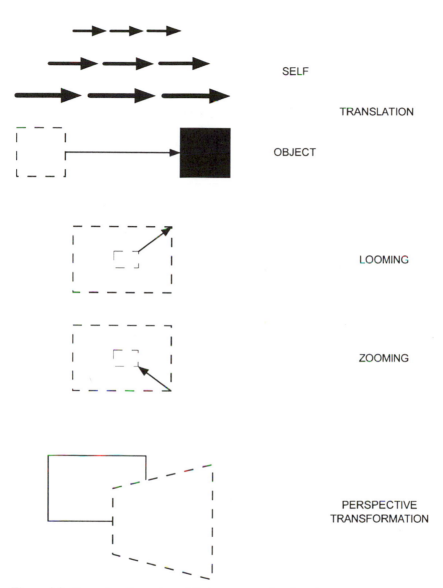

Figure 3.3. Examples of events and their corresponding invariants.

by means of successive overlapping samples of the ambient array. These samples result from the motion of trajectories of points of observations corresponding to the movement of their body. At the same time, *some* animals, by virtue of the differentially evolved state of their nervous systems, their size, form, and capabilities, are able to reveal patterns in the ambient optic array that *others* cannot reveal. In other words, *while they may be able to make the same successive samples, their ability to select or use the structure contained within*

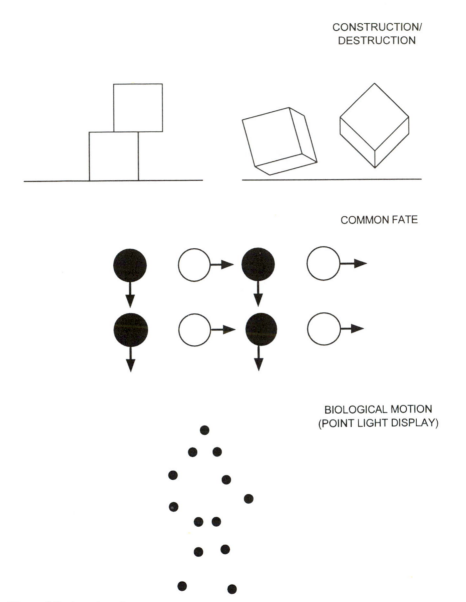

Figure 3.3. (*continued*)

those samples will differ. It is the *scaling of the kind of structure obtained during exploration of the ambient array to the properties of the animal* that Gibson tried to capture in his concept of *affordance:*

> Subject to revision, I suggest that the affordance of anything is a specific combination of the properties of its substance and its surfaces taken with reference to an animal. (J. J. Gibson, 1977, p. 67)

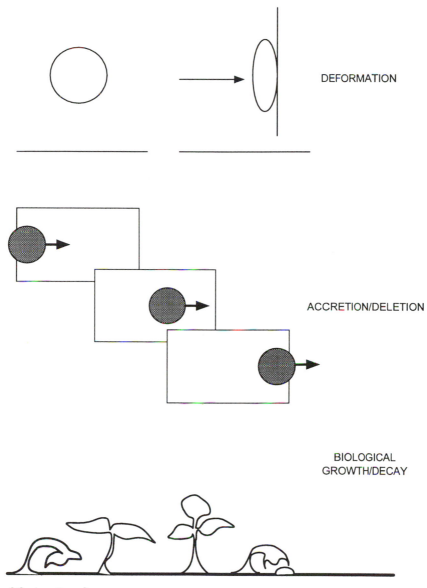

Figure 3.3. (*continued*)

Gibson made a preliminary attempt to describe some of the affordances of the terrestrial environment (see Table 3.4), relative to the media (air, water), substances, surfaces and their layout, objects, animals and persons, and releationships (e.g., concealment). Students of Gibson have gone in several directions in attempting to further operationalize the concept of affordance, and the way in which animals detect the affordances available in their own ecological niche. Common among these endeavors is the idea that what

Table 3.4. Affordances

Category	Affordance Relation	Action Mode Supported
Medium	Air (air spaces between obstacles and objects)	Respiration (for air breathing animals), unimpeded locomotion, visual exploration, exploration of vibratory events (sound fields), exploration of volatile sources (odor fields)
	Water	Respiration (for water-breathing animals), locomotion for aquatic and some other animals, limited visual perception at lower depths, considerable exploration of vibratory events at low frequencies, exploration of volatile sources, drinking for some animals, pouring from container, washing, bathing
Substances	Solids	Some afford nutrition. hard substances can be chipped, soft ones can be molded, elastic ones recover their original shape after deformation; afford manufacture, i.e., fabrication by hand
Surfaces and their layout	Horizontal, flat, extended, rigid surface	Affords support; permits equilibrium and maintaining of posture with respect to gravity
	Vertical, flat, extended, rigid	Downward slope affords falling if steep (the brink of a cliff is a falling off place). Barriers do not afford locomotion unless there is a door, gate, or bridge. There are ordinarily paths between obstacles
Objects	Detached objects	When scaled to muscular strength, afford lifting and carrying. When scaled to hand size, afford grasping and manipulation. Objects which afford (a) manipulation: sheets, sticks, fibers, containers, clothing tools, (b) wielding: club, hammer, lever, spear, needle, awl, (c)cutting: rigid objects with sharp dihedral angles, (d) throwing: missile, ball; with supplementary tools: sling bow, catapult, (e) knotting, binding, lashing, knitting, weaving, (f) trace making: stylus, brush, crayon, pen, pencil
	Other persons and animals	Mutual affordances: prey and predator, buyer and seller
Places	Eating place	Foraging for food
	Place of danger	Climbing to the brink of a cliff; locomoting to an area where predators lurk
	Place of refuge from predators	The home; a partial enclosure
	Place of concealment	Concealing oneself from an observer

Source: After J. J. Gibson, 1977, 1979.

distinguishes an animal's activity within a niche is exploration for a particular resource (sometimes called a trophic or nurturing substance, see, e.g., Purves, 1988) which supports the energetic requirements of that particular activity. I return to this notion after a discussion of Gibson's functional theory of the perceptual systems.

The perceptual systems. In his 1966 book, *The senses considered as perceptual systems*, Gibson attempted to eschew the traditional notion that the receptors were passive conduits for sensations in favor of the idea that *perception was an active process of detecting the patterns of structured energy in the ambient array*. Table 3.5 presents a summary of five ways in which the concept of perceptual system differs from that of the traditional sense. Fundamental to these is the idea that each perceptual system is a *mode* of activity, meaning that each perceptual system is distinguished by a function required for the survival of the animal (Gibson, 1966; Pick & Saltzman, 1978). For example, the basic orienting system is distinguished by its function of relating body position to gravity and the surface of support, while the auditory system functions to pick up the direction of an event. Clearly, though, given the emphasis on the active nature of perceptual exploration, hearing depends to some extent on basic orienting: to listen to a sound coming from a particular direction requires a postural adjustment of the body, i.e., an orientation.

Gibson has most extensively elaborated his theory with respect to the visual perceptual system. He notes that vision is useful for obtaining exteroceptive information (about the layout of the environment and about external objects and events) and proprioceptive information about the acts being performed. Lee (1978) suggests a modification whereby proprioception refers to the obtaining of information about the position and movement of parts of the body relative to the body. He introduces the term exproprioception to

Table 3.5. Five fundamental differences between a sense and a perceptual system

Sense	Perceptual System
Defined by a bank of receptors connected with a projection center in the brain. The definition of sense does not include the adjustments of the organ in which the receptors are incorporated	Defined by an organ and its active adjustments at a given level of functioning. At any level, incoming and outgoing nerve fibers are considered together so as to make a continuous loop (e.g., retinal receptors and visual projection areas are considered relative to active adjustments of the head and body as a whole)
Receptors only receive stimuli passively The inputs of a sense, its sensations, can be combined in accordance with the laws of association	Input–output loops obtain information actively With continuing experience, information is picked up in an increasingly selective way, i.e., each action in a loop is more precisely guided by the pattern scanned
Inputs have the qualities of the receptors being stimulated	Information is amodal and specific to the relation between the act of exploring the environment and the properties of things in the world
Attention occurs at centers within the nervous system. Increasing selectivity results from filtering of nervous impulses	Attention pervades the whole input–output loop. Increasing selectivity during exploratory activity results from changing resonance of the entire loop

Source: After J. J. Gibson, 1979.

refer to the obtaining of information about the position, orientation, or movement of the body as a whole, or part of the body, relative to the environment. These functions of vision are, again, based upon orientation of the body and, like hearing and the other perceptual systems, vision is closely related to basic orienting.

In addition to the functions that *distinguish* each as a mode, the perceptual systems share a *common function*: the detection of persistence and change in invariant structure of the optic array. By invariant, Gibson means a structure that is preserved despite a transformation. For example, in surface layout, an edge is an invariant form defined as a junction of two surfaces that make a convex dihedral angle, and specified by a particular patterning of the array. There are, similarly, invariants for events specified in the patterned array.

How can the perceptual systems, on the one hand, be specialized for detecting information specific to a modality and, on the other, detect information which is invariant across modalities? Gibson's solution is again a brilliant one. He argues that the patterning of the ambient array is amodal: more than one of the perceptual systems may detect the same patterning by exploring the array in the same way (since they are all based on the activity of the basic orienting system). Thus, an edge may be detected by the eyes or by the surface of the skin of the hand because *while the receptors transduce different energy fields, the active adjustments of the organs by the basic orienting system reveal the same patterns of successive and adjacent order in those fields.*

Gibson, influenced by the ideas of Lashley, proposed that during information pickup, the nervous system "resonates" (cf. von Holst on p. 41 of Chapter 2) to information. What made resonance work as a model for information pickup was the notion of a covariation between active exploration by a perceptual system and different inputs. In his review of Edelman's book *Neural Darwinism*, Reed (1989) makes the meaning of covariation more explicit than did Gibson, first, with respect to the active nature of the perceptual systems:

> Because perceptual organs are active, the same environmental configuration will lead to a variety of different "inputs" according to the different configurations and movements of the perceptual organs. But these different inputs will covary with the exploratory activities involved. For example, a single object can be felt with one hand or with two, with a single finger moving over it, or simultaneously by a number of fingers—and all these diverse input–output loops are parts of the process of perceiving one unified object. (p. 110)

Reed continues by considering the function of the neural ensembles underlying exploratory skills:

> Perceptual systems are made up of neural ensembles underlying exploratory skills integrated with ensembles underlying skills of information extraction. An equilibrium of activation across these ensembles—a resonant state—is only

achieved when there is covariance across the entire ensemble of activated groups. Such covariance means that a uniquely specific environmental object or event has been detected, although the particular combination of inputs and outputs constituting the detection may never have been previously experienced. (p. 111)

As we shall see in Chapter 4, such neural ensembles are the kith and kin of the functional collections of neurons proposed by Luria (1980; and see Kelso & Tuller, 1981), the model of control surfaces of cerebellar and related nuclei (Arbib, 1987; Churchland, 1989), and Edelman's theory of re-entrant signaling (Edelman, 1987), i.e., they are complex in composition, plastic in the variability of their elements, and possessing the property of autoregulation.

DEVELOPMENT OF EXPLORATION FOR AFFORDANCES IN HUMANS

Active exploration. Eleanor Gibson (1969, 1982, 1988) has used the concept of a self-tuning perceptual system and J. J. Gibson's ecological optics (especially the concept of affordance) as the foundations for her theory of perceptual development via active exploratory activity. Her summary of the exploratory activities of infants during the first year is presented in Table 3.6. Gibson proposes three phases (not stages, in the Piagetian sense but rather more like the organization of behavior in dynamic systems theory, e.g., Goldfield, 1989, 1990; Thelen, 1989a, 1990), and what distinguishes these phases is the increasing selectivity of the perceptual systems and the increasing postural control and mobility of the infant.

At each phase, the infant's increasing perceptual selectivity, postural control and mobility make it possible to discover new affordances. During the first phase, neonates actively explore by moving the head and eyes turning the

Table 3.6. Phases of infant exploration

Developmental phase	Characteristics
Exploration of events (birth to 4 months)	Very young infants explore immediate surround due to limited postural (i.e., eye-head, trunk) control. There is orienting to sounds accompanying events and use of haptic mouthing to discover object properties
Attention to affordances and distinctive features of events (5 to 8 months)	Improved postural control, reach, and grasp, as well as visual skills make it possible to discover new affordances and study distinctive features
Ambulatory exploration (9 months and on)	Increasingly independent mobility makes possible discovery of extended environments around corners, behind obstacles, and behind oneself, as well as investigation of affordances for hiding

Source: After E. J. Gibson, 1988.

head to a sound source (Field, Muir, Pilon, Sinclair, & Dodwell, 1980), and using the mouth for haptic exploration (Rochat, 1989). The transition to phase two at around four or five months is marked by new attentiveness to affordances and the distinctive features of objects. The transition comes about when several different subsystems (the visual perceptual system, the performatory system for reaching) each contributes to the infant's intentionality, the ability to use affordances to direct its activity. Self-initiated locomotion marks the transition to the third phase of development in Gibson's developmental model. In order to locomote, infants need to steer around obstacles and through apertures, and they must detect a safe surface of support for traversal (J. J. Gibson, 1988; Goldfield, 1989). Active locomotion seems to promote an infant's attention to this information, and to laws of control to simultaneously regulate steering, maintaining balance, and propulsion. The phases of exploration are examined in greater detail in the context of specific content areas in the chapters of Part III.

ACTION SYSTEMS

Taxonomies. The previous sections examined James Gibson's ecological approach to perception, and its extension by Eleanor Gibson to problems of perceptual development. The following sections further extend the work of the Gibsons by considering the relationship between habitats, as studied in the fields of ecology and developmental psychobiology, and the development of action systems. When Gibson (1966, 1979) created his taxonomy of perceptual systems, he did so in the context of an ecological approach, the extension of a study of the relation between animal and environment to perceptual behavior.

In ecology (as a branch of biology), a traditional approach to describing the diversity of life is to use taxonomies, classifications according to similarity or shared characteristics (Mayr, 1982). Here, I present a taxonomy of action systems, first introduced by Reed (1982), and modified in three specific ways. First, I do not include two of Reed's action systems, the semantic and play systems, respectively. These require special treatment because of the way that they have become appropriated during evolution and ontogeny for symbolization, and will be addressed elsewhere (see Chapter 13). Second, I extend Reed's analysis by considering the sequence of habitats (e.g., uterus, mother, social group) which are the milieu for each developing action system (Alberts and Cramer, 1988). Third, I propose rules for control of action in each developing action system (see Table 3.7).

Basic orienting. The basic orienting system "maintains a multicellular animal's functional orientation to gravity, and to the surfaces (ground, substrate) and media (air, water) of the environment" (Reed, 1982, p. 114). The resources potentially available for use by the basic orienting system are fundamental terrestrial persistences (diurnal cycles of light and dark, geographic invariances, gravity).

Appetitive. The appetitive action system is the means by which animals exchange energy with the environment via respiration, ingestion, and thermoregulation. The resources for appetition include nutrients, metabolites, and anti-metabolites.

Table 3.7. A partial list of rules for control of action in each of the developing action systems

Action System	Rules for Control of Action
Basic orienting	1. To maintain orientation, cancel optical flow by introducing appropriate changes in force 2. To introduce instability, allow flow to occur as follows (a) To start, make array flow (b) To keep moving, maintain flow (c) To change direction, magnify patch in optic array
Locomotion	1. To stand, keep feet in contact with a support surface; keep boundaries of the field of view oriented with the implicit horizon 2. To steer, keep center of outflow outside patches of array that specify barriers, obstacles, and brinks, and within a patch that specifies an opening 3. To approach, magnify a patch in the array 4. To enter an enclosure, magnify the angle of its opening to 180 degrees and open up the vista 5. To avoid collision, insure that there is a gain of structure inside the contour and not a loss outside 6. To avoid injury, keep optical structure of surface from magnifying to a degree that specifies contact
Appetition	1. To move hand or implement to food, minify the patch in the array specifying the hand or implement so that it makes contact with the food 2. To bring food to the mouth, magnify the patch in the array specifying the food so that it makes contact with the mouth 3. To taste an object, put it in the mouth and bring it into contact with oral mucosa
Performatory	1. To lift an object, grasp it and lift the arm so that the object no longer makes contact with a support surface 2. To drop an object, open grasped hand and release the object so that its optical specification is minified (and perhaps so that it makes a loud noise) 3. To throw an object held in the hand, release the object while the hand is moving away from the body so that the object minifies 4. To explore the texture of an object, place skin surface in contact with the object and move the skin surface over it
Expressive	1. To make another person approach, vocalize, and alternately magnify and minify their face (i.e, engage in en face play), smile and vocalize 2. To make another person relieve your feelings of discomfort, cry

Investigative. All of the perceptual systems, of course, are action systems. For this reason, the perceptual systems are here classified as investigatory action systems. What makes them action systems is that the process of perceiving requires the active orienting of the perceptual organs to the resources of ecological information.

Performatory. All animals have appendages by which they may alter aspects of the environment to suit their needs or goals. These include the mouths of fish, the claws and bills of birds, the hands of primates, the trunk of the elephant, and so on. All of these are used to structure available resources into habitats, such as shelters and nests, are used for foraging and to capture prey, and to make tools.

Locomotory. Locomotion refers to the capacity to move from place to place in order to explore for resources distributed throughout a given habitat. Locomotion is achieved in different ways within different media (air, water, and on the ground), but have in common the use of disequilibrium (falling) to initiate motion,

Expressive. Expressive acts communicate internal organizational states (affect, intention) via organized patterns of movement, often of the facial musculature.

HABITATS FOR ACTION SYSTEMS

Ontogenetic niches. I noted in Chapter 1 the significance of the concept of ontogenetic adaptation, a behavior which serves an immediate adaptive role, whether or not it anticipates a function that becomes adaptive at a later age (Oppenheim, 1981; Hall & Oppenheim, 1987). The complementary contexts for ontogenetic adaptation are the *ontogenetic niche*, what the animal does, its "occupation" (i.e., another term for a collection of action systems), and the *habitat*, an animal's "address, where it lives in space and time, its temperature, humidity, light level and cycle, energy sources, and distribution of resources" (Alberts & Cramer, 1988; West, King, & Arberg, 1988). Before proceeding to humans, let us briefly consider the ontogenetic niches and habitats of mammals in general, because we share the common heritage of a predictable sequence of niches:

> Fetal, newborn, infant, and juvenile mammals each inhabit distinctly different worlds, and each address requires a different occupation. In effect, the developing mammal occupies a predictable, discrete series of niches during its early life. (Alberts & Cramer, 1988, p. 4)

The general case: Animals. Each habitat consists of a particular distribution of resources with regions of higher or lower concentrations (cf. Kugler & Turvey, 1987). In newborn mammals, for example, the location of the mother's nipples is spatially distributed in a way that promotes the act of feeding, and various chemical, thermal, and tactile gradients guide the exploring nursling to the source of milk (Moltz, 1971; Rosenblatt & Lehrman, 1963). While habitats change, there is an invariant characteristic of action that provides continuity in development: spontaneous exploration of gradients for a particular concentration of a resource. Indeed, there may be persistent "styles" of exploration among individuals, which are evident in different habitats throughout the lifespan.

What changes developmentally and situationally may be the salience of the resource regulating exploration. So, for example, while the newborn mammal continues to nurse during infancy, at a certain point the nipple becomes less salient than other potential nutrients (Hall & Williams, 1983). There is a shift in regulation of exploratory behavior from one informational gradient to another because of a variety of growth-related changes, e.g., the body's changing energy requirements, the possibility of exploring a substance in a new way with the emergence of teeth for chewing, feathers for flying, or legs for walking (as in tadpoles).

Habitats for infant action. Table 3.8 offers a framework for considering the nature of the habitats within which humans develop during four periods: fetal, newborn, premobile, and independently mobile. These periods encompass roughly the first year of life. During the fetal period, the habitat is the uterus. It is characterized by an enclosure of a particular size and shape, containing a fluid medium which influences both fetal action and perception (see, e.g., Turkewitz & Kenny, 1982). The thickness and elasticity of the uterine wall determines that a certain amount of light and sound will be transduced into the uterus. In a sense, then, the uterus is an ambient array with its own unique reflective characteristics.

Within the uterus, several action systems are already functional. The basic orienting system allows the fetus to orient toward moderately loud sounds and light and away from intense stimulation, and maintain the limbs in a flexed posture (also accomplished to some extent by the constraints of the size of the uterus). In conjunction with basic orienting, the locomotor system (kicking) is used to reposition the body into the vertex (head-down) position prior to delivery.

During the newborn period, the mother's body is a primary habitat for adapting to environmental demands. The basic orienting system is used to bring the mouth to the breast, which then activates the appetitive system in sucking. The perceptual organs are used to explore the properties of the mother's skin, including its smell and taste, as well as its texture. The investigatory systems

Table 3.8. A sequence of developmental habitats in the first year

Developmental Period	Habitat (Character)	Basic Capabilities
Fetus	Uterus (shape and density of maternal abdominal wall; relative amounts of amniotic fluid; transduction of light and sound)	Orienting to light as well as speech and non-speech sounds
Newborn	Mother's body (sight of face, sound of voice, contact with skin, posture in holding baby)	Orienting to sounds, visual tracking, sucking, endogenous smiling, crying, vocalizing, kicking, ballistic reaching, elicited and spontaneous grasping and manipulation, imitating facial expressions
Pre-mobile	Immediate places where infant is sitting or lying, while stationary or while moved about; other adults, children, animals	Bringing objects held in hand to mouth, looking around, vocalizing, using hands to explore own and others' body and objects, listening to speech of others as well as self-produced vocalizations, producing facial expressions and exploring faces of others
Mobile (early)	Surfaces which afford crawling; small enclosures and low elevations; local environments	Crawling, creeping, assisted eating of solids with implements, using one hand for holding and at the same time using the other for manipulating, exploring facial expressions of others for affective information about the environment; laughing at visual incongruities
Mobile (later)	Distal environments, more varied substances and surfaces, wider range of people	Walking, running, climbing; independent use of implements for eating solids and liquids; holding objects in one or both hands while moving about; laughing with glee at accomplishments

are used for looking at faces, and listening to voices. Infants actively kick while supine, perhaps exploring their nascent locomotor capabilities. They also extend their hands, occasionally effecting contact with an object within arm's reach.

During the premobile period, stable posture achieved while sitting independently allows the performatory system to become dominant in exploring objects that are placed within the infant's reach. This exploration permits the mapping of action capabilities onto perceptual experiences in multiple modalities. Exploration also allows the infant to begin to expand the scope of action beyond the range of the reach of the limbs by capitalizing on gravity to propel objects. Infants appear to discover much about the possibilities of defeating the pull of gravity on the body, in anticipation of independent locomotion. In this premobile period, they bounce up and down on surfaces that are sufficiently elastic (e.g., mattresses, springy seats, and devices designed to entertain them such as swings and "Jolly Jumpers").

The period of independent mobility expands the infant's habitat to local environments deemed "safe" by adult caregivers. Indeed, much time is spent during social interaction in this period in identifying through referential games which objects and regions are safe for exploration, and which ones are not (e.g., "don't touch"). It is intriguing, then, that this period of independent mobility is one during which infants begin to exhibit fear at places which afford damaging falls (Bertenthal & Campos, 1987). During independent exploration while moving about, the infant may also come to perceptually differentiate body position and object locations within different local habitats. They become able to find objects hidden from them, and to anticipate the appearance of objects and events they have encountered before at a particular location (Goldfield & Dickerson, 1981).

DYNAMICS AND INFORMATION

Dynamics. The dynamic systems perspective discussed in Chapter 2 treats the actor on the model of a deterministic physical system. But it is, perhaps, the hallmark of human behavior that it is *non*-deterministic and goal-directed, influenced by intentional constraints and situational contingencies as much as by mechanistic laws. For example, despite the fact that walking at the natural frequency of one's limb system is energetically optimal and dynamically stable, it is quite possible to walk at a higher frequency when one is in a hurry or a lower frequency when out for an evening stroll. Nevertheless, it does appear to be the case that under free conditions, preferred gait frequencies are related to the natural frequencies determined by the length and mass of pendular legs (Holt, Hamill, & Andres; 1990; Hoyt & Taylor, 1981; Turvey et al., 1988). Further, one can show that within an adopted set of task constraints, such as walking at a fast rate, movement tends to be organized so as to capitalize on the inherent dynamics of the task. If actors are not deterministically driven by the dynamics, how can this be so?

Information. A distinguishing characteristic of biological systems is that they are not just physically but also informationally coupled to their environments, making use of information to guide their activities. This refers to Gibson's (1966, 1979) definition of *information* as a spatiotemporal pattern in an optic, acoustic, haptic, or chemical medium that is lawfully related to some property of the environment, the organism's movements, or the relation between the two. If such patterns uniquely specify behaviorally relevant properties of the current situation, then they can be used to guide efficacious action—the bottom line for both development and evolution.

As discussed above, Gibson emphasized the rich optical structure that is available to specify the layout of the environment (Lee, 1980), the observer's own locomotion (Warren, Morris, & Kalish, 1988), and even the functional properties or "affordances" of objects (Warren, 1984). Recently, Kugler and Turvey (1987) proposed that the underlying dynamics of action provide just this sort of information about movement itself. An organism that can haptically detect variables such as muscle force, cutaneous pressure, or rates of energy dissipation and "effort" during movement may be sensitive to the global dynamics underlying the task. Such "movement-produced information" is generated in the course of an action and is reciprocally used to coordinate and control subsequent movement. To understand how this information might be exploited in motor control and development requires a consideration of the nature of dynamics as information.

Dynamics as information. Relative to the three levels of dynamics introduced in Chapter 1, we can consider how the state of a system evolves over time from different initial conditions (see Table 3.9). At this level, the dynamics are often described as a potential landscape with hills (maxima)

Table 3.9. A dynamic view of information

Level	Description of Dynamics	Information
Components of state dynamics	How the state of the system evolves over time from different initial conditions, once parameter values are fixed	State space, whose dynamics are often described as a potential landscape with hills (maxima) representing high energy states and valleys (minima) representing low energy states
Assembled state dynamics	A function or equation that relates some of the system's df	Region of state space corresponding to a limited class of movements
Parameter dynamics	Parameters of the function (e.g., mass, length, stiffness, and damping of a mass-spring equation)	Parameter space, whose dimensions are the system parameters and some measure of resulting behavior such as energy cost
Graph dynamics	Bifurcational changes in the size, composition, and connectivity of functions at different time scales (e.g., skill acquisition, learning, and development)	The layout of bifurcations in the topologies of the behavioral forms of a given dynamical system

Source: After Goldfield, Kay, and Warren, 1993; Saltzman and Munhall, 1992.

representing high energy states and valleys (minima) representing low energy states. For example, the states of a mass-spring system are the possible positions and velocities of the mass; for the action system, this low-dimensional landscape may represent a subset of limb positions and velocities within the high-dimensional state space. The minima correspond to preferred states or attractors toward which the system is drawn, and can also be represented as stable trajectories in the phase plane. Changes in the system's ordinary parameters may affect the location of these attractors, but not the qualitative shape of the landscape, whereas changes in control parameters may alter the number, type, and layout of attractors. One can conceptualize a particular musculoskeletal organization as a *function* that relates some of the system's degrees of freedom, carving out a region of the state space that corresponds to a limited class of movements. Essentially, this function is a dynamic system that can be described by an equation such as that for the mass-spring system.

Attractors can take different forms, depending on the complexity of the system. For an undamped linear system such as the mass-spring, the landscape is flat and has no preferred states. This is because such a system has a stable natural frequency but no stable amplitude, and thus no stable trajectory in the phase plane. When the linear mass-spring is damped, a bowl-shaped minimum or potential well opens up in the landscape and the phase plane trajectory is a point attractor. This means the system has a single preferred state, in this case halting at the resting length of the spring. When a linear system is driven by an external forcing function, or when a nonlinear system (having a damping term involving squares, sines, etc.) oscillates autonomously, the landscape and phase-plane trajectory can be more complex, including limit-cycle attractors corresponding to stable oscillatory movements, and even non-repeating chaotic attractors.

There are two advantages to operating at the attractors for a given task. It is often pointed out that preferred movements are energetically efficient, and indeed there is a large literature showing that, for everything from walking to using a bicycle pump, actors freely adopt "optimal" movement patterns that require minimum energy expenditure. This supports the view that the action system tends toward attractors and adopts efficient parameter settings within the given task constraints. However, there are many small-motor tasks for which the energetic consequences of moving away from the preferred state are biologically insignificant in the context of daily metabolic fluxes, and it is difficult to rationalize them by traditional optimality criteria.

But there is a second advantage for operating at an attractor, namely, its stability. A minimum in the landscape provides a qualitative point that is easily detected, precisely recovered after perturbation, and reproducible on separate occasions. Contrast this with attempting to maintain a state upon the wall of a potential well, for which there is no intrinsic information in the landscape itself.

It has even been suggested (Beek, 1989) that human actors deliberately operate *near* but not locked onto attractors in order to continuously explore the information gradient for the attractor's location, because at the minimum itself, the gradient, and thus the information for its location, disappears.

It is worth emphasizing here that the dynamics of a particular task are defined over both the intrinsic dynamics of the action system and the constraints on that task provided by the environment (Warren, 1984). The intrinsic dynamics include the physical properties and resonances of a complex system of pendular limbs and adjustable spring-like muscles, whereas the environmental constraints include the material properties of objects and surfaces as well as the presence of a gravitational field. In effect, the goal of an action partitions the many variables of the organism and environment into a set that is relevant to the task at hand; they are called the *task constraints*.

In Gibson's (1979) terms, these properties constitute the *affordances* of the rattle, such as its graspability. Reciprocally, the intention also indexes the organism's complementary action capabilities, such as a prehensile grip and a rhythmic shaking movement, referred to as *effectivities* (Turvey et al., 1981). These factors together determine the underlying dynamics of the task. For example, whereas the structure of the arm's biokinematic chain naturally leads to a certain class of compound pendular movements, the rattle's length, mass, and orientation to gravity determine the natural frequency. Thus, the intrinsic dynamics of the action system must be taken together with environmental constraints to determine the underlying potential landscape.

The overarching point is that the gradients of the landscape provide *information* about the location and shape of attractors, i.e., the states of the action system that correspond to stable movement patterns. Further, minima in parameter space provide information about the optimal configuration of parameters for a particular task. In this sense, the dynamics serve not as causal forces that determine behavior, but as information that can be used to organize behavior.

Perception–action cycles. Among the questions which concerned Gibson, one of the most difficult was how perception guides movement and, conversely, how movement serves the generation and pickup of perceptual information (Beek & Bingham, 1991). In its original formulation by Gibson (1966), the concept of perception–action cycle was meant to convey the continuous cyclic relation between the detection of information and the exploratory and performatory activities which are used to guide action. In the context of the second round of Bernstein-inspired work, discussed in Chapter 2, the cyclic nature of perceiving and acting has been re-examined in dynamic terms (Kugler & Turvey, 1987; Shaw & Kinsella-Shaw, 1988; Swenson & Turvey, 1991). The challenge of this question in dynamic terms is how informational flowfields map onto force fields (Beek & Bingham, 1991).

Kugler and Turvey (1987) propose that the operation of perception–action cycles is driven by informational constraints on the muscular and nonmuscular forces involved in modes of action (or action systems). Patterns of information, defined in a qualitative geometry of forms (attractors and flow gradients), may be thought of as a family of solutions to the differential equations which describe the dynamics of action as described in Chapter 2. An attractor, described informationally, is a minimum surrounded by a potential well. An action system becomes coupled to particular geometries when the equation of motion that describes the system becomes bounded by the geometric form and restricts the trajectories of the system.

Note. The sections of this chapter from pp. 73 to 77 were written in collaboration with Bill Warren and Bruce Kay. I am, of course, responsible for any errors which remain. E.C.G.

CHAPTER 4

THE COMPONENTS OF ACTION SYSTEMS: SUBSYSTEMS AND THEIR INTERACTION

> Neurobiologists tend to suppose that the primary purpose of change in the nervous system is to encode experience. However, neural adjustment is necessary for at least one other reason: the body as well as the external environment changes. ... In order to monitor and motivate a body that is changing in both size and form, the nervous system must also change.
>
> Purves, 1988, p.16

> Nervous systems can be counted among the multivarious geometries (or boundary conditions) made available at the ecological scale. Some nervous systems bring more geometries, and more varied geometries, to bear than others and, therefore, condense out a larger variety of lawful regularities.
>
> Kugler & Turvey, 1987, p. 424

This chapter examines how the particular relation between body and brain that has evolved in humans supports the dynamic processes discussed in the previous chapters. In the first chapter, I highlighted the motor–action controversy, and observed that the information processing metaphor treated movement as the output of a motor program organized into a command hierarchy. A more traditional chapter on the nervous system in a book on "motor" development would focus on the anatomy of the perceptual and motor systems relative to a kind of flowchart of input–output relations (e.g., Brooks, 1986; Ghez, 1985).

As an action theorist, I approach this chapter in the Bernsteinian tradition, namely by emphasizing the cooperativity between body and brain. I examine the body–brain relation across different scales of size in the organization of action. For example, Purves and his colleagues (e.g., Easter, Purves, Rakic, & Spitzer, 1985; Purves, 1988) demonstrate that the connectivity of the brain is modifiable so as to be compatible with the changing size and form of the body. This and other examples demonstrate that, as a consequence of the way in which the brain is assembled, its organization is designed for *cooperation with* the properties of the body rather than to *command* the movement of the body (Fowler & Turvey, 1978).

Another theme concerns the emergence of organizational levels as a consequence of energy-sharing cooperativities in neural networks. Neural networks are massive interconections between microcircuits, and functional properties emerge via various processes at presynaptic and postsynaptic sites (Finkel, Reeke, & Edelman, 1989; von der Malsburg & Singer, 1988; Shepherd & Koch, 1990). Recalling the earlier distinction made between graph dynamics (responsible for changes in the size, composition, and connectivity of a system), state dynamics (the variables to be assembled), and parameter dynamics (processes that directly govern motion patterns in a system's parameters), I relate dynamics in networks at different levels as an attempt to show how graph dynamics may impose constraints on state and parameter dynamics. I offer this as an alternative to information-processing models whose levels are modeled on input–output relations in a hierarchy.

There has been a new questioning of the relevance of hierarchical models of brain function in favor of approaches which emphasize distributed parallel networks. In hierarchical models of cortical function, information flow is mainly unidirectional (Goldman-Rakic, 1988; Kelso & Tuller, 1981). By contrast, anatomical studies of thalamocortical, cortico-cortical, and cortical-subcortical connections reveals a picture of highly distributed parallel functional systems (Goldman-Rakic, 1988). When the brain is considered as a medium for condensing out low-dimensional "forms" from a high-dimensional space of energy flows, as Kugler and Turvey suggest above, the cooperativity between brain and body takes on new meaning.

IDENTIFYING THE SUBSYSTEMS

A first step toward articulating a theory of the cooperation between brain and body in the organization of action is to identify the subsystems of the human action system which cooperate. While any partitioning of the bodily systems is somewhat arbitrary, the functional distinctiveness of these subsystems is worth highlighting. Moreover, it should be emphasized that functional isolation of systems may emerge from the activity of dynamic systems. With these caveats in mind, in this section, I use the organizational scheme of identifying three subsystems: the link-segment, musculotendon, and nervous subsystems (excluding for convenience the circulatory system, as discussed by Bingham, 1988). The link-segment subsystem refers to the articulators, which comprise the bones as articulated segments and the joints as mechanical connections between the segments. Because the articulators are mechanical systems, they are characterized by inertial, centripetal, and Coriolis torques (forces)

(Bingham, 1988). The musculotendon subsystem comprises the actuators of the body, having both contractile and tendinous elements that actively and passively transduce forces. The mechanical energy produced by the actuators is derived from metabolites transported by the circulatory system (Bingham, 1988). And finally, impulse transmission to the muscles is actively regulated by the nervous system. Moreover, the structural and functional properties of the nervous system make possible the formation of maps, which may give the brain the capacity to create a "virtual" articulator in anticipation of actual movement (Jordan & Rosenbaum, 1989; Saltzman & Kelso, 1987)

Next, comes the question of how to relate each of these subsystems into a cooperative framework. As Bingham (1988) has noted, this question is a daunting one because of the potential complexity of dealing with the interrelationships of the subsystems and the influences of nonlinearities (see Table 4.1). In Chapter 2, I discussed dynamic systems, defined as the simplest and most abstract description of the motion of a system (Kelso & Kay, 1987;

Table 4.1. Nonlinearities of the subsystems

Subsystem	Nonlinearity
Link-segment	1. Inertia of link varies nonlinearity with its configuration (e.g., distribution of mass relative to momentary axis of rotation) 2. Variations in torque (inertia, velocity, centripetal, Coriolis) over a movement depend in complex ways on the joints and segments involved in a movement and on the particular ways they move
Musculotendon	1. The active contractile elements and passive elastic tendinous elements exhibit nonlinear force transduction characteristics (a) when stretched, tendon exhibits nonlinear stiffness in two discontinuously connected regions (b) contractile components exhibit nonlinear properties (i.e., isometric contractile force–length curve is nonlinear; muscles that are actively shortening produce less force than in isometric contraction; the form of the force–velocity curve is different entirely for lengthening muscle). The way each of these properties varies in relation to others over a movement determines amount of energy available for action
Circulatory	1. Blood flow within a muscle is heterogeneous according to (a) local capacity for flow determined by relative dilation of blood vessels in a muscle (b) global blood pressure (c) pumping action of muscular contraction which forces benous blood out of muscular vessels 2. Activity induces increase in blood flow, which increases power generated by the muscles
Nervous system	1. Impulse transmission of nerve cells include the following nonlinearities (a) all-or-none response to stimulation (b) absolute and relative refractory periods following a response (c) subliminal states of depolarization or hyperpolarization

Source: After Bingham, 1988.

Schoner & Kelso, 1988), as a macroscopic description of a complex system. A dynamic systems approach, then, holds the promise of dealing with this complexity. But how might dynamic systems elucidate the interrelationships between the subsystems?

The potential explanatory power in a dynamic systems approach comes from the possibility of transforming a "body-free" abstract dynamic description of a system (e.g., a description of control variables in a task space) into a body-specific system (e.g., a description of articulator variables in body space) by a change of variables (Saltzman & Kelso, 1987). Thus, it is possible to use the reduced dimensionality observable in dynamics to understand the high-dimensional variables comprising the other subsystems. This, then, is the second step proposed here for relating brain and body. It requires identifying the means for transforming the functions of one subsystem into a form commensurate with the others. This is done here with respect to the theory of task-dynamics developed by Elliot Saltzman and his colleagues (e.g., Saltzman & Kelso, 1987; Saltzman & Munhall, 1989). I will attempt to show that attractor dynamics evident in behavior (e.g., in the particular states that are stable out of a large number of possible states) are also evident in neural subsystems, suggesting common principles of organization in both (cf. Haken, 1983).

Task dynamics also introduces themes to be developed in the chapters which follow. For example, in Chapter 6, I discuss the evolution of complex functional systems at the cellular level in order to demonstrate that the close-packing of organelles with specialized functions resulted in the formation of symbiotic (energy-sharing) multifunctional systems (i.e., eukaryotic cells). I review evidence suggesting that aggregates of cells (e.g., in *Dictyostelium*) self-organize into a macroscopic "individual" capable of exploration for resources when local supplies are depleted. I then turn to the specializations of vertebrates in order to demonstrate that at the slower time scale of evolution, aggregates of body parts may enter into new organizations in order to adapt to changing "problems" of adaptation, including availability of resources and competition with other individuals for those resources.

Each of the action systems, too, is a macroscopic aggregation of microscopic components. But rather than being able to assemble a single function (e.g., locomotion) as in *Dictyostelium*, our bodily subsystems are able to assemble several action systems with differentiated functions. Infants discover how a hand may be a grabber or a pusher, how a leg may be a kicker or a lifter. Human action systems are, in other words, another manifestation of an energy-sharing strategy that has remained invariant throughout evolution, namely, cooperativity between subsystems (a) that are governed by physical law and (b) that can organize into many different configurations necessitated by the exigencies of living on a planet with limited resources.

In addition to providing a means for the assembly of macroscopic functions from microcomponents, task dynamics is also capable of addressing the tuning of action systems during performance, learning, and development by means of adjusting system parameters. In a developmental approach to task dynamics, for example, we can address how the perceptual systems may tune the parameters of action systems by examining how the infant may explore a "task space" to discover particular "regions" of stability (Newell, Kugler et al., 1989; Goldfield et al., 1993). If each observable region of stability is specific to the dynamics of the infant's own actions, then infants may use these dynamics as information (Kugler & Turvey, 1987) in order to maintain their activity within that observable region of stability. This active regulation of dynamics may also be assisted by another person, and I later examine how social regulation of adults may assist infants in exploring for regions of stability and instability.

THE PROPERTIES OF THE LINK-SEGMENT SYSTEM
AND BODY SPACE

Bony and spongy tissue: The skeleton. Bone performs four major functions in the human body: support, protection, anchoring (i.e., acting as a base for being pulled upon by the muscles), and storage and production of circulatory products (Shipman, Walker, & Bichell, 1985). The skeleton supports the soft tissues of the body and prevents its collapse against gravitational and other forces. In very small organisms (e.g., invertebrates), adhesion binds cells together. Indeed, the possibility of the decomposition of the bounded macroscopic individual into its microscopic components is part of the life cycle of certain invertebrates (e.g., *Dictyostelium*). However, over the course of metazoan evolution, large size has put animal bodies within the range of influence of gravitational forces (Bonner, 1988). Once in the range of gravitational forces, secreted calcium products may have been adapted for use as internal skeletal structures and shells surrounding the body for support and protection (Bonner, 1988).

Animals with more functional support structures and protective mechanisms gained a selective advantage in locomotion and defense against predators (Vermeij, 1987). The protective function has continued in the mammalian skeleton, and there has been increasing specialization in the protective "devices" which have evolved. For example, the ribs form a protective "cage" around the heart and lungs; the skull is a bony "shell" surrounding the brain; the joints and spongy skeletal tissue are "shock absorbers" modulating the impact of the body as it comes into contact with the support surface.

The same bony structures serve as anchors for muscles, making movement possible. Simply as a function of relative position of the points of attachment of the muscles to the bone, a single muscular function, contraction, becomes transformed into one of seven different actions: flexion, extension, abduction, adduction, rotating, gliding, and circumduction (Shipman et al., 1985).

When anchoring muscles, the rigidity of bone gives it the function of a lever, a rigid segment that moves about an axis. Depending upon the relative placement of its three components—power (force required to move a load), load (resistance), and fulcrum (point of movement)—a lever becomes capable of performing specialized kinds of work. The amount of force or power required for a given movement of a lever is a function of the ratio of load, length of the load arm, and length of the power arm

$$\text{power} = \text{load} \times \text{load arm}/\text{power arm}$$

where the power arm is the distance between power and fulcrum, and the load arm is the distance between load and fulcrum (Shipman et al., 1985). For example, the neck muscles holding the head level are first-order levers (like a seesaw), with a long load arm and the fulcrum at the first vertebra. By contrast, the use of the Achilles tendon to lift the body weight onto the toes is a second-order lever with the load between fulcrum and power, and the use of the biceps

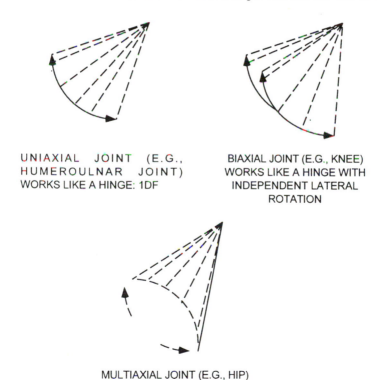

UNIAXIAL JOINT (E.G., HUMEROULNAR JOINT) WORKS LIKE A HINGE: 1DF

BIAXIAL JOINT (E.G., KNEE) WORKS LIKE A HINGE WITH INDEPENDENT LATERAL ROTATION

MULTIAXIAL JOINT (E.G., HIP) WORKS LIKE A BALL AND SOCKET

Figure 4.1. Three types of joint.

with the fulcrum at the elbow to raise a load held in the hand is a third-order lever (Shipman et al., 1985).

Lever systems consist of levers and joints, junctions at which two bones meet and are joined together or articulate with each other (Gowitzke & Milner, 1988; Shipman et al., 1985). Joints are classified according to the number of axes about which independent movement is possible (see Fig. 4.1), with uniaxial joints working like hinges, biaxial joints like a hinge mounted on a swivel, and multiaxial joints like a ball and socket.

There are other "machines" in the body, including the wheel and axle, and the pulley (Wells, 1971). The trunk, for example, is a wheel and axle device in which the force of the rotator muscles is applied to the spinal "axle". Other wheel and axle devices in the body include the head and neck, with force applied to the perimeter of the "wheel" by the sternocleidomastoid and splenius muscles and to the "axle" by the deep spinal muscles (Wells, 1971). A pulley is a device which changes the direction of force, either by allowing a greater angle of pull, or a totally different movement. Wells illustrates how, for example, the angle of pull of the gracilis muscle is increased via the bulging medial condyles of the knee over which the tendon passes just prior to attaching to the tibia (see Fig. 4.2).

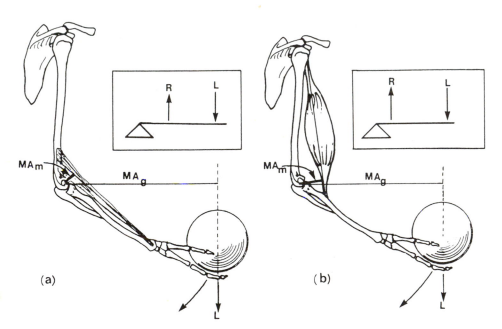

Figure 4.2. An example of a "machine" in the body: a second-class lever. L is a load or gravity as the moving force or effort. MA_g is the moment arm of gravity, and MA_m is the moment arm of the resisting muscle. The insets show equivalent lever systems of the second-class. (From Gowitzke & Milner, 1988. Copyright © 1988 by Williams and Wilkins Publishers. Reprinted by permission.)

Joints. Linking the bones of the human body are approximately 200 joints, classified into three groups (Enoka, 1988). Fibrous joints (such as the sutures of the skull) are relatively immobile, cartilaginous joints (such as the sternocostal) are slightly movable, and synovial joints are freely movable. The synovial joint is, thus, of most interest in understanding the biomechanical basis for machines in the body. The most notable characteristic of a synovial joint is its shock-absorbing properties. The articulating surfaces of the bones are enclosed within a fluid-filled joint capsule which absorbs impacts, prevents direct wear to the bones, and modifies the way one bone makes contact with another (Enoka, 1988). Bones grow by means of lengthening. This has an important impact on the potential power of the machines in the body (especially levers), since length is a critical variable in pendular systems.

Muscular contraction. If bones and joints make possible certain mechanical devices, then muscle provides the engine for the work performed by these devices (see Fig. 4.3). Muscles are "molecular machines that convert chemical energy, initially derived from food, into force" (Enoka, 1988, p. 103) (see Tables 4.2, 4.3a and 4.3b). This is evident in the molecular mechanism underlying the generation of force in the sliding filament model of muscular contraction (A.F. Huxley, 1974; McMahon, 1984; Squire, 1985).

According to the model, changes in muscle length occur when there is a sliding force generated between actin and myosin filaments. Nervous excitation of a muscle fiber causes calcium ions to be released which, in turn, effects the dynamics of myosin heads interacting with actin giving rise to filament sliding (Squire, 1985). Contractility is only one of the properties of muscle. The others include irritability (response to a stimulus), and conductivity (propagating a wave of excitation).

The muscles as springs. On the view that the nervous system is designed to take advantage of the properties of the body, what might some of these properties be? One suggestion is that the muscles behave like tunable springs (Feldman, 1986; Bizzi & Mussa-Ivaldi, 1989). A muscle is like a spring

Table 4.2. Two ways that muscles generate forces

Process	Principle
Motor unit recruitment	The motor unit with the smallest motoneuron is activated or recruited first and those of progressively increasing size are activated next (size principle)
Action potential frequency (rate coding)	The relationship between action potential frequency and muscle force is non-linear. For tonic motor units, the relationship is a ramp and plateau, but phasic units are linear

Source: After Carew and Ghez, 1985.

Table 4.3(a). Properties of muscle which influence the force that a muscle exerts when an action potential is propagated

Muscle Properties	Action Potential–Muscle Relation
Mechanical	
(a) Muscle length change (active element)	Development of force is based upon cross-bridge attach–detach cycles: greater number of cycles yield greater force. As muscle length changes, number of thin-filament binding sites change, and amount of tension changes. This is basis of length-tension curve
(b) Passive element	Muscle is composed of connective tissue which becomes like an elastic band and exerts a passive force that combines with cross-bridge activity
(c) Muscle length/torque	There are interactions between fiber arrangements, number of joints, moment arm, and muscle length resulting in different kinds of torque–angle relation
(d) Muscle length and load	There are different consequences of contraction depending upon relationship between muscle and load torques (isometric, concentric, eccentric)
Architectural	
(a) In series	There are specific effects of alignment of the force-producing units. The greater number of sarcomeres in series, the greater the change in length of the myofibril
(b) In parallel	Muscle fiber force is proportional to the number of myofibrils in parallel (measured by cross-sectional area)
(c) Angle of pinnation	A greater number of sarcomeres in parallel can be packed into a given volume of muscle
(d) Point of attachment	Points of attachment of the muscle relative to the joint determines the angle of pull of the muscle
(e) Proportion of contractile protein	The proportion of muscle length that contains contractile protein determines the proportion of muscle force (as comapred with other forces) that contributes to rotation

Source: After Enoka, 1988.

Table 4.3(b). Ways in which CNS may influence muscles in order to position a joint

Process	Benefit	Cost
Co-contraction (contracting both agonist and antagonist muscles)	Provides greater stability in response to unanticipated changes in external forces or loads	More energy costly and less efficient
Reciprocal innervation (Activation or shortening of one muscle which increases its stiffness and decreases its resting length, and relaxation of opponent muscles with decrease in stiffness and increase in resting length	More energy efficient	Requires that loads be accurately known

Source: After Carew and Ghez, 1985.

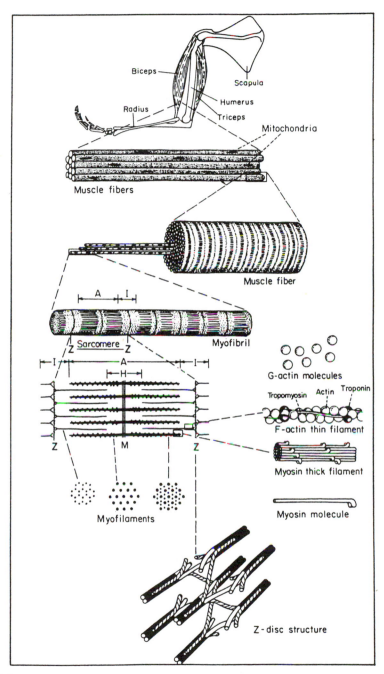

Figure 4.3. The organization of striated muscle structure showing the bands and proteins which make up the thick and thin filaments. (From McMahon, 1984. Copyright © 1984 by Princeton University Press, Inc. Reprinted by permission.)

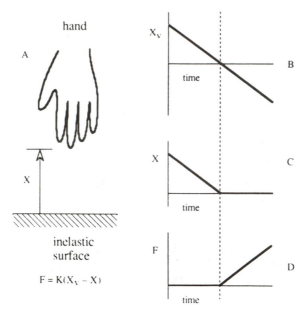

Figure 4.4. Diagram illustrating how virtual position may be used to control contact tasks. (A) The hand is controlled by a relation between force exerted, F, and the difference between a virtual position, X_v, and the actual hand position, X. (B) A trajectory of the virtual position, X_v, that could be used to move to a surface and exert force on it. (C) While the hand is not in contact, its actual position, X, tends to follow the virtual position. On contact, the position of the hand is constrained by the surface. (D) While the hand is not in contact, the force exerted by the hand, F, is constrained to zero. On contact, the force is proportional to the distance the virtual position moves "into" the surface. (Adapted from Bizzi, Hogan, Mussa-Ivaldi, & Giszter, 1992. Copyright © 1992 by Cambridge University Press, Inc. Reprinted by permission.)

in the sense that changes in length of both muscle and spring determines the force generated by them. Because muscles are arranged in pairs about the joints, postural control is achieved by the pulling forces of agonist and antagonist muscles.

In the model proposed by Bizzi and his colleagues (e.g., Bizzi & Mussa-Ivaldi, 1989), the neural signals to the muscles specify a series of postural equilibrium points, generating a reference path or "virtual trajectory" (see discussion below). The actual trajectory follows this virtual one because of the modulable elastic properties of the muscles (see Fig. 4.4). However, as Jordan and Rosenbaum (1989) observe, their model raises the question of how the virtual trajectories are actually generated. An answer following from task dynamics (e.g., Saltzman & Kelso, 1987; Saltzman & Munhall, 1989) is to assume that the same principles which apply to the intrinsic dynamics of the elastic properties of the limb also operate in a neurally instantiated task-based coordinate system (perhaps following connectionist principles).

THE PROPERTIES OF THE NERVOUS SUBSYSTEM

The nervous subsystem: Networks. There has been a traditional polarity of views in the history of the neurosciences on the relation between pluripotentiality and specialization of brain function. The great Russian neuroscientist Luria was a proponent functional pluripotentiality (see, e.g., Luria, 1980). This organizational principle implies that under certain conditions, a given function of the nervous system may be involved in other functional systems and may participate in the performance of other tasks. By contrast, other neuroscientists in the tradition of Broca and Geschwind (see, e.g., Geschwind & Levitsky, 1968) emphasize the apparent specializations of the human brain, evident in brain asymmetries.

A possible solution to the fight between these "foxes and hedgehogs" (Gardner, 1983) is to focus on the network level of organization (see Table 4.4). Pluripotentiality and specialization may, then, emerge from the massive interconnections between dendritic trees with local synaptic potentials, and the regulation of these potentials by neuroactive substances (see Fig. 4.5). Shepherd & Koch (1990) note that neurons possess a virtual "cornucopia" of different ionic currents, different in every major neuronal region in the central and peripheral nervous systems. The plethora of ionic currents result in widely varying electrophysiological properties and patterns of neuronal activity generated by cells in different parts of the brain. Each class of

Table 4.4. Levels of organization of the nervous system

Levels	Properties
Synapse	The elementary structural and functional unit for the construction of neural circuits
Microcircuit	The assembly of synapses into patterns of connectivity during development that produces functionally significant operations
Dendritic tree	Patterns of dendritic branching, unique to different types of neurons, impose geometric constraints which separate the activity in different branches from each other
Neurons	Different configurations of synapses, coupled with passive and active membrane properties, and the geometry of the dendrites, provide a rich substrate for carrying out neuronal computations
Local circuits	Circuits that mediate interactions within a region and which consist of longer-distance connections made by axons and axon collaterals within a given brain region
Interregional circuits	Patterns of synaptic connections and interactions characteristic of a given region
Network	Widely distributed circuits which show emergent properties not apparent or implied in constituent elements

Source: After Shepherd and Koch, 1990.

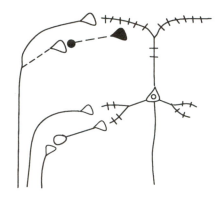 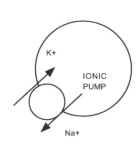

| INTEGRATIVE ACTIVITY OF NEURON (SYNAPTIC INTEGRATION) MADE POSSIBLE BY A BASIC CIRCUIT. GENERATION OF SYNAPTIC POTENTIALS OCCURS AT SITES ON DENDRITIC TREES. | REGULATION OF THE INTEGRATIVE ACTIVITY OF THE NEURON VIA MEMBRANE PROPERTIES AND NEUROTRANSMITTER ACTIONS |

Figure 4.5. Integration and regulation in neural networks. (Adapted from Shepherd & Koch, 1990.)

neuron is exquisitely "tuned" to do its particular task in the nervous system through its specialized ionic currents and by the precise modulation of these currents by neuroactive substances (Shepherd & Koch, 1990).

In addition to allowing us to break free of the confines of the localizationist–holist argument, an analysis of the nervous subsystem at the level of networks reveals three emergent functional properties that are well suited to the kind of cooperativity with the other subsystems argued for in this chapter. These emergent properties are:

1. *Stability*: amongst the large number of possible states of a network, only a few of these, its attractors, are stable (Hopfield & Tank, 1985; Sejnowski, 1986).

2. *Emergent forms* (*modes*): cortical maps are linked via parallel loops, and energy flow creates neural attractor dynamics (Sporns & Edelman, 1993). When coupled to the inherent dynamics of the musculotendon and link-segment systems, neural networks may act as "activation scores" which, by varying continuously in strength, may shape the articulators in particular ways (Saltzman & Kelso, 1987; Saltzman & Munhall, 1989).

3. *Adaptability:* network connectivity is modifiable to be compatible with changes in size and form of the body (Kaas, 1987, 1991; Purves, 1988). Limitation of some resource leads to competition among synapses and selection of the most vigorously growing at the expense of others (Edelman, 1988; Finkel et al., 1990),

Stability in rhythms produced by network activity. In simple nervous systems, such as that of the leech, there are two general processes by which neurons may produce rhythmic activity: (1) endogenous polarization rhythms that depend upon the intrinsic oscillatory propoerties of individual neurons, and (2) network oscillations that depend on connections linking a set of neurons (Stent, 1987). How might these latter network interconnections make it possible for a simple nervous system to generate stable rhythms? Stent (1987) discusses three types of networks controlling rhythmic output (see Fig. 4.6). The first, a self-exciting network, owes its rhythmicity to neuronal loops with positive feedback. However, these networks can only generate a single pair of complementary on–off phases of a duty cycle. In reciprocal inhibition

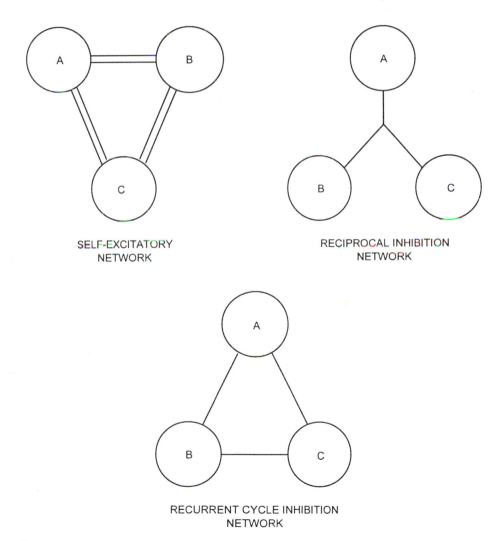

SELF-EXCITATORY
NETWORK

RECIPROCAL INHIBITION
NETWORK

RECURRENT CYCLE INHIBITION
NETWORK

Figure 4.6. Three types of networks in simple nervous systems. (After Stent, 1987.)

networks, two cells are driven by a third tonically active cell to produce alternating bursts. This network is limited to production of biphasic rhythms. A recurrent cyclic inhibition network is needed to generate polyphasic rhythms such as those seen in locomotion. In its simplest form, this network consists of an inhibitory ring formed by three tonically excited neurons inhibiting and receiving inhibitory input from each other (Stent, 1987).

In complex vertebrate nervous systems such as humans, evolution may have capitalized on these simple circuits by coupling them via reverberatory circuits so they form a highly parallel distributed network whose rhythmic output exhibits stability. An example of such resonance is the thalamic and neocortical neurons involved in the reverberation of sleep spindle oscillations (Steriade, Jones, & Llinas, 1990). Spindle activity can be evoked in cortical neurons by stimulating thalamocortical fibers or recurrent collaterals of corticofugal fibers. After cessation of stimulation, potentials within the same frequency range (7–14 Hz) as the stimulation may persist for seconds (Steriade et al., 1990). It is believed that these spontaneous bursts use the reciprocal pathways between the thalamus and neocortex to allow reverberations once they are set in motion.

Development of neural networks in humans may allow the physiological periodicities of aggregates of neurons to become coupled via these reverberatory circuits (Steriade et al., 1990). It has long been proposed that the primary purpose of sleep is to assist in the development of the central nervous system of the fetus and neonate (Roffwarg, Muzio, & Dement, 1966). One possible mechanism for this may be via spindle oscillations organizing thalamocortical circuits via modifications of synaptic activity. Thatcher (1991) cites studies of periodic increases and decreases in the magnitude or strength of cortico-cortical coupling during postnatal cerebral maturation. He considers these to be "waves" of maturation which behave as "traveling waves" which reflect dynamic equilibria between competing and cooperative neuronal networks.

Emergent forms: Neural networks and topographical maps. There is now considerable evidence that somatosensory and motor cortical areas form topographical "maps", and that these maps change as a consequence of competitive interactions at the synapses (Kaas, 1991; Merzenich, Kass, Wall, Nelson, Sur, & Felleman, 1983). The maps are referred to as topographic because the distance relation among cells is metrically deformed (P.M. Churchland, 1989). For example, in experiments with rats in which a motor nerve to muscles is sectioned, or a body part removed, the immediate effect is that stimulation of a site whose activation formerly moved the body part no longer does so. After several hours after the lesions, however, stimulation of these areas results in activation of new sets of muscles.

What is the function of these maps? From the standpoint of the task dynamic model to be developed in a later section, control of movement requires transformations between an abstract task-based coordinate system (a "virtual effector") and the real effector. The laminar structure of the cerebral cortex and the parallel fiber network of the cerebellum suggest two mechanisms by which such transformations may occur: vertically connected state spaces in cerebral cortical laminae and vector transformations in cerebellar networks. For example, Churchland (1989) proposes that via vertical axonal projections, cortical laminations transform points in one neural state space into another by means of the overall pattern of activation levels across the population of cells. Via this mechanism, a high-dimensional task would be handled by a very large number of low-dimensional state spaces, each massively connected via parallel circuits. One source of support for such a model comes from the work of Goldman-Rakic on the parallel circuits involved in the guidance of eye and hand movements. She presents evidence that guidance of hand movements by visuo-spatial information might be a "distributed" function of parallel parietal and prefrontal circuits.

Another mechanism, which may provide a second "style" of control supporting the cortical style of control, is cerebellar vector transformation (P.

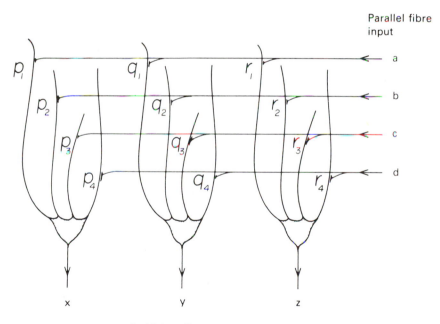

Figure 4.7. Neural implementation of coordinate transformations by means of matrix multiplication. The input vector (a,b,c,d) is physically represented by four spiking frequencies. Each input element synapses onto all of the output cells, and the weight of each synaptic connection implements the corresponding coefficient of the abstract matrix. Each cell "sums" its incoming stimulations and emits spikes down its output axon with a frequency proportionate to its summed input, resulting in the output vector (x,y,z). (Adapted from P.S. Churchland, 1986. Copyright © 1986 by MIT Press. Reprinted by permission.)

M. Churchland, 1989; Pellionisz & Llinas, 1979, 1985). Rather than spatial location of neural events as in cortical control, cerebellar control takes advantage of spiking frequencies in relevant pathways. These frequencies perform a biological equivalent of matrix multiplication (see Jordan, 1986, for a tutorial on matrices). This can be illustrated by a figure from Churchland (1989), who describes how the relation between parallel fibers and Purkinje cells make possible vector-to-vector transformation by matrix multiplication (see Fig. 4.7):

> The parallel input fibers at the right each send a train of electrochemical "spikes" toward the waiting dendritic trees. The numbers a, b, c, d represent the amount by which the momentary spiking frequency of each of the four fibers is above (positive number) or below (negative number) a certain baseline spiking frequency. The topmost input fiber, for example, synapses onto each of the three output cells, making a stimulatory connection in each case, one that tends to depolarize the cell body and make it send a spike down its vertical output axon. The output frequency of spike emissions for each cell is determined by the simple *frequency* of input stimulations it receives from all incoming synaptic connections, and by the *weight* or *strength* of each synaptic connection, which is determined by the placement of the synapses and by their cross-sectional areas. These strength values are individually represented by the coefficients of the matrix. *The neural interconnectivity thus implements the matrix.*

Adaptability in the nervous subsystem: Competition in neural networks. Edelman and his colleagues (e.g., Finkel et al., 1988) offer a theory of nervous system adaptability which involves selection processes during development and learning (see Fig. 4.8). During the latter, a process called group selection, groups of neurons, local clusters of hundreds to thousands of neurons which function as a collective (e.g., as a receptive field), compete with cells that belong in other groups. Such competition determines the functional properties of receptive fields (e.g., their size, location, and modality), and may play a role in the formation of topographic maps. The receptive fields are coupled to each other by "re-entry," phasic signaling along reciprocally connected projections.

While neuronal connectivity in topographic maps is established during development, adaptations with further experience involve selection via modification of presynaptic efficacy (the amount of transmitter released per depolarization) and postsynaptic efficacy (the locally generated voltage per amount of transmitter)(Finkel et al., 1988). This is evident in the possibility of altering receptive field maps after surgical changes in the body–brain relation (Kaas et al., 1983, Merzenich et al., 1983). For example, after transection of a peripheral nerve in the hand of a squirrel monkey, the cortical area formerly devoted to representation of the denervated part (a finger) switches to a representation of a new portion of the hand. Finkel and his colleagues argue

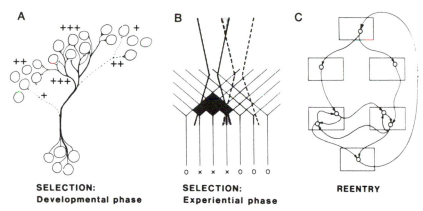

Figure 4.8. Schematic of the major processes of neuronal group selection. (A) During development, a primary repertoire of neuronal groups is formed. These groups arise from an initial phase of selection in the formation of neural connections. Variability in the anatomy is due to epigenetic mechanisms involving cell-adhesion molecules. Plus signs indicate the relative amount or distribution of CAMs on cells and fibers; solid lines are stabilized connections; broken lines are connections that have not been stabilized. (B) Selection of neuronal groups by patterns of extrinsic inputs. Hourglass figures represent groups that extend through all cortical laminae. Branching "Y"s represent thalamic afferents; those marked × receive coactive stimulation, those marked 0 do not. Group selection depends upon local coactivated input over time. (C) Reentry-anatomical projections between different repertoires carry out phasic signaling that coordinates the responses of the repertoires in space and time, allowing a unitary object to be recognized from the background and categorized. (From Finkel, Reek, & Edelman, 1988. Copyright © 1988 by Massachusetts Institute of Technology. Reprinted by permission.)

that rather than involving the sprouting of new neuronal processes, the changing representation is based upon "the emergence of anatomical connections which, although present, were previously too weak to be effective" (p. 150).

Purves and his colleagues (Easter et al., 1985; Purves, 1988) have further demonstrated that the connectivity of the brain is modifiable so as to be compatible with the changing size and form of the body. This research illustrates that as a consequence of the way the brain is assembled, its organization is designed for *cooperation with* the properties of the body. Consider, for example, the neuromuscular requirements of animals with motor units of different size. Purves (1988) notes that muscle mass constitutes a constant proportion of mammalian body weight (40–45 percent), so that homologous muscles in an elephant are larger than those of a mouse. Nevertheless, there is a disproportionately small number of primary motor neurons in very large mammals (Morgane & Jacobs, 1972) and this implies that each motor neuron in a large animal must innervate many more muscle fibers than homologous ones in a small animal. In other words, larger animals have larger motor units because of increased *divergence* (Purves, 1988) (see Fig. 4.9). An important consequence is a "power gain:" in large animals the motor

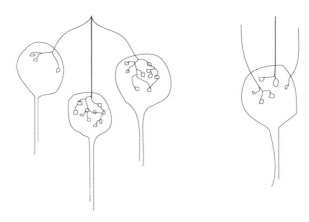

DIVERGENT INNERVATION: MORE
CHARACTERISTIC OF LARGER
ANIMALS. LARGER MOTOR
UNITS RESULT IN POWER
AMPLIFICATION

CONVERGENT INNERVATION: IN
LARGE ANIMALS,
HOMOLOGOUS NEURONS IN
DIFFERENT INDIVIDUALS VARY
GREATLY IN THEIR FORM
(WHILE THEY ARE STEREOTYPED
IN SMALL ANIMALS).

Figure 4.9. Divergent and convergent innervation. In divergent innervation, each nerve cell axon usually innervates many target cells (e.g., effector cells) in a one-to-many relationship. In convergent innervation, each target cell may be innervated by many different neurons. (Adapted from Purves, 1988. Copyright © 1988 by Harvard University Press. Reprinted by permission.)

neurons generate more force in the muscles innervated than in large animals. The power gain in larger animals suggests that phylogenetic modulation of divergence establishes thresholds for muscle recruitment that are scaled to changing body size.

Another mechanism for scaling brain and body is *convergence*, the number of axons that innervate each nerve cell (see Fig. 4.9). Convergence depends upon the geometry of the postsynaptic cell: geometrically simple neurons are innervated by a single input, but those with complex dendritic arbors are innervated by different axons (Purves, 1988). Modulation of dendritic form "changes the number of inputs that neurons receive, the character of their activity, the manner in which they integrate the synaptic information that impinges on them, and the size of the neural units in which they participate" (Purves, 1988, p. 73).

What kinds of modulation between neurons and target muscle cells exist during ontogeny? Purves (1988) offers evidence that while several different axons innervate mammalian neonatal muscle fibers, there is a transition in postnatal life to a one to one relationship between motor axons and muscle fibers (Van Essen, 1982). Purves (1988) demonstrates that the transition from multiple to single innervation is accomplished by neural competition for a limited resource (a trophic substance).

Adaptation: Boolean networks. Like Edelman, Kauffman (1989, 1990, 1991) places biological adaptation in the context of the process by which Darwinian selection may act upon self-organizing systems in order to tune attractors to local requirements. Kauffman uses Boolean networks to model self-organization and selection. An advantage of Kauffman's model for the present purpose of understanding cooperativity between brain and body is that Boolean networks have a natural link to the kinds of nonlinear dynamic systems which we will use to describe action systems.

Kauffman adopts Boolean networks because they offer a solution to a problem about complex systems first proposed by Ashby (1960), an early systems theorist. In modeling mechanical systems on biological ones, Ashby wished to know how to build complex systems of many interacting parts in such a way that alterations in one part of the system did not propagate uncontrollably and break apart the system's functional integrity. Ashby proposed that a potential solution to controlling a complex system was to include variables which have partially constant responses as their input values change. The meshwork created by a large number of these variables "wall off and hence functionally isolate clusters of variables which cannot communicate to one another through the walls of constancy" (Kauffman, 1989, p. 664). The point worth emphasizing here is that the architecture of Boolean networks instantiates functional modularity by means of transient walls of constancy between the many variables of the system.

The functional modularity of certain Boolean networks offers a design for neural network architecture that establishes a natural link with the concept of coordinative structure introduced in Chapter 2. In both Boolean network and the dynamic systems of coordinative structures, cooperative organization among elements is achieved by softly assembled constraints, rather than by structural assembly of fully independent subsystems. With a common dynamic basis for both neural network architecture and the equations of motion which generate observable action, it is possible to have a common metric for identifying organizational principles at both macroscopic and microscopic scales. As we observe changes in the size, composition, and connectivity of the equations of motion describing action, it may be possible to infer how the architecture of neural networks may grow, shrink, or be partitioned in new ways during development (Saltzman & Munhall, 1992).

EXPLORING THE RELATION BETWEEN THE SUBSYSTEMS

Inverse dynamics. One approach to an understanding of the interaction between the subsystems in the generation of goal-directed acts involves the use of a methodology, inverse dynamics, in which "the motion of the mechanical system is completely specified and the objective is to find the forcing functions causing the motion" (Vaughn, Davis, & O'Connor, 1991). In inverse dynamics, joint reaction forces, the net forces generated by bone on bone contact between adjacent body segments, are used as a measure of this forcing function.

However, before describing this procedure, it is useful to consider some standard terminology in the biomechanics literature for describing a mechanical system. Biomechanists often use a free body diagram, a simplified "stick figure" which isolates the articulators from their surroundings, to illustrate the interaction between the forces acting on the system. The external forces and moments acting on it are then drawn to scale with arrows representing the length and magnitude of forces (force vectors) acting on the system (Enoka, 1988). External forces are those exerted from outside the system, excluding internal forces (due to bone, ligament and muscle) (Enoka, 1988). In order to examine the contribution of the muscular force across a joint, it is necessary to define it as an external force by identifying a net muscle force and joint reaction forces of adjacent body segments (Enoka, 1988).

Once a segment is defined in this way as a mechanical system, it can be treated like any other physical body, subject to the three laws of Newton (Gowitzke & Milner, 1988):

1. *The law of inertia:* A body remains at rest, or in a state of uniform motion in a straight line unless acted on by an applied force.
2. *The law of force, mass, and acceleration:* If a body of mass, m, has an acceleration, a, the force acting on it, f, is defined as the product of its mass and acceleration.
3. *The law of action–reaction:* To every action there is an equal and opposite reaction.

The various forces acting on the body are considered with respect to these three laws. For example, a ground-reaction force, defined from Newton's third law, is an expression of the relation between the articulator and support surface (Enoka, 1988).

Vaughn et al. (1991) describe one set of procedures for deriving joint reaction forces. They use anthropometric measures (body segment masses and lengths) in regression equations to predict the masses and moments of inertia of each body segment in question. Kinematic data is used to predict the position of internal landmarks (e.g., joint centers). The joint centers are then used to predict positions of segment centers of gravity, (an abstract "balance point" around which all the particles of the object are evenly distributed and moves when the body segments are moved relative to each other; see Enoka, 1988) and calculate velocities and accelerations of the positions. The data on segment masses and moments of inertia, segment velocities and accelerations, and ground reaction forces are substituted into equations of motion to yield resultant joint forces and movements (the presumed forcing function).

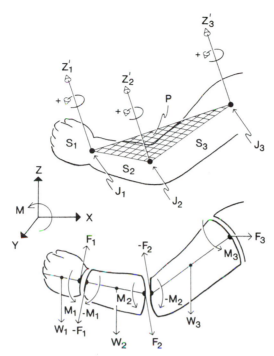

Figure 4.10. Interpretive and free-body diagrams of a model of an infant's upper extremity. The upper diagram shows the limb positioned in an inertial (X,Y,Z) coordinate system with a positive torque (M) defined. The upper extremity is modeled as three interconnected rigid segments (S_1 hand, S_2 forearm, and S_3 upper arm) with frictionless joints (J_1 wrist, J_2 elbow, and J_3 shoulder). At each instant in time during a reach, a moving local plane (P) is calculated so that the plane contains the X,Y,Z coordinates of each of the three joint centers (J_1, J_2, J_3). The planar torques at the wrist, elbow, and shoulder are calculated with respect to joint axes (Z_1',Z_2',Z_3') that pass through each joint and are perpendicular to the moving local plane (P). The lower portion of the figure is a free-body diagram of the upper extremity. Depicted are forces related to the hand, forearm, and upper segment weights (W_1,W_2,W_3) acting at their respective center of mass, and the wrist, elbow, and shoulder joint reaction forces (F_1,F_2,F_3) and torques (M_1,M_2,M_3). (From Zernicke & Schneider, 1993. Copyright © 1993 by the Society for Research in Child Development. Reprinted by permission.)

A second approach to deriving equations of motion is discussed by Zernicke and Schneider (1993) (see Fig. 4.10 and Table 4.5). While the goal of Vaughn and his colleagues is to use inverse dynamics to infer the nature of the locomotor programming by which an "idea" is converted into a pattern of muscle activity, the goal of inverse dynamics for Zernicke and Schneider is based more on a Bernstein-inspired partitioning of forces. Recall from Chapter 2 that Bernstein emphasized how motion-dependent forces of multiple interconnected links were blended into the neuromuscular system in order to control movement. Inverse dynamics, as Zernicke and Schneider use it, then, is predicated on a partitioning of all of the forces acting on a segment: gravitational, motion dependent, and muscle.

Table 4.5. Steps for deriving equations of motion according to a biodynamic approach to inverse dynamics

---

1. Perform a rigid body analysis of a limb's dynamics by constructing a free body diagram. The diagram isolates the segment of interest with all external applied forces.
2. Use anthropometric data on segmental masses, center of mass locations, and moments of inertia in order to calculate joint forces and torques.
3. At each of the joints of the limb segments, calculate
    (a) net joint torque: the product of segmental moments of inertia and angular accelerations that act at a joint
    (b) gravitational torque: a passive torque from gravity acting at the center of mass of each segment
    (c) motion-dependent torque: torques arising from mechanical interactions among segments in a linked system
    (d) generalized muscle torque (calculated as a residual of the other torque components): forces arising from active muscle contractions, and from passive deformation of muscles, tendons, and ligaments.
4. Formulate inverse dynamics equations of motion to test models of neuromotor control (e.g., minimization of mean-squared jerk for the production of smooth movements).

Source: After Zernicke and Schneider, 1993.

Problems with a biomechanical approach. There are at least two problems with solutions to the inverse dynamics problem based solely upon finding forcing functions presumed to be causing underlying motion. First, there is evidence that, at least for manual tasks, control structures must be considered not only in a joint space of forces (torques), but also in the extrinsic coordinates of the external surroundings, i.e., within a "hand" space (Rosenbaum, 1991). For example, if planning is based upon the extrinsic coordinates of hand space, the hand should move in a straight line. The results of animal and human studies indicate that hand trajectories during reaching, pointing, and drawing consist of a series of straight line segments (Morasso, 1981; Abend, Bizzi, & Morasso, 1982). There is also evidence for joint-based planning on similar kinds of tasks (Hollerbach, Moore, & Atkeson, 1987; Soechting & Lacquaniti, 1981), suggesting that both joint and hand spaces are used in control.

A second and related problem concerns learning and development. In the biomechanical approach, forcing functions are like motor programs: they are *a priori* prescriptions for how to move the body, rather than *a posteriori* stable forms that emerge with changes in components. Because a forcing function is specified by an executive (i.e., derived by the experimenter), it is a fixed solution to each set of extant forces. It is not clear, however, how a new forcing function is selected with learning and development.

Autonomous control structures, proposed by Turvey and his colleagues as the basis for action systems address both of these problems. The assembly of control structures is construed as a self-organizing system which emerges as a consequence of a variety of constraints, including intention:

> On the basis of the cognitive constraints on the movement that are specified by the intentional state of the actor, synergies are formed between an actor's muscles, joints, and the force-producing mechanisms of the neural and metabolic machinery to produce autonomous control structures that are responsible for the execution of a movement. (Schmidt, Treffner, Shaw, & Turvey, 1992, p. 67)

Other constraints on the assembly process include growth-related properties of the body (see, e.g., Thelen & Fisher, 1982), changes in the ability to produce muscular force, either as a result of increasing muscle strength or development of the nervous subsystem. Moreover, the assembly process occurs at multiple time scales, including performance, learning, and development.

Following the "soft" assembly of a control structure governing the cooperativity among components, the actor is conceived of as exploring the actions made possible by the control structure. It is in this sense that the actor's own actions become informative for tuning the control structure to the particular requirements of a task. As was noted in Chapter 3, for each setting of parameters at a particular value, a region in state and parameter spaces specifies an attracting region with a specific stability. The actor is viewed as manipulating the parameters of the control structure to move toward an optimal equilibrium state.

The equilibrium-point hypothesis. A research group at MIT (e.g., Bizzi, Hogan, Mussa-Ivaldi, & Giszter, 1992) offers another solution to the inverse dynamics problem which, they claim, avoids the need for any inverse computations of kinetics. This solution is based upon the equilibrium-point hypothesis: a virtual trajectory, a time sequence of central commands giving rise to a set of virtual positions, or attractors, influences the actual position of the arm, which is governed solely by inertial and viscous properties. In their view, the CNS expresses a sequence of of equilibrium positions, the virtual trajectory, and the spring-like properties of the muscles (see above) transforms the difference between actual and desired limb positions into a restorative force. The result is a motion which is inexact, but does not require complex computations. While equilibrium-point control has been shown to be adequate for movements at moderate speeds, it requires a modification for faster movements which includes position and velocity feedback signals (McIntyre, 1988, 1990; McIntyre & Bizzi, 1992).

Feldman and his colleagues (e.g., Feldman, 1986; Flanagan, Ostry, & Feldman, 1990) propose an alternative account of equilibrium-point control. Rather than relying upon changes in muscle activation to shift equilibrium, Feldman argues that central commands control the equilibrium point of the system by setting motoneuron recruitment thresholds, or lambdas (expressed

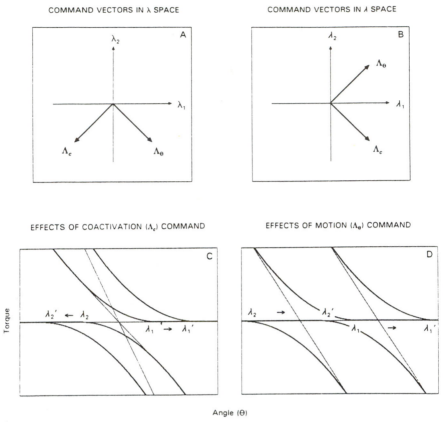

Figure 4.11. The lambda model of equilibrium control. Coactivation (λ_c) and movement (λ_θ) command vectors for single joint motion shown in linear lambda coordinates (*a*) and angular lambda coordinates (B). Each lambda in (C) and (D) is associated with an invariant torque–angle relationship (thick curves) which summate to give the net stiffness (thin diagonal lines). (From Flanagan, Ostry, & Feldman, 1990. Copyright © 1990 by Elsevier Science Publishers. Reprinted by permission.)

biomechanically as an invariant force–length or torque–angle characteristic). Central control consists of a set of vectors which specify the rate and direction of shift in equilibrium point (see Fig. 4.11). Specific motor functions are controlled via selection of various combinations of lambdas. But how can one relate central control vectors to body coordinates?

Task dynamics. Saltzman and Kelso (1987) have offered a set of techniques for transforming an abstract dynamic model of a control system into a description of real articulator motions under particular task constraints. In their task-dynamic approach to modelling skills (see Table 4.6), such as reaching and speaking certain sounds (Saltzman & Munhall, 1989) one first identifies (e.g., for reaching) an abstractly defined goal location or task space

Table 4.6. Examples of levels in task-dynamic explanations of reaching

Level	Description	Device
Task space	Global layout of attractors (time invariant dynamic regimes) and values to tune parameters to current task demands	Abstract terminal device independent of any particular effector system
Body space	Body space dynamic parameter x (location of the task space origin in body space coordinates) and 0 (orientation angle between task space reach axis t_1 and body space axis x_1)	Current spatial location between performer's effector system and the task space. Task space is embedded in a shoulder-centered coordinate system
Task network (joint variables form of massless model arm)	A network of task- and context-specific dynamic relations among the model arm's articulator-kinematic variables	Body-space dynamic regime is defined with reference to the motions of the abstract terminal device (still disembodied from the effector system), i.e., the model arm's kinematic variables (lengths but no masses)
Articulator network (real arm)	A network of articulator dynamic relations among the real arm's joint variables (torques or forces)	Specification of control parameters for a real effector so that it will behave like the model effector (i.e., one which exhibits forces)

Source: After Saltzman and Kelso, 1987.

(the target of a reach) and terminal device, and an appropriate type of task-dynamic topology (see below).

Since the abstract task space is defined independently of any particular effector system, the second step is to transform the dynamic regime into body space (e.g., an arm), based upon the spatial relationship between the end effector and the joints (e.g., a shoulder-centered coordinate system). The body space variables are related to the task variables by a task network, and an articulator network (where a network is understood to be a relation among variables). To examine how a real arm accomplishes reaching, the variables that describe a model arm at the task dynamic level (simulated on a computer) are manipulated until it performs particular task-specific skills as does a real arm. The temporary reorganization of articulators so that their relations match the surface relations of objects in the environment results in the transformation of the effector (in this case the arm) into what Saltzman and Kelso call a special-purpose device.

To specify how a special-purpose device is assembled, it is necessary to define an appropriate task-dynamic topology along each task axis. The different topologies refer to a small set of possible attractors, discussed earlier in Chapter 2. Each attractor has a surrounding basin of attraction which identifies all of the possible trajectories which converge on the attractor. The basin of attraction, in other words, is an abstract geometric image of a control system governing a particular task-specific coordination. Reaching, for example, is governed by point-attractor dynamics:

> Task-specific coordinations can follow from the simple control of initial conditions that put the system into the basin of a given attractor. The act will then (self) organize by converging onto the attractor. Consider reaching for an object on a table. Very many reaching movements, starting at very many different places within the vicinity of the object, can converge on the object. In dynamic terms one would say that reaching, regardless of when, where, and with which parts of the body it is conducted, has the features of a system governed by a spatially defined point attractor. (Turvey et al., 1991, pp. 7–8)

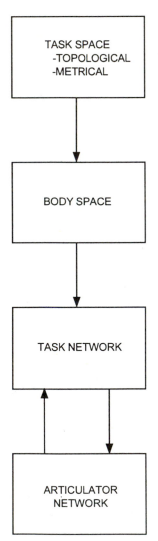

Figure 4.12. A task-dynamic analysis of skilled action. (After Saltzman & Kelso, 1987. Copyright © 1987 by the American Psychological Association, Inc. Reprinted by permission.)

A. CHARACTERIZE THE "MODEL" REACHER

1. IDENTIFY THE TASK SPACE

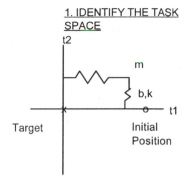

THE REACH AXES IN TWO DIMENSIONS (t1,t2) IDENTIFY A "VIRTUAL" REACHER, AN EFFECTOR NON-SPECIFIC POINT ATTRACTOR WITH 2 DF DEFINED BY 2 UNCOUPLED EQUATIONS OF MOTION (SINCE THERE ARE TWO REACH AXES). THE EQUATIONS OF MOTION CONSIST OF A RELATION BETWEEN MASS, STIFFNESS, DAMPING, AND THE REACH AXES.

2. TRANSFORM THE TASK SPACE INTO A BODY (SHOULDER) SPACE BY ROTATING IT RELATIVE TO SHOULDER (x1,x2) AXES

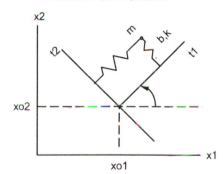

THE TRANSFORMATION OF TASK SPACE INTO BODY SPACE INVOLVES A COORDINATE ROTATION. ROTATION LOCATES THE VIRTUAL REACHER IN A SPATIAL COORDINATE SYSTEM ANCHORED TO THE SHOULDER. THE ORIENTATION IS REPRESENTED BY COUPLING THE EQUATIONS OF MOTION.

Figure 4.13. Task dynamics as applied to the task of reaching. (After Saltzman & Kelso, 1987. Copyright © 1987 by the American Psychological Association, Inc. Reprinted by permission.)

While an attractor exerts control over the trajectories within its basin of attraction, there are other influences competing with the attractor that influence the geometry of each trajectory. In order to explain the ontogeny of action systems, it will be necessary, therefore to both identify the attractor dynamics and the other factors influencing observable trajectories.

Let us consider each of the levels of task dynamics in greater detail. I do so here with reference to the two fundamental dimensions of action: postural control and movement. A classic set of studies on adult postural control by Nashner and his colleagues (e.g., Nashner & Woollacott, 1979; Nashner &

3. IDENTIFY CONTROL PARAMETERS
TO BE USED AS CONSTRAINTS ON
ARTICULATORS. THIS MODEL
ARTICULATOR SPACE IS CALLED A
TASK NETWORK.

BODY SPATIAL VARIABLES (X) ARE
EXPRESSED AS FUNCTIONS OF
JOINT VARIABLES OF A MASSLESS
"VIRTUAL" OR "MODEL" ARM. tHESE
ARE DERIVED USING A STRICTLY
KINEMATIC (MASSLESS)
TRANSFORMATION WHICH
EXPRESSES BODY SPATIAL
VARIABLES AS JOINT ANGLE
COORDINATES (∅).

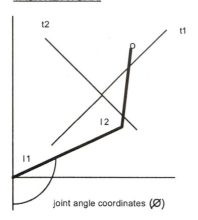

joint angle coordinates (∅)

B. CHARACTERIZE THE ARTICULATOR DYNAMICS OF THE
REAL ARM (I.E., ONE WITH MASSES WHICH GENERATE
TORQUES).

1. IDENTIFY THE PASSIVE
MECHANICS OF THE REAL ARM,
ASSUMING FREE LINKAGE (NO
CONTROLS), FRICTIONLESS JOINTS,
AND NO GRAVITY.

THE EQUATIONS INCLUDE
VARIABLES FOR INERTIAL, CORIOLIS,
AND CENTRIPETAL TORQUES.

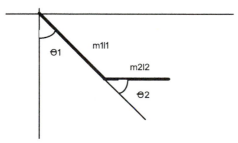

Figure 4.13 (*continued*)

McCollum, 1985) finds that when standing posture is experimentally
perturbed, there are rapid postural adjustments characterized by fixed ratios
among the responding muscles, suggesting that the muscles are organized into
functionally appropriate postural synergies. Saltzman and Kelso (1987) explain
these postural synergies as "emergent properties of the task dynamically
organized postural system" (p. 99). They first define a postural task space, a
two-dimensional point attractor for which specific damping and stiffness
parameters define point-attractor topologies along each axis (see Figs 4.12 and

4.13). This task-space dynamic regime may be transformed into body-space form by transforming the coordinates system so that the origin coincides with the center of the support base. The body-space dynamic regime is transformed into an equivalent task-network form by mapping the coordinates onto a model (virtual) effector system with four segments (foot, shank, thigh, and torso) and three joints (ankle, knee, and hip). Finally, an articulator network for the actual body is defined relative to the task network for the model body. The task network is used to both "actuate and modulate" the real body's behavior, while the ongoing behavior of the real body is used to modulate the task network.

In support of the claim made by Reed (1982) that movement is the transition between stable postures, there is evidence in the motor control literature that movement is the outcome of a series of equilibrium positions (Bizzi, Accorno, Chapple, & Hogan, 1982; Feldman, 1986). Task-dynamics uses the same kind of model of transforming dynamic regimes in different coordinate spaces in order to account for movement as related to control of equilibrium positions of the muscles. During reaching, point-attractor dynamics can account for *equifinality*, whereby the task mass comes to rest at the target regardless of initial position and velocity despite transient perturbations along the way, and *straight-line trajectories* during unperturbed motion. The point-attractor dynamics are transformed into body space by embedding the attractor in a shoulder-centered coordinate system, expressing these body coordinates according to a model arm's kinematic variables, and specifying damping and stiffness parameters for the real arm.

Part II
Assembly and Tuning at Different Time Scales

All living things are highly ordered systems: they have intricate structures that are maintained and even duplicated through a precise ballet of chemical and behavioral activities. Since Darwin, biologists have seen natural selection as virtually the sole source of that order. But Darwin could not have suspected the existence of self-organization, a recently discovered, innate property of some complex systems. It is possible that biological order reflects in part a spontaneous order on which selection has acted. Selection has molded, but was not compelled to invent, the native coherence of ontogeny, or biological development. ... We may have begun to understand evolution as the marriage of selection and self-organization.

Kauffman, 1991, p. 78

The first part of the book addressed the problems of assembly (coordinative structures in Chapter 2) and tuning (perceptual regulation in Chapter 3) at the time scale of performance (i.e., adult skill acquisition). In this part, I introduce the dimension of different time scales to the examination of skill acquisition. Here, I discuss the longer time scales of learning, development, and evolution. The emphasis of the book is on human infant development, but before proposing a theory of the development of human action systems during infancy, I first present a rationalization for the processes of assembly and tuning as a more general problem in the study of biological morphogenesis.

In the above epigraph, Kauffman beautifully articulates the central premise of the developmental model presented in this book, namely that the development of action during human ontogeny is achieved by the dual processes of self-organization (pattern formation) and selection. In this part, I develop a model of the development of action systems based upon (1) the idea that the starting point for development is spontaneous activity regulated by the structured properties of the surround, or pattern formation (see, e.g., Murray, 1989), and (2) the idea that nature is a "tinkerer" (Gould, 1977, 1982; Reed, 1985).

Kugler and Turvey (1987) (see also Schmidt & Turvey, 1989, and Turvey et al., 1991) propose a morphogenetic model which explains the stability and reorganization of dynamic "forms" controlling action. In their model, a "form" (called a mode or dynamic regime) emerges from the competitive interaction of two or more force systems. The action systems which emerge during ontogeny are the "forms" of interest in this book.

The Kugler–Turvey perspective is related to the study of morphogenesis in biological systems, as exemplified by D'Arcy Thompson. During a period of Darwinian hegemony, D'Arcy Thompson published the first edition of his classic *On growth and form* (1917). He was considered a heretic because he suggested that natural selection operated only to eliminate the unfit, and was not a progressive force in evolution (as Darwin argued). Instead, Thompson proposed that changes in structure arise by "direct adaptations" (Bonner, 1974), in which organic form results from physical forces acting on responsive matter. Thompson also introduced a geometry of growth, allometry, as a tool for the study of the regulation of growth.

Biologists influenced by both Darwin and D'Arcy Thompson (see, e.g., Bonner, 1988; Buss, 1987; Gould, 1980) have recognized that evolutionary and developmental processes are organized into hierarchies, and that certain processes operate at some scales and not others. One must be careful, however, about what is meant by a hierarchical relation of individual units and populations of units. Gould (1980) notes, for example that the action of genes is mediated by a "kaleidoscope" of environmental influences, embryonic and postnatal, internal and external. Selection does not work directly on parts, but rather accepts or rejects collections of interacting parts because of the advantages they confer.

The approach to the development of action systems which I introduce here heeds Gould's caveat by treating populations of interacting elements as coalitions in which each element may be engaged in a large variety of functions (Turvey et al., 1978), and by assuming that morphogenesis occurs simultaneously at the evolutionary, ontogenetic, and microgenetic time scales (Johnston & Turvey, 1980). Unlike a hierarchy, a coalition makes no assumption of immutable dominance of one part of a system over the other (Shaw & Turvey, 1981). As discussed in Chapter 1, I adopt three levels of organization in discussing the coalitional organization of action systems in this book: graph dynamics, responsible for changes in the size, composition, and connectivity of the set of equations used to represent the system, parameter dynamics, processes that govern motion patterns in a dynamic system's parameters, and state dynamics, the trajectories of changing states in real time.

In Chapters 5 and 6, I discuss the complementary processes of spontaneous pattern formation and selection as central themes for understanding the nature of the process of development in the assembly of action systems. In Chapter 5, I summarize arguments supporting the view that pattern formation in both physical and biological sytems emerges as a consequence of spontaneous motility of stochastic elements enveloped by a mechanical surround (Murray, 1989; Oster & Alberch, 1982). However, as I emphasize in Chapter 6, while morphogenesis is able to account for the generation of *possible* spatiotemporal patterns, there must additionally be a selective process which fits these patterns to *actual* local conditions of resource availability. This selective process at the time scales of ontogeny and performance is perceptual exploration, driven by cooperation and competition between different parts of a complex system.

Chapter 7 uses these dual processes of assembly and tuning as the basis for a theoretical model of the development of action systems during human ontogeny. Each action system is an assembly of variables from different parts of a complex system (Saltzman & Kelso, 1987; Saltzman & Munhall, 1989; Turvey et al., 1988). The effectors may be thought of as "machines" in the body (Wells, 1971), capable of doing different kinds of work (see Chapter 4). The same body part may be transformed into different kinds of machine: the hand a "grabber" or a "pointer", the leg a "kicker" or a "lifter" (Turvey et al., 1981). Thus, a family of actions may be functionally equivalent (e.g., writing the letter A with a pen held in the hand, mouth, or foot) (Turvey, 1977) , because the same dynamic regime is assembled, but the components from which it is assembled are different. A challenge for a developmental theory of action is to explicate how a particular kind of action system may be assembled from different body subsystems in order to perform different kinds of work (e.g., point-attractor dynamics coupled to the arm and hand for reaching).

CHAPTER 5

SPONTANEOUS PATTERN FORMATION

When we see how the branching of trees resembles the branching of arteries and the branching of rivers, how crystal grains look like soap bubbles and the plates of a tortoise's shell, how the fiddleheads of ferns, stellar galaxies and water emptying from the bathtub spiral in a similar manner, then we cannot help but wonder why nature uses only a few kindred forms in so many different contexts.

Stevens, 1974, p. 4

Much of the design of organisms reflects the inescapable properties of the physical world in which life has evolved, with consequences deriving from both constraints and opportunities.

Vogel, 1988, p. 4

In this chapter and the one which follows, I present background for a theory of the development of action systems based upon two processes: *assembly*, the spontaneous formation of pattern, and *tuning*, the means for transforming these patterns into specialized forms adapted to local resources. This chapter focuses on the former. The theme of spontaneous pattern formation is applied to the work of Gibson and Bernstein by emphasizing the ways in which each addresses *how nature has capitalized on physical law in building complex biological systems for perceiving and acting*. Gibson, for example, showed how the sensory organs evolved to detect patterned energy fields (see Chapter 3), while Bernstein demonstrated that mammalian nervous systems evolved a style of control of action which harnesses reactive and other forces generated during motion of the articulators with respect to a support surface (see Chapter 2). Here, I turn more generally to the question of how evolving biological systems may have capitalized on physical law by discussing two aspects of pattern formation: resettable clocks and morphogenesis. I then make the claim that perception–action systems, specialized biological systems, both act like resettable clocks and exhibit morphogenesis.

The discussion of clocks and morphogenesis is based upon the dynamic systems perspective on order in physical and biological systems developed in Chapter 2 (see, e.g., Haken, 1983; Kugler et al., 1989, 1990; Thelen & Ulrich, 1991). Following Kugler and Turvey (1987), I argue that physical law has constrained the evolution of human action systems so that they are capable of spontaneous order, but must be regulated by perceptual information to be adaptable to local resources. The theme of this chapter is that action systems are biological systems which couple neural attractor dynamics to biomechanical devices in order to do work. Before presenting a rationale for building a theory of action upon a foundation of physical and biological self-organization, let us consider the sense in which action is a form of morphogenesis.

ACTION AS MORPHOGENESIS

Bernstein redux. The phenomenon we wish to understand is the emergence of low-dimensional forms in human action. Bernstein (1967) recognized that action was a process of morphogenesis. For example, when he used kinematic descriptions (cyclograms, or moving "stick" figures) of adult and child locomotion, the motion revealed particular "forms" which unfolded over time. However, Bernstein lacked the quantitative tools of modern dynamics (e.g., Abraham & Shaw, 1987) to be able to specify the origin and ontogeny of these forms. The ideas of Kugler et al. (1982) were a beginning of more than a decade of studies which have extended Bernstein's analysis via the tools of dynamics. These studies have in common the theme that stable forms of coordinated action may best be construed as a geometry created and maintained by dissipative processes.

As stated earlier, one of the goals of this book is to demonstrate how the spontaneous activity of humans, evident even in the fetus, are low-dimensional forms that emerge from dynamic processes. Observed actions are a product of muscular forces patterned by the form of the body and by forces acting on the body (e.g., gravity). The body may give form to forces in two ways: as a layout of gradients and as a mechanical matrix (cf. Gibson's patterning of the ambient optic array). Body gradients are a consequence of asymmetries in rate of growth in different parts of the anatomy. Lateral asymmetries in posture, for example, create a gradient which is a distribution of forces relative to the layout of the skeletomuscular links, while differences in the size of the body segments (e.g., shoulder to elbow versus elbow to wrist) create a gradient which distributes forces proximo-distally.

The body may also act as a mechanical matrix, warping the forces generated muscularly as a function of the composition of the body tissues and as a function of "machines in the body" (Wells, 1971), such as bones which act like levers, muscles which act like springs, and joints which act like pulleys and wheels on an axle (as discussed in Chapter 4). These simple machines may also self-assemble into more complex devices capable of sustained oscillation, like a clock, and these clocking systems may themselves be assembled in different ways to perform complex coordinated activities.

THE EMERGENCE OF SPATIAL PATTERNS AND CLOCKS

Pattern formation at different scales: Physical systems. Careful observers of the physical world, from the philosopher Heraclitus to the physicists Arthur Iberall (e.g., Iberall & Soodak, 1987) and Ilya Prigogine (e.g., 1980) to James Gibson (1979) have stated their wonder over the fundamental phenomenon in nature that all things are becoming or flowing, and yet exhibit similarities. This is captured elegantly by Stevens (1974) in the chapter epigraph. Like Stevens, we are all struck by the similarities of patterns in different materials, and at different scales of size. Here, I explore the possibility that the unifying theme in the similarity of patterns is that *form emerges naturally when particular boundary conditions are imposed on thermodynamic systems*. After exploring this theme for physical systems, I turn to biological ones, in order to address to what extent nature proceeds as an engineer, as physical biologists would argue, or whether the additional constraints of historical contingency imply that nature's design is tampered by the requirement to assemble new functions from old parts under local conditions of availability of resources.

I begin my examples of pattern formation at the cosmic scale and progress through ever-decreasing scales of size as a means of illustrating how ordered structures at multiple scales of size arise from the flow of energy in thermodynamic systems in far-from-equilibrium states. Figure 5.1 is of large-scale eddies in the atmosphere of the planet Jupiter. Computer simulation studies by Metcalf and Riley (in Prigogine, 1980) use a model of two layers of fluid flowing at different velocities to demonstrate that small perturbations of the mixing layer evolve into large-scale vortices.

Planting our feet here on earth, and without the aid of a telescope, we may observe another kind of pattern (see Fig. 5.2) that is a consequence of the way in which atomisms of soil aggregate during thermodynamic flow, what is called "patterned ground" (Krantz, Gleason, & Caine, 1988). Patterned ground refers to "natural regularities defined by stones, ground cover or topography that assumes forms such as circles, stripes and polygons" (p. 68). Krantz and his colleagues offer some specific examples of patterned ground that result from repeated freeze–thaw cycles in water-laden ground. As was the case for the vortices on Jupiter, the emergence of order is a consequence of flow, here convective flow that occurs when a fluid is heated from below. Patterned ground is particularly interesting because the emergent pattern persists even when the flow process which created it has ceased.

The persistence of a free convection pattern in the material of the ground surface is instructive for understanding biological pattern formation. In the formation of patterned ground, the layer of freezing and melting water sits atop the ground surface. Free convection becomes possible in the thawing ground

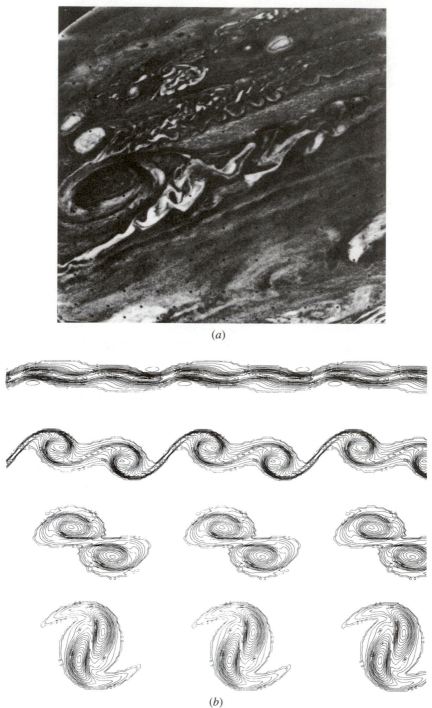

(a)

(b)

Figure 5.1. (a) Photograph and (b) computer simulation of eddies in the atmosphere of Jupiter. (From Prigogine, 1980. Copyright © 1980 by W.H. Freeman and Co. Reprinted by permission.)

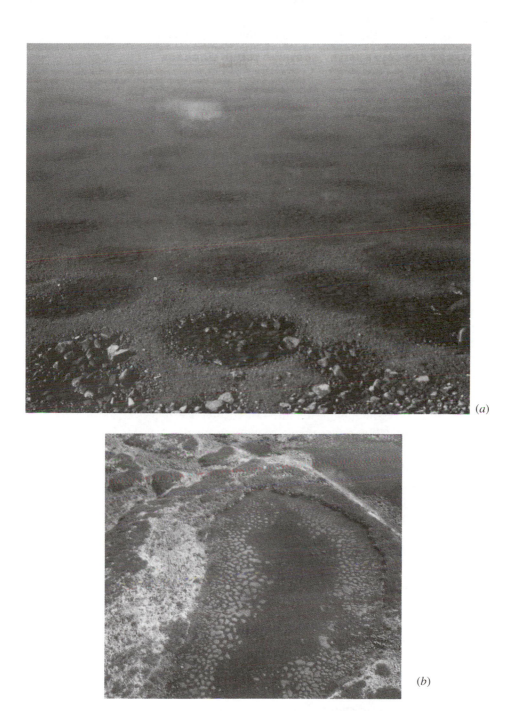

(a)

(b)

Figure 5.2. (*a*) Patterned ground in pits of stones near the shoreline of the Amphitheatre Mountains of Alaska. (*b*) Underwater patterns occur only where the water is shallow enough to freeze into the lake bed. (From Krantz, Gleason, & Caine, 1988. Copyright © by Scientific American, Inc. Reprinted by permission.)

when the ice is covered with warmer water: the denser water sinks to the thaw front, cools, and rises again. This cycle establishes continuosuly circulating cells. How, then, is a persistent pattern sculpted in the ground surface? Krantz and his colleagues suggest that geophysical (mechanical) processes reproduce the convection cell geometry on the ground surface when stones get pushed into the trough of the thaw front, and frost heaves may then pull the stones to the surface (cf. W. Beek, 1990). As we shall see below, the formation of biological patterns in layers, as in skin and feathers, seems to follow similar principles.

Spatial pattern formation in biological systems: Fractal anatomy. With the discovery of fractal geometry by Mandelbrot (see, e.g., Mandelbrot, 1982), scientists had a new tool for measuring the organizational complexity of high-dimensional objects, such as the branching of blood capillaries, and the tree-like structure of the cerebellum (Glass & Mackey, 1988; Goldberger, Rigney, & West, 1985; Jurgens, Peitgen, & Saupe, 1990; Nelson, 1992). Natural fractals are characterized by a structure with variable detail present over a range of scales. From an adaptive standpoint, the fractal geometry of living systems is yet another manifestation of an organization with a multiplicity of scales that can function over a wide range of spatial and temporal demands.

Fractals are structural equivalents to turbulence in dynamical systems. Fractal structure contains the features of turbulence that is a consequence of structural organization rather than a dynamic process (Nelson, 1992). As such, fractal geometry offers improved efficiency in systems involved in sustaining energy flows (such as the circulatory and nervous subsystems). Nelson (1992) observes that the hallmark feature of the developmental changes in the cerebellum is the progressive branching structure as white matter is distributed throughout the cerebellar volume. Like other fractal structures, the geometric complexity of this branching maximizes distribution of white matter within a finite volume.

Clocks as chemical oscillators. We saw in the sections above that when thermodynamic systems are constrained by certain boundary conditions, there is a spontaneous formation of pattern. In this section, I further consider the nature of the spatiotemporal patterns that are made possible by self-organizing biological systems. Here, I turn to the temporal domain, and clocks (see also, Glass & Mackey, 1988). What are clocks? According to Moore-Ede, Sulzman and Fuller (1982), a fundamental property of clocks is that *they convert a nonperiodic source of energy into a self-sustaining periodic output.*

Work in the field of chemistry suggested the possibility of a chemical clock around 1950. A chemical oscillator that fit the above criterion of a clock was discovered in 1950 by the Russian chemist Boris Belousov. As is often the case when a radical breakthrough occurs in science, his discovery was rejected outright by mainstream investigators. When Belousov added together some commonplace chemicals, including an acid and a metal ion catalyst, cerium, the reaction did not go to equilibrium, as expected. Instead, it alternated between one concentration of ions and another with remarkable regularity for up to one hundred cycles before the reactants were exhausted. This chemical oscillation is now called the Belousov–Zhabotinskii (BZ) reaction (see Fig. 5.3).

The significance of such chemical oscillation for our concerns in this chapter is threefold: (1) the BZ reaction occurs as a physical system that may be harnessed by living tissue to act as a biological timekeeper, (2) there is a natural coupling between the self-organizing system and ambient energy, and (3) when considered within the mechanical boundary conditions of the enclosure of the reactants (e.g., a circular Petri dish), an emergent property of

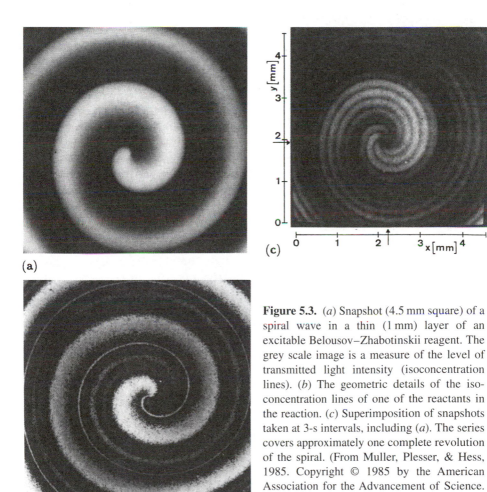

(a)

(b)

(c)

Figure 5.3. (*a*) Snapshot (4.5 mm square) of a spiral wave in a thin (1 mm) layer of an excitable Belousov–Zhabotinskii reagent. The grey scale image is a measure of the level of transmitted light intensity (isoconcentration lines). (*b*) The geometric details of the iso-concentration lines of one of the reactants in the reaction. (*c*) Superimposition of snapshots taken at 3-s intervals, including (*a*). The series covers approximately one complete revolution of the spiral. (From Muller, Plesser, & Hess, 1985. Copyright © 1985 by the American Association for the Advancement of Science. Reprinted by permission.)

the periodicity of the reactants is pattern. It is this first characteristic that we shall pursue next.

Biological timekeepers: The possible origins of tuning. While clocks had been hypothesized in living systems for centuries (Linnaeus in 1751 proposed a flower clock identifying the periodicity of petal opening and closing), it was not until fairly recently that scientists identified biological clocks in organisms ranging from insects to humans. Living forms, having evolved on a planet with regular periods of light and dark, use clocking for a variety of biological regulatory systems, including action. In this section, I consider how living tissue has evolved the capability for timekeeping. The starting point in an ecological analysis of the problem is the relation between earth, sun, and moon. The earth, rotating on its polar axis once every 24 hours, is itself a kind of clock: the boundary between light and dark, moving across the landscape in the same sequence, is literally an earth-scaled transformation of solar radiant energy (cf. Gibson's notion of ambient light). As the earth rotates, the light–dark boundary follows a path across a sequence of habitats at its leading edge and on the opposite side of the globe brings a sequence of habitats into darkness. Early sundials were a kind of scaled down version of the path of the light–dark boundary.

Once humans began to travel outside their local habitats (e.g., in circumnavigating the earth), a paradox became apparent: when traversing a distance at the spatial scale of the planet, travelers' local experience of time was based upon *their* relationship to the cycles of the sun in a particular local environment. However, relative to someone in a fixed locale, the passage of time was different. For example, Pigafetta, a crewman with Magellan who diligently kept a written log of the passage of days, found that upon landing at the Canary Islands, his record did not correspond to local time (Winfree, 1988). Why did Pigafetta not notice the loss of small amounts of light in a day as he monitored the day–night cycle? As Winfree notes, it was because of the resetting of Pigafetta's biological clock to local changes. Pigafetta's paradox, the unnoticed vanishing of a full day from the calendar, experienced by the many other sea travellers who followed, led to the establishment of time zones dividing the globe into equal meridians, and an international dateline at which a correction is made for the consequence of travel on the experience of the passage of the light–dark boundary (i.e., the experience of the passage of time). How have biological clocks with resettability evolved?

As we shall see in Chapter 6, because nature is a "tinkerer," the evolutionary process by which living matter assumes the properties of physical systems under the constraints of limited resources results in imperfect devices. In the case of physiological clocks, the fundamental imperfection is a mismatch between the periodicity of the earth's rotation and the capability of biological systems to keep time as they become capable of traveling outside their local habitats. Biological clocks may have evolved with the fundamental property of phase resetting as a way of adapting to the time-delay required for slower biological processes to model physical ones. This is illustrated in processes ranging from the flowering and fruiting of trees to the growing and shedding of antlers by reindeer. In all of these processes, exposure to light nudges the clock a bit ahead or behind its natural rhythmicity (Winfree, 1988).

Chemical oscillation responds to external perturbation (e.g., a pulse of ultraviolet light) in a characteristic way: it undergoes phase resetting. Resettability seems apparent throughout the evolution of biological clocks. Winfree notes that during the complex chemical reactions that led to the first biological clocks, there probably was little chance that equilibrium was stable. We have evidence of this in the far from equilibrium systems observable today at the planetary scale and in chemical reactions such as Belousov–Zhabotinskii, discussed above. It seems reasonable to suppose, therefore, that in the primeval soup there were a diversity of forms of biological clocks (Winfree, 1988).

A critical implication for perceiving and acting of phase resetting in the evolutionary history of biological systems is that perception–action systems may have incorporated cells capable of resettability, e.g., the suprachiasmatic nuclei of the visual system. But what kind of clocks are action systems? During our evolutionary history, the increasing size of the body, and requirement for locomotion as local resources become depleted may have transformed the nature of the clocking mechanism so that there was compatibility between the microscopic functioning of component cells and the macroscopic (pendular-type) clocking apparent in locomotion and other action systems. In communities of unicellular organisms such as swarms of blue-flashing *Gonyaulax polyedra*, we see contemporary versions of primeval clocking capable of phase-resetting. *Gonyaulax*, however, is a sea-organism and, thus, is passively moved from place to place by the ebb and flow of the tide. With the evolution of communities of cells such as various forms of slime mold, the cooperation between cells made active transport possible (see earlier discussion of *Dictyostelium*, p. 81).

The study of biological clocks has stimulated a search for neural clocks underlying complex coordinations such as locomotion. These putative clocks have been called central pattern generators (CPGs), functional neural subsystems that are contained entirely in the central nervous system, and that can produce rhythmically patterned motor outputs without the use of timing information from sensory receptors (Camhi, 1984). An assumption of many neuroethologists (e.g., Camhi, 1984; Dean, 1990) is that order at the behavioral level is driven by neural clocks, perhaps intricately interconnected with each other. However, Camhi (1984) notes that for even an apparently simple behavior such as leech swimming, the multicellular control system is so complex that if one were to draw the complete circuit diagram, it would appear nearly unintelligible.

Order out of chaos. An alternative approach to modeling the neural contributions to observable behavioral order has been to assume that it is not interconnected clocks that are the basis for order, but rather, "neurocircuits" which emerge from the variability inherent in collections of neurons. Consider, for example, the work on the invertebrate mollusc (sea slug) *Pleurobranchea* by Mpitsos and colleagues. The feeding behavior of the sea slug is instructive because of a peculiarity of its anatomy: for coordination to occur between the jaw and mouth, the brain must receive information about activity of the buccal ganglion (controlling the opening and closing of the jaws and a tongue-like structure). One group of 15–20 neurons, the buccal-cerebral neurons (BCNs), are the only ones that send axons from the buccal ganglion to the brain.

When Mpitsos, Creech, Cohan, and Mendelson (1988) recorded from the neurons and nerve bundles between ganglia, they found that BCNs have multiple functions, but their most important feature is that function emerges from the interrelationship or context of firing of the individual neurons (p. 166). BCNs, in other words exhibit order in the context of their variability. There are two findings in their data that illustrate this point. First, patterns of responses can be established in different ways. For example, while a BCN may initially have a strong influence on pattern formation, when other BCNs become active, this effect is lost. Second, individual neurons can exhibit different functional properties within different patterns (i.e., a sensitivity to initial conditions). For example, a BCN and motoneuron may change their phase of activity as a consequence of the preceding activity.

Mpitsos et al. (1988) interpret their data relative to the concept of attractor, discussed in chapter 2 in the context of dynamic systems. With respect to neural networks, attractors are defined as "energy states that form and constrain the integrated activity within a limited parameter space defined by the phase portrait" (p. 183). In particular, they suggest that a *chaotic attractor* is what best characterizes the pattern-generating mechanism in the sea slug, since, their results suggest that the BCN pattern is unpredictable but deterministic, the feature that defines chaotic attractors.

Transitions. A second problem which arises from the assumption that neural order alone underlies behavioral order is to account for abrupt transitions between ordered states, as in locomotor gaits in vertebrates. Many contemporary investigators have adopted a tripartite model for the control of locomotion based upon a clock at the center of a servocontrol system (Gallistel, 1980; Goslow, 1985). The tripartite model is used as evidence that functional interconnections of hierarchically organized components make gait transition possible. But lack of progress in identifying the "circuitry" as well as

Bernstein's problem of context-conditioned variability has impeded progress (Goslow, 1985, p. 363).

By contrast, starting with the assumption that transition between ordered states might be based upon the inherent variability in neural activity has resulted in some promising results. Freeman (1991; Skarda & Freeman, 1987) has studied the role of the brain in olfaction by measuring the collective activity of neurons comprising the olfactory system in rabbits. He argues that the spontaneous activity of collectives of neurons results in ordered patterns which uniquely specify a scent and distinguish it from others. The collective behavior of neurons is derived by recording from a spatial array of electrodes implanted in the olfactory bulb and cortex of rabbits during conditioning trials. When an animal inhales a familiar odorant, all of the recorded waves of electrical activity suddenly become more regular. When the amplitude of each wave is plotted on the same axes, they form distinctive contour maps.

Freeman (1991) accounts for the order apparent in such records with a model of selective strengthening of the synapses connecting neurons within the olfactory bulb and cortex. Strengthening occurs when the sensitivity of postsynaptic cells to excitatory output (gain) is increased so that the input generates a greater dendritic current. When gain is primed by arousal and by excitatory input, a bulb wide "burst" of collective activity occurs. The burst is a spontaneous ordered structure which emerges when the priming amplifies the collective activity of the neurons into a far from equilibrium state. When far-from-equilibrium, the cell assemblies "jump globally and almost instantly from a nonburst to a burst state and then back again" (p. 82).

By using phase portraits (see Chapter 1) to plot the amplitude data so that it reveals the shape of successive cycles of activity (see Fig. 5.4), Freeman (1991) provides evidence that this collective bulbar activity is *chaotic*: the phase portraits reveal particular shapes interpreted as attractors which form under the influence of particular odorants. Freeman goes on to suggest that the olfactory bulb and cortex may maintain many chaotic attractors, one for each odorant an animal or human being can discriminate. But chaos is evident in the olfactory system even when no odorant is presented. Thus, its source is not simply the priming of arousal and excitatory input. The source of chaos emerges from the organization of the brain itself, i.e., when areas of the brain excite each other strongly enough so that they cannot settle down or agree upon a common frequency.

However, the dynamic regime of chaos itself may not be the basis for the possibility of computation in neural networks. Within the chaotic regime, small changes in the activity of any element may trigger an "avalanche" of changes or "damage" which rapidly propagates throughout the system. Conversely, within the ordered regime, alteration of a small number of elements only alters the behavior of a few neighboring elements. Instead, as Kauffman (1992) argues, complex adaptive systems such as molecular regulatory systems and

Figure 5.4. Phase portraits made from EEGs generated by a computer model of the brain reflect the overall activity of the olfactory system at rest (above) and during perception of a familiar scent (below). The more circular shape of the lower portrait indicates greater order during perception than at rest. (From Freeman, 1991. Copyright © 1991 by Scientific American Inc. Reprinted by permission.)

nervous systems may inherently operate within the phase transition zone between the regimes of order and chaos. The nervous system, in other words, may operate within a third complex regime poised on the edge of chaos (Kauffman, 1992). We further pursue this possibility below.

Pattern formation in networks. As animals became larger during the evolution of life forms on earth, their brains grew in complexity. The past decade has seen an explosion of interest in neural net models which attempt to understand how ordered patterns form in such complex systems. Neural nets rely on the dynamics of the activity of vast numbers of interconnected elements with parallel architectures rather than on programs in order to perform computations (P. S. Churchland & Sejnowski, 1992). Attempting to model a complex system which exhibits graph dynamics, i.e., grows a particular architecture which is then capable of adaptive changes when placed in particular ecological niches, presents one of the greatest challenges to this field. There are presently a number of promising approaches to this problem, e.g., Edelman's theory of neuronal groups (Finkel et al., 1988), connectionist models capable of development and learning (Jordan & Rosenbaum, 1989; Jordan & Rumelhart, 1992; Mjolsness, Sharp, & Reinitz, 1991), Kauffman's Boolean networks (Kauffman, 1989, 1990, 1991; Kauffman & Johnsen, 1991), and artificial life, the study and creation of human-made systems that behave like living systems (Farmer & Belin, in press; Ray, 1992). Here, I will briefly discuss the work of Edelman and Kauffman, respectively, because of their emphasis on Darwinian principles and the applicability of their ideas to human action systems.

Edelman's theory is actually a set of models governed by the principles of Darwinian selection. Its principal strength is in its links between actual processes of morphogenesis and the processes modeled by computer simulations. Its major weakness is in links between the architecture of the nervous system and the presumed behavioral functions performed by the brain (see, e.g., Reed, 1989). The units of selection are groups (local clusters) of neurons which share many functional properties. Initial pattern formation occurs via morphogenesis regulated by a small set of cell adhesion molecules, or CAMs. The result of initial proliferation and regulated neuronal migration is a primary repertoire of neuronal groups. During postnatal experience, particular groups are selected over others in competitive fashion, a feature of many similar models (see, e.g., Changeux, 1985). A third process, reentry, coordinates the individual regions established during the developmental and experiential phases of selection.

Kauffman (1989, 1991, 1992, 1993) offers an alternative proposal for how natural selection acts upon the self-organized behavior of random, disordered, parallel processing networks. He argues that morphogenesis is a self-organizing process that creates attractors and adaptive landscapes (state and parameter spaces). Morphogenesis may be modeled by Boolean networks, idealizations of a wider class of nonlinear dynamic system. Boolean networks consist of elements which switch each other on and off.

In Kauffman's view, natural selection tinkers within a space of different Boolean networks. Each Boolean network has a fitness landscape for a desired property. While morphogenesis creates attractors, adaptation is a process, visualized in parameter space, which confines trajectories in state space within certain limits. The capacity to adapt is governed by the correlation structures of fitness landscapes. A correlated landscape is one in which alterations in one part of the system do not cause drastic changes in many or most properties of the integrated system. This is achieved by a particular network architecture in which there are modules. When such modules are each influenced by only a few others, they remain coupled and can integrate, but will not destabilize successes achieved and accumulated in other modules. The kind of modularity Kauffman argues for is not a structural one, but rather a floating functional one. This is achieved by "transient walls of constancy" which keep forming between the many variables of the system. These walls functionally isolate clusters of variables.

We have seen how the nervous system may operate at the edge of chaos. However, as brains began to grow in size during evolution , so did the bodies that moved those brains around through the environment. The modes of action (action systems) that have emerged in animals and humans may, therefore, be a consequence of mechanical constraints of the body imposed on neural systems capable of generating chaos. For example, at the level of mobile creatures that locomote on land and fly through the gaseous medium of the air, it is often argued that locomotion is achieved by the coupling of neural oscillators to a mechanical device (a wing or leg) that pushes or pulls the body relative to the surface or medium (see, e.g., Grillner, 1985; Gallistel, 1980; Wilson, 1980). But a point not adequately emphasized is that with size increase, we see the beginnings of a fundamental change in the kinds of clocks that are coupled together. As the mass of the body became increasingly influenced by gravitational and reactive forces with increases in size (Bonner, 1988), neural oscillators appear to have become coupled to the articulators to form clocks that are regulated by escapements (Kugler & Turvey, 1987).

Pendular clocking. A research program by Turvey and his students (e.g., Schmidt, Beek, Treffner, & Turvey, 1991; Turvey, Rosenblum, Kugler, & Schmidt, 1986; Turvey, Schmidt, Rosenblum, & Kugler, 1988) offers evidence that the rhythmic behavior of terrestrial animals is typified by what they call pendular clocking. Pendular clocking refers to cooperation among the variables of a complex system which create periodic motion in a pendular system. The system consists of both mechanical and neural processes: the limbs are treated as pendula (with measurable mass and length), and the energy-converting processes at the neuromuscular junction act as an escapement, injecting energy into the pendular cycle in order to offset frictional losses and sustain periodic motion. Clocking, in their view, is a soft assembly of neural processes whose underlying dynamics are the basis for cycle duration. The escapement is a functionally distinct assemblage of components whose activities are evident in the phasing of muscular activity.

One source of evidence for the claim that mammalian action is governed by pendular clocking is the finding of independence between the *timing* of interlimb coordination (the pendular component) and the *phasing* of muscular activities (the engine component) driving the individual limbs. For example, Turvey et al., 1986, 1988) report a lawful relationship between pendulum mass and length and period of oscillation when humans swing at the wrists two hand-held pendulums. This relationship holds whether the motion of the pendulum is in phase or out of phase. Thus, periodic timing is indifferent to phase. However, even though periodic timing is common in the two phase relations, how these common dynamics are constrained differs between the two phase relations. This is evident in the temporal "noise" of the neuromuscular mechanism, as measured by the period variance attributable to the clock and engine processes (a method developed by Wing & Kristofferson, 1973). Turvey et al. (1986) found that clock variance is greater for systems during out-of-phase coordination, but that engine processes were not affected by phase, indicating that intended phase acts as a constraint on clock states.

IMPLICATIONS OF SCALE: THE WORK OF D'ARCY THOMPSON

A motivation for considering above examples of patterns in physical and biological systems is to make the point that *physical processes with common dimensions related by a common function are dynamically similar up to some scale value.* This was an insight of D'Arcy Thompson in his principle of dynamical similarity (discussed earlier). Like Gibson (see Chapter 3), D'Arcy Thompson recognized that "the effect of scale depends not on a thing in itself, but in relation to its whole environment or milieu" (p. 17). In particular, D'Arcy Thompson offered two scaling laws: (1) surfaces are proportional to the squares of length, and (2) volumes are proportional to the cubes of length.

Now, it is important to note that the forces governing bodies act relative to these laws. So, for example, a certain material with a particular tensile strength may be able to resist bending or crushing under a load only up to a certain size. Increase the size while maintaining the same geometry and the structure will collapse. Thus, an important implication of the relation between size and surface or volume is that *changes in geometric form result as a natural consequence of the nonequivalent rate of change in dimensions. Conversely, in order to maintain constancy of function with an increase in size, it is necessary to change the shape of the field.* As we shall see later, the interaction between geometries which grow at different rates may be capitalized upon in nature as a means for implementing evolutionary changes.

Thus far in this chapter, I have been considering the possibility that the origin and evolution of living, open systems may be traced to the physics of the forces enveloping those life forms (see the chapter epigraph from Vogel). In the sections which follow, I consider the opportunities made available to living tissue by physical forces. Then, in Chapter 6, I examine the historical constraints on these opportunities, and suggest that ontogeny plays a special role in mediating evolutionary constraints in the assembly of action systems

Direct adaptation. In his classic work, *On growth and form,* D'Arcy Thompson offers some unique insights for understanding the relation between the form assumed by living tissue and the fields described by physicists. D'Arcy Thompson's work was overshadowed by biologists who turned to genetics to address questions about morphogenesis, largely as a result of early interest in the synthetic theory of evolution, the marriage of Darwinian theory and Mendelian genetics (Mayr, 1982).

For D'Arcy Thompson, the form of living tissue, like that of inanimate matter, is a diagram of the forces acting upon it. Living tissue, of course, consists of atomisms (cells) which are open to energy exchanges with the environment. The cells proliferate into an astronomical number of copies of themselves, and the ensuing population of cells is regulated by both genetics and an epigenetic landscape of fields. D'Arcy Thompson only hinted at the nature of these fields, and it has taken the tools of modern biology to begin to identify them (see below).

Like other scientists of great insight, D'Arcy Thompson was adept at seeing patterns. He recognized the patterns common in the mechanical stresses on inanimate materials, and in the growth of form under the same physical forces. So, for example, he considered the evolution of the form of the bones of animals with reference to the tension and compression resulting from heavy loads on beams and girders. In animals such as birds, the hollow of the bone is empty, but in the weight-bearing bones of larger animals, the hollow space is filled with living tissue (marrow) as well as a fine network of tendrils or "trebeculae." He realized that the arrangement of the bony trabeculae was "nothing more nor less than a diagram of the lines of stress, or directions of tension and compression in the loaded structure" (p. 232).

He also astutely recognized the relation between physical forces in diffusion processes and the formation of biological structure. For example, the physical process underlying the formation of cells in fluids (the Benard convection) was proposed to underlie certain familiar geometric forms, e.g., the honeycomb of the bee (see Fig. 5.5). As he progresses through the chapters of

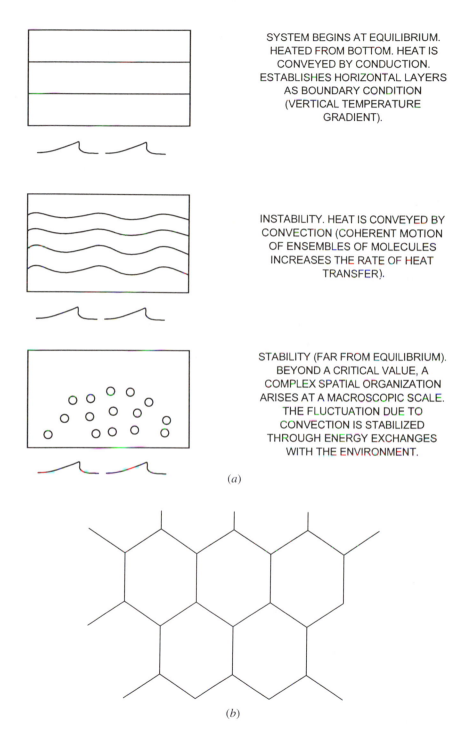

SYSTEM BEGINS AT EQUILIBRIUM. HEATED FROM BOTTOM. HEAT IS CONVEYED BY CONDUCTION. ESTABLISHES HORIZONTAL LAYERS AS BOUNDARY CONDITION (VERTICAL TEMPERATURE GRADIENT).

INSTABILITY. HEAT IS CONVEYED BY CONVECTION (COHERENT MOTION OF ENSEMBLES OF MOLECULES INCREASES THE RATE OF HEAT TRANSFER).

STABILITY (FAR FROM EQUILIBRIUM). BEYOND A CRITICAL VALUE, A COMPLEX SPATIAL ORGANIZATION ARISES AT A MACROSCOPIC SCALE. THE FLUCTUATION DUE TO CONVECTION IS STABILIZED THROUGH ENERGY EXCHANGES WITH THE ENVIRONMENT.

(a)

(b)

Figure 5.5. (a) Benard convection and (b) portions of a honeycomb both exhibit hexagonal patterns due to mechanical constraints on flow.

the book, D'Arcy Thompson identifies other physical forces that are presumed to be at work in the evolution of forms such as spicules, skeletons, and spirals.

On size and form. D'Arcy Thompson also emphasized the significance of the nature of the material being subjected to physical forces by noting that, while curvature in flexible structures is the result of bending, curvature in rigid substances such as shell, tooth, and claw, must have resulted from growth. A fundamental contribution to the understanding of the relationship between growth and form was his demonstration that *size imposes specific constraints on shapes.* As succinctly stated by Vogel (1988):

> Without a doubt, nothing is more important in determining how size affects biological design than the relationship between area and volume. Contact between an organism and its surroundings is a function of its surface, while its internal processes and structure depend mainly on its volume. (p. 39)

Implications. There is an invaluable lesson for students of the development action to be learned from the distinction between the emergent patterns emphasized in studies of chaos, and the scale considerations of D'Arcy Thompson's work. The observable patterns in physical processes such as patterned ground were seen to be a consequence of the sandwiching of a convective process with objects whose size make them subject to the laws of classical mechanics. While structures created by thermodynamic processes exhibit self-similarity at all scales, those materials driven by thermodynamics but subject to enveloping mechanical constraints must change their form beyond a certain scale. The work by Turvey and his students suggests that in order to study the way in which the brain and body cooperate in the development of action, we need to understand how mechanical motion is patterned by enveloping fields. A clue to how this goal might be accomplished comes from the study of morphogenesis in the field of developmental biology.

TWO MODELS OF MORPHOGENESIS

It is argued in modern developmental biological accounts of pattern formation (e.g., Gilbert, 1988) that (1) genes regulate the production of cells by means of transcriptional and translational control of mitotic division, (2) each of the cells produced is motile and is unique in its ability to bind to other cells, and (3) post-translational regulation by means of gradients of diffusible substances or by mechano-chemical interactions at the cell surface is responsible for epigenetic pattern formation (Edelman, 1988; Gilbert, 1988; Murray, 1989).

Two kinds of models have been proposed for the post-translational regulation of pattern formation during embryogenesis: reaction–diffusion models and mechano-chemical models. Both share a common critical feature: *they involve cells whose patterning is dependent upon the geometry and scale of the matrix within which they are moving.* Moreover, because these processes involve the imposition of boundary constraints on flow, they may reflect a general feature of self-organizing systems. That is, *the laws governing the emergence of spatial and temporal patterns of large populations of motile elements within the boundaries of a patterned field may apply equally well to cells during morphogenesis, and to kinematic flow in the organization of action.*

Reaction–diffusion (Turing) models. In the Turing model, also called the chemical pre-pattern view (Turing, 1952, Wolpert, 1978), the process of morphogenesis is separated into sequential steps. First, a chemical morphogen (identity unspecified) establishes a gradient of chemical concentration. This is accomplished by a reaction–diffusion process. In a reaction–diffusion process, one begins with two morphogens that can react with each other and that diffuse at varying rates. Because the diffusion rates are not equal, once the diffusion process begins, it can rapidly destabilize equilibrium because the reaction rates may not be able to adjust quickly enough to reach equilibrium. In reaction–diffusion models, it is assumed that one morphogen is an activator, and the other an inhibitor. Murray (1988) offers an analogy between the reaction–diffusion process and firefighters trying to extinguish a blaze:

> The analogy involves a very dry forest—a situation ripe for forest fires. In an attempt to minimize potential damage, a number of fire fighters with helicopters and fire-fighting equipment have been dispersed throughout the forest. Now imagine that a fire (the activator) breaks out. A fire front starts to propagate outward. Initially there are not enough firefighters (the inhibitors) in the vicinity of the fire to put it out. Flying in their helicopters, however, the firefighters can outrun the fire front and spray fire-resistant chemicals on trees; when the fire reaches the sprayed trees, it is extnguished. The front is stopped. If fires break out spontaneously in random parts of the forest, over the course of time several fire fronts (activation waves) will propagate outward. Each front in turn causes the firefighters in their helicopters (inhibition waves) to travel out faster and quench the front at some distance ahead of the fire. The final result of this scenario is a forest with blackened patches of burned trees interspersed with patterns of green. (p. 82)

Thus, particular chemical wavelengths are amplified, and others are suppressed. But the critical point is that which of the reactant peaks survive is dependent upon the size and shape of the tissues in which the oscillating reaction is occurring. Reaction diffusion models have been used to explain pattern formation in several aspects of embryological growth, two of which will be discussed here as examples. Both emphasize the constraints of size and shape on pattern.

The first application of reaction–diffusion I will discuss is with respect to segmentation of the *Drosophila* embryo (Gilbert, 1988; Kauffman, Shymko, & Trabert, 1978; Meinhardt, 1984). Kauffman et al. (1978) used Bessel functions (complex equations) as a model of insect body segmentation. They propose that which wavelengths of reaction diffusion persist as a function of length of a growing structure. Each of the Bessel functions is believed to establish a boundary. Cells are presumed to aggregate relative to these boundaries, and this is the basis for formation of body segments.

The second application concerns a question that even Aesop appreciated: How did the leopard get its spots? Again significant in the answer to this question is the way in which the geometry and scale of the enveloping surround within which reaction–diffusion takes place determine how the regular alternating colors of a chemical color change are patterned. Murray (1988) points out that the way in which patterning of a clock-like alternation of color occurs is akin to the mathematical problem of describing the vibration of thin plates or drum surfaces: if a surface is very small, it will not sustain vibrations; they dissipate quickly. A minimum size is therefore needed to drive any sustainable vibration. Since vertebrate bodies are assemblies of cylindrical forms, the geometric constraint on pattern formation is the cyclinder. When Murray performed computer simulations of reaction–diffusion constrained by the geometry of a tapered cylinder he found what is apparent in nature: it is possible for a spotted animal to have a striped tail, but impossible for a striped animal to have a spotted tail (see Fig. 5.6).

Mechano-chemical model. While Murray (1988), in his earlier work, and others have been enthusiastic about reaction–diffusion models, the model is somewhat problematic in two regards. First, despite many years of searching, it has not been possible to identify the chemical morphogen which is presumed to lay down the "pre-pattern" followed by motile cells (although protein gradients specified by genes may create the polarity of oocytes, see, e.g., Melton, 1991; Schindler, 1990). And second, it is well recognized that during embryogenesis, there are significant mechanical effects on the shaping of form. Murray (1989), therefore, proposes a model for pattern formation that avoids the problem of specifying the chemical morphogen for pre-pattern formation by having pattern formation and morphogenesis (the form shaping movement of cells) occur simultaneously.

At the heart of the model is an interaction between cell motion and the mechanical properties of the extracellular matrix (ECM). Consider, for example, the process by which mesenchymal (fibroblast) cells establish patterns during vertebrate embryogenesis. Mesenchymal cells have two fundamental properties (see Fig. 5.7): they are motile and they secrete fibrous

Figure 5.6. How the leopard got its spots. The diagram depicts a model of how scale affects patterns generated within the constraints of a particular shape. Increasing the scale and holding all other parameters fixed produces a remarkable variety of patterns. The model agrees with the fact that small animals such as the mouse have uniform coats, intermediate-size ones such as the leopard have patterned coats, and large animals such as the elephant, are uniform. (Adapted from Murray, 1988. Copyright © Scientific American Inc. Reprinted by permission.)

material that becomes the extracellular matrix. Their motility is made possible by long finger-like protrusions (lamellipodia), which grab onto adhesive sites within the ECM and pull themselves along. As they do so, the traction exerted on the matrix generates gradients in the matrix density. These gradients are the adhesive sites for subsequent cells to grab onto. Cells move up the adhesive gradient because they can get a stronger grip on a more dense matrix. The traction, thus, generates a pattern of stress and strain on the ECM as a viscoelastic tensor. Traction, Murray argues, is the predominant force acting on the ECM because the time scale of cellular motion is very long (hours), and the spatial scale is very small (millimeters) (i.e., the traction forces occur within a very low Reynolds number regime).

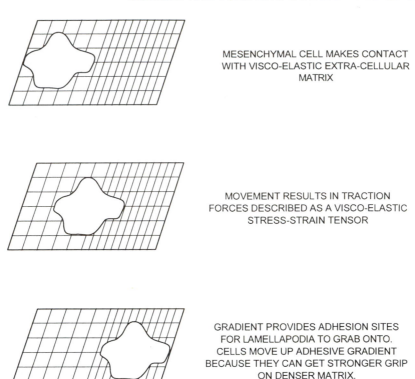

MESENCHYMAL CELL MAKES CONTACT
WITH VISCO-ELASTIC EXTRA-CELLULAR
MATRIX

MOVEMENT RESULTS IN TRACTION
FORCES DESCRIBED AS A VISCO-ELASTIC
STRESS-STRAIN TENSOR

GRADIENT PROVIDES ADHESION SITES
FOR LAMELLAPODIA TO GRAB ONTO.
CELLS MOVE UP ADHESIVE GRADIENT
BECAUSE THEY CAN GET STRONGER GRIP
ON DENSER MATRIX.

Figure 5.7. Pattern formation by mesenchymal cells. (*a*) After Murray 1989. (Copyright © 1989 by Springer-Verlag Press. Reprinted by permission.)

Mesenchymal cells are in proximal contact with another kind, the epithelial cell, forming two layers in vertebrate skin. While mesenchymal cells move, epithelial cells do not, but rather are packed together in sheets. Spatial patterns in populations of epithelial cells are made possible by cell deformations (see Fig. 5.8). Murray (1989) demonstrates that the formation of periodic patterns of feather germs in chicks is a consequence of the *influence of the traction forces of the mesenchymal cell layer on the deformability of the epithelial layer* (see Fig. 5.9). The patterning is a consequence of cell migration along a gradient of traction forces, and aggregation at sites where there is the greatest possibility for adhesion. Tension lines then develop, joining the cell aggregation centers. Thus, the gradient of stress and strain generated by mesenchymal traction with the ECM is the basis for deformation of the epithelial layer, determining the location of a feather germ.

The emergence of pattern in the interaction between the thermodynamics of cell motion and the mechanical properties of the extracellular matrix is illustrative of the manner in which the geometry of a field (the ECM) establishes a boundary condition on thermodynamic flow and, in com-

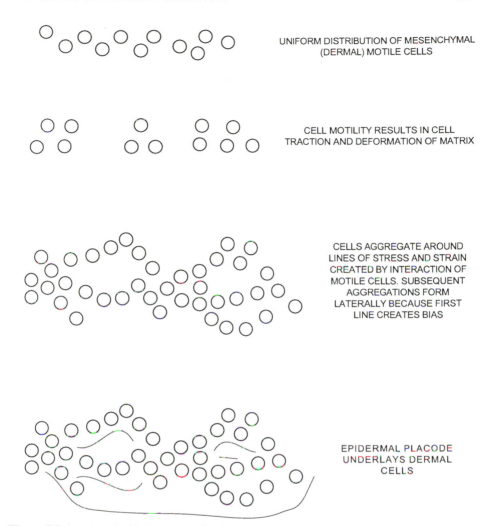

UNIFORM DISTRIBUTION OF MESENCHYMAL (DERMAL) MOTILE CELLS

CELL MOTILITY RESULTS IN CELL TRACTION AND DEFORMATION OF MATRIX

CELLS AGGREGATE AROUND LINES OF STRESS AND STRAIN CREATED BY INTERACTION OF MOTILE CELLS. SUBSEQUENT AGGREGATIONS FORM LATERALLY BECAUSE FIRST LINE CREATES BIAS

EPIDERMAL PLACODE UNDERLAYS DERMAL CELLS

Figure 5.7 (*continued*) (*b*) After Oster & Alberch, 1982. (Copyright © 1982 by Indiana Society for Evolution. Reprinted by permission.)

plementary fashion, the thermodynamics of the cell (i.e., secretion of the ECM material, metabolic activity) establishes the initial conditions for the mechanical properties of the field. However, geometric boundary conditions need not occur in layers. For example, Murray (1989) applies the mechano-chemical model to cartilage formation during vertebrate limb formation. Cartilage (which later ossifies into bones) is made up of chondrocytes, a type of mesenchymal cell. But unlike the case of feather patterning, the geometric boundary conditions on cell aggregation are not in layers, but are due to the cross-sectional shape of the limb (see Fig. 5.10).

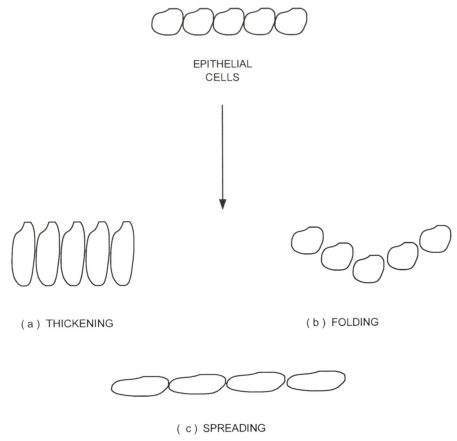

EPITHELIAL
CELLS

(a) THICKENING   (b) FOLDING

(c) SPREADING

Figure 5.8 Spatial patterns in epithelial cells formed by different kinds of deformation. After Oster & Alberch, 1982. Copyright © 1982 by Indiana Society for Evolution. Reprinted by permission.)

What is significant about the thermodynamics of chondrocyte motility within an envelope of cylindrical form is that it illustrates how mechanical forces establish the initial conditions for the formation of the axial shape of a limb and how, in turn, the geometry of the axial surround acts as a boundary condition for bifurcations in the thermodynamic flow of chondrocytes. As described by Murray (1989):

> The axial cell aggregations are influenced by the cross sectional shape. . . . As the cells condense into a single aggregation they generate a strong centrally directed stress. . . . This radial stress deforms the already slightly elliptical cross section to make it even more elliptical. This change in geometry in turn induces a secondary bifurcation in two condensations because of the changed flatter geometry of the cross section. (p. 559)

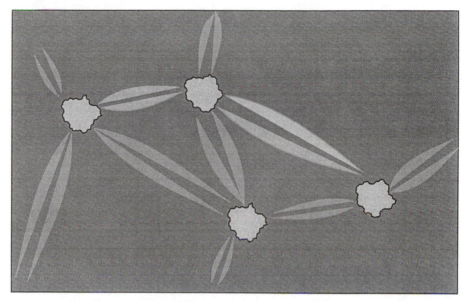

Figure 5.9. Mesenchymal cells on an elastic substratum. The strong tractions generated deform the substratum and create compression and tension wrinkles. (After Murray, 1989. Copyright © Springer-Verlag. Reprinted by permission.)

CONSTRAINTS OF SPACE AND TIME ON MORPHOGENESIS

Scale considerations. How, then, might one reconcile these two models? Both provide a means of self-organization based upon the geometry and scale of the extracellular environment within which cell motility is regulated. A possible solution is suggested in the work of Vogel (1988). In keeping with the tradition of D'Arcy Thompson that links biological forms to lawful transformations following the influence of physical forces, Vogel (1988) examines a fundamental link between two physical processes, diffusion and convection. In particular, he makes the intriguing argument that the origin of convective systems (e.g., mechanical systems such as pumps) is a result of the limitations of diffusion (i.e., diffusion only works effectively at short distances).

Diffusion is a process in which the distance of travel of a molecule is dependent on time, following a "random walk" process. The rate of movement of particles on the average away from a point as a result of a random walk is inversely proportional to the square of the distance from that point, or LT^{-1} (Vogel, 1988). This inverse relationship is especially significant for complex biological systems, since, as such systems grow in size, the span between the most distal points represents a substantial journey for diffusing molecules.

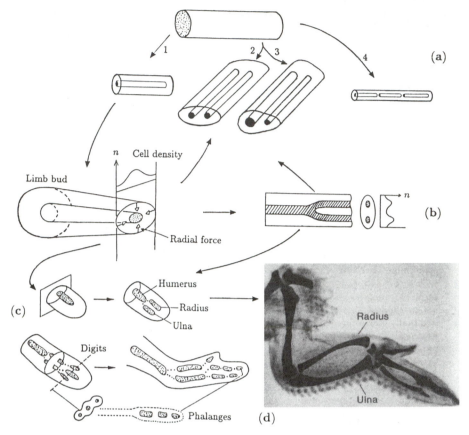

Figure 5.10 Geometric boundary conditions on cell aggregation due to the cross-sectional shape of the limb. Initially, a single condensation path, path 1, will be produced, for example, the humerus in (*c*). A more elliptical cross-section allows two aggregations to form with an aerofoil-shaped domain producing unequal condensations, paths 2 and 3 (for example, the radius and ulna in (*c*). (*b*) Shows how the mechanical mechanism influences cross-sectional form and hence induces the required sequence of chondrogenic patterns. As the cells form the central condensation their tractions deform the limb thus making it more elliptical. At a critical ellipticity the pattern bifurcates to two condensations. (*c*) The schematic bifurcation sequence of chondrocyte (mesenchymal) cell aggregations which presage cartilage formation in the developing chick limb. (From Murray, 1989. Copyright © 1989 by Springer-Verlag, Inc. Reprinted by permission.)

How might internal systems circumvent the limitations of diffusion? Vogel argues that fluid transport systems evolved as a general solution to the size constraints imposed by diffusion. A fluid transport system is "any system in which internal convection reduces the effective distance between two parts of an organism or between the organism and the external environment" (Vogel, 1988, p. 172). I extend this argument here by proposing an hypothesis, namely, that *the complementary processes of neural flow and mechanical action (i.e., the hybrid nature of action systems) arises from the sandwiching of thermodynamic processes (the nervous system operating at the edge of chaos) with the mechanical properties of the body.* Action systems, I argue, are macroscopic transport systems which have evolved to move complex neural systems through patterned environmental fields. Such movement may allow internal gradients of the nervous system to self-organize (be attracted) into one of a small number of stable states. This is, I believe, precisely what Gibson meant when he described perceptual systems as active: the receptors transduce ambient gradients only when they are transported through an array. But for such a neural-mechanical system to function, there must be some principled basis for their cooperativity. In the next chapter, I discuss the evolution of energy-sharing as a response to animals functioning in an environment with limited resources.

Implications for evolution and development. We have just seen that spatial scale imposes constraints on morphogenesis. There is also evidence that morphogenesis is constrained by processes operating at different time scales. Morphogenesis, *per se*, while capable of accounting for biological patterns, does not operate alone in the assembly of complex biological systems undergoing evolution and development. For example, in embryogenesis, while spontaneous cell motion under the constraints of gravity is capable of initially specifying the axis of the amphibian egg, such specification can occur even when the effects of gravity induced motion are experimentally controlled (Vincent, Oster, & Gerhart, 1992). Newman (1992) suggests, therefore, that the "generic" process of morphogenesis has, during evolution, become coupled to genetic processes. These genetic processes are assemblies of intricately organized macroscopic structures which have evolved to carry out highly specific functions (Newman, 1992). In the next chapter, I consider this argument further with respect to the evolution of specializations in multi-cellular animals, in general, and, special-purpose devices for perceiving and acting, in particular.

CHAPTER 6

SELECTION AND THE EMERGENCE OF SPECIALIZED FUNCTIONS

> Darwin's work explains how the parts of orchids are so arranged that they facilitate the transfer of pollen by insects. He demonstrates that such adaptations arose through the modification of some pre-existing part, so that a structure which originally subserved a given function comes to do something quite different and unrelated.
>
> Michael Ghiselin, 1969, p. 136

In Chapter 5, I examined how the assembly of coordinative structures was an example of spontaneous pattern formation (biological morphogenesis). Morphogenesis of action is the process by which the microscopic degrees of freedom of the body self-assemble into macroscopic units. As we shall see in this chapter, there is also a fundamental question of "how" in all complex biological systems, the means by which coordinative structures become useful for special functions, i.e., to serve as special-purpose devices. In order to address this question, I discuss the significance of Darwinian selection on the self-organization evident in morphogenesis, with respect to both graph dynamics (the time scale of ontogeny and evolution) and parameter dynamics (the time scale of learning).

At the graph dynamic level, selection reduces the dimensionality of the population of cooperative microscopic elements by assembling a subset of these elements into a cooperative macroscopic system. This is evident, for example in the emergence of "frozen elements" in the architecture of Boolean networks (Kauffman, 1989), which may be a reasonable model for actual neural networks, as well as in changes in the coupling of dynamic systems. Presumably, graph dynamic processes in development are best observed over the extended time span of longitudinal obervations, and this has implications for developmental methodology. At the level of parameter dynamics, selection is a *regulatory process* that allows "tuning" of patterns of activity to the exigencies of local resources. In observing infants, we may observe such regulatory processes in perceptual exploration and perceptual learning.

The role of selective processes in the development of action systems. A key to making the case that selective processes occur during the development of action is identifying the inherent variation available in excess degrees of freedom of a complex system. In answering the question "Why is it easy to control your arms?" Peter Greene (1982) notes that the large number of degrees of freedom of complex systems does not complicate control, but rather allows selection of a small subset of degrees of freedom which are useful for particular tasks. The complex physical arm can become many different "virtual arms," each one capable of a specialized function. Consider, then, the question of how infants learn to control their arms. During development, spontaneous activity (e.g., limb trajectories) may be interpreted as a source of microscopic variation and the basis for self-organization of cooperative ensembles (coordinative structures with attractor dynamics). Selection is the process of tuning the coordinative structures via perceptual exploration of different parameter values.

In dynamic terms, the restricted "solution space" created by selective processes results from task constraints on the intrinsic dynamics of a system of pendular limbs and spring-like muscles. The solution space may be described with reference to both state and parameter spaces. An infant learning to reach or locomote may explore state space to locate a low-dimensional attractor, defined by an equation of motion. The exploration of parameter space may be described as a varying of the parameters of the equation of motion, and observation of the resulting behavior of the system. A surface in the parameter space reflects the consequence of various settings. Parameter tuning adjusts movement to local conditions of the task and adapts to changing conditions. Consider the example of learning to reach with the hand for an object approximately at arm's length. The spontaneous (initially ballistic) extensions of the arm reflect the assembly of a "transporter," a special-purpose device useful for getting the hand to the object. Visual information about the object's size, distance, and orientation are used to eliminate certain trajectories via tuning of the parameters of the equation of motion describing the system.

The origins of cooperativity in perceiving and acting. An overriding concern in this section of the book is to show that the processes by which human action systems develop are embedded in the more general principles of the evolution of multicellular organisms living in a world of limited resources. Towards this end, I examine the origins of reduction of the dimensionality in biological systems by reviewing complex energy-sharing relationships in the evolution of multicellular organisms (Margulis, 1981; Margulis & Sagan, 1986) and through discussion of selection in Boolean networks (Kauffman, 1989, 1991). I then examine regulation of cooperativity with respect to perceptual organs. I argue that action systems share organizational principles with other complex multicellular systems (e.g., colonies of cells). *Action* *systems are macroscopic functional specializations that emerge from a symbiotic (energy-sharing) relationship in microscopic populations of neuromuscular elements. Action systems are held together by informational boundaries that are created by the intentions of the actor and by perceptual input. The relatively small number of action systems that emerge is a reflection of limited environmental resources.*

DARWINIAN THEORY

Natural selection. Darwin's theory of natural selection is based upon two processes: variation (for achieving diversity), and selection through survival (for achieving fitness). As we have just seen in Chapter 5, there is substantial evidence that interactions between genetic and epigenetic processes yield variation in biological systems. Selection is an ordering of this variability: those dynamic transformations (or, more traditionally, those phenotypes, the visible characteristics, morphology, functions and behaviors) which are adaptive (i.e., better suited to current ecological pressures) will give the individual (a bounded population of genes and epigenetic processes) greater probability of survival.

Population thinking. Because Darwin was influenced by the economic views of Malthus, evolutionary theory has a natural proclivity for economics. Ghiselin (1969) calls Darwin's adoption of Malthusian "population thinking" a revolution in metaphysics, because it led Darwin to conceive of biological groupings in a way totally different from the traditional taxonomic approach. In this new way of thinking, a population is an integrated system, existing at a level above that of the biological individual.

Adaptation. In the context of the belief systems of the nineteenth century, Darwin introduced the concept of adaptation as an alternative to the notion of "argument from design" (the idea that things are the way they are because they were pre-ordained and reflected the work of an omniscient creator). The meaning of adaptation can be explicated with reference to the distinction between natural selection as an engineer and as a tinkerer. As noted in the epigraph from Ghiselin at the head of the chapter, Darwin repeatedly emphasizes the structural and functional imperfections of the living world, e.g., in his work on orchids. He offers many examples in nature of the oddities and strange solutions that "a reasonable God would never have used" (Jacob, 1982, p. 34).

The reason for these oddities, as Jacob notes, is that evolution is a tinkerer: "it works on what already exists, either transforming a system to give it a new function or combining several systems to produce a more complex one" (p. 34). Stephen Jay Gould (1980) offers several illustrations of such tinkering in order to demonstrate that the contrivances which have evolved are solutions to problems posed by the requirements of survival in the natural world. The essence of these adaptations is that they are specialized means for (a) insuring reproduction, and (b) establishing means for conversion of particular resources into useful energy in the competition for limited resources. Indeed, *establishing symbiotic relationships with some aspect of the environment in order to insure reproductive success and a share of limited resources is a general theme guiding the form and function of adaptations.* Below I will suggest, following Buss (1987), that such constraints on adaptation may stem from the competing teleomatic "goals" of reproduction of the germ line and motility for exploration of local concentrations of resources.

Significantly, the adaptations which emerge from such cellular competitions are also observable in the relation between morphology and behavior at a more macroscopic scale. Consider two of Gould's examples of adaptations: Darwin's orchids and the panda's thumb. Gould notes that Darwin recognized self-fertilization as a poor strategy for long-term survival:

> since offspring carry only the genes of their single parent, and populations do not maintain enough variation for evolutionary flexibility in the face of environmental change. Thus, plants bearing flowers with both male and female parts usually evolve mechanisms to ensure cross-pollination. Orchids have formed an alliance with insects. They have evolved an astonishing variety of contrivances to attract insects, guarantee that sticky pollen adheres to their visitor, and ensure that the attached pollen comes in contact with female parts of the next orchid visited by the insect. (Gould, 1980, p. 20)

The kinds of adaptations that have evolved in orchids are illustrations of tinkering: *Epipactus* uses enlarged versions of petals as a trap (see Fig. 6.1) which forces the insect to brush against pollen masses in order for it to escape,

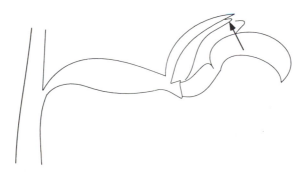

Figure 6.1 Marsh *Epipactus*. Runway of labellum is initially depressed after insect lands and then is raised after insect crawls into cup below. (After illustration by D. L. Cramer in Gould, 1980. Copyright © 1980 by Stephen Jay Gould. Reprinted by permission

other orchids develop series of complex folds, again adaptations built from petals, that lead insects to both nectar and pollen.

As a naturalist in the great Darwinian tradition, Gould noticed in observing the behavior of a feeding panda that they seemed to use an apparently flexible thumb to hold stalks of bamboo in their paws and strip off the leaves by passing the stalks between the thumb and remaining fingers. But as Gould discovered, the panda's thumb is not, anatomically, a finger. It is constructed from a bone called the radial sesamoid, normally a small component of the wrist. The panda's thumb did not arise *de novo*. Instead, its muscles and bones are familiar bits of anatomy remodeled for a new function.

Competition for limited resources. One of the fundamental linkages between a Darwinian "view of life" and the ecological approach proffered here is Darwin's recognition of the importance of the natural setting of plants and animals for their evolution. Bonner notes, for example that for Darwin: "it was not possible to separate the process of evolution from the surroundings in which it occurred" (Bonner, 1988, p. 19). A consequence of this fundamental mutuality between evolution and environment is that in any one habitat there is a limited supply of energy, leading inevitably to enormous competition among organisms for those resources (Bonner, 1988). Indeed, competition, in Darwin's view, was one of the prime moving forces in natural selection.

Bonner discusses three ways in which competition drives natural selection in an ecological niche. First, successful individuals that exploited available resources were the ones that reproduced. Second, members of different species, where one has adaptations for preying on another (consuming it as food energy), motivate escape to niches that allow avoidance of predation and competition. This results in an increase in species diversity. And finally, a third result of competition is that it promotes instances of organisms living together in an energy-sharing arrangement that benefits at least one of them.

EVOLUTION AND ONTOGENY

Heterochrony. Even before Darwin's *Origin of species* (1872), there was an appreciation in the German biological school of *Naturphilosophie*, as well as among the French transcendentalists, of the significance of development for evolution (Gould, 1977). It was within this tradition, and soon after publication of *Origin* that Ernst Haeckel proposed his "biogenetic law," the idea that an individual repeats the most important changes in form evolved by its ancestors.

Haeckel's view, in other words, was that the ontogenetic changes observed in an individual's development was caused by the phyletic sequence of adults that preceded it (e.g., the gill slits of human embryos as features of ancestral adult fishes). However, as Gottlieb (1987), and Gould (1977), have observed, Haeckel overlooked the fact that while the phyletic line of succession of zygotes ran parallel with the adult sequence, the similarity between zygotes in this phyletic line was steadily diverging. Indeed, the recurring theme in work since the time of Haeckel is that *developmental change is necessary for evolution to occur*. For example, von Baer (1828) showed that there were early ontogenetic similarities in related species, and that as ontogeny proceeds, these similarities diverge from each other. Later, Garstang (1922) proposed that later evolving ontogenies are modifications of earlier occurring ones, as a consequence of an altered zygote. Expression is not merely terminal addition, as Haeckel would have it. Expression represents changes in earlier stages of ontogeny by means of embryonic mutation.

De Beer (1958) offers another argument in favor of the view that developmental change is the mechanical cause of evolution: the order in which characters appear in phylogeny is not always faithfully reproduced in ontogeny. For example, prior to mammals, teeth evolved before tongue, but in contemporary mammals tongue develops before teeth. This is, apparently, a retardation of the appearance of teeth relative to the tongue under some selective pressure.

A fundamental contribution of de Beer was his concept of heterochrony, that *alteration and reversal of ontogenetic sequences is a major mechanism of evolution*. With the concept of heterochrony, ontogeny assumes its deserved status as the process by which genetics and environment are involved in the assembly of each individual. In de Beer's view, evolutionary change derives from ontogenetic changes in the timing of various aspects of individual development in descendants as compared to ancestors (Gottlieb, 1987). Changes in timing (heterochrony) produce a different-looking phenotype by means of a stage's growth rate being either accelerated or retarded relative to other stages. Modern studies of morphogenesis trace their heritage to this latter line of thought (e.g., Murray, 1989; Oster & Alberch, 1982), but continue to acknowledge the significance of Darwinian selection.

What, then, is the significance of these two trends in evolutionary thinking, morphogenesis and Darwinian selection, for understanding the development of action systems in humans? I argue here that (1) development of action is a form of morphogenesis, i.e., action is the product of a self-organizing process in which there is initially a proliferation of patterns, (2) selection of action occurs when a collection of microscopic elements in a number of subsystems (see Chapter 5) are assembled into a macroscopic collective under local conditions of resource allocation, thus reducing the initial proliferation of patterns (i.e., reducing dimensionality), and (3) the macroscopic collection of parts adapts to existing resources via perception–action (regulatory) cycles. These, I believe, are complementary processes in the organization of action systems, and give action systems the fundamental characteristic of being self-organizing and tunable.

ENERGY SHARING AS THE BASIS FOR COOPERATIVITY

The origins of cooperativity in biological systems. In this section, I examine the origins of cooperativity in the earliest biological systems in support of the idea that cooperativity has remained invariant during evolution as a style of organization for action systems. I begin by considering the endosymbiotic theory of Lynn Margulis (1981) and others (see, e.g., volume by Dyer & Obar, 1985):

> The nucleus and cytoplasm of eukaryotes originally comprised a prokaryote which entered into a symbiotic relationship with an aerobic bacterium (the mitochondrion), a photosynthetic bacterium (the plastid), and a motile spirochete bacterium (the motility organelle or undulipodium). (Dyer & Obar, 1985, pp. 4–5)

This theory is of special interest here because it suggests a general principle in evolution and development: *energy sharing between specialized functional entities is made possible when particular boundary conditions are imposed.* As we shall see, for the earliest multicellular organisms, this boundary was the cell membrane. But as I will argue later in this chapter, smart perceptual mechanisms (Turvey, 1988) give the populations of cells participating in human action the capability for assembling and decomposing transient boundaries in informational arrays. In other words, perception may make it possible for populations of cells to isolate their energy flows from other populations and, in so doing, create boundaries for differentiated functional activities.

Margulis and Sagan (1986) suggest that under conditions of starvation and desiccation, some protists not only made physical contact to share nutrients, but indeed engaged in cannibalism (eating members of their own species). They speculate that because protists had already evolved a mechanism to prevent digestion of their own internal contents, when they encapsulated another protist, such a mechanism would keep the predator from actually digesting it. This led to instances of "doubled forms" with small genetic differences between the two. These differences may have allowed the double form to outcompete single conspecifics because with less surface area per unit volume, it might have better tolerated starvation or desiccation.

Energy conversion. A significant advance in these evolving eukaryotes was when they encapsulated protomitochondria as an "on board" energy supply for oxidation of carbohydrates to carbon dioxide. According to Margulis

(1981), in its protomitochondrial free-living form as a eubacteria, mitochondria had already evolved a dissipative pathway for energy consumption based upon oxygen. Protoeukaryotes which had evolved in the same era were anaerobic microbes. The symbiosis was presumed to have occurred under the selective pressure of increase in atmospheric oxygen during the Proterozoic Aeon: the eubacteria "sought" an energy-sharing relationship because they could not survive in the increasingly oxygen-rich atmosphere.

The theme here is not that one function becomes enslaved by another, but that the relationship is mutually advantageous. This is expressed beautifully by the eminent pathobiologist and essayist Lewis Thomas (1974):

> The usual way of looking at mitochondria is as enslaved creatures captured to supply ATP for cells unable to respire on their own or to provide carbohydrate and oxygen for cells unequipped for photosynthesis. This master–slave arrangement is the common view of full-grown biologists, eukaryotes all. But there is the other side. From their own standpoint the organelles might be viewed as having learned early how to have the best of possible worlds, with least effort and risk to themselves and their progeny. (p. 84)

Locomotion. Undulipodia is a term used to describe cilia, flagella, and related motility organelles of eukaryotes (Margulis, 1981). The origin of undulipodia in the symbiosis between protists and spirochetes (highly motile unicellular bacteria) proposed by Margulis (1981) is not only fascinating in its own right, but also may provide some more general insights into the process by which biological systems for locomotion in complex metazoans such as humans are assembled during development (see Chapter 10). While we often think of locomotion as a unitary capability, its apparent origins in the symbiosis between protists and spirochetes suggests instead that *locomotion is a capability that arises from an energy-sharing symbiosis between a functional entity specialized for propulsion and one specialized for altering direction of motion.* Consider, for example, *Mixotricha paradoxa*, a flagellate with four undulipodia and covered with thousands of hair-like projections. These projections are actually swarms of spirochetes. What is peculiar about *Mixotricha* is that, unlike other large flagellates, it swims at a constant speed in a straight line. This movement continues even when the flagella are motionless. *Mixotricha* is, thus, propelled by the undulations of the attached spirochetes, and the flagella serve to alter the direction of movement. I will propose in Chapter 7, and in the third part of this book, that such energy-sharing symbioses have remained as a useful strategy in the assembly of complex biological systems. *Action systems, I will argue, are assemblies of different functions that are held together by energy-sharing symbioses.*

While energy-sharing symbioses may have remained as an invariant means of increasing complexity, size once again changes the picture. A feature of the energy-sharing relationships among large aggregates of cells is that when

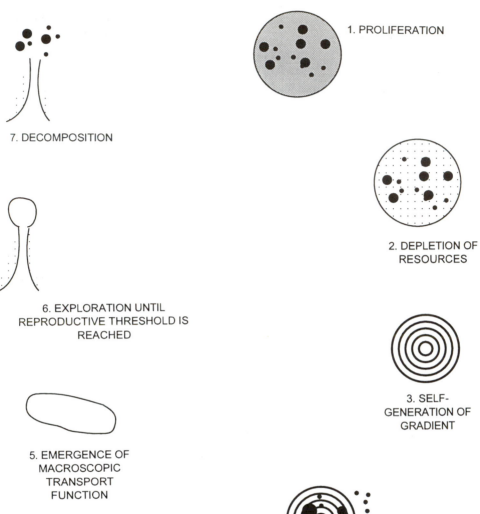

1. PROLIFERATION

7. DECOMPOSITION

2. DEPLETION OF
RESOURCES

6. EXPLORATION UNTIL
REPRODUCTIVE THRESHOLD IS
REACHED

3. SELF-
GENERATION OF
GRADIENT

5. EMERGENCE OF
MACROSCOPIC
TRANSPORT
FUNCTION

4. AGGREGATION AT
SINGULARITY

Figure 6.2. *Dictyostelium discoideum*, or slime mold, exhibits self-organization of its component amoeba cells. (1) When coming out of spores the amoeba multiply as unicellular organisms. (2) The amoeba cease to reproduce when they deplete local nutrients. (3) Release by some amoeba of a chemotactic substance, cyclic AMP creates a center of aggregation. (4) The other cells respond by moving toward the centers and relaying signals to the periphery. (5) The initially isolated cells form a mass composed of several tens of thousands of cells, differentiation occurs, and a "foot" forms. (6) The foot supports a round mass of spores which multiply as soon as they come into contact with a nutrient, and (7) form a new colony of amoebas which live in one region until nutrient resources are depleted. (After Garfinkel, 1987, and Prigogine & Stengers, 1984.)

local resources become depleted, individual cells operating in the diffusive range (see Chapter 3) may temporarily form a macroscopic aggregate, bounded by a membrane, in order to locomote to a new region of resources. This is illustrated by the life cycle of the slime mold *Dictyostelium* (Garfinkel, 1987; Schaap, 1986) (see Fig. 6.2).

The slime mold is notable because it spends part of its life as an individual (an amoeba), and part as a colonial organism. When in its single-celled phase, the single-celled animals live their own lives, eating and locomoting as individuals. But when the food supply becomes depleted, production of cyclic AMP results in aggregation into colonies of thousands of cells, which then differentiate into functional organs, such as a foot and fruiting bodies. Most remarkably, when in the colonial phase, the aggregate of cells is able to move together over macroscopic distances. In other words, during this phase the slime mold uses its foot to locomote as a single individual.

The emergence of ontogeny and the differentiation of new functions. While colonial organisms such as *Dictyostelium* used cooperativity successfully to locomote in order to explore for new resources, other cooperative strategies evolved which allowed for the differentiation of action systems persisting during an entire life span. The key to the possibility for differentiation into new functions rested with the emergence of ontogeny.

Margulis (1981) and Buss (1987) present a cogent case for the origins of multicellularity (metazoan organisms) and of the origins of development as solutions to a fundamental problem that plagued protoctists (all protists and their multicellular descendants, exclusive of animals, plants, and fungi): how to both move independently and continue to be capable of mitotic division. Both the undulipodia and mitotic spindle grow from the same "microtubule organizing center" (MOC) or centrioles. Since the undulipodia and mitotic spindle simultaneously need to move through the fluid surround, there is a competition for the MOC. How can organelles of motility and feeding (such as undulipodia) be retained if their components are also to be used for mitotic cell division? One solution is to maintain unicellularity and somehow temporally separate the two functions, i.e., divide at one stage and be motile at another. A second solution is to establish a two-celled organism, with one cell maintaining the capacity for cell division while the other retains motility (Buss, 1987). This solution may have resulted in the process of ontogeny.

Implications of the evolution of energy-sharing and controlled energy dissipation: The possibility of controllable special-purpose devices. In summary of this section, I propose the following implications of the evolution of energy sharing:

1. Limited resources results in the aggregation of cells into cooperative systems with differentiated functions.

2. With increasing size and the evolution of ontogeny, multicellular animals evolved bodies capable of operating in the macroscopic range, and internal systems which continued to operate in the diffusive range.

3. Because the transport of animal bodies, having a macroscopic spatial scale, is governed by gravitational and elastic forces, the neural line of cells inside the body evolved to harness these forces in order to satisfy the goals of the macroscopic individual. This may have resulted in the "harnessing" of macroscopic "machines in the body," or special-purpose devices by populations of neurons.

THE ENVIRONMENT AND SELECTION

As I indicated earlier, Darwin recognized the significance of the environment as a constraint on variation. There have been a variety of theoretical attempts to specify precisely how environmental information is involved in the regulatory processes of biological selection (see, e.g., information theoretic approaches by Brooks & Wiley, 1986, and work in ethology by Schone, 1984). Each of these is distinguished by a particular view of the nature of information. I will argue in this section that only an ecological definition of information, detected by perception–action cycles, and directed by ecological law, adequately specifies the role of information for selection.

Laws of perceptual coupling. Warren (1988a) offers an analysis of the information animals use to guide local action cycles in the service of a particular global action mode by proposing an ecologically based terminology for laws of control. These laws express a relation between the information available in optical flow, and the forces generated by locomoting animals. Warren begins with the assumption that movement of an animal through the environment corresponds to a global transformation of the optic array. An animal intending to maintain its global orientation, he argues, simply applies the force required to cancel the change in optical flow. This is a law of control:

$$\delta F = g(\text{delta flow})$$

where g is the global activity of exploring the optic array.

Warren (1988a) offers an illustration of the global action modes, local action cycles, and affordances supporting these activities for the case of flight control in the fly (cf. Collett & Land, 1975). His model considers the relation between the information in optical flow needed to support local cycles of the fly's activity within a global action mode (e.g., ambient orientation) and the forces the fly must generate to achieve these activities. Here, I will only describe the case of hovering, within the global action mode of ambient orientation. When hovering, the fly acts so as to cancel any global optical flow by producing a total upthrust (U) with the left (L) and right (R) wings, thus restoring orientation, according to the law:

$$\delta(U_L + U_R) = k/c \; \delta y$$

where k is a drag constant and c is a distance scaling factor.

Recalling Gibson's assumption that all animals evolved to orient to optical flow, the illustrations of Reed and Warren further highlight his claim that the information specified in the ambient array is potentially available to all locomoting animals, and that orienting to that information and locomoting are fundamental action modes that are *universal* to all animals. It is also clear from these examples that what *distinguishes between* animals is the particular ordering of local action cycles nested within a global action mode (consider, e.g., the local action cycles of the worm as compared with the fly during the global mode of orientation).

The ordering of local action cycles is based upon the organismic "priorities" of the animal, e.g., its metabolic state, its growth status, and the capabilities of its action systems, in using the resources available (Goldfield, 1983; Goldfield & Shaw, 1984). The relation between these *organismic* properties and the *material* properties of the environment constitute an elaboration true to what Gibson meant by affordance. Consider, again, the affordances available to the fly. Nectar-bearing flowers afford feeding for flies because they have particular structures for ingesting and metabolizing nectar. Similarly, a flower is large with respect to the fly, and so affords landing. To the extent that a fly can detect these properties of objects relative to its own action capabilities, it may be said to perceive the affordances of its environment and can act on them (Warren, 1988a).

EVOLUTION OF MODES

Modes and resources. Reed (1985) links Darwin's theory of the competition for resources to the evolution of specialized modes of competition for using those resources. Central to the synthesis of ecology and dynamics in this book is the definition of *resources as potentials*, and of *action systems as modes of resource use* (Kugler & Turvey, 1987; Reed, 1985). Reed (1985) defines a resource as "anything that can be incorporated into, and thereby contribute to, the furtherance of a biological process," but notes that a resource is a potential: "it can, but it *need* not, become incorporated into a process" (p. 360).

Following Gibson's strategy of beginning with the properties of the environment (in this case resources) in order to rationalize distinctions among functional systems, Reed suggests that a resource is *specific to* the process it supports. As Gibson had done, Reed offers a taxonomy of resources and the processes supported by them (see Chapter 3). Action systems are defined by Reed (1985, 1988a) as modes of resource use. The distinction between modes is based upon the specificity of a mode for use of a particular resource. At the same time, there are many resources multiply specific to the mode.

Consider first the Darwinian view of the relation between the availability of resources and the adaptation of specific behaviors (Reed, 1985). In studies of earthworms Darwin (1882/1904) discovered two distinct functional activities in the way in which worms burrow a tunnel: (1) maintaining a specific diameter of tunnel width by means of both compression of the walls and bodily secretions, and (2) lining the burrow with leaves to reduce friction on the worm's soft body. He then performed experiments on how the worm adapts its behavior to available resources. When pine needles were deposited near some burrows, the worms used these as a lining, but oriented them so the sharp points were pressed into the walls so as not to puncture their skin.

In Reed's interpretation of experiments such as these, burrowing is a *mode of resource use, a specific use of the affordances of the substrate to guide a behavioral cycle*. As Gibson had done in his descriptions of the environment, Reed proposes that there are lawful uses of resources characteristic of distinctive *global action modes* (see Table 6.1) within which are nested *local* activities. In the case of the global action mode of burrowing, for example, the local activity is a digging cycle defined relative to a substrate (the ground) that permits (affords) both penetration and extension of the body into it. The worm seems to be guided by a law about the relation of the tunnel width to the properties of its own body (e.g., its shape, size and resistance to puncture), and the result is a tunnel that is both structurally stable and reduces friction on the skin surface.

As a second example of resource use by animals in their natural habitat, Reed (1985) considers the predator–prey relation. Here, the local activity cycle is more extended in both space and time than was the case for the worm, and there are multiple nestings of affordances which support the local activity cycles: the cycle of pursuit by a predator, for example, is supported by the affordances of potential prey (its succulence, size, strength, and capability for escape) (see Fig. 6.3).

But what information available to the predator specifies when to terminate the local cycle of stalking and initiate the cycle of pouncing? The answer to this question rests with an explication of the distinction between global and local structure in the optical flowfield to which the predator is oriented. Consider again the ambient optic array surrounding an animal. The global action mode of locomoting reveals global structure in the flowfield: all vectors in the field magnify concurrently, but at one point in the field, the point toward which the animal is approaching, the velocity is zero. Local structure is nested within global:

Table 6.1. Burrowing and predation as modes of resource use

Global Action Mode	Local Action Mode	Affordances of Substrate	Ecological Perceptual Law
Burrowing	Digging cycle	A substrate affords burrowing if its surfaces and substances permit both penetration and further extension into the substrate without collapse	Maintain a tunnel width slightly larger than one's diameter through the tunnel
Predation	Search and general orientation	A substrate affords search and general orientation when its substances and surfaces permit elevation above the ground plane and access to a path for pursuit and capture	Seek places from which prey can be observed and pursued
	Orientation to prey	An object affords being eaten by an animal if it is succulent and its surfaces and substances can be decomposed into metabolites by the action of mastication, ingestion, etc.	Seek whatever information is available that specifies prey
	Pursuit and capture of prey	An object affords pursuit and capture if it is succulent, if it moves at a velocity that does not exceed that of the predator, and if it affords pouncing	
	Interception		Move so as to have the prey object getting closer at an acceptable rate
	Stalking		Use movements and postures that will be non-alarming to prey
	Pouncing		Locate

Source: After Reed, 1985.

Some substantial surfaces are displacing relative to the point of observation. These local movements give rise to localized disturbances in the optical flowfield. Think about it this way: As a player moves forward, say, in a soccer game to get to a loose bouncing ball, there is *simultaneously* a symmetry (pattern) defined globally over the optical flowfield specifying the player's forward movement and a symmetry (pattern) defined locally specifying an object moving in a certain way that is being approached by the player. (Kugler and Turvey, 1987, p. 102)

The local structure, in other words, consists of the kinds of ecological events described by Gibson. Of particular importance for the predator–prey relation is the local flow pattern produced by approaching objects:

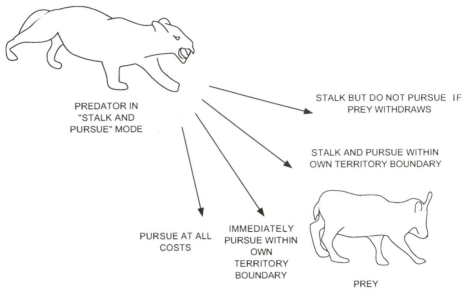

Figure 6.3. The predator–prey relation.

The object in question gives rise to one of the cones that has its apex at the point of observation. Let the object approach the point of observation at a constant speed. As it does so, the corresponding optical solid angle magnifies. ... The inverse of the relative expansion velocity is an important temporal quantity. In fact, it is the time elapsing before the object contacts a plane located at the point of observation. (Kugler & Turvey, 1987, p. 102)

Lee (1974, 1990) has called this macroscopic optical property *tau* (see Fig. 6.4). The significance of tau is that it directly specifies when an object will be at the observer's present location. Reed suggests that the perceptual law for predation, "locate oneself in a position for which prey is catchable" can be written in terms of units of tau:

If a pounce is made from a running start, information based on time to contact could be used both for initiating the pounce and for controlling movements prior to the pounce. If a pounce is made from a relatively static posture (as is often the case), then information functionally equivalent to time to contact is available visually. This is what Lee (1974) calls "body-scaled information;" that is, information about how many body lengths (or step-lengths) stand between a static observer and some surface in the environment. (Reed, 1985, p. 378)

Throughout evolution, certain resources have regulated species-specific morphogenetic processes that are already prepared at birth to detect specific resources. Such resources have remained relatively invariant for the species during its history (e.g., the morphology of the body relative to gravity).

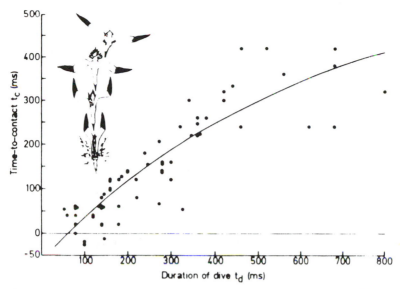

Figure 6.4. The plummeting dive of a gannet as illustrative of the optical variable tau, or time to contact. (From Lee, 1990. Copyright © 1990 by Lawrence Erlbaum Associates Inc. Reprinted by permission.)

However, there are other resources which are more transient and which are specific to the unique activities of an individual, and ontogeny is a process which allows further regulation of modes to these resources. A taxonomy of resources for each of the action systems is presented in Table 6.2.

Consider, for example, milk, a resource that is used by young mammals for life-sustaining processes. The evolution of of an oral apparatus and internal organs for the digestion of milk are already functional at birth, as are behavioral acts that direct oral activity to the source of milk. But the appetitive mode consists of additional behavioral acts (e.g., orienting, respiration) that must be coordinated during postnatal experience relative to the availability of the milk

Table 6.2. A taxonomy of resources for each of the action systems

Action System	Resources Used
Basic orienting	Fundamental terrestrial persistences, e.g., geographic invariants (sky, land, water) and their interfaces, gravity, diurnal and other cycles
Locomoting	Distribution of resources (scattering, patchiness, cluttered objects in places, event-specific locales, surfaces and media of support)
Appetition	Molecular resources (nutrients, metabolites)
Performatory	Modifiable substances and surfaces (moveable, malleable, attachable, and decomposable objects)
Expressive	Emotional states (affective situations, social relations, mutual intentionality)

Source: After Reed, 1985.

and to the state of hunger of the nursling. Certain properties of the nipple and milk (e.g., Lehrman & Rosenblatt, 1971), as well as maternal behavior, must therefore *direct* the nursling to the resource, but it is the spontaneous cycle of activity that allows the nursling to *explore ways to approach and use the resource*. In other words, while the motivational, directive aspects of a mode of activity may already be adapted to a resource as a consequence of species evolution, the multiple specificity of that resource leaves open the future possibility of discovering new uses for it. It is in this dual sense of a resource directing an animal's behavior and spontaneous exploration allowing the detection of other potential uses of a resource that cycles of activity may be nested within a mode of action.

SPECIAL-PURPOSE DEVICES IN EVOLUTIONARY AND ONTOGENETIC CONTEXT

Vertebrate specializations. One way to approach the development of special-purpose devices is with respect to changes in body morphology. A fundamental assumption of both Darwinian evolution and dynamic systems approaches to development (see Chapter 1) is that the selective process works on what is available in the component subsystems. Darwinians call this mosaic evolution (Radinsky, 1987), recognizing that the mosaic of components changes its organization as a consequence of both competition for limited resources and the opening up of new opportunities. The result is a "functionally competent arrangement of parts" (Vogel, 1988).

The vertebrate body plan has been one such arrangement (see Fig. 6.5), and the discussion of early vertebrate and mammalian evolution which follows is based largely on Radinsky (1987), and Hildebrand (1985). In an ecological niche of a water medium rich with circulating organic particles, the earliest vertebrates, small, mobile, aquatic filter-feeders evolved a barrel-like structure at the head end that served as a strainer for food-gathering. Because of their small size, these animals had a high ratio of surface area to body volume, so that respiration was possible through blood vessels in the skin. The propulsive system of the earliest vertebrates used a long series of muscles on each side of the body, the myomeres. The only internal supporting structure of the body was a longitudinal rod of elastic tissue, the notochord. Its stiffness prevented the body from telescoping when the myomeres contracted, and its elasticity acted as an antagonist to the myomeres.

At the head end of the body, the spinal cord, running parallel to the notochord, expanded into a center for integrating information picked up by three receptor organs clustered in the head. The olfactory system was originally based upon olfactory cells lining a small sac into which water flowed through a nostril at the front of the head. There were presumed connections between the

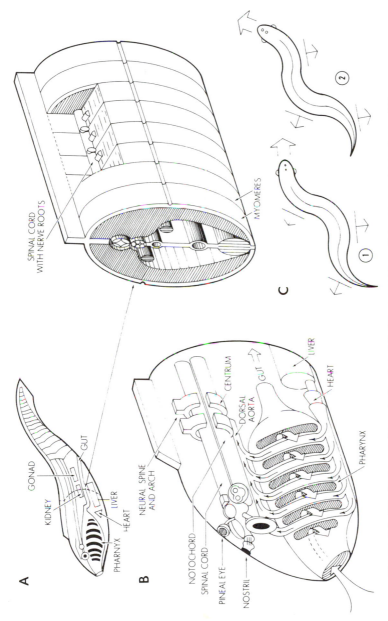

Figure 6.5. The basic vertebrate body plan. (A) Reconstruction of the ancestral vertebrate. (B) Major systems in head and trunk regions. (C) Top view of body showing how lateral undulations produce backward and sideway thrusts against the water. (From Radinsky, 1987. Copyright © 1987 by The University of Chicago Press, Inc. Reprinted by permission.)

SPINAL CORD
WITH NERVE ROOTS

MYOMERES

C

①

②

A

GONAD

KIDNEY

GUT

LIVER

HEART

PHARYNX

B

CENTRUM

DORSAL
AORTA

GUT

LIVER

HEART

PHARYNX

NEURAL SPINE
AND ARCH

NOTOCHORD

SPINAL CORD

PINEAL EYE

NOSTRIL

157

receptors and a pair of olfactory bulbs, forming the forebrain. The visual system consisted of light-sensitive cells arranged in a sheet (the retina) as part of two large lateral eyes and one very small median (pineal) eye. And third, the acoustico-vestibular system used hair cells to detect sound waves and turning movements of the head.

In addition to a nervous system which integrated and regulated bodily activities by means of fast-travelling neural impulses, an endocrine system regulated certain body functions via hormones circulating in the blood. An outer membrane of skin protected the body from damage and invading parasites, maintained internal fluid balance, and contained receptors for haptic exploration of the environment. An aid to fighting invading bacteria and viruses, the immune system, was composed of leukocytes specialized to manufacture antibodies.

Mammalian evolution from this vertebrate body plan consisted of specializations that gave animals a selective advantage in competition for resources and allowed these animals to take advantage of new opportunities emerging with the opening of ecological niches. Their principal difference from reptiles was a more active life, especially changes in locomotion and feeding, driven by a relatively high, constant metabolic rate. Given the relation between energy dissipation and the formation of new structures, this changed metabolism may have opened up new opportunities for specializations.

The continuing specialization of mammalian locomotion involved a change in limb posture from sprawling to semi-erect (Radinsky, 1987). With elbows pointing out and backward, and knees out and forward, the hands and feet were placed closer to the body's center of gravity. This opened up the opportunity for a reduction in the size of the large ventral muscles previously required just to hold the body up off the ground. With a greater range of mobility, new foods became available and the teeth, jaws, and jaw musculature changed to allow new forms of feeding. As the jaw became strengthened, some of its small bones came to lie in the middle ear cavity and were used for better amplification of sound. As the new foods supported higher metabolism, reptilian scales were replaced with a mammalian covering of hair, an excellent insulator. Moreover, some hairs on the face (vibrissae) developed tactile functions. A concomitant of changes in receptor and effector organs was a fivefold to tenfold increase in mammalian brain size as compared with mammals.

Specializations in clocking. It is apparent in studies of morphogenesis (e.g., in the growth of sheets of epithelial cells) that biological form may be varied by means of regulating rates of cell division (Oster & Alberch, 1982). The selective process apparently tinkers with the timing of cell divisions in order to create new forms. How might we conceptualize the components of action systems in such a way that a similar process of tinkering with timing relations in action might be possible? One approach is suggested by recent work by Turvey and his students (e.g., Turvey et al., 1988) which examines action systems in the context of time allometry (see also Calder, 1984). In their analysis, all human action is based on a flexibly assembled dynamic regime, the pendular clocking mode. This dynamic regime has the following properties:

1. It is a regular periodic displacement of a point mass (e.g., a body segment) about a fixed axis of rotation relative to two conservative forces, gravity and an elastic force.
2. The work done in overcoming the two conservative forces during periodic displacement is recoverable and stored as potential energy.
3. The regular periodic displacement is achieved and sustained by contractile muscular force, usually close to resonance.
4. The elastic potential force is provided by the animal's tissues (muscular and tendinous).
5. The regular periodic displacment may be regulated by neural processes.

Turvey and his colleagues offer evidence that the pendular clocking mode is a preferred period for all instances of mammalian locomotion, e.g., during walking, trotting, and cantering, and that the difference between animals is due to the lengths of their limb segments. They plotted periodic times of these three major quadrupedal gaits as a function of hindleg length and body mass (Pennycuick, 1975) and found that in each gait, periodic time scales close to length to the 1/2 power. Moreover, the elastic restoring force in a given gait is the same constant multiple of the gravitational restoring torque associated with the magnitude of each animal, despite wide differences in animal size and shape (Turvey, 1988). These results suggest that neural control mechanisms may select different patterns of locomotion by regulating the tunable parameters of the pendular clocking mode.

Smart perceptual instruments. It follows from the work of Gibson, discussed in Chapter 3, that the perceptual organs are capable of becoming a variety of special-purpose devices for intrinsic measurement of the ongoing dynamics of the action system, or what Runeson (1977) and Turvey (1988) call a "smart perceptual instrument." An example of a smart perceptual instrument is the haptic system, a collection of mechanoreceptors distributed throughout the body (Kugler & Turvey, 1987). If we conceive of the forces acting on the body as a "layout" of gravitational and elastic potentials, then, there are varying influences on the distribution of mechanoreceptors. The structured array of tissue strains as a hand wields an object, for example, may be represented by an inertia tensor, a layout of moments of inertia (resistance to being rotated) (Burton & Turvey, 1990). As used by Burton and Turvey, the inertia tensor is a 3 by 3 matrix of resistances to rotational acceleration about each axis of the wrist, yielding moments of inertia (the diagonal terms of the matrix) and products of inertia (off-diagonal terms). This structured array of moments has been shown to be useful for detecting the tissue deformation consequences of wielding hand-held objects.

As we shall see in Chapter 9 of this book, the use of the mouth for haptic exploration is very highly developed in the human newborn. This suggests that the mouth may be the prototypic smart perceptual instrument in humans, and probably in all mammals. It is well documented that infants will modify their nutritive sucking to varying properties of a nipple placed in the mouth. It is possible that the informational basis for such modification is an inertia tensor characterizing the receptor surfaces of the mouth. This possibility remains to be explored.

ASSEMBLING AND DECOMPOSING TRANSIENT BOUNDARIES

Boolean networks revisited. The functional modularity and field-like nature of Boolean networks as applied to neural nets, introduced in Chapter 4, may have a natural affinity with the pendular clocking mode and smart perceptual instruments. The attractors in a state space of the neural network may have the same underlying dynamics as the pendular clocking mode and, therefore, be able to couple to it in order to do work. Similarly, the exploration of parameter space during the adaptation of a network may be able to harness the dynamics of a smart perceptual instrument. A key component in the cooperation between subsystems adapting in an informational field (the environment), then, may rest with the capability of neural nets to create temporary functional modularity in a meshwork of connected variables (an internal field capable of generating its own dynamics).

Networks. In this section, I consider the Kauffman network (see Chapters 4 and 5) in greater detail in order to examine how the evolutionary trend in symbiosis discussed earlier in this chapter may have been continued in the assembly and decomposition of boundaries in complex neural networks. Here, I use the language of dynamic systems introduced in Chapter 2 to describe the behavior of a complex system, a network, where coupled components influence one another's activities.

The network architecture may be depicted with reference to attractors in state space (the trajectories of variables kept within a certain limited boundary), parameter space (basins of attraction created by extrinsic changes in the values of a system's parameters) and fitness space (the relation between a target pattern of network activity and the current pattern during a particular state cycle).

Boolean networks are random parallel processing networks which are idealizations of a wider class of nonlinear dynamic system. They consist of elements which switch each other on and off. Random Boolean networks are capable of generating attractors in state space, basins of attraction, and fitness landscapes (useful variations) as well as permitting Darwinian tinkering within a fitness space of Boolean networks via alterations in input connections. These networks are governed by the parameters N, the number of binary variables, and K, the number of variables which control activity. Adaptation at different time scales is the dual process of self-organization of basins of attraction which

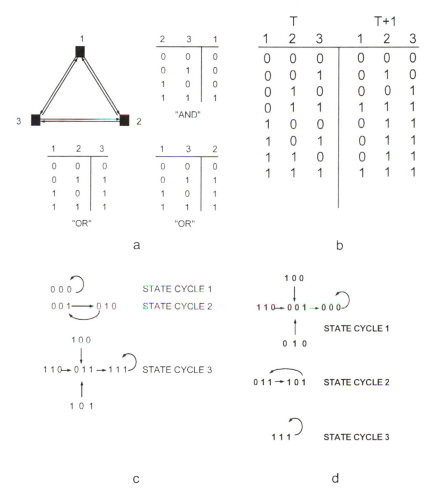

Figure 6.6. (*a*) The wiring diagram in a Boolean network with three binary elements, each an input to the other two. (*b*) The Boolean rules of (*a*) rewritten to show for all $2^3 = 8$ states at time T, the activity assumed by each element at the next time moment $T + 1$. Read from left to right this figure shows the successor state for each state. (*c*) The state transition graph, or behavior field, of the autonomous Boolean network of (*a*) and (*b*), obtained by showing state transitions to successor states connected by arrows. (*d*) Effects of mutating the rule of element 2 from "OR" to "AND." (Adapted from Kauffman, 1993. Copyright © Oxford University Press, Inc. Reprinted by permission.)

confine state-space trajectories within certain limits, and selection which alters input connections relative to some optimality criterion.

Let us first consider the dynamics of connectivity which make Boolean networks capable of self-organization (see Fig. 6.6). Each variable in a Boolean network is regulated by some other variables in the network which serve as inputs. A variable may assume a value of 1 (active) or 0 (inactive). Whether a variable switches in value from one moment to the next is determined by a Boolean function, a logical switching rule. One switching rule is the Boolean "OR:" an element with two inputs may be active at the next moment if either one or the other or both inputs is active at the current moment. An alternative rule, "AND," is defined by an element being active at the next moment only if both inputs are active at the present moment. As a dynamic system, a Boolean network passes through a succession of states (its trajectory). Because Boolean networks are autonomous (i.e., have no inputs from outside the system), they exhibit a finite number of states and the system must always pass from one state to a successor state. For this reason, state cycles are the dynamic attractors of Boolean networks.

The link between self-organization and selection in Kauffman's networks is established by the relation of modular subsystems in state space and fitness landscapes in parameter space. Both spaces are assembled simultaneously during morphogenesis. Self-organization is achieved when the connectivity is such that the attractors spontaneously "box" themselves into small volumes of state space. Kauffman demonstrates that such attractors are created in random Boolean networks with two inputs ($K=2$, the number of inputs regulating a given binary element). In such networks, global order reflects simple local constraints when there is high connectivity. This is because the fairly stable behavior of a local cluster of elements blocks the propagation of alterations through it. These blockages "wall off and hence functionally isolate clusters of variables which cannot communicate to one another through the walls of constancy" (p. 664)

When a $K=2$ network is assembled during morphogenesis, the functional modularity of the state space has associated with it a parameter space with a particular kind of landscape which determines how adaptive processes may operate. Selection acts on self-organized connectivity established during morphogenesis. More specifically, the walls of constancy assembled in state space correspond to a landscape with a rugged structure that hinders "adaptive walks." With a parameter space created by morphogenesis, adaptation is "a process which searches in parameter space for parameters yielding 'good' attractors in the underlying integrated dynamic system." Kauffman proposes that random Boolean $K=2$ networks are appropriate descriptions of neural nets. He suggests that attractors in neural networks are chaotic in the absence of some further ordering principle, and that learning (adaptation) is that principle. During learning, there may be changes in synaptic weights between pre- and post-synaptic neurons, and the kinds of changes occurring during learning may be constrained by landscapes in parameter space.

CONCLUSIONS: LESSONS FROM EVOLUTION FOR UNDERSTANDING THE ONTOGENY OF ACTION AND PERCEPTION

The major message of this chapter has been that evolved forms are not ideal, but rather, are approximate solutions to a changing environment. There must, therefore, be a regulatory process in evolving systems which can adjust the timing of pattern formation in both "clocks" (see Chapter 5) and body morphology so that they are scaled to the exigencies of a local environmental niche. We saw that the regulation of timing in morphogenesis of the body plan is a likely candidate for such scaling. What kind of regulatory process is compatible for pattern formation of action systems?

In this chapter, I examined the evolution of multicellular complexity. There is support for the idea that as systems capable of movement and still capable of development have become more complex, a variety of regulatory systems have evolved. With the appearance of vast numbers of eukaryotic cells, likely to deplete local resources, undulipodia permitted the entire cell to follow gradients of energy, and keep the system from going to equilibrium. Metazoans, and the appearance of distinct somatic and germ cell lineages opened up the possibility of a mobile soma in the convective range exploring the environment for energy, inside of which were networks of organelles operating in the diffusive range and relatively isolated from the macroscopic movements of the soma. I would argue that the neural, link-segment, musculotendon, and circulatory systems comprising action and perceptual systems (see Chapter 4) are a continuation of this trend in evolution of *regulatory systems based upon a mobile soma in the macroscopic convective range with microscopic cell networks inside them operating in the diffusive range.*

CHAPTER 7

THE ONTOGENY OF ACTION SYSTEMS: A THEORY

Compared to many animal species, human infants are motorically immature at birth, but they are surely not motionless. Young infants lack both control of and strength in the large antigravity muscles and are quite helpless in the face of the formidable tasks of supporting a relatively large head and fat body. Nonetheless, they show considerable movement in the face, the head, the limbs, and the trunk, especially when in certain states or when placed in facilitating postures.

Thelen, Kelso, & Fogel, 1987, p. 48

We don't simply see, we look. The visual system is a motor system as well as a sensory one. ... These adjustments of the perceptual system are often, especially in early life, exploratory in nature because the young creature is discovering optimal means of adjustment.

E. J. Gibson, 1988, p. 6

OUTLINE OF THE THEORY

This chapter builds a theory of the development of action on the concepts of self-organization and selection in a mosaic of subsystem components developed in the previous two chapters. Here, I address questions such as: What is the role of spontaneous activity in development? Why do certain cooperativities and not others stabilize? What is the role of perception for the development of action? What is the basis for the emergence of novel behavioral forms (skills)?

The earliest actions of humans, I argue, exhibit the properties of self-organizing systems and exhibit attractor dynamics: (1) they are spontaneous, (2) their trajectories exhibit variability, and (3) they reveal specific spatio-temporal patterns (in dynamic descriptions derived from their kinematics). The earliest actions are only *approximate* solutions to the various adaptive tasks which confront the newborn in the sense that they are not yet fully useful in performing these tasks. The actual means for performing tasks, which may be described abstractly by equations of motion, must be assembled during ontogeny. They are *task-specific devices* which result when the equations of motion are parameterized by means of the infant's spontaneous exploration of his or her own body, exploration of the environment, and social regulation by adults.

In Chapter 2, I discussed how dynamics places motor behavior in the context of natural physical law. However, biological systems differ from mechanical systems in two important respects. First, they are intentional systems whose actions are goal-directed. A goal is a boundary constraint on the assembly of an action system, which thence behaves as a dynamic system. Second, biological systems are regulated by information in Gibson's (1966) sense—visual, auditory, haptic, somatosensory, and vestibular patterns of stimulation—that informs the organism about the state of the environment and the body.

Human action systems appear to be assembled during ontogeny according to the same principles of morphogenesis governing other biological systems. For example, the properties of the body (e.g., its mass, shape, and size) transform trajectories into useful spatiotemporal patterns. In the same way that interaction between cell motion and the extracellular matrix generates gradients that create patterns during morphogenesis of body structure (see Chapter 5), the body as a mechanical matrix, and nervous system as an energy matrix transform motion into subsets of low-dimensional patterns. However, as was the case in morphogenesis of body structures, only a subset of all possible patterns is useful given particular local conditions. Competition and cooperation within the nervous system, based upon changing patterns of connectivity, may act to select from these patterns.

In outline form, the theory I propose for the development of action systems hinges upon the way in which perception–action cycles (see Chapter 3) are used to assemble task-specific devices (see Chapter 4). Two processes are proposed in the developmental transformation of spontaneous activity into a task-specific device: (1) *assembly* of a system with low-dimensional dynamics, and (2) *tuning* of the system via exploration to refine and adapt the movement (see Fig. 7.1). Assembly is a consequence of self-organization. An assembled action system establishes a temporary relationship among the components of the subsystems (see Chapter 4), transforming these microcomponents into a task-specific device such as a kicker, walker, or shaker (Bingham, 1988; Saltzman & Kelso, 1987). Once assembled, the parameters of this dynamic system can be tuned by the infant to adapt the movement to particular conditions.

It is instructive here to recall the distinction made in Chapter 1 between three levels at which dynamics may be considered: graph, parameter, and state dynamics, respectively. At the graph level, task-specific devices (functions, or equations of motion for a dynamic system) are assembled from the many components of the action system. Assembly is a process of adopting different

ASSEMBLY:

THE GATHERING TOGETHER OF AVAILABLE
DEGREES OF FREEDOM INTO AN ACTION SYSTEM, A
DYNAMIC SYSTEM WHICH YIELDS A STABLE ACTION
PATTERN, OR ATTRACTOR

TUNING:

ACTIVE EXPLORATION OF UNDERLYING DYNAMICS IN
ORDER TO MODIFY PARAMETER SETTINGS GIVEN TASK
DEMANDS

Figure 7.1. The processes of assembly and tuning underlying the development of each of the action systems to be discussed in Part III.

functions over the degrees of freedom available and exploring the attractor layout of each that emerges. Then, the parameters on the function are tuned to yield a movement adapted to the task at hand. When performing the task, the dynamic system evolves through a series of states to an attractor or stable movement pattern. It is the capability for spontaneous motion and the use of perceptual systems to explore the dynamics inherent in this motion that makes the assembly of action systems possible. Let us consider this assembly–exploration–selection process in greater detail.

Assembly via spontaneous motion. From the fetal period onward, humans are capable of spontaneously moving the articulators, but do not yet know the variety of ways these articulators may be used to perform different tasks (Smotherman & Robinson, 1988). Because the articulatory and neuromuscular components have the potential to generate many different body segment trajectories, these spontaneous activities generate high-dimensional "state spaces" (the possible states of the measured variables) which reveal to the infant what the body is doing. However, there are specific constraints, such as the architecture of the nervous and musculoskeletal systems, the infant's posture while moving, and the mass of the limbs, which conspire to reduce this dimensionality so that low-dimensional dynamics are apparent in infant behavior.

In adult studies of rhythmical movements, the emergence of low-dimensional dynamics is seen as a consequence of the formation of macroscopic organizations of neural, muscular, and skeletal components (see, e.g., Bingham, 1988; Kay, 1988; Kay et al., 1991). These organizations are the *coordinative structures* discussed in Chapter 2. There is already considerable evidence from adult studies that depending upon the task, humans turn their effectors into a variety of task-specific devices, e.g., "an arm can become a retriever, puncher or polisher; a leg may become a dancer or swimmer; the speech organs may become talkers, singers, chewers, or swallowers" (Saltzman & Kelso, 1987, p. 85). The chapters of Part III examine how infants begin to discover the body's potential for becoming a variety of special-purpose devices.

Exploration of dynamics. Earlier chapters discussed the assumption that the nervous system is designed to cooperate with the natural properties of the body (Bernstein, 1967; Goldfield, 1990). Control over movement, in this view, is not determined by a prewired mechanism, but rather, emerges naturally from the dynamics of sufficiently complex systems (Kelso & Kay, 1987). The actor is viewed as actively exploring the properties of the body during motion so the system can sustain that motion and create new forms from it (Warren, 1988b). While it is well recognized by developmentalists that infants actively explore objects and events (see, e.g., E. J. Gibson, 1988), little attention has been paid to the information available to the infant in his or her own acts. The information specific to dynamics takes the form of a relation between the variables of the system, described by an equation of motion. The goal of exploration by an actor may be to discover how to harness the energy being generated by the ongoing activity, so that the actual muscular contribution to the act can be minimized (cf. Schneider, Zernicke, Ulrich, Jensen, & Thelen, 1990; Schneider & Zernicke, 1992).

An approach based upon *assembly of low-dimensional systems* and *exploration of the dynamics of these systems* lends itself particularly well to developmental questions. The components of the subsystems—limb segments of particular length and mass, and muscular and tendinous elements with particular stiffness and damping characteristics—may undergo specific growth and experience-related changes that effect dynamics and lead to predictable changes in the behavior of the system. So, for example, if a limb is being controlled as if it were equivalent to a physical device like a pendulum, then increasing the length of the moment arm (either naturally or experimentally) would be expected to reduce the period of the system given a constant muscular force. The change in period is potentially useful information about the properties of the arm and loads held in the hand. During perceptual exploration of the effector while it behaves like a particular kind of task-specific device, the nervous subsystem may actively adjust the parameters of this device (such as stiffness) so that the spontaneous motion may be transformed into action that is useful for achieving particular goals.

The remainder of this chapter presents illustrations of how spontaneous activity may be transformed into useful goal-directed activity. I show here (1) that spontaneous activity in the context of a structured surround (the body, the environment) results in pattern formation, or *assembly* (in this case, of a closed set of effector trajectories), much akin to the process of morphogenesis discussed by biologists (see, e.g., Murray, 1989), and (2) that such forms are well suited to a wide variety of potential goals and, as a consequence, specific subsets of these forms which are useful in particular contexts must be *selected* from all potential forms .

Five propositions are offered for how action systems are assembled and how they are modified to fit local conditions once assembled. A central theme of the theory is that *all action systems are emergent forms, cooperative energy-sharing arrangements of available components that are assembled as a consequence of self-organization, and regulation at different time scales.* These five propositions stem from the levels of analysis of dynamic systems (state, parameter, and graph dynamics) introduced by Saltzman and Munhall (1992), and discussed in Chapters 1, 2, 3, and 4, as well as the considerations of biological morphogenesis and selection in Chapters 5 and 6.

This statement of the theory may be examined with respect to each of the following:

1. *Self-organization*: As a consequence of producing variable trajectories under specific constraints and intentions, the microscopic components of action become assembled into coordinative structures which exhibit attractor dynamics.
2. *Body and environment as a structured surround*: Particular postural configurations, biomechanical properties, and influences of environmental forces (gravitational, elastic, Coriolis) on the body all act as a structured surround which transforms spontaneous motion into "families" of trajectories that define a function.
3. *Regulation of assembly at multiple time scales*: Tuning of an assembled function is regulated by processes which can be observed longitudinally during ontogeny, during perceptual learning, and during performance.
4. *Information*: In the high-dimensional space of possible postures and movements, only certain regions are stable and functionally useful. Perceptual exploration of information specific to behaviorally relevant aspects of dynamics reveals these stable regions. Other forms of information (e.g, about events, substances and surfaces, affordances) are also available to be picked up by active perceptual systems.
5. *Tinkering*: The subsystems as well as the habitats which gradually become available during development are "resources". Action systems are assembled from whatever resources are available.

PROPOSITION 1: COORDINATIVE STRUCTURES WITH ATTRACTOR DYNAMICS EMERGE FROM SPONTANEOUS MOTION

A starting assumption is that many of the earliest activities of humans are generated by coordinative structures. What would constitute evidence for such a claim? Recall from Chapter 2 that coordinative structures can be modeled as equations of motion of a dynamic system, with characteristic attractor dynamics. In the dynamics literature, modeling strategies have been developed which make it possible to identify the presence of attractors. However, little research has been done on the question of whether infant behavior exhibits attractor dynamics (see work by Robertson et al., 1993 in Chapter 7). Another approach is to look for some of the distinctive signatures of collective variables defined over more microscopic elements. Collective variables exhibit entrainment, or the kinds of interactive influences discussed by von Holst (see Chapter 2), they enter preferred stable states, and they exhibit abrupt phase transitions. Does spontaneous activity during early human infancy exhibit these properties?

Magnet effects: Influences of one rhythm on another. Let us first consider whether the earliest spontaneous rhythms exhibit interactive or magnet effects. Dreier et al. (1979), for example, examined the relationship between sucking bursts and pauses and patterns of respiration in full-term and preterm infants as young as 34 weeks of conceptional age. They found that normal full-term infants showed a small but consistent alteration of breath durations with the onset of non-nutritive sucking bursts, so that the alternation of bursts and rest periods superimposed secondary frequency on the respiratory pattern (see Fig. 7.2).

Wolff and White (1965), Bruner (1973b), and Gregg, Haffner, and Korner (1976) have all demonstrated that newborn visual pursuit is more effective while sucking on a pacifier than when not sucking, and Mendelson and Haith (1975) and Mendelson (1979) report that the size of the vertical component of newborn eye movements during scanning of a simple display are significantly less variable when sucking on a pacifier than during a sucking pause.

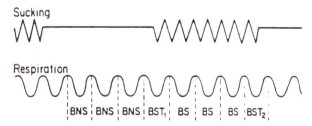

Figure 7.2. Diagram of non-nutritive sucking burst and associated categories of breath intervals. Breath intervals were scored as occurring as follows: (1) non-sucking (BNS), (2) sucking onset (BST1), (3) sucking (BS), and (4) sucking offset (BST2). On the sucking curve, points of maximum downward deflection, representing times when the pacifier was maximally compressed for each suck, are the sucking peaks used to determine suck interval durations and the times of sucking "onset" and "offset". On the respiration curve, points of maximum upward deflection, representing times of maximum inspiration for each breath, are the respiration peaks used to determine breath interval durations. (After Dreier, Wolff, Cross, & Cochran, 1979. Copyright © 1979 Elsevier Press Inc. Reprinted by permission.)

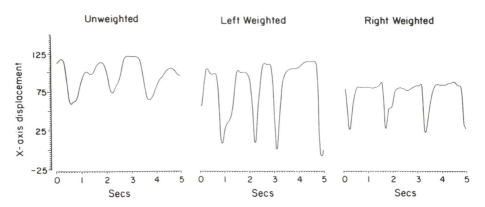

Figure 7.3. Horizontal (*x*-axis) excursions of the right leg of a 6-week-old infant (dry condition) when the legs were unweighted, and when the left and right legs were weighted. (*X*-axis displacement is expressed in arbitrary units). (From Thelen, Skala, & Kelso, 1987. Copyright © 1987 by The American Psychological Association.

The work of Thelen and her students on neonatal kicking also supports the notion that locomotor rhythms exhibit magnet effects. Thelen, Skala and Kelso (1987), for example, added a small weight to one leg of 6-week-olds and examined the influence on the non-weighted leg. They found that weighting resulted in a decrease in rate of kicking by the weighted leg, and an increase by the weighted leg (see Fig. 7.3). Thus, even with greater loads on the muscles, the interactive influence of one rhythm appears to maintain coordination with another.

Preferred regions of state space. A second index of an attractor is its stability. A geometric measure of the stability of a movement is its topology in an abstract state space, the phase-plane (a plot of position versus velocity). Consider the trajectory of the knee during kicking. If the trajectory is not random, the plot will consist of a filling in of a particular region of the plot. Heriza (1988, 1991) has shown that in very young infants, the excursion of the knee during kicking resembles the classic phase portrait of a periodic attractor (see Fig. 7.4). While trajectories of the leg are variable, they remain within a limited region of the phase plane.

Abrupt phase transitions. A third marker of an attractor is the presence of abrupt phase transitions between stable states. Studies of respiratory patterns in infants consistently indicate that there are systematic and discontinuous changes in the phase relation between respiratory muscle groups during the transition from active to quiet sleep (Curzi-Dascalova & Plassart, 1978). Curzi-Dascalova and Plassart (1978) examined the relation between quiet and active sleep and rhythmic movement of thoracic and abdominal muscles during

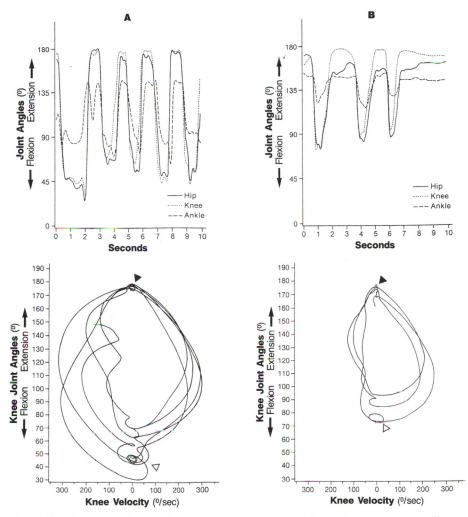

Figure 7.4. Full-term infant at 40 weeks gestational age. Top figure shows angle–time diagram of the displacement of the hip, knee, and ankle joints. Bottom figure illustrates corresponding phase-plane trajectories of the knee joint amplitude of movement and peak velocity. The filled triangle indicates the beginning of flexion movement; the open triangle represents peak flexion. Phase-plane trajectories proceed clockwise, by definition. (From Heriza, 1991. Copyright © 1991 by The American Physical Therapy Society. Reprinted by permission.)

vegetative respiration (for life support). Chest and abdomen maintain an invariant phase relation during most of quiet sleep, but are out of phase by 180 degrees in active sleep. In a followup study comparing full-term and preterm infants, Curzi-Dascalova (1982) found that even the preterm infants showed in-phase movements of thoracic and abdominal muscles in state 1, and out-of-phase movements in state 2. The out-of-phase pattern also appears to occur during crying. Langlois, Baken and Wilder (1980) examined respiratory phase during crying and found that as in state 2, the thoracic and abdominal muscles were out of phase. Respiration, thus, seems to be a dynamic system which undergoes abrupt phase transitions. As discussed in Chapter 9, respiration may also be a substrate for the assembly of differentiated functions of the oral effectors.

PROPOSITION 2: THE BODY AND ENVIRONMENT AS A STRUCTURED SURROUND

What gives the abstract dynamics of task space the familiar look of concrete acts such as reaching for a ball, or walking across the floor. In other words, what makes attractor dynamics useful for a body with a particular morphology? According to the task-dynamic approach, discussed in Chapter 4, for attractor dynamics to be useful as a control structure, there must be system components which transform the abstract dynamics of task space into body and environment related coordinates (Saltzman & Kelso, 1987). This transformation process is like the patterning of spontaneous motility of cells during morphogenesis in the formation of embryonic tissue, in the sense that the body and environment act as a surround, which can be described by a layout of forces in body and environment centered coordinate spaces.

In Chapter 5, I suggested that the body may pattern spontaneous attractor dynamics in two ways: (1) body posture may act as a layout of equilibrium points which dissipates forces in particular ways; (2) body tissues which have variable density and viscosity, or compliance, may dissipate forces in particular ways. An example of the former is the patterning of movement that occurs when the newborn is lying in a supine posture. Supine newborns typically adopt a posture in which the head is turned to one side (usually the right), with the ipsilateral arm extended and the contralateral arm flexed (Turkewitz, Gordon, & Birch, 1965). A consequence of spontaneous arm movement while in this posture is that the infant is more likely to see the ipsilateral hand (Michel, 1981), perhaps facilitating eye–hand coordination on one side earlier than the other.

How can we categorize the forces acting on the body? Bingham (1988) refers to these as "incidental dynamics" and offers three categories: (1) inertial, dissipative and mechanical constraints (e.g., pumping air into a bicycle tire, swinging open a door, carrying a bucket of paint by the handle), (2) potentials able to absorb, store and/or passively return energy to the muscular forces (e.g., gravitational potential and the elastic potential of springs, as in bouncing a ball or juggling), and (3) independent sources of energy (e.g., shaking someone's hand).

There is some evidence that human infants may learn to harness forces acting on the body during spontaneous kicking. Using the technique of intersegmental dynamics, Schneider, Zernicke, Ulrich, Jensen, and Thelen (1990) were able to determine the net torque, or the sum of all forces causing the angular movement of a human infant leg segment, and partition it into its consituents. Newtonian equations of motion (see Chapter 4) were used to calculate torques arising from (1) the effects of gravity (GRA), a constant torque acting through the center of mass, and (2) motion-dependent torques (MDT), resulting from velocities and accelerations of the segments. A residual torque was then obtained by subtracting GRA and MDT from the net torque. This residual torque was used as a measure of muscle (MUS) torque, the result of active muscular contraction. The way in which muscle forces interact with shifting passive flexor and extensor torques while stepping on a treadmill illustrates the cooperation and competition of intrinsic dynamics and forces acting on the body.

When the infant is stepping on a treadmill, the contact of the foot with the surface of the belt provides perceptual information about the speed of the treadmill. Thelen and Ulrich (1991) showed that infants are able to adjust their treadmill steps to the speed of the treadmill. During a fast step, GRA provides the most important flexor influence early in the swing phase, aided by MUS. By the time the thigh reversed direction in preparation for foot fall, MUS and GRA acted cooperatively to oppose the flexor influence of MDT. Then, during the rest of the swing phase, MUS continued to counterbalance MDT while GRA remained an extensor influence. By contrast, during a slow step, MUS became a dominant extensor torque prior to reversal of the thigh to oppose GRA and MDT. Thus, infants adjust MUS to the changing conditions of the task.

The effects of growth-related changes in the distribution of body tissue on the appearance of certain forms of action are illustrated by a series of early studies of Thelen on the relation between body fact, muscle strength and stepping. Thelen, Fisher, Ridley-Johnson, and Griffin (1982) found that infants who were relatively heavier for their length stepped less than those with a lean build. Thelen, Fisher, and Ridley-Johnson (1984) then further tested the consequences of differential growth rates on stepping by experimentally manipulating the mass of the legs, either by adding weights or by testing while the legs were submerged in water. They found that during age 2 to 4 weeks, a period of especially rapid weight gain (e.g., increase in fat fold), there was a 26 percent decline in average number of steps. At 4 weeks, stepping frequency was related to weight and ponderal index rate gain, and those infants who gained most weight stepped less. When weights which simulated 2 weeks of growth were added to the legs of 4–week-olds, their stepping declined 32 percent, and when infants' legs were submerged in water, reducing the effects of mass, the average step rates nearly doubled. Thus, the patterning of stepping is influenced by the composition of body tissues.

Changes in the "form" of action may also result from changes in size which require a "rescaling" of the system according to the laws relating length and volume (D'Arcy Thompson, 1942), and with a redistribution of body mass as body proportions change (Thelen, 1983), as well as from changes in the nervous system and the environment. There is little known about the consequences of anatomical growth for rescaling of control structures. A particularly fascinating illustration of this problem, which awaits careful study, is the restructuring of the anatomy of the rib cage, and the descent of the larynx down in the pharynx to the point where it can no longer form a sealed airway from the nose in infants between birth and three months (Lieberman, 1985). The neural control system that regulates breathing restructures at this point to allow mouth breathing. Are there changes in respiratory stability which may mediate such control system restructuring?

PROPOSITION 3: REGULATION OF ASSEMBLY AT MULTIPLE TIME SCALES

The temporal nesting of behavioral rhythms. One of the significant discoveries of research on behavioral rhythms is that rhythms have characteristic periods which range from hours to seconds (Moore-Ede et al., 1982; Robertson, 1988, Robertson et al. 1993; Stratton, 1982) (see Fig. 7.5). This range of periods may be one window on the time scale of various functional activities of animals which have evolved within particular ecological niches. For example, the diurnal rhythm reflects a basic energy-conservation function in which animals alternate sleep and wakefulness. During waking hours, animals feed and explore the environment for its resources, and during sleep, the various systems of the body use the acquired resources to better adapt itself to the local habitat. Each action mode, such as feeding, has its own serial ordering specific to the waking needs of the animal. Waking activity, therefore, may be considered as a set of goals (activation scores) which influence the activation of particular modes of coordinated behavior.

Based in part upon the earlier work of Piaget, one of the first attempts to consider the possible significance of behavioral rhythms for the organization of early infant behavior came from studies of rhythmic behaviors apparent during sleep and wakefulness (Wolff, 1987, 1993). Prechtl and Beintema (1964) and Wolff (1966) demonstrated the predictable co-occurrence of a collection of behavioral and physiological rhythms during various phases of the sleep–wake cycle. These authors referred to such collections of behavioral rhythms as behavioral states (Prechtl, 1974; Prechtl & O'Brien, 1982). More recently, Wolff (1987) has proposed a taxonomy of five behavioral states (see Chapter 1).

Wolff (1987) distinguishes between two usages of the term "behavioral state." As an independent variable, behavioral state is used as a means of ordering otherwise unexplained variation in observed behavioral and physio-

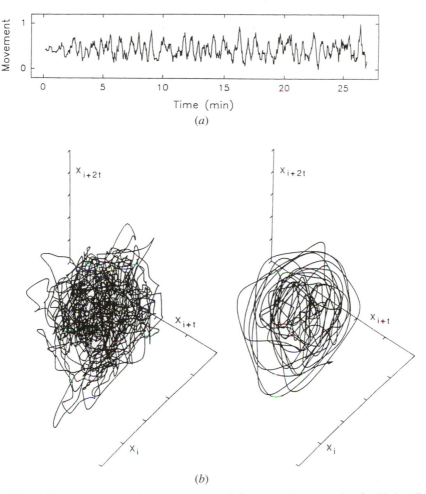

Figure 7.5. (*a*) Movement time series from an awake infant studied two months after birth. After detrending, the data were rescaled to the interval (0,1). In this illustration, the time series has been smoothed with a 15-second moving average. (*b*) The same time series embedded in three dimensions (time delay = 15 seconds) and projected onto two dimensions. Successive points along the trajectory have been connected with a cubic spline and suppressed with a low-pass filter (frequency response = 0.1 at 3 cycles/min). (From Robertson, Cohen, & Mayer-Kress, 1993. Copyright © 1993 MIT Press. Reprinted by permission.)

logical dependent variables. As a dependent variable, behavioral state refers to the collection of variables which intervenes between nonlinear input–output relations such that there is no one-to-one correspondence between input and output. When considered in the latter usage of collections of behavioral and physiological rhythms, behavioral states exhibit the property of entering into a small number of "preferred" configurations.

The first appearance of these organized patterns or behavioral states is evident in both ultrasound studies of fetuses and in studies of low-risk premature infants. Nijhuis, Martin and Prechtl (1984) and Van Vliet, Martin, Nijhuis, and Prechtl (1985) report, for example, that there is no evidence of fetal behavioral states until 38 weeks. Prechtl, Fargel, Weinmann, and Bakker (1979) similarly found that among low-risk premature infants the rhythms of respiration, rest and activity, and eye movements that define sleep states do not coincide at all before 35 to 37 weeks. The preferred modes or states of sleep and wakefulness first appear at about 36 postconceptual weeks when respiration, heartrate, eye movements, and EEG become temporally linked to form the familiar pattern of quiet and active sleep and wakefulness (Dittrichova, Brichacek, Paul, & Tautermannova, 1982; Karch et al., 1982; Parmelee, Wenner, Akiyama, Schultz, & Stern, 1967). This pattern becomes consolidated during the first six months of life (Coons & Guilleminault, 1982, 1984; Roffwarg et al., 1966).

There is differential elicitability of "reflexive" behaviors and the expression of specific postures as a function of behavioral state, once they appear. Consider, for example, the proprioceptive and vestibular reflexes (Prechtl, 1972). In state 1 and wakefulness, the Moro and tendon reflexes are readily elicited, but during state 2, they are markedly diminished. The exteroceptive skin reflex, the rooting response, by contrast, is absent in both sleep states (Lenard, von Bernuth, & Prechtl, 1968; Prechtl, Vlach, Lenard, & Grant, 1967; Vlach, von Bernuth, & Prechtl, 1972). Posture is also state-specific. During the transition from waking activity to state 2 sleep, for example, there is a loss of active posture. In supine, the baby's face falls to the side, the arms fall gently with the fingers open to a semi-flexed tonic posture, and the legs become more abducted and exorotated (Casaer, 1979). During state 1 sleep, by contrast, infants show more symmetrical arm flexion and leg adduction. During active (state 2) sleep, there are fine movements of the fingers and toes as well as smiles and grimaces not present in state 1 (Schulte 1974; Wolff, 1966).

Preferred configurations of the variables which are components of specific behavioral states are also apparent in the tendency of particular collections of rhythms to remain temporally linked despite external perturbation. Wolff (1966) provided an early demonstration of the relative resistance against external perturbation of state-specific behaviors when he exposed neonates in different behavioral states to a continuous monotonous sound—"white noise." During state 2, white noise converted irregular respirations to regular respirations within a brief interval, but during drowsiness or waking, the same white noise caused a transition to state 1 sleep in only half of the infants. In vigorously crying infants the white noise was effective in shifting the behavioral state to sleep in only 25 percent of infants. The same white noise was relatively ineffective in producing any behavioral state changes when the infant was in state 1 sleep. Whether the white noise was turned on at the beginning, middle, or end of a cycle of state 1 sleep had no substantial effect in prolonging its typical period of 21 minutes. Thus, the configuration of behaviors that constitutes state 1 sleep is more resistant than the other states to the same external perturbation.

PROPOSITION 4: EXPLORATORY ACTIVITY REVEALS STABLE REGIONS IN DYNAMIC GEOMETRIES

One of the premises of the theory of development of action systems proposed here is that infants explore the dynamics of their own action and may discover information specific to stable regions in the high-dimensional spaces of possible actions. The presence of an attractor may guide the infant to optimize the function assembled during spontaneous activity. To examine this possibility, Goldfield, Kay, and Warren (1993) gave infants the opportunity to learn the dynamics of a mass-spring system: their own body suspended from a spring of known stiffness and damping. The infants were observed longitudinally once each week over a period of several weeks as they learned to bounce while suspended in a harness attached to a spring.

Specific predictions were developed about how infants learn to bounce when they become part of a mass-spring system, based upon considerations from dynamic systems (see Chapter 2). We first attempted to identify a low-dimensional description (a function) of what is assembled during spontaneous movement, namely, a task-specific periodic kicking device. As a first approximation, we can model this function by the following equation:

$$m\ddot{x} + b\dot{x} + kx = F_0 \cos(\omega t)$$

Here, the mass parameter, m, represents the mass of the infant, and the stiffness, k, and damping, b, parameters represent the characteristics of the infant bouncer's spring. The infant's kicking is represented by the driver of the right-hand side; the actual vertical motion of the infant is represented by x and its time-derivatives. The free parameters that the infant may be controlling appear to be the driving force, F_0, and the forcing frequency, ω: how much force to apply and how fast.

This equation has a very clear optimality property, resonance. For any given driving force, the amplitude of the mass's oscillations is maximal at a specific frequency; conversely, a given amplitude requires minimum driving force at this frequency (Kugler & Turvey, 1987). This value is termed resonant frequency, and it is close to the natural frequency of the undriven system. One possibility is that infants search frequency space until they find the resonant frequency. During ground contact, it is unlikely that the infant's legs are acting as pure force applicators, but more like springs with the joints and muscles having stiffness and damping characteristics of their own. That is, the infant's legs are contributing their own stiffness and damping to the situation.

The muscles also act as a transmission between the actual force-generating mechanism (sliding filaments) and the load that they are moving (the infant's body). It is well known from engineering theory (e.g., Ogata, 1970) that the maximum power can be transmitted to the load if the impedance properties of the transmission (the muscles) are matched to the impedance properties of the load. That is, the infant contributes to the stiffness of the entire system, and she will transfer maximum power to her body's mass if she matches leg stiffness to that of the attached spring. When impedance matching holds, then, the total stiffness of the stiffness is twice that of the physical spring. The natural frequency of the total system is square root of 2 times that of the simpler driven system.

The appropriate phasing of kicking may be intrinsically specified for the infant by the moment of foot contact with the ground, or some equivalent property such as the moment of maximum foot pressure or maximum leg flexion. The haptic closing of the loop turns a linear externally driven mass-spring into an autonomous limit-cycle with the intrinsic timing determined by foot contact, a characteristic of nonlinear oscillators. (An analogous example is learning how to "pump" on a playground swing, where the timing of leg flexion and extension is intrinsically specified by the peaks of swinging, perhaps via vestibular stimulation).

Once this kicking device is assembled, tuning its parameters yields other effects. For a given kicking force, the height of bouncing increases as the frequency of kicking approaches the resonant frequency of the system. This resonant frequency depends upon both the stiffness of the spring and the legs: when leg stiffness matches spring stiffness, the infant achieves maximum amplitude for a given force. Thus, tuning the system involves a search of frequency-parameter space, where the ratio of force to bounce height provides a "cost function" that defines an attractor in parameter space. Fortunately, the task dynamics are relatively simple, with a single basin of attraction in a two-dimensional space. In theory, the infant may perceive this landscape via haptic information about force and visual information about amplitude, and follow the gradient to the attractor (see Chapter 3).

Goldfield, Kay, and Warren (1993) used the above considerations to make specific predictions about the development of infant bouncing over a period of longitudinal observations:

1. There should be an early "assembly" phase of sporadic, irregular kicking without sustained bouncing.
2. Emerging from this should be a tuning phase of more periodic kicking during which the forcing frequency and leg stiffness vary, yielding high variability in period.
3. Once the infant has locked onto a stable attractor, a sustained bouncing phase should occur with the following characteristics:
   (a) oscillation at the resonant frequency

(b) increase in amplitude, due to operating at resonance
(c) decrease in variability of period, due to operating at a stable resonant frequency.

Eight infants served as subjects. Their mean age at the observation on which they exhibited the longest string of successive bouts was 244.4 days (SD = 26.7). Each infant was observed once each week for at least six weeks, and was weighed at the first and last observations. We determined the stiffness and damping coefficients of the spring by the dynamic method. The computed spring stiffness was 523 N/m. The logarithmic decrement method indicated that damping was so small that it did not contribute appreciably to the observed oscillation.

A *bounce* was scored as a complete cycle of vertical displacement in which the knees flexed so that the body moved toward the floor, and then extended so that the body moved away from (and sometimes off) the floor, and then back towards the floor. A *bout* was defined as a continuous series of bounces with no pauses during any part of a cycle; the number of bounces in a bout is termed bout length. The session during which the the longest bouts occurred was defined as the *peak* of bouncing.

The mean number of bounces per bout is a measure of the infant's discovery of the resonance peak. Fig. 7.6 presents this measure with individual subject data aligned by the session in which the peak bounce occurred. There was a significant effect of bout length for sessions –2 to peak, with the peak bout length significantly different from both preceding sessions, but these were not different from each other. In the early sessions, infants kicked irregularly, with only one or two bounces per bout. This is consistent with the interpretation

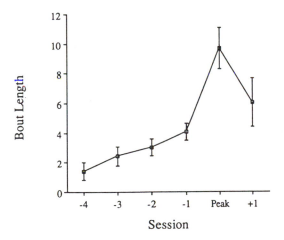

Figure 7.6. Mean number of bounces per bout for sessions –4 to peak. Error bars indicate ± 1 SE. (From Goldfield, Kay, & Warren, 1993. Copyright © 1993 by the Society for Research in Child Development, Inc. Reprinted by permission.)

that they experiment with the system through spontaneous activity. Bout length increased gradually over the next several sessions up to a mean of 4.2 bounces, consistent with a tuning phase in which the infants explored the properties of the spring, until bout length suddenly doubled in the peak session to 8.7 bounces. Translated into dynamic terms, the sudden emergence of sustained bouncing may indicate that the infants locked onto the attractor. Finally, after reaching a peak, the bout length began to decline in subsequent sessions. Thus, once the task was mastered, it became less "interesting."

There was also an increase in amplitude over sessions, consistent with the hypothesis of a "resonance peak" observed when a system is driven at its resonant frequency. While mean period did not vary over sessions, within-bout variability in period decreased significantly. Thus, whereas the average behavior of the system remained in the same ballpark, the decline in variability is consistent with a process of exploring frequency-stiffness space and homing in on a stable attractor.

To determine whether this preferred frequency corresponded to the resonant frequency of the system, we first compared the observed period in the peak session to the period predicted by the external spring alone, with no stiffness contribution from the infant's legs. Predicted period was computed from the equation

$$\omega_0 = \sqrt{k/m}$$

using the the infant's mass, m, the empirically determined spring stiffness constant, k, and a damping coefficient of zero. In all cases, each infant bounced with a shorter period than predicted by the inert mass-spring.

We next added a second spring to the model on the hypothesis that the infant's legs act like a spring that matches the impedance of the external spring. According to the model, the value of total stiffness doubles, and the predicted period decreases by a factor of the square root of 2. The observed and predicted periods for the two-spring model are in close agreement for each of the subjects. The results may be interpreted as follows: the infants home in on the attractor in frequency–stiffness space, matching the impedance of the spring to yield maximum energy transfer, and driving the system at the resulting resonant frequency to yield maximum amplitude for minimum force.

These findings may have general implications for the study of developing action systems. In the course of learning a task, the infant actor may try out different musculoskeletal organizations, explore parameter space, and probe the resulting landscapes, in each case being guided by the dynamics of the task. Consider again the role of exploration at the three levels of task dynamics. At the highest level, the infant may experiment with different combinations of musculoskeletal components, in effect adopting different functions over the degrees of freedom of the action system, and explore the attractor layout that emerges. The process is essential to the self-organization of a task-specific device. This implies that one of the functions of spontaneous activity in infancy is to explore possible organizations by allowing the free interplay of components and becoming sensitive to the types of global attractors that emerge.

At an intermediate level, the infant explores parameter space, varying the parameters of a particular function. This process involves becoming sensitive to the landscape in parameter space and identifying the configuration of parameters that is best for a given task. At the lowest level, the actor lets the system evolve to states that correspond to a particular attractor. This is crucial for finding stable movement patterns and subsequently tuning parameters to adjust them to the task.

PROPOSITION 5: ACTION SYSTEMS ARE ASSEMBLED FROM A MOSAIC OF AVAILABLE COMPONENTS

During the 1940s, a dominant theme in the study of behavioral development was that development reflected a maturational unfolding (Gesell, 1946) and that a careful description of the observed sequence of developmental change would provide adequate evidence of this unfolding process. For example, Gesell asserted that observable sequences of development in crawling reflected the tandem principles of developmental direction (the cephalocaudal gradient of growth) and reciprocal interweaving (a developmental fluctuation in dominance of flexors versus extensors and in unilateral versus bilateral muscle groups). At the same time, McGraw (1945) used similar data to support the argument that purposive behavior was controlled by the cerebral cortex, that reflexive behavior was controlled by subcortical nuclei, and that the ontogeny of locomotion reflected the gradual control over the latter by the former. Both Gesell and McGraw, in other words, assumed that observable motor behavior was a direct reflection of the developing brain.

By contrast, I assert here that developmental changes in action capabilities reflect the interaction of several subsystems, a mosaic of components, each with its own rate of growth. Consider, for example, the interaction between the nervous and musculoskeletal systems (see Chapter 4). Even though musculoskeletal movements are most often progressive and change in a linear fashion (e.g., the stage-like progression of postural control), the growth of the brain is not at all progressive. Brain growth involves not only addition, but also deletion of neural elements throughout early genesis by mechanisms such as cell death, axon retraction, and the appearance and removal of transient brain structures (Bekoff, 1981; Cowan, Fawcett, O'Leary, & Stanfield, 1984; Nowakowski, 1987).

In addition to these characteristics of brain growth, there are also changes with growth in the characteristics of the geometry of the skeletomuscular system, the strength of the muscles, and the mass of the body. These changing properties of the body are sources of what Bernstein (1967) and Turvey et al. (1982) call context-conditioned variability: a given innervational state does not have a fixed movement consequence. For example, pectoralis major changes its role as a function of the angle of its pull with respect to the axis of the joint.

During development, not only are there different movement consequences from the same muscle activation, but also, different muscle activations result in the same movement consequences, depending on the effects of gravity and passive torque on limb mass. The earlier example from the work of Thelen and her colleagues on infant kicking illustrate this point. Thelen et al. (1984) w ere able to demonstrate that the rapid deposition of fat relative to muscle during the first 8 weeks of life rather than the appearance of a new neuromotor function was responsible for the so-called "disappearing" stepping reflex. As the mass of the body increases, the same muscle activation has different movement consequences: the same activation no longer results in a kick because of increased resistance on the muscle.

A lesson from Bernstein and Thelen, therefore, is that infants capitalize on inherent variability in order to perform coordinated task-specific activities. At first blush, this seems to contradict the most fundamental traditional data in the study of motor systems, namely, the description of behavior according to stages. However, while the classic investigators of motor development (e.g., Gesell, 1946; McGraw, 1945) emphasized invariant stage sequences in describing infant locomotor behavior, they also recognized the individuality of growth. For example, Gesell (1946) notes: "The different modes by which children learn to walk and to run are impressive for variety of style. ... Nature is infinite in variety and variability. Even identical twins are not perfectly identical" (pp. 323–324). Neither Gesell nor McGraw, though, provided a means for understanding how behavioral development, which is intrinsically variable, results in stable patterns.

The proposition of subsystems with uneven rates of growth provides a framework for understanding how the variability so often observed in the way in which infants attempt to use their bodies to locomote may be implicated in skill acquisition. Variability may be a reflection of the "soft assembly" of components (Kugler & Turvey, 1987; Kugler et al., 1982) whereby a biokinematic system may be "assembled temporarily and for a particular purpose from whatever neural and skeletomuscular elements are available and befitting the task" (Kugler & Turvey, 1987, p. 3).

At a particular point in development, the infant uses whatever means he or she has available to accomplish a task, and as individual elements change, the organized behavior as a whole changes. This is the source of observed variability. Moreover, a small change in one of the elements may drive the organization of the system as a whole into a new configuration:

At developmental transitions, one or several components of the complex system may act as control parameters, including variables in the context or the environment. Although all of the elements or subsystems are essential for the systems output, only one or a few of the subsyetms will trigger transitions, which in turn will lead to system-wide reorganization. (Thelen, 1989a, p. 89)

A stage of behavior, in this view, may reflect a stable (albeit transitory) state resulting from the particular interaction of components, each of which has its own rate of growth. The stages of prone locomotion described by Gesell and McGraw, then, may not reflect a lock-step progression of postures resulting from maturation, but rather, a preferred way to accomplish a particular task, given certain existing capabilities.

What are the locomotion-relevant capabilities of the young infant which both exhibit variability and interact functionally with each other? Goldfield (1989) has proposed three capabilities underlying prone locomotion in infancy: (1) orienting, the use of the eye–head system to maintain balance while the chest and abdomen are lifted off the support surface, (2) propulsion, use of the legs for rhythmic kicking against the support surface, and (3) steering, use of the hands to change the direction of body movement. Observed stages of prone locomotion, in this view, reflect the way in which the infant uses these three capabilities together in order to accomplish a particular task: steering the body through the environment (for further discussion, see Chapter 10).

Part III

The Action Systems

In this part, I use the ecological, dynamic, and developmental foundations of the previous chapters to explicate the five propositions of Chapter 7 with respect to the following action systems: basic orienting, eating and drinking, locomotion, manipulation, and emotional expression. My focus here is on the infancy period.

Chapter 8 examines basic orienting. Like Reed (1982), I consider the basic orienting system, the action system responsible for postural control, as a basis for the others. But how, precisely, are other action systems related to basic orienting? The key to answering this question, I believe, is in the relation between postural disequilibrium and attractor dynamics. While posture has traditionally been thought of as a static state (e.g., Magnus, 1925), I adopt the approach here that posture is dynamic, and emerges from both muscular forces and the extant forces acting on the body to initiate, maintain, change, or halt a movement. Posture is a matrix for the distribution of forces (analogous to the influence of the extracellular matrix on cell motility). Reed (1982, 1988a), taking the view that postures are dynamic, argues that movements are transitions between postures. Here, I extend that argument by proposing that each part of the body which maintains a stable relationship with another body part, or with the environment, may be thought of in a dynamic sense as an emergent stable consequence of competing influences (cf. Feldman, 1986; Kugler et al., 1989/1990). Changes in the strength of any of the competing influences results in a shift from one stable posture to another (a new layout of attractors), and a new family of possible movement trajectories.

From a developmental standpoint, the attractor dynamics of spontaneous movements may be considered as *ontogenetic adaptations* (see Chapter 1), in the sense that each may serve a specific function at the particular point in development where they are evident. Developmental changes in postural control, however, may transform these ontogenetic adaptations so that they continue their preadapted function, but in a way that may make them seem to "disappear". In their place, we see the appearance of "emergent" forms, the action systems described in the following chapters.

With a dynamic basis for all acts, regardless of their function, it becomes possible to treat each of the action systems as dynamically equivalent. So, for example, as an infant attempts to maintain balance while sitting without support, one might describe this functionally as basic orienting. And, as the infant allows the body to fall forward in a controlled way in order to begin to crawl (Goldfield, 1989) one might call this goal-directed act locomotion. In both instances, the basis for control is the relation between the body and the support surface: the infant must control the forces required to oppose gravity. The only difference between sitting and crawling is the goal which allows the infant to relax control over certain muscular forces that were operative in sitting. In other words, I make the case in these chapters that (1) what binds action systems together is that they have a common abstract basis in dynamics, and (2) what differentiates action systems into different functional organizations are the goals and other influences on the body which transform these dynamics in particular ways.

It should be noted that this is much the same strategy that Gibson adopted in his treatment of the relation between information and affordances. I propose here that the relation between dynamics and goals is identical to the relation between amodal information in an ambient array and affordances, respectively. Both goals and affordances relate actor and environment. A goal may be thought of as means for modifying existing force fields acting on the body and as means for creating new force fields in order to act with the body (see, e.g., Kugler et al., 1989/1990), given a particular task. In this view, the principal difference between the goal of sitting up and the goal of locomoting is the particular way in which a set of extant forces is warped in order to create a particular dynamics. New goals may arise for a variety of reasons, including brain development, new requirements of the body for resources, and changing opportunities that emerge through social interaction and entry into new habitats.

The specific process by which goals influence attractor dynamics was introduced in Chapters 2 and 4, and extended to development in Chapter 7. In the chapters of this Part, I consider the *mutual influences of organismic and social regulation of attractor dynamics as the basis for development of differentiated action systems*. Chapter 9, for example, examines the attractor dynamics of respiration and oral activity, and how changes in goals associated with metabolic requirements, changes in the morphology of the oral effectors, and nursing practices, result in changes in feeding behavior. Mammalian ingestion is a cooperative pattern of oral effectors which involves the coupling of two distinctive acts, each with its own dynamics: attaching to the nipple and sucking (see, e.g., Bosma, 1967). Brake et al. (1988) have demonstrated that in rats these two components become coupled only when the animal is hungry and awake, and when there is maternal nursing. According to the approach proposed in this book, the intentions of the animal and social regulation modify the dynamics of these two activities so that they become coupled to each other into a useful cooperative pattern for feeding.

In Chapter 10, I turn to locomotion and specifically consider how forces acting on the body transfer a stable posture into an unstable one and create a disequilibrium. Postural disequilibrium is, I argue, one impetus for emergence of a new locomotor pattern. Specifically, I discuss the transitions from quadrupedal stance to crawling, and standing to walking. In both instances there are periods when postural stability acts as a kind of stable platform from which to explore the consequences of *controlled falling*. Controlled falling may be a fundamental means for transforming the dynamics of spontaneous kicking, already evident in the earliest days of life (Thelen, 1983), into a *useful* functional system. I also examine the perceptual control of locomotion and address how the infant may use optical flow to regulate controlled falling.

Chapter 11 highlights manipulation and tool use, and addresses the question of how objects held in the hands may be controlled as extensions of the body. One theme of this chapter is the relation between the symmetry of body morphology, and functional asymmetries of the nervous system (e.g., the asymmetric tonic neck response). I argue that lateral asymmetry is another means by which the infant's spontaneous activity may introduce instability in a controlled way in order to establish new organizational patterns. A second theme of the chapter is the abstract similarity between biological articulators and physical devices. With the body conceived of as a collection of abstract biophysical devices, such as levers and pulleys, objects held in the hand fall easily within that domain as an additional class of devices to be controlled.

Chapter 12 reviews a topic which especially fascinated Charles Darwin: emotional expression. My approach for treating emotional expression as an action system follows from the insights of Peter Wolff (1987, 1991) on the subject. The emotions are not traits, but rather are stable organizational patterns that emerge from the dynamics of the component systems which underlie emotional expression. After reviewing some of Darwin's influential ideas, as well as controversies such as whether neonates are capable of imitation, I present a detailed analysis of the emergence of emotions as differentiated forms of waking activity in the early months of life.

CHAPTER 8

BASIC ORIENTING

Any given action is therefore seen as made up not of mechanically specific displacements, but of functionally specific components which themselves would count as actions. These components are of two kinds. First, an actor must obtain a relatively persistent orientation to the environment, supporting her weight, balancing all the forces acting on her body and limbs, and keeping her perceptual systems tuned to the available information. Second, an agent modulates changes in this persisting orientation so as to effect desired changes in her relations to the environment, such as moving from place to place.

Reed, 1988b, p. 49

INTRODUCTION

Orienting as a foundation. Gibson (1966) recognized that orientation was the foundation upon which all perceiving and acting rests. He distinguished relatively permanent orientation to the earth (gravity and the support surface), temporary orientations to events and objects being attended to, oriented locomotion (ranging from simple tropisms to homing and migration), and geographical orientation (see Fig. 8.1). Reed (1982) bases his outline of a theory of action systems on this idea, and in this chapter, I consider the ontogeny of basic orienting, and the function of basic orienting for the ontogeny of other action systems. Moreover, I make the claim here that the types of orientation distinguished by Gibson have an ontogenetic course that is based upon transitions to new habitats (see Table 8.1).

During the transition from fetal to postnatal life, the neonate encounters a habitat that is quite different from the uterus: he or she must adapt to breathing air, must react to disequilibrium of bodily posture, and must begin to use the invariants of perceptual information which will persist throughout the life span (e.g., the horizon). With increasing postural control during the first half of the first year, infants must master temporary orientations, i.e. become able to control the muscles in order to maintain both static and dynamic equilibrium. Here is when the infant learns to keep the head oriented in an

PERMANENT ORIENTATION	TERRESTRIAL ANIMALS MAINTAIN PERMANENT ORIENTATION TO THE EARTH (I.E., TO GRAVITY AND THE SUPPORT SURFACE)
TEMPORARY ORIENTATION	ANIMAL ADOPTS TEMPORARY ORIENTATIONS TO EVENTS AND OBJECTS WHENEVER THESE ARE ATTENDED
ORIENTED LOCOMOTION	LOCOMOTING DEPENDS UPON ORIENTING OF THE PERCEPTUAL ORGANS OF THE HEAD (E.G., IN LOOKING AND LISTENING)
GEOGRAPHICAL ORIENTATION	ANIMALS FIND THEIR WAY TO A GOAL OVER LONG DISTANCES (E.G., DURING HOMING AND MIGRATION

Figure 8.1. Gibson's four types of orientation.

upright posture, learns to sit upright, and begins prone locomotion. These attempts at orienting reveal information for the control of temporary orientations, most notably properties of optical flow (Bertenthal & Bai, 1989; Warren, 1988a). With self-generated mobility during the second half of the first year and into the second year, infant locomotion becomes oriented, i.e., the intention to locomote to a particular location orients the eye–head system in a way that steers the body in a particular way and guides hand placement on the support surface, and eventually foot placement (Goldfield, 1989). Finally, during the latter part of the second year, orientation becomes increasingly guided by geography, the spatial location between habitats (see, e.g., Pick, 1990).

Table 8.1. Fundamental transitions in basic orienting during the first 36 months of human life

Developmental Period	Transition to New Habitat
Fetal to postnatal life	Permanent orientation: From liquid to gaseous medium; introduction of gravity; permanent orientation to perceptual information in terrestrial environment
12 weeks to 7 months	Mastery of temporary orientations: Postural control results in revealing new disequilibria
7 to15 months	Oriented locomotion: Self-generated activity maps endogenous states onto action-specific information (affordances)
15 to 36 months	Geographical orientation: Spatial orientation to different habitats and relations between them

Table 8.2. Changing tasks and resources in the first year which regulate action cycles during basic orienting

Developmental Period	Resource	Task of Basic Orienting
Fetus	Informational gradients in the uterus (chemical, haptic, auditory, e.g., maternal voice and heartbeat)	Positioning the body so the head is in a vertex position for delivery
Perinatal	Voice and face of adult	Orienting the head to the face and voice of another person.
	Breast, nipple	Orienting mouth to breast and nipple
3 to 6 months	Support surface; information specifying egomotion. Information specifying displacement, invariant object properties	Maintaining upright (sitting) posture. Orienting eye–head system
6 to 12 months	Objects scaled to body properties	Maintaining upright posture while leaving hands free to explore

As is evident in the epigraph from Reed (1988b) at the head of the chapter, orienting is postural control with respect to specific aspects of the environment. After introducing contrasting perspectives on orienting, I examine an implication of this quote by considering the different tasks of orienting that must be mastered by the human infant (see Table 8.2). I propose that within each of these task spaces, the infant orients to some specific invariant and/or affordance. What changes with development is not only the infant's postural control (and the consequent redistribution of forces), but also the infant's attending to a particular informational resource in the task space specifying the variability to be controlled.

CONTRASTING PERSPECTIVES ON ORIENTING

Orientation: The postural reflex tradition. Following the work of Sherrington (1906), Magnus (1925) proposed that orientation of the head on the trunk was fundamental for maintaining postural control. In his classic developmental work from a neurological perspective, Peiper (1963) was influenced by Magnus, and conducted a comprehensive examination of postural reflexes in newborns (see Table 8.3). He offers the view, still widely held among neurologists and physical therapists (see, e.g., Capute et al., 1982, ch. 13) that "primitive" reflexes of position and movement allow the newborn to react to the influence of gravity well before voluntary control of orientation in holding the head up, sitting, standing, and locomoting. These include: the Moro, tonic labyrinthine, asymmetric tonic neck, Galant, crossed extension, stepping, upper placing, lower placing, and positive support reflexes. Capute (1979) argues that

Table 8.3. Reflexes in newborn and older infants

Postural reflexes	
Asymmetric tonic neck	Relative to head orientation, ipsilateral arm and leg extended, contralateral arm and leg flexed
Tonic skin	Elicited by stimulation of the skin and cause tonic flexion or extension of the limbs and tonic flexion of the spine
Tonic palmar grasp	Elicited by pressure on the palm; leads to tonic flexion of second to fifth fingers
Plantar grasp	Elicited by pressure on sole; leads to flexion of five toes; functional significance related to arm and leg suspension
Spinal	Stimulation of dorsal skin in lumbar region by pinching or tickling; quick contraction of dorsal movements
Neck righting	When placed on back, turning head sideward results in whole body following the rotation
Body righting	With infant on side and legs grasped turning pelvis to other side, trunk and head roll to other side
Gravity reflexes	
Labyrinthine righting	In newborn, if placed prone on surface, head is lifted with a jerk, and falls again immediately
Chain	Through raising the head, position of neck, trunk, arms, pelvis and legs is regulated
Supporting reaction	Usually elicited by the weight of the body which presses the limbs against the support surface; causes a supporting tonus in the muscles of the extremities, which makes standing possible

Source: After Peiper, 1963.

since these "primitive" reflexes ordinarily disappear between three and six months of age, their continued presence beyond this period signifies the presence of a severe motor disability, such as cerebral palsy.

Other recent work distinguishes three types of orienting via postural reflexes: equilibrium, righting, and protective reactions. Equilibrium reactions are responses to loss of balance which results when the body's base of support is disturbed by a push, pull, or tilt (Bobath, 1980); righting reactions are presumed to maintain alignment to gravity and keep body parts in alignment with each other after rotation (Chandler et al., 1980; Effgen, 1982), and protective reactions are more local responses. Equilibrium reactions are seen as the integrating mechanism for the ontogeny of postural stability in prone and supine posture, sitting, quadrupedal support, and standing (Shumway-Cook, 1988). So, for example, before a child can sit, he or she must first have developed mature equilibrium while prone.

Orientation: Active posture, function, and a systems approach. There has been recent criticism of the approach which treats posture as a static state and assumes that primitive reflexes are the basis for postural control. Reed

(1988a), for example, argues that rather than being passive reactions that work against gravity, dynamic posture works *with* gravity to achieve functional actions. The source of information about the relation of the body to the environment is not just the vestibular system, but rather, all of the perceptual systems. As Reed notes, the emphasis should not be on the achieving of a stable state, but on the dynamic process of making forces acting on the body compatible with the task at hand.

Similarly, postural reflexes are not manifestations of a physiological reflex arc, but rather, are a fragment of a functional action system which is variable with respect to neural pathway, but specific to a functional task (Anokhin, 1974; Berkenblit et al., 1986; Reed, 1982). Shumway-Cook (1988) further elaborates this distributed control (systems) alternative to the reflex-hierarchical view by examining the contribution to the equilibrium function of various components of postural control, each with its own rate of growth (see Fig. 8.2).

An ecological approach to orienting. The Gibsonian approach to orienting stands in marked contrast to the classic work of Frankel and Gunn (1940) and the more recent extension of their work by Schone (1984). According to Schone, animals orient to physical energy—radiant, chemical, thermal and mechanical. But, as Gibson (1966) argues, the nature of information is more complex. A lower-order control holds for animals with less highly evolved nervous systems who can detect only simple invariants, but animals with more complex nervous systems, who can detect higher-order invariants, are capable of a second level of control.

A second difference between a Gibsonian approach to orienting and the one proposed by Schone (1984) concerns the way in which an animal's "central dispositions" influence the nature of orientation. Schone's work builds upon that of von Holst. According to von Holst and Mittelstaedt (1973), orientation is directed by the relation between a central disposition and a signal from the effectors concerning the consequence of motion. Von Holst (cited in Schone, 1984) describes the mechanism underlying orienting with respect to an "efference copy", a kind of central image of the motor signal. When the effector is activated, its associated receptors are stimulated and bring about "reafference". Reafference, in other words, is afference that is a consequence of oriented efference. Afference based upon stimulation *imposed* by external influences is called exafference. The implication of this model is that orientation depends upon a specific central disposition (itself dependent upon both endogenous and exogenous factors).

As Warren (1988a) observes, however, there *is* no predictable relation between motor commands and optical results, and hence the origin of accurate expectations is not accounted for by such a model. Instead, as noted by Gibson, "neural input caused by self-produced action is simply different from the neural

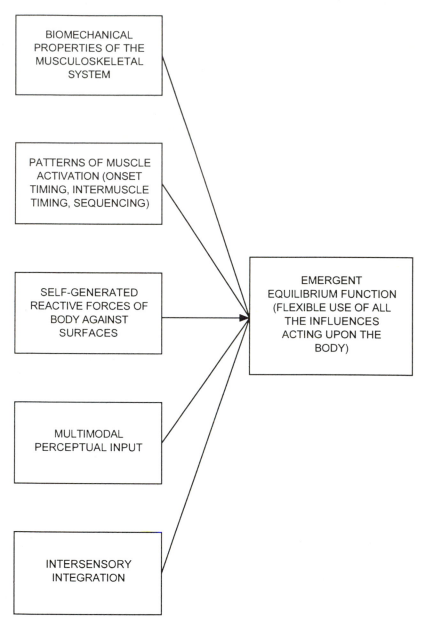

Figure 8.2. A systems model of posture and balance control. (After Shumway-Cook, 1988.)

input caused by the intruding stimulus. The two kinds of input are different in their sequential properties, they are different kinds of transformation or change, and the simultaneous pattern of nerve fibers might be widely dispersed" (p. 39). Since Gibson's death, his students have been developing a theory of orientation based upon the ecological approach to perception.

Laws of control for orientation. Warren (1988a), in building upon Gibson's insight that optical information specifies the relation between actor and environment (see Chapter 3), proposes that "perception is best characterized not by a servomechanism that matches current and desired flows, but by a system that achieves meaningful states of affairs that are specified by flows" (p. 347). Since *changes* in the relation between actor and environment are directly specified by *changes* in optical flow, then *orienting may be thought of as all of the actions which generate forces cancelling changes in flow (optical, haptic, etc.).*

To illustrate how orientation is achieved *vis à vis* the properties of optical flow, Warren (1988a) offers an illustration of visual control of insect flight. Within the global action mode of orienting, the fly engages in a variety of nested local action modes, including hovering, cruising flight, approach, and landing (see Collett & Land, 1975). Each of these modes constitutes a distinct way that the fly orients to its environment, and depends upon a "choice" of a path through a "landscape of multiple branching channels" (cf. the choice points identified by Kugler and his colleagues in Chapter 3). The critical meaning of these choice points is that once an action mode is temporarily selected, the orienting behavior of the fly is "governed by highly systematic laws of control until it is superseded by a new action mode and its accompanying laws of control" (Warren, 1988a, p. 350).

Let us consider Warren's example in greater detail. In the fly, movements are described with reference to a body-centered coordinate system with six degrees of freedom: pitch (up-down rotation about the lateral axis), yaw (side-to-side rotation about the vertical axis), roll (rotation along the longitudinal axis), and translation (lateral, vertical, and forward motion). To produce motion, the body must generate a particular set of forces. Translations are produced by regulating the *sum* of the forces of the actuators (wings, legs), and rotations by regulating the *difference* between them.

Given this regulation of motion by the application of particular combinations of forces, Warren proposes two general laws of perceptual control. Relative to initial values

1. Changes in the *rate* of (optical) flow regulate changes in the net magnitude of force
2. Changes in the *direction* of (optical) flow regulate changes in the direction of force.

Recalling that the fly's global mode of ambient orientation includes hovering, cruising, approach, and landing, how do laws of visual control obtain? Table 8.4 presents a summary of the laws of control for each of these modes. Warren notes that even in an insect such as the fly, movements are not causally determined responses to a given stimulus. They are actions taken

Table 8.4. Modes of orienting by the fly and laws of control

Mode	Goal of Orienting	Control Law
Hovering	To maintain constant position with respect to visible surroundings, acting so as to cancel any global flow	Change the upthrust so that it is equal to the upward flow (scaled to distance and the species-specific properties of the body)
Cruising	To translate linear paths with respect to the surrounding environment	Make the array flow at a rate corresponding to forward motion, while at the same time maintaining ambient orientation
Approach	To cruise toward a more or less stable object so that its longitudinal axis is oriented toward it	Magnify a patch in the optic array while cruising and maintaining ambient orientation
Landing	Decelerate during approach	When time-to-contact reaches a particular value, decelerate by decreasing forward thrust (or upthrust) to maintain rate of change of optical expansion and insure a soft landing

Source: After Warren, 1988a.

relative to the affordances of the environment and the fly's choices (see Chapter 3):

> For example, in cruising flight, the optical expansion produced by approaching a surface yields a change in course to avoid collision. Yet in landing mode, the same optical pattern yields deceleration and leg extension to achieve a soft collision. ... The fly's selection of an affordance to be realized thereby determines the current action mode and the operative control laws. (Warren, 1988a, p. 361)

These illustrations of orienting in the fly highlight the centrality of orienting for the kinds of activities characteristic of the insect's niche. But the same holds true for other animals and for humans. The goal-directedness of action requires that acts be oriented with respect to particular objects, places and events comprising niches.

THE ONTOGENY OF HUMAN BASIC ORIENTING: THE FETAL PERIOD

Fetal life. Fetal life and the transition to the postnatal environment are starting points for the analysis of basic orienting in humans. It is often assumed that some degree of very early experience takes place during human fetal life, e.g., maternal–fetal communication of daylength (Reppert & Weaver, 1988) and effects of transmission of low-frequency sounds on the auditory system

(De Casper & Fifer, 1980; Fifer & Moon, 1988). One of the fundamental environmental constraints in fetal life is the relationship between the body morphology of the fetus and the size, shape, tissue properties, and activity of the mother's internal organs. What effect, if any, does fetal posture relative to the intrauterine environment have for understanding the "givens" of the basic orienting system in the transition from prenatal to postnatal life? Is the fetal experience of the direction of gravity based solely upon information from the otolith organs or "graviceptors", or might the fetus use information such as the direction of the maternal heartbeat and/or voice to provide a fundamental frame of reference that is more useful for adaptation to the postnatal social environment. It is often noted that newborns quiet to the sound of the maternal heartbeat and voice (Salk, 1962), but is it also possible that fetuses actually orient to these sounds?

According to Stoffregen and Riccio (1988), orienting is "controlled interaction between an organism and a surface (or surfaces or medium) of support, so as to maintain dynamic equilibrium with respect to the forces acting on the organism" (Stoffregen & Riccio, 1988, p. 7). While the traditional view of orientation is that detection of gravitoinertial forces (the direction of gravity) by the otolith organs are used for perception of the phenomenal upright, Stoffregen and Riccio demonstrate that the otoliths actually show poor sensitivity to gravity. Instead, they argue that the upright that is relevant to postural control is the *direction of unstable equilibrium (or falling)*, i.e., changing accelerations characteristic of the body falling during most motions, e.g., walking.

The Stoffregen and Riccio analysis has interesting implications for the transition of the fetus from a liquid to gaseous medium at birth, since there are different patterns of acceleration in water versus air. Because water imposes a viscous drag on the body, acceleration, and motion in general, is more gradual than in air. There are also differences in the torque acting on the body under water. On land, gravity is resisted by the support surface, but in a liquid medium the force of gravity is opposed by buoyant forces of the water. In the "fetal position" *in utero*, the human fetus is in a posture which minimizes the distance between the centers of gravity and buoyancy, and so the body is at a state of neutral equilibrium. In this condition, the direction of gravity is irrelevant to orientation and the liquid environment *in utero* acts as a medium of support.

The uterus as a habitat. What is the uterus like as a habitat? Let us first consider the acoustic information available (see Fig. 8.3). There are two sources of of acoustic information that have been identified as salient for fetal development: internal sounds (pulse, digestion) and maternal speech. By inserting a small microphone into the amniotic cavity near the fetus's head, after rupture of the amniotic membranes, it has been possible to make *in utero*

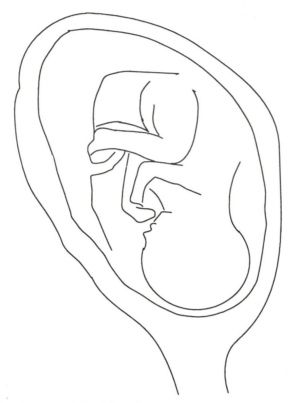

Figure 8.3. The uterus as a habitat for orienting.

recordings of the fetal acoustic environment. The following sounds are audible
to adult listeners: maternal pulse, very low-frequency vascular sounds, and,
most notably, maternal voice (Fifer & Moon, 1988).

Turkewitz (1988) proposes a model of the developing uterus as a slowly
inflating balloon which has very different acoustic properties at different
degrees of inflation. Early in pregnancy, the uterus is a relatively small
chamber. Because the uterine wall is relatively thick and unstretched, it acts as
a poor transmitter of externally produced sounds. In other words, at this stage
in development, the uterus is a habitat dominated by internally generated
sounds (e.g., heartbeat and gastrointestinal noises) and a relatively small
proportion of externally generated sounds. Later in development, when the
uterus becomes filled with a fluid-filled amnion which stretches the uterine
walls, it becomes an amplifier of external sounds; thus increasing the mix of
maternal speech sounds and the sound of the maternal heartbeat. Moreover,
maternal speech may become particularly salient because it is additionally
transmitted to the uterus via conduction along the vertebral column, and
because it is accompanied by multimodal information such as pressure changes

in the fluid medium with diaphragmatic movements accompanying maternal speech.

The increasing size of the fetus and the gradual filling of the intrauterine cavity has specific consequences for fetal posture. The size and shape of the uterus comes to both restrict global movement (Hofer, 1988), and constrain the limbs into a posture of semiflexion. Michel (1987) proposes that intrauterine position may contribute to postnatal posture via influence on the elasticity of the skin and muscles, as well as via calibration of general "set points" of the muscle spindles. For example, there is evidence in ultrasound recordings at various times during pregnancy that the head of the fetus is frequently oriented away from the midline (de Vries, Visser, & Prechtl, 1982).

THE TRANSITION FROM FETAL TO POSTNATAL LIFE

Change in medium. Following the transition to the extrauterine environment, there is an immediate increase in degrees of freedom of head movement that results from removal of the fetus from the constraints provided by the size and shape of the uterus and the support provided by the fluid medium of the amniotic sac. While postnatal behavioral states assist in regulating postural organization to some degree (see Chapter 7), the newborn's head control and the coordination of eye and head movement remain poorly developed (Goodkin, 1980; Casaer, 1979). This section examines how the newborn's early efforts at head control, changing orientations of the body relative to gravity, and neurological development transform fetal orienting to the new habitat of the extrauterine environment. More specifically, I consider (1) the induction of functionally specific muscle groups during specific behavioral states and orientations of the body, (2) early coordination of eye and head movement, (3) the relative importance of visual and vestibular information, and (4) the relation between changes in eye–head coordination and the infant's use of information.

The induction of functional patterns in groups of muscles. Casaer (1979) conducted a comprehensive study of the adjustments of newborn posture due to changes in behavioral state and orientation to the environment. Orientational influences on posture are apparent when one compares the organization of different muscle groups in prone versus supine. While supine, the newborn often lies with his face partially to the side (usually the right). The most common supine postures are flexion of the arms at the elbows and the legs at the hips, and an asymmetrical tonic neck (i.e., fencing) posture (see Fig. 8.4). These two supine postures are relatively transient and flow smoothly into movements such as putting the hand to the face or mouth.

Figure 8.4. Neonatal postures. The figures on the left depict postures during sleep, and on the right postures during wakefulness. (After Casaer, 1979. Copyright © 1979 Spastics International Medical Publications, Inc. Reprinted by permission.)

The finding that supine newborns are more likely to turn their head and/or eyes rightward has a long history and is well-documented (Gesell & Ames, 1950; Liederman & Kinsbourne, 1980; Turkewitz, 1977, 1980; Turkewitz, Gordon & Birch, 1965). Liederman and Kinsbourne argue that dextral bias of head orientation results from an asymmetry in the tonic activation of the neck muscles, and that afferent input has, at best, a phasic modulating influence on asymmetry. Turkewitz (1980) asserts, however, that tonic asymmetry has a "priming effect" on afferent input: developmentally earlier stimulation resulting from differential experience of the head to one side results in increased responsiveness to somesthetic stimulation on that side. There are several studies which tend to support that view (see Michel, 1987, for a review).

Though common in a supine posture, the tonic neck pattern is rarely seen while the newborn is prone. Indeed, there is often a crossed flexion or crossed extension posture (e.g., arm flexed, contralateral leg extended) (Peiper, 1963). It is interesting to note the presence of this crossed pattern at birth, since it is evident during locomotion. In Chapter 10, I consider whether this early pattern may induce the coordinative relation apparent in prone locomotion (and see Goldfield, 1989). The frequent head lifts apparent while prone, moreover, do not exhibit the pervasive dextral asymmetry seen while supine. Rather, lifting the head has the consequence of moving it from side to side so that it comes to rest at the midline.

The classic descriptions of motor development summarize trends in the infant's achievement of posture as progressing from cephalo-caudal to proximo-distal (e.g., McGraw, 1945). More recent work (e.g., Scherzer & Tscharnuter, 1982; Woollacott, 1990) considers development of postural control relative to the reactive forces generated by the three orientational planes of the body: control in the sagittal plane is achieved through extension and flexion against gravity, in the frontal plane through lateral flexion, and in the transverse plane through rotation within the body axis. In the terminology used by neurologists and physical therapists, the control of these reactive forces in three planes is referred to as righting and equilibrium reactions.

Whereas the prone newborn is able to lift the head against gravity, the 4-month-old is able to maintain the face in a truly vertical plane, and extends the arms at the elbows in order to push the body off the ground against gravity. Gradually, the infant becomes able to move the head while keeping shoulder girdle and trunk stable. Between 5 and 8 months, the infant achieves complete antigravity extension, in what is referred to as the Landau reaction (Scherzer & Tscharnuter, 1982): neck, trunk, and legs extend such that the infant can stabilize the pelvis while raising the head and chest.

Supine newborns are most likely to keep the head at midline during crying or sucking. The month-old infant becomes able to maintain the head at midline while quiet and alert as a consequence of more active flexion against gravity. This midline orientation of the head then occasions the hands coming together at midline and promotes perceptual exploration of the hands. Coryell and Michel (1978) examined the relationship between supine head orientation during the first three months, and the amount of visual experience infants had with their right and left hands. As in other studies, infants exhibited a predominantly dextral bias, and this preference remained stable throughout the first 12 months. Infants who held their heads consistently to one side also tended to exhibit an asymmetric tonic neck response (ATNR) on that side. The ATNR position preference placed the infant's right hand within their visual field significantly more often than their left. Coryell and Michel conclude that head orientation, via the ATNR, biases visual experience of the hands, and may give one hand an advantage in eye–hand coordination tasks.

Early coordination of eye and head movements. Gibson (1966) has argued that one consequence of humans having their eyes set in front of the skull is that they must turn the head in order to look around, i.e., to explore their environments. While Gibson focused on information pickup as one consequence of looking around, he did not address the effect of looking around on the postural biasing of the muscles via the ATNR. The process by which infants coordinate eye and head movements may be influenced by their active looking around, but also, perhaps by another active system of the head, the mouth. While at first blush it may seem odd to discuss the mouth when discussing eye–head coordination, such oddity is mitigated when one considers the effects of sucking on posture. Casaer (1979) for example, finds that the temporal succession of the tonic neck posture and the activation of non-nutritive sucking when the hand goes to the mouth has the effect of changing posture so that the head becomes centered and the arms flex at the elbow with the hands at midline. The sucking rhythm, in other words, is associated with a shift from asymmetrical to symmetrical posture.

Here, then, we are confronted with an interesting juxtaposition: the ATNR promotes head turning to one side, while spontaneous mouthing promotes a symmetrical posture. What might be the significance of these two complementary influences? One possibility is that a competition between these two influences on head turning creates a partitioning of space at the midline. This is supported by a study by Bullinger (1981). At 20 days old, babies will turn their heads to follow a mobile from the position of rightward orientation until they reach the midline. They do not cross the midline, but instead return the head to the original position.

There is another influence of sucking that suggests it may compete with the ATNR in regulating active orienting during early infancy: sucking influences the temporal organization of looking. Wolff and White (1965), Bruner (1973a) and Gregg, Haffner, and Korner (1976) all demonstrate that visual pursuit of the newborn is more effective when the infant is sucking on a pacifier than when it is without a pacifier. Mendelson and Haith (1975) and Mendelson (1979) find, moreover, that the size of the vertical component of eye movements in the newborn are significantly less vulnerable to perturbation during scanning of a simple visual display when they are sucking on a pacifer than during a sucking pause.

Here, then, we see an example of the assembly of a coordinated pattern of eye–head activity during the first three months that emerges from the competition between two systems: the tonic asymmetric biasing of the head and the phasic attraction of the sucking rhythm. It is important to note that one need not assume that the control over orienting exhibited by the infant results from a new capacity for representation (Piaget, 1954). Instead, the model offered here suggests that new patterns of cooperativity in the infant's orienting skills emerge as a consequence of the competition between systems with opposing tendencies.

Visual–vestibular interactions. There is some capability for postural compensation of the head to visual events, even in newborns. Jouen (1988) used a sequential pattern of lights to specify forward or backward sway to a group of 3–day-olds seated with air bags placed behind their head to measure change in pressure. These newborn babies made postural reactions of the head to these visual events, suggesting an early perception–action coupling. Jouen (1984, 1990) has also studied the relative importance of visual and vestibular interactions in the head righting response during experimental manipulations of body tilt (via a tilting chair). In a preliminary study, Jouen (1990) examined the amplitude of head righting (degree of deviation from the vertical) in 3- and 4-month olds either when the body was tilted without visual reference, or with a single red light as a visual reference. As measured by amplitude of head righting, compensatory reactions to the body tilt was better in the older infants, especially in the visual reference condition. In a second experiment, Jouen (1984) manipulated orientation of the visual reference via a patterned field in horizontal, vertical, or lateral direction for infants distinguished by the degree to which they could organize a postural adjustment of the head (righting response). Jouen reports that infants with better postural control are more sensitive to orientation of the visual pattern. These results may reflect experience with head control on the ability to explore the environment for visual information, as well as increasing proprioceptive inputs from the neck muscles (Woollacott, 1990).

FROM FLEXION AND EXTENSION AGAINST GRAVITY TO CONTROLLED MOVEMENT

On the possible significance of postural instability for the development of new forms of action. In the developmental theory outlined in Chapter 7, dynamic stability was proposed as (1) emerging from the layout of potentials in parameter space, and (2) a source of information about ongoing dynamics that is useful for tuning the parameters of the system so that they are optimal for particular tasks. While much emphasis was placed upon the stability emerging in oscillatory acts (e.g., finger oscillations in adults; Haken et al., 1985), stability has as much relevance for understanding the development of posture. Indeed, postural instability may be one determinant of the emergence of new forms of action (cf. Reed, 1988a).

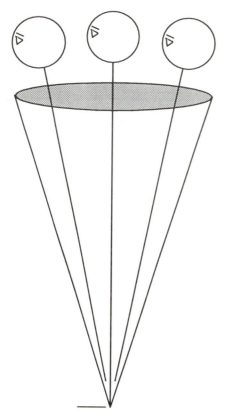

Figure 8.5. Stability cones. In the case of rotations about the ankle, stability limits enclose areas of movement in which postural adjustments are effective. (After McCollum & Leen, 1989. Copyright © by the Helen Dwight Reid Educational Foundation. Reprinted by permission.)

Postural stability may be explicated with reference to a diagram of the body balanced against gravity, taken from the work of McCollum and Leen (1989) (see Fig. 8.5). Any displacement of the body (an inverted pendulum) away from the vertical causes an angular acceleration that must be compensated for by applying torque at the affected joint (e.g., the ankle in the case of rigid sway about the ankle). The limiting factors in determining which perturbations can be reversed are the latency between the perturbation and muscle activation, and mechanical properties of the body. What is most interesting about this conceptualization is that it demarcates a boundary, the stability limit of the stability cone, outside of which certain muscular forces will not be able to restore postural equilibrium. Here, as in oscillatory motion, there is information in dynamics that directly specifies the efficacy of a particular action.

The postural control that develops during the middle of the first year may be analyzed with respect to control over forces acting upon the body relative to the sagittal, frontal, and transverse planes (Scherzer & Tscharnuter, 1982), forming a postural work space. In the development of postural control described below, there are two notable trends. First, the achievement of stability makes possible a new set of movements which use that stability to anticipate and counteract muscular forces. Second, the achievement of a new means of postural control opens up new possibilities for perceptual exploration of the capabilities of the body.

When prone, infants begin to show the so-called Landau reaction, an extension against gravity in the sagittal plane. It becomes possible for the infant to raise the head and chest because coordination between the axial extensors and flexors stabilizes the pelvis. The extension of the hips then makes it possible to bring the legs together, facilitating weight-shifting to one side in the frontal plane. This extension, in turn makes possible controlled rolling, crawling and creeping in the transverse plane (see Fig. 8.6).

When supine, flexion against gravity allows sustained midline orientation of the head, producing the symmetrical posture noted by Gesell and others. Once the head can be stabilized in this way, infants begin to spend considerable amounts of time exploring the hands held at midline and the feet brought towards the head. Infants then are able to cross the midline with their hands and feet, resulting in lateral weight shifting and a resulting axial rotation of the trunk. Here again, each postural achievement opens up new possibilities for action and exploration.

One of the most striking achievements in postural control during this period of infancy is independent sitting. Initially, when infants briefly begin to sit unassisted, the lumbar spine remains somewhat rounded (Scherzer & Tscharnuter, 1982). To assist in maintaining balance infants may either prop themselves up with the hands or hold both arms in the "high guard" position. Coordinated activation of the extensors and flexors of the trunk and hips allow the infant to control sway of the trunk and head. For example, flexion at the hips combines with full extension of the lumbar spine (Scherzer & Tscharnuter,

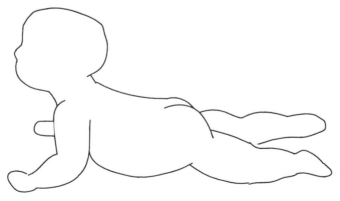

Figure 8.6. The so-called "chain reaction" of extension against gravity requires coordination between axial extensors and flexors (abdominals, extensors of spine and hips) and enables the infant to stabilize the pelvis and raise the head and chest off the support surface. (After Scherzer and Tscharnuter, 1982. Copyright © by Marcel Dekker. Reprinted by permission.)

1982). With improved trunk balance, there is a narrowing of the base of support, as the legs are brought closer together and extended at the knees. Here, again, trunk control frees the hands for manipulation while in a sitting position.

The significant role of vision in sitting is apparent in the influence of head righting on trunk control. Butterworth and his colleagues (e.g., Butterworth & Hicks, 1977) conducted early studies of the influence of optical flow on infant sitting in a swinging room. We saw in Chapter 3 that Gibson identified a global flow of optical texture that is specific to the direction and velocity of movement. In the context of a moving room, an experimental apparatus used to create optical flow patterns, the flow may be specified by movement of either the whole room, front wall, or side walls. Butterworth and his colleagues found that infants were sensitive to changes in optical flow while sitting by moving the head in the direction opposite to the flow. A more recent study by Bertenthal and Bai (1989) further addresses the role of optical flow for controlling posture while sitting. When infants of three ages, 5, 7, and 9 months, respectively, were placed in a sitting posture within the moving room, only the 9-month-olds showed significant postural resposiveness to the movement of the front wall alone. Five-month-olds showed little response in any condition, while 7-month-olds responded to the whole room. Bertenthal and Bai relate the developmental trend to the development of sitting unsupported, which has a mean age of occurrence on the Bayley exams of 6.6 months, and to the onset of crawling.

Other investigators address the cooperation of the muscles that make possible the postural compensation in independent sitting. In a longitudinal study of 2- to 5-month-olds, Hartbourne, Giuliani, and MacNeela (1987) distinguished a developmental trend in the order of muscle activation of the back and hip. At 2 to 3 months, order of muscle activation was highly variable but by 5 months, there was a preferred pattern of muscle activation. Woollacott, Debu, and Mowatt (1987) examined the development of postural stability in sitting by means of presentation of sudden perturbations of a platform used to support an infant seat. In 3- to 5-month-olds, there was a wide variety of response patterns. Even with visual information about sway, responses were variable. By 5 months, without any visual frame of reference, a backward movement of the platform resulted in forward sway and neck muscle activation to compensate for the sway. This suggests that during the period from 3 to 5 months, infants have an opportunity to explore the limits of the stability cone and visually tune the assembled coordinative structures. Once infants could sit independently, there was temporally organized muscle activity in the neck and trunk with or without visual information specifying direction of motion.

Does vision play any other roles during this period? One possibility is that the various affordances for approach, manipulation, etc. attract the infant to approach objects, events, and persons and in so doing change equilibrium setting. How does this happen? One of the variables in the equation of motion for a point attractor is equilibrium position. Changes in equilibrium setting may act as a control parameter for systems exhibiting point-attractor dynamics. At equilibrium, all forces act equally at a point. A change in equilibrium setting reflects the redistribution of influences on the system.

Postural disequilibrium may, thus, be one means by which the infant is able to make a transition between a stable posture and a movement. There are periods in development when infants become able to maintain postural stability, and it is from these postures that they may attempt to perform new movements. For example, when infants are able to sit independently, the configuration of the body becomes a kind of platform from which to explore the consequences of controlled falling onto the hands (Goldfield, 1989; Kamm & Thelen, 1989). Here, there is a competition between the intrinsic dynamics involved in preventing body sway (and falling) and information specifying something interesting in the environment which affords approach, manipulation, etc. (see Chapters 10 and 11).

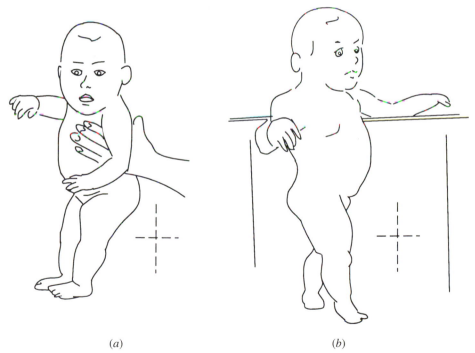

(a)   (b)

Figure 8.7. (a) During early phases of supported standing, the infant is unable to bring the hips forward for vertical alignment of feet, hips, and shoulders. Weight bearing on the heels occurs with the knees in neutral extension. (b) While supporting herself, the infant moves between extended and flexed postures (toe standing and squatting). The center of gravity is now brought forward (eight months). (After Scherzer and Tscharnuter, 1982. Copyright © by Marcel Dekker. Reprinted by permission.)

THE TRANSITION TO STANDING

A final freeing of the hands. The upright posture of standing is the culmination of postural control against gravity for bipedal humans. Of course, highly skilled individuals may eventually be able to balance the body on one hand or on the toes of one foot, but for the rest of us, standing upright on two feet is a major achievement. Standing independently recalls, perhaps like no other skill, the phylogenetic transitions in action systems which were so significant for human evolution (see Chapter 10). The significance of that event for humans may have been a fundamental freeing of the hands for other uses than postural support and locomotion. The continuing use of the hands just prior to standing independently attests to their importance in postural control.

Peiper (1963) offers a classic description of the transitional period prior to standing independently during which the infant relies upon the hands in using supporting objects while upright. This transitional period involves gaining mastery over pulling up by means of using the arms, holding on while stooping to grasp an object on the ground, and "coasting":

> The mother places the infant near some supporting object before he is able to get up unaided. Only when he feels halfway safe does he dare to let loose with one hand and to grasp for something. Bending down is especially difficult. Gradually the infant develops the faculty of moving along a suitable object, such as a railing, by repeatedly changing the position of the hands. (p. 230)

More on the development of standing is presented in the context of locomotor development in Chapter 10.

CHAPTER 9

EATING AND DRINKING

This reciprocal circuit of sensory-elicited oral motion effecting further apposition experience in the tongue, lips and palate is the essential mechanism of the infantile suckle and oral positional mechanisms. It is also the background of development of biting and chewing and, distinctively in the human and some other primates, of the greater array of oral manipulations of food and of speech sounds which are made possible by the differential enlargement of the oral cavity compared with the tongue.

Bosma, 1967, p. 98

Issues. In his paper for the First Symposium on Oral Sensation and Perception, James Bosma identifies a central issue to be addressed in this chapter: how does infant appetitive behavior develop in the context of the other functions served by the oral articulators? Like another effector organ of the body, the hand, the mouth may be used for multiple functions or "effectivities" (see Table 9.1): a detector (of what is in the mouth), sucker, explorer, chewer, biter, and speaker. In this chapter, I will make the claim that the multiple functions of the oral articulators may emerge from activation influences on attractor dynamics (Saltzman & Munhall, 1989).

A second issue examined here concerns the relation between the earliest patterns of sucking and later ingestion. We saw in previous chapters that while

Table 9.1 Effectivities of the mouth as an active perceptual-motor organ

Effectivity	Description
Detector	Detecting the soluble and volatile components of a substance and its material qualities, like consistency, before swallowing it
Sucker	Means of feeling and sucking the mother's nipple; means for ingesting
Explorer	Explores objects brought to the mouth
Vocalizer	Produces vowel and consonant sounds
Chewer	Use of gums and teeth via jaw action to crush edibles for ingestion
Biter	Use of gums and teeth via jaw action to grip and tear edibles

Source: After J. J. Gibson, 1967.

attractor dynamics can account for order in a behavior such as sucking (Crook, 1979; Wolff, 1968), attractor dynamics must be serially modulated for controlling the sequence of behaviors that comprise eating. I propose here that the earliest forms of appetitive behavior observed in the human neonate already consist of behaviors exhibiting attractor dynamics. Sucking, swallowing, and breathing form a coordinative structure that maintains stability despite perturbation (see, e.g., Dreier et al., 1979). However, orienting to the nipple and attaching to it must be serially ordered with this coordinative structure in order for feeding to succeed. Moreover, during later feeding, nutritional needs, changes in the availability of semi-solid and solid food, patterns of nursing, the size of the oral cavity, and the eruption of teeth all change the requirements for serial ordering of behavior. Chewing must become an intrinsic part of the eating sequence. How does this transition from sucking fluids to chewing solids take place?

As with other action systems, I argue here that the earliest pattern of sucking may be an ontogenetic adaptation which insures that a particular function, necessary for survival, will be evident, but which is only a temporary solution to the task of learning to eat. The attractor dynamics governing sucking may be used to drive the ontogenetically assembled coordinative structures for chewing and swallowing. As I will show, this appears to happen by about six months of age. In order to develop this argument, I first present background on the attractor dynamics involved in sucking, the multiple functions of the mouth, the development of taste, the growth of the oral cavity, the changing metabolic requirements of the infant, and changes in nursing during infancy (the availability of different foodstuffs).

THE ORAL ARTICULATORS

The mouth as a haptic organ. In a chapter entitled "The mouth as an organ for laying hold on the environment", Gibson (1967) discusses haptic exploration with the oral effectors (see Table 9.2). He argues that the mouth, tongue, and lips, like the hands, are used to explore perceptually:

> By laying hold of something, a person can detect its size, its shape, its surface texture and its material substance or consistency. ... As part of its function in testing food substances, the tongue plus the oral cavity are sensitive to size, shape, texture, consistency, and temperature. (p. 130)

The tongue. Of all the oral articulators, the tongue is most like the hand in that it is highly flexible and multifunctional, it is used for grasping and pointing, and it is an exquisitely sensitive haptic organ. The tongue of the newborn is densely innervated with a variety of nerve endings (papillary, fibrillar extensions, networks, free endings, and branched terminations),

Table 9.2. Information available about a substance in the mouth

Properties of substance	Effect on body organ
Soluble fluid (sapid)	Stimulates receptors int he tongue and nearby tissue lining the mouth
Volatile properties	Stimulates receptors in the olfactory cavity above the mouth
Relative temperature	Stimulates tongue and mouth
Surface texture	Registered by mouth palpation which detects such properties as slippery, smooth, or rough
Consistency	Registered by chewing, which detects such properties as viscosity, elasticity and soft, hard, or brittle
Shape, size, specific gravity, and wholeness or granularity	Registered by the haptic action of the mouth

Source: After J. J. Gibson, 1967.

making it a sensitive organ for detecting thermal, tactile, and chemical gradients (Bosma, 1986). This haptic organ is, at the same time, a performatory system. It comprises extrinsic muscles which attach to the skeleton (cranium or mandible) at one end, and intrinsic muscles with no such attachment (Bosma, 1986). The arrangement of muscles of the tongue into two physiological distinct regions (medial and lateral) contribute to the peristaltic component in specific ways. A peristaltic wave that progresses in a posterior direction exerts successive negative and positive pressure on the nipple, conveying expressed milk toward the pharynx (Erenberg, Smith, Nowak, & Franken, 1986). These muscles transform the tongue into a highly flexible articulator and at the same time make possible rapid and directed movements within the oral cavity.

Classic cineradiographic studies (Ardran, Kemp, & Lind, 1958; Bosma, 1967) as well as more recent video, ultrasound and fiber-optic recording (Bosma, Hepburn, Josell, & Baker, 1990; Eishima, 1991; Erenberg et al., 1986) illustrate the articulatory prowess of the tongue during feeding at the breast (suckling and swallowing) by the human neonate (see Fig. 9.1). Suckling consists of two phases: (1) a lowering of the jaw with forward and downward displacement of the tongue body, and (2) elevation of the jaw with upward and dorsalward displacement of the tongue (Bosma, 1967). These have the consequence of creating a suction which draws the fluid into the mouth.

The coordination of the muscles of the tongue, pharynx, and lips also make possible a temporal pattern of co-articulation that appears to be necessary for sucking and swallowing:

> If infants are suckle feeding from a freely open nipple, they may express milk directly into the pharynx. ... In this circumstance, the actions of swallow are coincident with the suckle phase of mouth opening and tongue lowering and protrusion. Thus, the dorsal portion of the tongue is involved in swallow, while the remainder of the tongue is participating in suckle. (Bosma, 1967, p. 101)

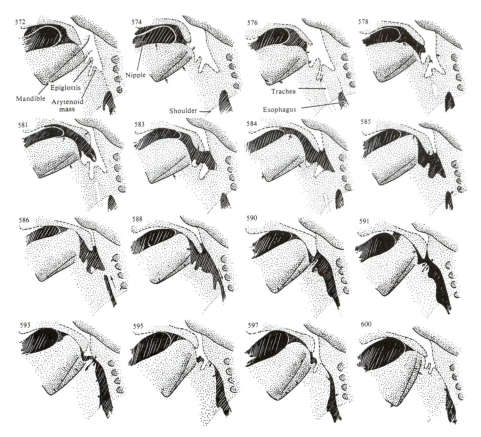

Figure 9.1. Cineradiographic demonstration of suckle feeding. A barium mixture was used, and filming was at 50 frames per second. In frame 572, the undistorted nipple is in suckle position within the mouth, surrounded by barium. The barium bolus is retained by apposition between the pharyngeal palate and tongue. The pharynx is open in respiration. In frames 574 to 584, the mandible and tongue are elevated and the nipple is compressed. The reciprocal phase of suckle performance is shown in frames 585 to 600, in which the mandible and tongue body are displaced inferiorward, allowing the nipple to resume its original contour. (From Bosma, 1986. Copyright © 1986 The Johns Hopkins University Press. Reprinted by permission.)

The tongue is additionally involved in pharyngeal airway maintenance: in the infant who is quiet (either with eyes open or closed), the tongue maintains apposition with the soft palate and, thus, maintains an airway.

Eishima (1991) reports a comparison of sucking when nipples with different hole sizes were used. This study demonstrates that the perceptual–exploratory capabilities of the tongue influence its articulatory configuration. When presented with a nipple having no hole, the tongue surrounds the nipple completely, and creates strong peristaltic movements. By contrast, when the nipple has a large hole, the tongue does not surround the nipple: it is either flat or irregular in shape and does not work to squeeze out the milk.

It is also evident that the tongue serves the function of basic orienting when one considers its role during chewing. Chewing must be coordinated with the cyclical activity of the mandible in order to direct its force in an appropriate way to crush the food held in the mouth. Prior to chewing, the tongue is brought into a position which brings the high density of receptors at its tip into initial contact with the food.

The tongue, then, is an articulator that is transformed into a variety of task specific devices: a basic orienting device during search for the nipple, a pumper used for sucking and swallowing, and a transporter of food within the mouth during mastication. How are these devices used during the development of eating?

EARLY EATING

Components of early eating. Prechtl (1958; and see Crowell, 1967), has identified four components of early breast feeding: (1) orientation of the head to bring the mouth into contact with the breast, (2) opening of the mouth and grasping with the lips once there has been contact with the breast, (3) sucking once the mouth areas are stimulated, and (4) swallowing movements. As I suggested earlier, the basic orienting system provides the foundation for appetition, since it directs the oral articulators to the resource (milk) which affords eating. We may typically think of the orienting response as a reflex-directed searching for the breast. However, Prechtl (1958) distinguishes such directed orienting from a rhythmic nondirected rooting activity that is evident in the earliest episodes of orienting toward the breast and persists through the first month. In rhythmic rooting, the head is turned from side to side, either when the central part of the mouth and lips are touched, or when the infant is very hungry. By contrast, directed head turning is more often elicited when the neonate is touched near the corners of the mouth.

Why do these two different patterns occur when oral activity elicited in different ways? One possibility concerns the face as a layout of receptor surfaces and the directionality of an orientation. When the corners of the mouth are touched, the receptors are stimulated to one side of the midline, and point attractor dynamics may direct the head to turn to one side. However, the midline may be a saddlepoint for the influences of point attractors to either side of the midline of the somatotopic map of the face (see discussion of saddlepoints in Fig. 2.3). Thus, when the stimulation occurs at the midline, the receptors may trigger activation of a limit-cycle attractor which oscillates between the competing influences of receptor fields mapping the mouth.

Sucking: One mode or two? When a "blind" nipple is introduced into the mouth of a neonate, there ensues a vigorous sucking characterized by a distinctive temporal pattern: the sucks occur at a regular frequency of about 2 Hz, and exhibit short bursts separated by pauses (Wolff, 1968, 1972). By contrast, when fluid is introduced through the nipple, the sucking slows to a frequency of about 1 Hz (Burke, 1977; Crook, 1979; Crook & Lipsitt, 1976). Wolff proposes what might be called a dual-mode model of sucking. Nutritive sucking is one mode of rhythmic sucking, common among all mammals, that is used for ingesting nutritive substances. Its slower rhythm reflects coupling via magnet effect of a central oscillator to the swallow reflex. A second mode, non-nutritive sucking, is notable for its resistance to perturbation and its influence on other ongoing rhythms, such as respiration. Lipsitt and his colleagues propose an alternative hypothesis, here called the single-mode model. They explain these two distinct patterns with reference to a single

NON-NUTRITIVE
SUCKING:

2 HZ RHYTHM ONLY
EVIDENT IN HUMANS;
DECLINES DURING
SECOND SIX MONTHS OF
INFANCY

NUTRITIVE SUCKING:

1 HZ RHYTHM; SLOWER
THAN NON-NUTRITIVE
SUCKING BECAUSE OF
COUPLING OF ORAL
ARTICULATORS WITH
SWALLOW REFLEX

WOLFF: DUAL MODE HYPOTHESIS

NON-NUTRITIVE AND NUTRITIVE SUCKING:

SINGLE MODE GENERATES BURST-PAUSE
PATTERN ON DRY NIPPLE; WHEN FLUID IS
INTRODUCED, BURST LENGTH INCREASES AND
PAUSES SHORTEN; SLOWER RATE OF NUTRITIVE
SUCKING REFLECTS SAVORING OF FLUID

LIPSITT-CROOK : HEDONIC HYPOTHESIS

Figure 9.2. Neonatal sucking. One mode or two?

"pacemaker" whose temporal pattern adapts to the presence or absence of fluid. When there is no fluid, a burst–pause pattern is evident, but when fluid is introduced, the neonate savors the taste of the fluid and this both increases burst length and shortens pauses (see Fig. 9.2).

The models differ most clearly in their explanation of why nutritive sucking is slower than non-nutritive sucking. Lipsitt et al. (1976) suggest that the change in rate reflects "an adaptive gustatory phenomenon wherein the sweet fluid is savored by a slower sucking rate" (p. 305). Wolff (1973) attributes the slower rate to the state-dependent coupling of sucking to the swallow reflex as a function of sensory feedback. Having been influenced by the work of von Holst, Wolff proposes that as the infant draws milk from the nipple, the swallowing reflex interacts with sucking activity by a "magnet effect." When the milk stops flowing or the infant falls asleep at the nipple, he continues to suck without forming a vacuum. The swallowing reflex is no longer activated and sucking shifts to the non-nutritive mode.

Wolff's observations of the transition from an eating mode to a non-nutritive sucking mode suggest that state-specific changes in the coupling of the attractors of sucking and swallowing may be conceptualized as a change in parameterization influences on the articulators. As a source of parameterization, behavioral state *might serve as an ontogenetic adaptation for maintaining early coordination of the multiple functions performed by the mouth.* For example, respiration is a vegetative function served by the oral articulators and the muscles of thorax and abdomen. Non-nutritive sucking appears to periodically "entrain" the temporal pattern of respiration. Dreier, Wolff, Cross, and Cochran (1979) report that normal full-term newborns in regular sleep show small but consistent changes of breath duration during non-nutritive sucks: there is a shortening of breath intervals in the middle of sucking bursts and a lengthening of breath interval spanning the end of sucking bursts.

The state specificity of hand–mouth coordination. In Chapter 7, I discussed the state-specificity of certain neonatal postures as an illustration of the process by which serial activation of articulator dynamics was evident in newborn behavior. A series of studies by Rochat and Blass and their colleagues (e.g., Rochat et al., 1988; Blass et al., 1989) further illustrate how behavioral rhythms may influence parameterization during appetitive behavior. Of interest in these studies was the relative incidence of mouthing (chewing, sucking, lip puckering) and hand-in-mouth (HIM) behavior (when any part of the hand was inside the mouth) as a function of an experimental procedure in which there was delivery of sucrose solution to the oral midline (see Fig. 9.3).

Twice as much mouthing and HIM was evident during delivery of sucrose than during either a presucrose baseline period or at sucrose termination. The

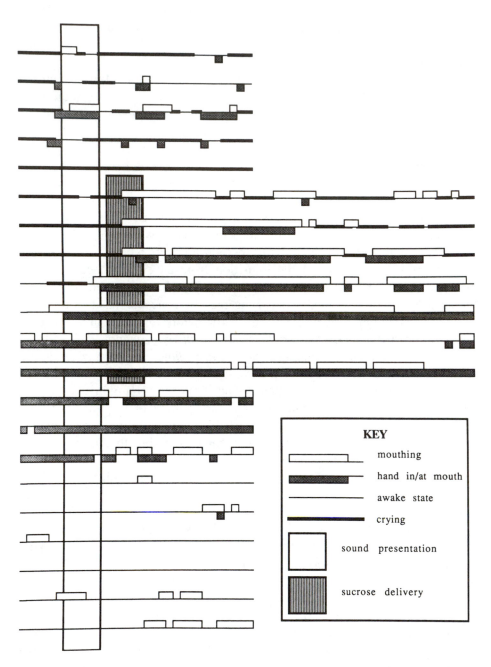

Figure 9.3. Time-line representation of a typical hand-in-mouth (HIM) baby. (The entire width of the figure represents 2 minutes. Each horizontal line follows its predecessor in time). (From Blass, Fillion, Rochat, Hoffmeyer, & Metzger, 1989. Copyright © 1989. American Psychological Association.)

amount of HIM remained elevated throughout sucrose delivery, but mouthing was only elevated at the point of delivery and subsequently declined. The coupling of mouthing and HIM exhibited a rapid onset and offset: it was engaged and disengaged within two minutes of sucrose administration and termination, respectively.

These results suggest that sucrose elicits mouthing, and that mouthing recruits the hand to the mouth, i.e., that sucrose influences the coupling between suckling and using the hand for eating. Blass et al. (1989) suggest that a possible mechanism for engaging hand–mouth coordination is a threshold for mouthing that must be reached before the hands are brought to the mouth.

How might we understand these results in dynamic terms? Mouthing, a rhythmical behavior precedes HIM. Recall from the earlier discussion of the work of Casaer (1979) in Chapter 8 that during mouthing, the arms are most often in a semi-flexed posture. This suggests that the attractor dynamics of mouthing are associated with particular stiffness parameters of the limbs, with the consequence that the arms bend at the elbow, and the hands tend to move toward the face with muscle activations. Thus, when sucrose promotes mouthing, it may also parameterize the limbs in a particular way so action is directed *toward* the body.

A study by Buka and Lipsitt (1991) supports the idea that the attractor dynamics of mouthing is associated with specific limb parameters. A cylindrical rod suspended from a pressure transducer was placed in the hand of neonates during two sucking conditions: with no fluid available and with sucrose solution available. Variations in strength of grasp were dependent upon whether the infant was sucking for the sweet fluid or not. When they sucked for sweet fluid, they grasped the bar with greater pressure. Moreover, the pressure increases were coincident with sucking bursts.

THE TRANSITION FROM NEONATAL ORAL ACTIVITY TO CHEWING

Oral reflexes and chewing. The classic descriptions of chewing by Gesell and Ilg (1937) identify its milestone appearance between 5 and 8 months. However, there has been little research on the relationship between neonatal oral activity and chewing as it is used for eating. Sheppard and Mysak (1984) have approached this question by exploring the relation between what they call the "oral reflexes" (rooting, biting, mouth opening, lip, lateral tongue, and Babkin reflexes) and later chewing. Their study was done in the context of the "controversy" over whether reflexes play a role in organizing voluntary behavior or must wane for voluntary behavior to emerge. Infants were studied longitudinally between 1 and 35 weeks using the procedures of (1) touching different parts of the mouth with a pressure aesthesiometer (to elicit reflexes) and (2) placing a 0.5-cm cube of banana on the lateral part of the gingiva.

CHEWING

A.

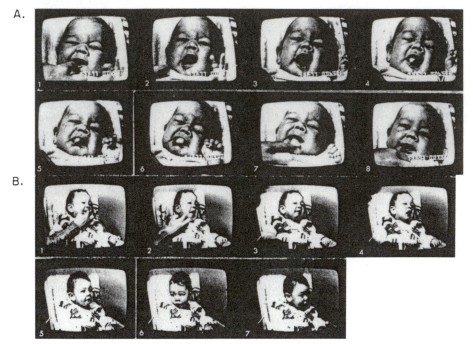

B.

Figure 9.4. Photographs of selected frames from videotaped chewing trials, subject M.A. (A) 8 weeks. (1) The banana cube had been placed in the cheek. (2–4) Centering phase included initial, ipsilateral lip deviation followed by lip deviation to the left and transfer of the bolus to the midline. (5) A brief processing phase during which the bolus was shifted anteriorly is followed by (6,7) resolution phase and ejection of the bolus. Duration of total response and return to inactive postures (8) was 5 sec. (B) 35 weeks. (From Shepperd & Mysak, 1984. Copyright © The Society for Research in Child Development. Reprinted by permission.)

Sheppard and Mysak (1984) report that it was possible to elicit all of the oral reflexes throughout the 8 months of testing, but that the reactions were "more subtle" between 5 and 8 months (see Fig. 9.4). During this same period, they observed some specific changes in chewing. To facilitate description of these changes, they divide chewing into three phases: (1) centering, transferring the bolus of banana to the midline using lateral tongue movements, (2) processing, consisting of rhythmical cycles of mandible elevation and depression in combination with various lip and tongue movements, and (3) resolution, a break in the rhythmical processing cycles during which the bolus is swallowed or ejected from the mouth.

Whereas certain aspects of chewing (cyclical mandible elevation and depression, lateral tongue movements, and transport of the bolus from lateral to medial oral position) were evident even at one week, three emergent aspects of chewing did not occur until between 21 and 31 weeks: lateral and protrusive mandible movements, mandible elevation and depression at a speed of 1 Hz, and mastication, the application of a crushing force to the bolus.

While Sheppard and Mysak discuss their findings in the reflex tradition, their descriptions of observed behavior suggest that the oral activities had rhythmical qualities. For example, as they elicited a response, they observed what they call "reverberating response sequences" (repetitions of two or more responses). These occurred in all biting and 23 percent of other reflexes, and peaked between 10 and 14 weeks. Even the earliest chewing activity in response to banana placed in the mouth resulted in cycles of mandible elevation and depression, with a frequency of between 0.36 Hz at week to 1.1 Hz at 31 weeks. Indeed, in their concluding comments, Sheppard and Mysak note "comparison of infantile oral reflexes and chewing reveals an underlying similarity. Both behaviors consisted of a similar repertoire of generally cyclical, complementary sequences of craniofacial movements" (p. 842).

There were, however, significant functional differences between early oral activity and later chewing. Chewing is distinguished by the *transport* of the bolus in the mouth *in preparation* for mastication and swallowing. Thus, the receptor surfaces of the tongue allow it to act as a detector and transporter, while the mandible acts as a crusher, and the lips and pharynx as a pumper. This implies that in order to understand what is developing during this period, one needs to consider the multiple effectivities of the oral effectors.

THE TRANSITION TO INDEPENDENT EATING

Earlier views. Gesell and Ilg (1937) conducted an oft-cited longitudinal study of developmental changes in eating behavior, and their descriptive findings are summarized in Table 9.3. For example, they describe the

Table 9.3. Developmental changes in action of oral and manual articulators during breast and bottle feeding

Developmental Period	Behavior
Neonate	During sucking, chin makes wide excursions, surface of tongue is brought flat against nipple; swallowing is closely merged with sucking; hands rest on chest
4 to 12 weeks	Tongue curling allows better approximation with the nipple. Tongue movement becomes more forward and backward
16 to 24 weeks	Lower lip becomes more active and nipple is held more firmly; resists withdrawal of nipple; increased strength of sucking; hands fairly active, occasionally patting and grasping, and fingering breast or bottle
28 to 36 weeks	Sucking and biting of the nipple; hands show more prehensile and manipulatory activity; infant may hold bottle alone for part of feeding
40 to 52 weeks	Can manage bottle alone, tilting it as it empties, and retrieving it if it drops

systematic changes in the use of the tongue and lips for ingestion, and of the hands for holding breast or bottle and, eventually, for using implements (cup and spoon) for bringing food to the mouth. Consistent with his other work on behavioral development during this era, Gesell attributes such changes to neuromaturational growth. The neuromotor organization in general proceeds in a head to foot direction: lips, tongue, and pharynx come first, and then the tongue undergoes gradual differentiation.

At the opposite extreme of explanations of the development of appetitive behavior during infancy is that the infant must learn the associations between the time, place, and circumstances of a meal and the use of the oral articulators to satisfy the appetite. Appetite is considered a mental construct incorporating memory, symbolic representation, perception, and affect. The brain is said to act as an integrator between the various physiological and psychological mechanisms involved in the regulation of food intake (Wright & Crow, 1982).

Exploration for affordances. An alternative to both the maturational and cognitive views of appetitive behavior is to consider changes in the performatory and exploratory skills of the oral apparatus, especially the tongue. According to Eleanor Gibson's phases of exploration, discussed in Chapter 3, neonates explore events. With respect to appetitive exploration, the events would include the flow of milk into the mouth. Neonates may use the tongue to explore the properties which remain invariant and change during the flow of liquid. In this regard, the flow of liquid may be equivalent to optical flow explored by the visual system. For example, Hall (1975) suggests that for breast-fed babies, eating from the first breast is ended with milk rich in fat and protein, then starts on the second breast with thin and watery milk. The changes in the composition and taste of the milk, she suggests, are detected by the infant and specify when to stop eating. This might account for the increased tendency toward rapid weight gain and risk of obesity in bottle-fed infants who do not have this information available to them.

Several studies have chronicled the transition from exploration for events to exploration of affordances. Some studies have used the cross-modal transfer paradigm. Meltzoff and Borton (1979), for example, report that 1-month-olds visually prefer the shape and/or texture of an object they previously explored with their mouth only. E. J. Gibson and Walker (1984) found that infants of this age subsequently discriminated object softness from rigidity after having explored different objects with the hand or mouth.

Rochat (1987) has adopted a somewhat different approach. He compared manual and oral positive pressure responses of newborns, and 2- and 3-month-olds, when applied to objects varying in their elasticity or rigidity. Rochat specifically modeled the study on the affordances of the breast for suckability. He argued that if the object was elastic like a nipple, the infant should respond orally to its affordances for sucking, and show a more oral activity than manual activity when the object was rigid. By contrast, if the object is rigid, the infant should respond to its affordances for graspability, and show more manual activity than oral activity. This is indeed what he found for the neonates, using the measure of frequency of positive pressure (squeezes). However, while at birth "the function attached to a modality influences the nature of the infant's discriminative response" (Rochat, 1987, p. 447), this was no longer the case at 2 and 3 months. Rochat interprets the developmental change as follows:

> These results suggest that the developmental trend observed is based on a change within the oral modality. The nutritional function of the mouth might be less dominant by 3 months when the infant is less engaged in sucking responses. ... From the less dominant nutritional function of the oral system (less sucking) emerges new interactions with the object and new grounds for discrimination. (pp. 447–448)

By around 5 months, the nascent attentiveness to affordances during exploratory activity identified by Rochat (1987) and others has blossomed. Interestingly, this occurs at a time (1) when the tongue is becoming increasingly mobile, and (2) just prior to the appearance of the infant's use of the mandible not only for 1-Hz rhythmic opening and closing, but also its use as a crusher. This new exploration for affordances also occurs at around the time that most infants have had solid foods introduced into their diet (Wright & Crow, 1982). How might increased skill at exploring for affordances with the tongue be related to the differentiated use of the mandible and jaw for crushing and chewing, and the lips and pharynx for chewing and swallowing?

We saw earlier that the 1 Hz rhythm was characteristic of the earliest nutritive oral activity of sucking, and could be characterized as a limit-cycle attractor. At the same time, the 2-Hz rhythm for non-nutritive sucking declines. This suggests that there may be a changing pattern of parameterization of the articulators during this period, so that the 1-Hz rhythm "captures" the articulators for chewing. The reason for this changing parameterization may be a combination of changes in the properties of the articulators, and the availability of solid foods. It also may reflect the dictum of new functions from old parts. Here the 1 Hz may be coupled to the articulators used for chewing. The result is that there is a new serial ordering of articulator dynamics appropriate for the available affordances.

Appetite, then, is the intention which determines the parameters of temporal activation of the sequential ordering of the articulators given particular affordances: opening the mouth and drawing the food into the oral cavity, orienting the tongue to the food so that it can be transported to the crushing surfaces, exploring the properties of the food so that detection of a size which affords swallowing results in a cessation of chewing and the initiation of swallowing. In this sense, appetite may be a graph-dynamic process which, like earlier neonatal behavioral states, serves the function of serially ordering the attractor dynamics of the articulators.

Hunger and the appetitive mode. There are at least two implications of special-purpose devices for eating (chewing, swallowing, transporting with the tongue) being sensitive to graph-dynamic changes in activation of the appetitive mode: (1) there should be observable changes in parameterization of the articulators as a function of hunger (operationally defined as time since last feeding), and (2) there should be increased resistance of coordinated patterns to perturbation. Both of these are supported by longitudinal observations reported by Wolff (1987), who examined three measures of parameter changes relative to time since last feeding: vigor of protest to interruption of feeding, anticipatory behavior before feeding, and rooting.

Wolff first examined how 1- and 3-month-old infants responded to the interruption of feeding at the beginning (after two or three swallows), middle, and close to the end of feeding, while they were still awake and alert. Near the end of a meal, there was hardly any protest at any age. At the beginning of a meal, 1-month-olds cried vigorously, but 3-month-olds rarely cried at all.

He also examined the influence of hunger on bottle-fed infant's anticipatory behavior (spontaneous mouthing, tonguing, mouth searching or rooting, and hand–mouth contact) when either placed in a feeding position or being shown the bottle. Neither posture nor the sight of the bottle produced any anticipation in newborns, but by the end of the second week, at the beginning of feeding there was anticipation at change in posture without seeing the bottle. It was not until 6 or 8 weeks that sight of the bottle alone at the beginning of feeding influenced anticipation.

In his examination of rooting, Wolff stimulated four "cardinal points" (at the two corners of the mouth and the upper and lower lips) as well as four adjacent sites. Prechtl had reported previously a specific state-dependent change in rooting: neonates turned their head toward the site of stimulation when awake, but away from the site when in irregular (state 2) sleep. Wolff found that during the period between the second and eighth week, the frequency of rooting responses during wakefulness and the radius of skin sensitive to stimulation were greater before than after a meal. Moreover, after the meal, waking infants usually rooted only when the lateral corners of the mouth were stimulated. And, finally, the latency of rooting was always significantly shorter before than after a meal. Wolff interprets these results as follows: "Thus hunger had a graded effect on rooting, relative to the area of facial skin that was sensitive to adequate stimulation" (p. 92). Considered together, the influence of hunger on behavior revealed in these experiments supports the idea that hunger may be thought of as a graph-dynamic process, influencing the parameterization of assembled coordinative structures.

The appetitive mode and maternal behavior. A shared feature of the earliest appetitive behavior of mammals is maternal regulation of the suckling of their young. The serial ordering of maternal behavior within the ecological niche characteristic of a species can be described by gestural scores. The serial ordering of maternal behavior creates temporal "windows" within which the behavior of their young is regulated in particular ways. Brake (1991), for example, describes how rat suckling, distinguished by different rates of sucking (intermittent arrhythmic, rapid, and slow) is promoted by the maternal

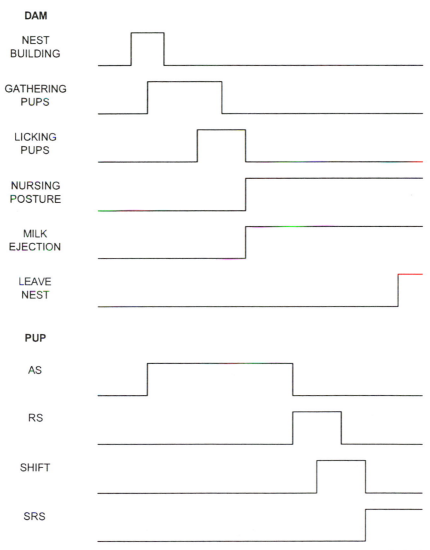

Figure 9.5. The way in which different rates of suckling by rats (intermittent, arrhythmic (AS), rapid (RS), and slow) is regulated by the maternal activities of nest building, retrieval and gathering, licking, assuming a nursing posture, and milk ejection. (After Brake, 1991.)

activities of nest building, retrieval and gathering, licking,'assuming a nursing posture and milk ejection (see Fig. 9.5).

In humans, the caregiver adjusts the temporal organization of behavior so that it is compatible with, and also anticipates the achievements of the developing child (see, e.g., Hodapp, Goldfield, & Boyatzis, 1984; Hodapp & Goldfield, 1985; Kaye, 1982; Rogoff, 1990). One example of the the earliest maternal regulation of sucking is Kaye's observations (Kaye, 1977; Kaye and Wells, 1980) of mothers "jiggling" their babies during many pauses that follow a burst of sucking. Kaye found a significantly higher probability of a burst following the maternal activity of jiggling and stopping, than either while jiggling or if there was no jiggle. Thus, the infant's pauses tend to elicit the mother's jiggling and cessation of jiggling elicits the next burst of sucking. The implication of the close relationship between maternal regulation in mammals and the behavior of their young is that the appetitive mode originates as a shared process, with the control of its temporal structure only gradually assumed by the young.

INDEPENDENT EATING

Transition. The transition to independent eating, like other skills, is a slow process in humans (Stevenson, Roach, ver Hoeve, & Leavitt, 1990). It occurs during the second half of the first year, and is characterized by increasingly active participation of the infant as well as by increased infant vocalization. Like the temporal pattern evident in the earliest maternal regulation of sucking, there is also a patterned, rhythmic interaction during this transition period (see Fig. 9.6):

> Following infants' acceptance of food, mothers of term infants immediately suppressed further offers of food, suggesting sensitivity to the infants' immediate need to complete one mouthful before tackling another. Mothers then touched their infants, usually with a spoon to remove any food that was not swallowed; looked away from their infants, usually to refill the spoon; looked back toward their infants; and, finally, offered an additional spoonful of food. (Stevenson et al., 1990, p. 66)

Gesell's observations of use of cup and spoon. Gesell and Ilg (1937) present a detailed description of the early use of cup and spoon (see Table 9.4). From 4 to 12 weeks, drinking is very similar to sucking and is accompanied by similar posture (e.g., head movements). The tongue is well-protruded and assumes a "half-moon" shape. Between 16 and 24 weeks, body movement increasingly anticipates the cup with the head reaching and an open mouth. Jaw movements are less extensive, but sucking-like movements are still used and there continues considerable spilling. It is during the period from 28 to 36

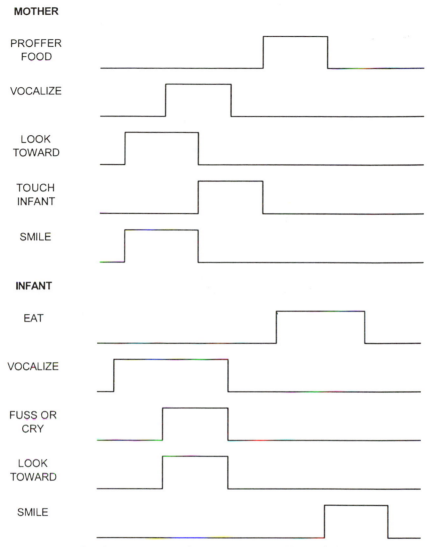

Figure 9.6. The role of maternal regulation during the transition to independent eating. (After Stevenson, Roach, ver Hoave, & Leavitt, 1990.)

weeks that the infant spontaneously reaches out for a cup, and is more likely to bring the median portion of the lips to the cup rim. The infant begins to be able to interrupt drinking after one or two swallows.

Spoon feeding often begins by around 16 weeks, with the infant seated while supported in some fashion. Gesell and Ilg report that the infant looks at the spoon and from spoon to dish, opens the mouth as the spoon approaches, and closes the lips firmly on the spoon. Infants may kick their legs actively, wave their arms, or pat the food tray of a high chair. By 28 weeks, Western

Table 9.4. Developmental changes in the use of cup and spoon

Developmental Period	Cup	Spoon
4 to 12 weeks	Oral pattern identical with sucking; tongue is well protruded and the lower jaw makes wide excursions	
16 to 24 weeks	Sucking pattern continues with increased contraction of cheek muscles at corners of mouth	Opens mouth each time spoon touches it and closes lips firmly on spoon. Tongue frequently projects as spoon is withdrawn
28–36 weeks	Shows awareness of function of cup and anticipates it by bending forward and opening mouth	Brings head forward to receive spoon, bending trunk and then sitting upright; removes food quickly from spoon by pressing lips against it and drawing head away; beginning of chewing with lateral tongue movements
40 to 52 weeks	Mobility of tongue tip allows true drinking behavior, but cheek muscles are not fully coordinated with lips and tongue and infant may sputter and blow bubbles; with satiety, infant plays with cup by biting, banging, rotating, shifting it from one hand to the other	Takes food rapidly; draws in lower lip as soon as food is removed; explores food in mouth by definite chewing movements, often pouting the lips; may interrupt meal momentarily by razzing (vibrating tongue while compressed between lips); manipulates empty spoon in various ways; transferring it from hand to hand; drops it onto dish; uses spoon to rub food back and forth or mash it in hand
Second year (about 65 weeks)	Well-defined self-management of cup; demand to hold it; some difficulty with lifting and adaptively tilting the cup; uses palmar push at sides of cup rather than fingers	In grasping, infant first holds lower third of handle, but only at 2 years holds end; seizure is usually pronate and palmar but varies; difficulty with filling spoon

infants are likely to be seated in a high chair and reach with the mouth while the hands are held fisted at the shoulders or resting on the tray. Infants bring the head forward and bend the trunk at the waist to receive the spoon. This is the period when chewing movements become apparent.

Anticipatory mouth opening. Since the early observations by Gesell and Ilg, there has been little study of the organization of action during eating. A recent exception has been a study by Connolly and Dalgleish (1989), discussed in Chapter 10. Whereas even neonates are able to bring the hand to

Figure 9.7. Anticipatory mouth opening when using a spoon.

the mouth, Connolly and Dalgleish report that it is not until later during the first year that infants visually monitor a spoon held in the hand as well as anticipate the spoon's arrival by opening the mouth (Fig. 9.7). They examined the activity of transporting food from a dish to the mouth using a spoon held in one hand. They measured the body-related position of the spoon at which the mouth opened in anticipation. Between 12 and 23 months, the variability of the position at which the mouth opened decreased, and became more likely to occur about halfway between the dish and mouth (see Fig. 9.8). Older infants were more likely to watch the spoon over a longer portion of the journey from dish to mouth, and for a longer period of time. With increasing age, visual monitoring was more likely to continue until the mouth opened in anticipation of the spoon's arrival. This suggests that infants may be increasingly likely to use some optical variable, such as tau, to control mouth opening at a time scaled to the amount of time it takes to open the mouth, given a particular velocity of the spoon.

Task dynamics of using a cup. We saw in Gesell and Ilg's account that learning to use a cup to drink liquids is a difficult task. Is a dynamic approach useful for explaining the difficulty that young children have in using a cup to drink liquids? Consider the task further: in bringing the cup to the mouth, the goal is to move the cup with the hand from its initial position (say, on a table top) to the final position of the mouth without spilling the liquid in the cup.

DEVELOPMENTAL
PROGRESSION

RATE LIMITERS

INCREASED USE OF ONE
HAND; CONSISTENCY IN USE
OF PARTICULAR GRASP
PATTERNS

CONTROLLING THE HOLDING OF
THE SPOON WITH THE HAND

INVOLVEMENT OF
CONTRALATERAL HAND TO
PUSH FOOD ONTO THE SPOON
OR TO HOLD ONTO THE DISH

LOADING FOOD ONTO THE SPOON

USE OF VISUAL INFORMATION
TO MONITOR ORIENTATION OF
SPOON LOADED WITH FOOD
BEING TRANSPORTED TO
MOUTH

TRANSPORTING THE LOADED SPOON
FROM DISH TO MOUTH WHILE
MAINTAINING A CONSTANT ORIENTATION
TO AVOID SPILLAGE

SHOULDER FLEXION AND
HEAD MOVEMENTS
INCREASINGLY USED TO
EMPTY SPOON ONCE IT IS IN
THE MOUTH

EMPTYING FOOD FROM SPOON INTO
MOUTH

Figure 9.8. The possible rate-limiting factors during the development of learning to use a spoon to eat semi-solid food. (After Connolly & Dalgleish, 1989).

This task translates into the ability of the action system to control the articulators using an equation of motion *which incorporates the constraints of cup orientation.* Saltzman and Kelso (1987) have modeled the task of bringing a liquid-filled cup to the mouth, and their approach is instructive for evaluating the hypothesis that developmental change in drinking from a cup involves adding the constraint of maintaining orientation of cup.

Recall from Chapter 4 that the task-dynamic approach involves writing an equation of motion (a set of constraints) which relates attractor dynamics in a task space to the orientational axes of the body and the joint variables of the effector system. We know from longitudinal observations of young children that even very young infants can bring the hand to the mouth using the kind of straight line trajectory that is evidence of point-attractor dynamics (see Rochat studies above). Thus, we can write an equation of motion for bringing the hand to the mouth with the additional constraint of maintaining a particular orientation of the cup. Clearly, becoming skilled at bringing a liquid-filled cup to the mouth requires learning, and the simulations suggest that what the infant must learn is how to use multiple frames of reference to relate the cup to the mouth (a body space) and relate the liquid to the cup.

We saw in Chapter 8 that one of the later developing aspects of basic orienting is relating the body to positions in the environment. A study by Goldfield (1983) suggests that the ability to simultaneously orient to two complementary frames of reference develops at around 18 to 20 months. Infants were given two tasks which abstractly required the infants to orient an activity occurring within one frame of reference to another activity in a complementary frame of reference. One task involved using the long end of a tool (a "rake") to remove a cookie placed in the middle of a long transparent cylinder. In the second task, infants were given a picture that was oriented relative to their point of view and asked to show a picture to a person seated facing them. For the picture to be oriented to the observer, the infant had to turn it by 180 degrees before showing it. It was not until between 18 and 20 months that infants both oriented the long end of the rake to fit into the cylinder and get the cookie, and turned the picture so that it was oriented to the observer when they showed it. Thus, the developmental changes involved in bringing a liquid-filled cup to the mouth may reflect not only use of vision to guide the hand to the mouth, but also a more general developmental change in the nature of basic orienting.

Table 9.5. Cycles of eating mode nested within orienting mode

Mode	Cycles within Mode
Orienting	1. Orienting to gravity. Hold back and head sufficiently erect for food to pass down throat 2. Orienting to support surface. Adjust body posture and end effector to surface supporting food and utensils 3. Orienting to food. Bend forward to meet food
Eating	1. Transport food. Bring food to mouth (a) solids-grasp with hands or use implement (b) bring liquids to mouth in vessels 2. Apportion food. Take correct amount of food into the mouth 3. Serially order eating and breathing. Temporally sequence chewing and swallowing with breathing

The nested cycles of activities involved in eating. We have just seen that bringing a cup to the mouth is a skill that can be explained within the domain of task dynamics. But using a cup to drink liquid is only part of the nested cycle of events that constitutes independent eating. Consider some of the descriptions of eating by Reed (1988b) (see Table 9.5). There are three aspects of eating that organize the flow of nested activities during eating: preliminaries and set up, eating, and maintaining posture while eating. Eating is composed of a number of cyclic components, postures, and movements, facilitating a variety of subsidiary functions, all of which are constrained by perception to serve an overall function (see Fig. 9.9).

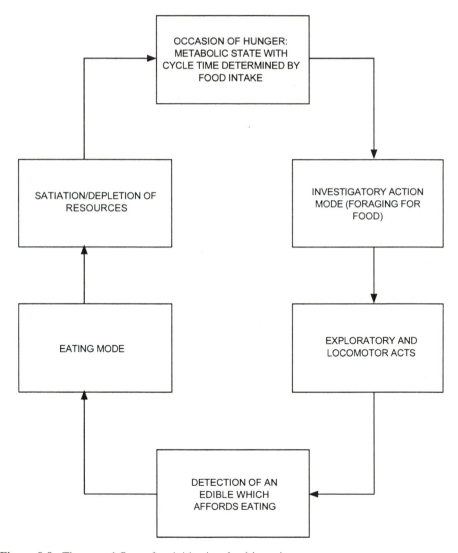

Figure 9.9. The nested flow of activities involved in eating.

When children learn to eat, as when they learn other skills (see, e.g., Hodapp & Goldfield, 1985; Hodapp, Goldfield, & Boyatzis, 1984), they are assisted by adults in each of the three organizational aspects of eating. First, the meal is prepared and placed in front of the child either in a container or directly on a table top. In cultures that use implements, these are also provided. The infant is seated in a posture which promotes reaching for the food and bringing it to the mouth. While infants are initially fed by the parent, they often learn to eat independently by means of games which give the child experience with adjusting the timing of opening the mouth for the arrival of food (e.g., "here comes the airplane into the hangar") relative to the optical flow of the approaching food. Adults gradually release control of the nested cycles of events so they are performed independently.

CHAPTER 10

LOCOMOTION

The purpose of locomotion is to transport the body across the ground. It entails repeated patterns of using, abandoning, and regaining a balanced stance on the ground successively with the alternate legs.

Brooks, 1986, p. 181

A standing posture can be modelled as an inverted pendulum on a small base, thereby having a small stable region. ... To maintain this static equilibrium, the basic requirement is to keep the body's center of gravity over the quadrilateral base of support provided by the feet. ... We can also approach the edge of the base of support, that critical boundary between standing and falling, in a controlled manner by shifting our weight around. Apparently, a standing human senses the region of stability and the critical boundary by means of propriospecific information. ... During the initiation of gait, the system must move off the stable region and cross the critical boundary, making a transition from stationary stance to a new periodic regime.

Warren, 1988b, p. 374

The mature step cycle of human walking emerges from an intimate link between stance and transport. We see in the earliest spontaneous movements of the legs in the fetus and newborn that there is inherent temporal order (Provine, 1988; Robertson, 1988). Yet, a complete account of locomotor development must also consider how these early spontaneous patterns become nested within the postural matrix of the basic orienting system. The "milestones" of locomotor development, recognized even in the ancient riddle of the Sphinx, all involve changing orientations of the body to the surface of support under the influence of a gravitational field: crawling on all fours, standing with support, standing unassisted, and walking.

I first consider the evolution of walking in humans as a way of highlighting the consequences of changes in upright posture for locomotion (Lovejoy, 1988), and offer a brief comparative look at neural as well as postural and biomechanical influences (Hurov, 1991; Brakke & Savage-Rumbaugh, 1991; Rollinson & Martin, 1981) in primate locomotion.

The theoretical framework presented in Chapter 7 is then used to examine how the changing postural matrix of the human infant makes walking possible. Toward this end, I first examine the attractor dynamics of early kicking and show how it may be an ontogenetic adaptation for the fetus which persists during the early postnatal months (Prechtl, 1981). Changing postural constraints on the muscles may, in turn, provide the opportunity for exercise and strengthening of the muscles, but during the early months of infancy, rate of fat deposition may outpace muscle strengthening (Thelen & Fisher, 1982). For this reason, the early spontaneous pattern of stepping, the so-called "stepping reflex" (Zelazo, 1983) may disappear when the infant is in an upright posture.

The elegant series of studies on interlimb coordination by Thelen and Ulrich and their colleagues is reviewed as a way of illustrating that temporal patterning is not simply a consequence of muscle activation, but rather emerges from a variety of forces acting on the limbs (Schneider et al., 1990; Thelen & Ulrich, 1991; Ulrich, 1989). I then consider data from a longitudinal study which I conducted in order to examine the role of the changing use of the hands for the development of crawling (Goldfield, 1989). Crawling appears to be a skill which emerges when other developing capabilities (balance, propulsion, and steering with the hands) become useful as an ensemble. When infants begin to crawl, their perception of affordances relevant to locomotion begin to show some specific changes (Bertenthal & Campos, 1984, 1987; E. J. Gibson, et al., 1987; Gibson & Schmuckler, 1989).

There appear to be complementary influences of the nervous subsystem, which exhibits inherent asymmetries, and the link-segment and musculotendon subsystems, which exhibit bilateral symmetry. Because these systems exert opposing influences on the limbs (e.g., muscle torques versus gravity), there are periods when infants assume relatively symmetrical postures, and movement exhibits dynamic equilibrium (e.g., during the stages of prone rocking and early standing). The inherent asymmetries of the anatomy of the nervous system (Rosen & Galaburda, 1985) may serve a specific function at these junctures: namely, driving the posture into a relationship of dis-equilibrium with the surface of support, and promoting falling and forward motion. Postural instability may, in other words, be a formative influence in motor development.

We will see that mature walking by the young child requires such a long developmental history because of the tapestry of changing postural and biomechanical influences on the spontaneous temporal patterning of kicking. By the time children show a mature gait, they have mastered (1) maintenance of support of the upper body against gravity during stance (i.e., to prevent collapse of the lower limbs), (2) maintenance of upright posture and balance (i.e., to prevent falling over in the anterior–posterior or lateral directions, and (3) control of foot trajectory to achieve safe ground clearance and a gentle heel or toe landing (Winter, 1989).

CONSTRAINTS ON LOCOMOTION

New functions from old parts. Lovejoy (1988) chronicles the anatomical changes associated with the transition from quadrupedal gait in primates to upright walking in humans. What is common in all of these changes is that *a particular part of primate anatomy which had served the propulsion function has become transformed in humans to perform the function of stabilization in bipedal gait* (see Table 10.1). Stabilization is necessitated by the greater instability (sway) inherent in bipedalism: the forces acting on a standing biped introduce the possibility of pitching froward with each step, and with falling to one side. For example, the gluteus maximus has been transformed to counteract falling forward with each step, while the hip extensors serve to prevent the pelvis and trunk from tipping toward the unsupported side at each step.

Given these anatomical adaptations for bipedalism, why do human infants require such a long period of development before they are capable of bipedal

Table 10.1. New function (stabilization) from old (propulsion) in the evolutionary transition from quadrupedal to bipedal gait

Anatomy transformed	Quadruped	Biped
Gluteus maximus	Minor muscle	During locomotion, upright trunk flexes forward at each foot strike because of momentum. Gluteus maximus prevents trunk from pitching forward
Ilium of the pelvic innominate bone	In quadrupedal primates, the ilia are no longer than in humans, lengthening the torso, and adding to the mechanical disadvantage of the gluteus maximus. Iliac blades are flat and lie in a more or less single plane across the back of the torso	Much shortened ilium shortens the torso and brings the trunk's center of mass much closer to the hip joints, reducing the mechanical disadvantage of the gluteus maximus. Each ilium is also rotated forward
Anterior gluteals (gluteus medius and minimus)	These muscles contract between attachment points near the top of the ilium and on the outside of the upper femur (serve as hip extensors and with a long ilium give the muscles a large range of contraction)	Hip extensors contribute little to locomotion, and instead act as abductors, preventing the pelvis and trunk from tipping toward the unsupported side at each step
Hamstring muscles	Connect lower pelvis to the back of the femur and serve as hip extensors	Hamstrings serve to control limb, not extend it. Extended limb (like a long pendulum) has a large moment of inertia. The hamstrings are used to decelerate the leg once it has completed its forward arc

Source: After Lovejoy, 1988.

gait? One aspect of the answer may rest with the concept of neoteny. While the shape of the bones and the position of muscle attachment to the bones that increase stabilization in adults is already present at birth, the structural composition of bone and muscle strength required for bipedal gait does not fully develop for several months after birth. The nascent state of bone and muscle in the neonate may be a consequence of retaining fetal characteristics for several months after birth. Bone may remain relatively soft and flexible for reasons relating to the delivery process, e.g., to facilitate compression of the skull during vaginal delivery, and to promote flexibility so that the limbs can be tightly flexed into the "fetal posture" prior to delivery. Muscle may remain relatively weak so that the forces generated by spontaneous movements (such as kicks) are scaled to the uterine environment. Intrauterine kicks need to be sufficiently vigorous to orient the body into the vertex position (see Chapter 8), but must not be so strong that the forces damage fragile maternal internal organs.

The evolutionary transformation of anatomy originally used for propulsion into means for stabilization highlights the significance of postural control for the development of controlled movement during human ontogeny. As we shall see, the incorporation of postural control strategies within locomotor timing patterns accounts well for the observed stages of locomotor development.

TEMPORAL PATTERNING AND CONSTRAINTS

Neural contributions to temporal patterning: Spinal pattern generators and supraspinal control. One approach to identifying the relation between both the invariant temporal patterning and adaptive postural control in early human locomotor development is to apply insights from neurophysiological studies with animals to infant behavior. Hans Forssberg and his colleagues (Forssberg, Stokes, & Hirschfeld, 1992), for example, have been inspired by Grillner's work on central pattern generators in cats and lower vertebrates (e.g., lampreys) (e.g., Grillner, 1985) to look for evidence that ontogenetic changes in human locomotion reflect the gradual increase of descending supraspinal control of spinal generators. To find evidence for spinal pattern generators, classic studies by Grillner used the "fictive" locomotion paradigm in which the cat's spinal cord was isolated from supraspinal influence by spinal transection and from phasic sensory information by curare immobilization of leg muscles) (see Fig. 10.1). Under these conditions, temporal sequencing of muscles was still evident following administration of DOPA. Forssberg draws parallels between these animal studies and humans. Because fetuses as young as 10–12 weeks gestational age kick their legs during a period when descending fibers are unmyelinated, he proposes that spinal generators are responsible for this behavior.

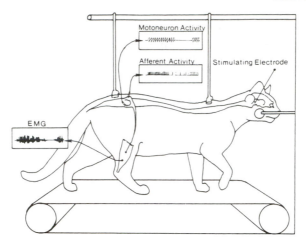

Figure 10.1. Controlled locomotion of a cat whose midbrain has been sectioned, studied on a treadmill. Repetitive stimulation of various locomotor regions in the midbrain results in descending activity, which excites the central pattern generators. As the animal walks, trots, or gallops, simultaneous records from isolated motoneurons (top), afferents (middle), or hindlimb muscles (bottom) may be made. (From Goslow, 1985. Copyright © 1985 by Harvard University Press. Reprinted by permission.)

Other animal studies by Shik and Orlovsky (e.g., Shik, Severin, & Orlovsky, 1966) have found that locomotion could be activated in decerebrate cats by electrical stimulation of areas of the brainstem. More recent work suggests that the brainstem apparently initiates and controls the speed and force generated at the spinal level (Garcia-Rill, 1986). But the brainstem does not prescribe details of locomotion. Rather, diffuse activation of spinal pattern generators results in highly ordered behavior. (For a dynamic interpretation, see below.) The brainstem is also involved in adapting stereotyped spinal patterns to the demands of the environment via peripheral feedback (via the rubrospinal and vestibulospinal tracts) (Mori, Matsuyama, Takakusaki, & Kanaya, 1988). The cerebellum also is involved in adapting locomotor movements. More specifically, the dorsal spinocerebellar tract is apparently involved in reporting on peripheral events, since deafferentation of the hindlimbs results in cessation of activity in this tract (Arshavsky & Orlovsky, 1985). Forssberg and his colleagues again draw a comparison between these studies of supraspinal influences and the ontogeny of locomotion in postnatal human infants (see also Sutherland, Olshen, Cooper, & Woo, 1980). They summarize the developmental trend in locomotion along the dimension of complexity (i.e., the number of Fourier coefficients needed to represent a pattern): young infants exhibit simple limb movements due to simultaneous contraction of the muscles, but after the first year, these simple patterns become more complex. This transition from simplicity to complexity results from the increasing influences of higher brain centers on spinal circuits. There are three specific influences proposed to develop between 6 and 12 months: descending brainstem systems turn on and off spinal generators, supraspinal processes such as equilibrium control make bipedal balance possible, and synchronized muscle activity is transformed into plantigrade gait.

Biomechanical constraints on temporal patterning. Following the lead of Bernstein, some researchers have been skeptical of the view that neural signals are the sole means of accounting for the inherent order of limb and trunk movements during locomotion. The physiological approach constitutes what Fowler and Turvey (1978) call an "air" theory, in contrast to Bernstein's "ground theory" of coordinated action. In the former, the individual is treated as if, in a sense, suspended in the air without regard to external and body-generated forces, while in the latter, the individual is described in terms of relationships among forces supplied reactively by the environment and muscularly by the body. One consequence of adopting a ground theory is a questioning of the assumption that observed developmental changes in postural organization arise solely as a result of cortical maturation. Research with human infants (described below) demonstrates that growth-related changes in body morphology are a constraint on the temporal patterning of the legs during kicking and stepping.

Morphological constraints. Study of animals suggests that body morphology is another constraint on locomotion. For most amphibians and reptiles, as well as 16 orders of mammals, gait is symmetrical, i.e., footfalls of the two feet of a pair are evenly spaced over time, and only in some animals is gait asymmetrical (Hildebrand, 1985). While Grillner and others argue that evolutionary modifications of gait selection reflect a change in the nature of the descending influences on central pattern generation, Hildebrand (1985) discusses ways in which stability and economy of effort impose morphological constraints on neural activation of the muscles. One constraint that arises from efforts to maintain stability is that footfalls must be timed so as to maximize the number of feet on the ground at any one time, and to favor those placements of three supporting feet (forming triangles or tripods) that enclose the largest base of support. A second constraint dictated by stability considerations is that the center of gravity must move within the base of support.

The relative distribution of body weight also plays a role in gait selection. Primates and other mammals differ in the distribution of their body weight, with the center of gravity in primates located further back in the body than in non-primate animals (Kimura, Okada, & Ishida, 1979). Indeed, it is possible to experimentally induce a monkey-like gait in the domestic dog by adding weights to the animal's hindquarters, thus shifting the center of gravity backwards (Tomita, 1967). Ontogenetic shifts in gait selection during locomotion in non-human primates appear to be greatly influenced by a shift in the center of gravity. Rollinson and Martin (1981) observed locomotor development in two species of monkeys. They found a transitional gait or "bob walk" which was a mix of lateral and diagonal sequences, and attributed this to head size. The relatively large head size of monkeys at birth in comparison to body size changes during this period and contributes to a shift in center of gravity and concomitant shift in gait.

Another morphological constraint on gait selection discussed by Hildebrand (1985), Alexander (1989) and others (e.g., Taylor & Heglund, 1982) concerns how animals "recycle" energy during locomotion, i.e., the nature of the exchange during each locomotor cycle between gravitational potential energy (as for a pendulum) and the storage and subsequent recovery of elastic strain energy in tendons and other tissues (as for a spring). Hildebrand (1985) considers the limbs as inverted pendula (cf. Cavagna, Heglund, & Taylor, 1977; McCollum & Leen, 1989), and the tendons and ligaments as springs. In trotting, hopping, and running, there is a minimum exchange of kinetic and potential energy because of the phase relations of the legs acting as inverted pendula, and because the long tendons of the ankle and knee extensors store elastic strain (Alexander & Bennet-Clark, 1977).

Lessons from robotics: Capitalizing on mass-spring systems. As in physiology, attempts in the field of robotics to create mechanical analogs of motile insects have sought the constraints which transform the output of endogenous oscillator circuits into organized patterns of gait. Significantly, however, in building devices which must function under specific terrestrial (and extraterrestrial) conditions, scientists in robotics have begun to confront not only internal or computational sources of constraint on locomotion, but also the constraints of morphology (e.g., different numbers of legs), biomechanics (e.g., the reactive forces generated by a biokinematic chain), and the informational structure of the ambient optic array (e.g., information which specifies that a surface affords support for a body with certain properties but not others).

For example, attempts by Raibert (1986a,b; Raibert & Sutherland, 1983) to build mechanical devices capable of dynamic balance have been most successful when they have capitalized on the properties of energy dissipation of an oscillatory system. Raibert has devised a computer-controlled "hopper" which mimics the mass-spring properties of the mammalian leg during vertical oscillations on a support surface. Three separate servocontrols are used for hopping in place as well as for changing position. The first controls the height of the hopping motion by adding or removing energy from the motion to make up for the energy dissipated during the hop; the second provides for balance by positioning the mechanical "foot" so the next landing is made in a balanced posture; and the third swings the leg forward at the hip in preparation for the next landing.

Raibert (1986a) makes an observation which has more general implications for devices, mechanical or biological, which capitalize on oscillation to achieve locomotion with dynamic balance. He found that it was not necessary to explicitly program the hopper to swing the leg back and forth. The swing was, instead, a natural outcome of the interplay of the servocontrols for balance and attitude. As we shall see below, infants appear to discover a similar strategy as they explore the motion of their spontaneous kicks.

THE HUMAN INTRAUTERINE ENVIRONMENT

Kicking as a fetal ontogenetic adaptation. Oppenheim (1981) proposes that the earliest kicking by the fetus is an ontogenetic adaptation for orienting the body into the vertex (head at cervix) position. But why does this ontogenetic adaptation begin at 28 weeks? One possibility is that the timing of maturation of the neural circuitry for kicking is scaled to body growth within the uterus. In this view, kicking begins because it becomes useful for locomotion relative to a surface of support: the body has grown sufficiently to fill the uterus and, as a consequence, the uterus may act as a surface which affords locomotion. It is between 28 and 36 weeks that fetuses actively kick, and also during this period that they succeed in changing their orientation to vertex. Thus, kicking may serve the specific function of orienting the body in anticipation of delivery (Oppenheim, 1981). This possibility is supported by the report of Langreder (1949) that babies born with paralyzed limbs are likely to be in an abnormal position at birth. Moreover, once they are in the vertex position (by around 36 weeks), there is a decrease in kicking, which may preserve this posture. Stable sleep–wake states emerge at around 36 weeks (Nijhuis, Martin, & Prechtl, 1984) and could serve to modulate posture and kicking at this time.

TRANSITION TO THE POSTNATAL ENVIRONMENT

The role of reflexes and spontaneous behavior in locomotor development. In Chapter 1, I discussed the relation between spontaneous order and regulation as a central issue in motor development. This issue appears in a different guise in the study of locomotion, namely, in the relation between the earliest locomotor reflexes and perceptually guided locomotion. Neurophysiological (Grillner, 1985) and neurological (Capute, Shapiro, Accardo,Wachtel, Ross, & Palmer, 1982) perspectives distinguish reflexes and temporally ordered behavior, respectively, according to their origins in the nervous system. For example, the spontaneous temporal order of the locomotor step cycle is traced to central pattern generators, while termination or prolongation of the cycle is regulated by spinal reflexes (Brooks, 1986). This distinction between rhythm and reflex has led to a controversy with respect to the development of locomotion, namely, whether there is continuity between early reflexive and later instrumental control over locomotion (see, e.g., Thelen, 1983; Zelazo, 1983), or whether the two are concurrent (McDonnell, 1979; McDonnell & Corkum, 1991).

In this section, I make the argument that whether a behavior appears reflexive or rhythmic may depend upon the parameter settings of an equation of motion that is the underlying control structure governing behavior (see Chapter 2). Reflexive and rhythmic behaviors may be emergent properties of this control structure and, when treated as such, the controversy over continuity versus concurrency may disappear. How can different settings of a parameter such as stiffness in an equation of motion result in different behavior?

McMahon (1984) demonstrates that stiffness regulation in the stretch reflex, can either damp out intrinsic oscillation or cause oscillations to grow. Whether an end effector oscillates reflects a balance between the function of the muscle spindles and tendon organs that regulate stiffness:

> afferent activity from both spindle receptors and tendon organs balances in such a way that neither muscle force nor muscle length should be considered the controlled quantity—rather, it is their ratio, the change in force per change in length, which appears to be fixed at a nearly constant value by the stretch reflex. (p. 149)

For example, consider the limb as a pendulum. Muscle force acts to supply restoring torque, and if it is proportional to muscle stretch, harmonic oscillation results. But when the stretch receptors controlling muscle force are regulated by rate of change of muscle length, damping stabilizes the oscillation.

Let us consider how stiffness regulation of oscillation may account for the data presented by Zelazo (1983), Thelen (1983), and McDonnell and Corkum (1991) on the role of reflexes in locomotor development. Zelazo (1983) offers a cognitivist interpretation of the effect of exercise on the neonatal stepping reflex. It had been a well-documented phenomenon that the so-called "stepping reflex" of newborns declines to a very low level or "disappears" by four or five months of age. In a now-classic study, Zelazo, Zelazo, and Kolb (1972) found that by using daily practice of stepping on a support surface while supported under the arms, it was possible to maintain the stepping pattern beyond that point, and accelerate the onset of voluntary walking. According to Zelazo (1983):

> The infant's newly emergent ability to generate specific associations quickly may allow the necessary integrative ability to permit the onset of independent walking. The rapid generation of associations may be necessary to elicit the correct motor adjustments needed to acquire balance and posturing. (p. 121)

Thelen (1983) offers several arguments against Zelazo's cognitivist interpretation. The most telling is her demonstration with kinematic and EMG data that supine kicking and upright stepping are identical movement patterns motivated by the same neural pathways. This presents a paradox: if they are the same, why does upright stepping disappear while supine kicking continues. The answer, Thelen suggests, has to do with body build: as infants mature the mass of their legs increases dramatically, and they do not have sufficient muscle strength to lift the legs when upright. She demonstrates this point by experiments which mitigate the effects of added mass (placing the legs in water), and experiments which add mass to babies who are still able to kick while upright. Babies with decreased load step more frequently, and babies who have mass added become unable to step. In other words, the stepping is context-specific.

Thelen also argues that the cognitive achievement Zelazo pinpoints at 12 months, the voluntary motive to move forward, is evident much earlier in infancy. Indeed, she suggests that the motivation to move forward is part of a very general motivation to explore in humans as well as in all but the most primitive animals. Why, then, do infants walk independently at about one year? Thelen (1983) suggests:

> What does contribute to this developmental milestone is the maturation of subcortical, and possible spinal pattern generating centers, and their integration with developing mechanisms for maintenance of balance in both static posture and during movement. At the same time, body proportions rapidly change to favor erect stance despite the inherent mechanical difficulties of such a posture. (p. 159)

The above discussion of parameterization is an extension of Thelen's point about the multiple determinants of independent walking. Spontaneous temporal order emerges from state dynamics, while reflex-like control emerges from parameter dynamics. Viewed in this way, the earliest neonatal reflex behavior may be interpreted as a dynamic system with parameters (e.g., stiffness) already established within a certain range of species-specific values. Spontaneous temporal order may be interpreted as the same dynamic system, but with parameters whose settings remain plastic. The two kinds of parameter settings, species-specific ones and more flexible ontogenetic ones, may be concurrent during certain periods in development. When infants explore the properties of their own body during kicking, the flexible parameters become more useful and (perhaps as a consequence of competition among widely distributed neural networks), these may come to control behavior. There is also continuity in development because the same dynamic system, i.e., the same collection of variables described by an equation of motion, governs behavior. The "reflex" look of behavior is an emergent consequence of parameters with species-specific values, while the "voluntary" appearance of the behavior reflects the possibility of selecting parameters that are useful for achieving particular goals.

A dynamic strategy for studying the development of stepping. Thelen and Ulrich (1991) adopt a dynamic strategy for understanding the development of treadmill stepping (see Table 10.2). They first identify a collective variable: alternating steps:

> Alternation requires an informational link between the legs such that the dynamic condition of one leg is used to regulate initiation and trajectory of the second leg. Single, parallel, and double steps may be purely mechanical, that is determined strictly by the potential energy stored by the stretched leg and the spring-like action of the limb when released. Thus, selecting alternating steps as a dependent variable captures the cooperative ability of the system to respond to the imposed task. (p. 52)

The nine infants in the study displayed a similar developmental pattern between 1 and 9 months: an initial period of only a few alternating steps, followed by a brief period of decline in steps and then a more steady increase lasting several months. During this same period, the stepping repertoire became dominated by alternating steps. Detailed kinematic analysis of relative phasing of bilateral steps in four of the infants indicated that each more closely approached the ideal phase lag of 0.5 (calculated on the basis of a ratio of step onset to cycle duration) after 4 months. By 6 months, this value stabilized and infants decreased the variability of their phase lags.

In the same way that developmental time was considered a "scalar" for the onset of the 0.5 phase cycle, belt speed of the treadmill was also used as a scalar to examine the effect of speed on phase. In mature locomotion the

Table 10.2. A dynamic systems research strategy for studying treadmill stepping

Strategy	Data to Evaluate Treadmill Stepping
1. Identify the collective variables of interest	Phasing of alternating steps on the treadmill
2. Characterize the behavioral attractor states at particular points in time	Stability of phasing as determined by within and between subject variability
3. Describe the dynamic trajectory of the collective variable	Individual longitudinal trajectories of phasing over time
4. Identify points of transition (characterized by loss of stability)	Variability within an individual's performance
5. Identify potential control parameters	Correlation between the time-dependent profile of the collective variable and putative control parameter
6. Manipulate putative control parameters to experimentally generate phase transitions	Not yet studied

Source: After Thelen and Ulrich, 1991.

duration of the step cycle depends upon the speed of forward motion. In the experimental situation used by Thelen and Ulrich (1991), belt speed could be systematically manipulated to examine whether treadmill stepping was a product of belt-independent pattern generation, or was determined by the belt as a driver. Thelen and Ulrich report that even in the early months, infants adjust cycle duration to the speed of the treadmill, suggesting that treadmill stepping is an attractor. If so, then stepping should be less vulnerable to disruption by perturbation.

Thelen and Ulrich introduced different kinds of experimental perturbations via the split-belt treadmill. One was a speed change after the first 5 s of a trial. They report that if the infant was producing alternating steps at the onset of perturbation, adjustment was immediate and rapid. In a second kind of perturbation, one leg was driven at twice the speed of the other by appropriately

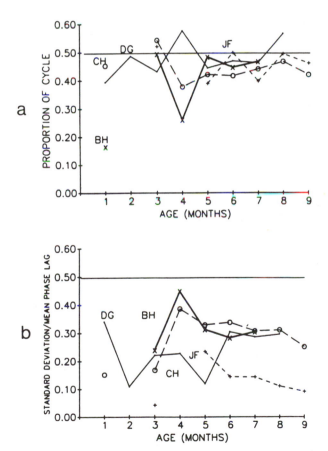

Figure 10.2. Mean relative phase lag (*a*) by infant and age pooled over trials, and (*b*) standard deviation/mean phase lag during infant treadmill stepping. (From Thelen & Ulrich, 1991. Copyright © 1991 by the Society for Research in Child Development. Reprinted by permission.)

adjusting the two belts. The results may be seen in Fig. 10.2. Phase lags approached the mature 0.5 of the cycle with increasing age, most notably at 5 months.

The final step in their research strategy involves identification of the putative control parameter underlying the abrupt phase shift at 5 months. They examined the relationship between the onset of the 0.5 phase lag and four possible control parameters: motor maturation (as measured by Bayley scale performance), body build characteristics, arousal level, and posture of the legs. Leg posture showed the strongest association with number of alternating steps, suggesting that it acted as a control parameter for treadmill stepping. What specific aspects of postural control are involved? Thelen and Ulrich suggest that the orientation of the leg and foot in relation to the moving belts played a crucial role in whether infants responded to the treadmill with alternating steps:

> If ... treadmill stepping is elicited either by the dynamic stretch of the leg backward on the moving belt or by some threshold value of the hip position, relative to the trunk. then the spring tension on the leg must permit this leg stretch. (p. 86)

Thelen and Ulrich note that newborns exhibit a characteristic flexor dominance in their limbs that only gradually wanes during the first 6 months (e.g., at around three months, the flexion phase of kicking and stepping is initiated by active muscle contraction, while leg extension results largely from passive elastic and inertial forces; Schneider et al., 1990). Thus, competition between flexors and extensors appear as a likely control parameter for treadmill stepping. Might this competition between flexors and extensors in different postural configurations be a more general control parameter in the development of locomotion?

TRANSITION TO INDEPENDENT MOBILITY: CRAWLING

Crawling: The classic observations. During the 1930s and 1940s, Arnold Gesell and Myrtle McGraw conducted a set of heroic descriptive studies of infant locomotion, deeply embedded in the scientific *zeitgeist* of the era. McGraw (1945) was greatly influenced by the contemporary studies by Conel (1929) of postmortem infant brain characteristics, such as myelination. She argued that purposive behavior was controlled by the cerebral cortex, reflexive behavior was controlled by subcortical nuclei, and that ontogeny of locomotion reflected the gradual control of the former over the latter. Gesell, a physician (see Gesell & Ames, 1940), drew upon more general principles from biology on growth. He asserted that observable changes in behavior reflected general principles of growth. These included the principles of developmental

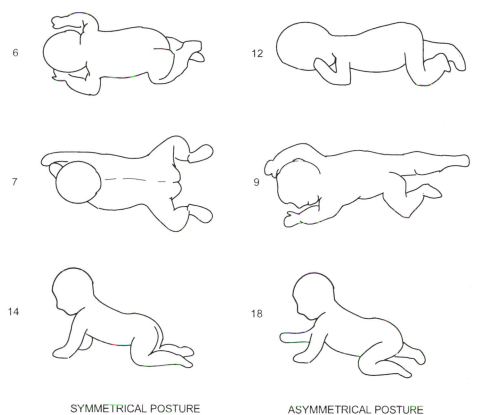

SYMMETRICAL POSTURE   ASYMMETRICAL POSTURE

Figure 10.3. The stage model of Gesell and Ames showing differences in lateral asymmetries during stages in the development of crawling. (After Gesell & Ames, 1940.)

direction (the cephalocaudal growth gradient) and reciprocal interweaving (a developmental fluctuation in dominance of flexors versus extensors and in unilateral versus bilateral muscle groups). He used these principles to organize his observations into a sequence of maturational stages (see Fig. 10.3).

Another look at crawling: A changing postural matrix. In a longitudinal study which I conducted (Goldfield, 1989, 1990, 1993), each of 15 infants was observed for a minimum of four weeks prior to the first time they were observed to crawl. This allowed a scoring of the ways in which they attempted to locomote prior to crawling. The definition of stages of prone locomotion proposed by Gesell and Ames (1940) was used to identify any of 10 different ways in which infants tried to locomote while prone (see Table 10.3).

The number of different ways infant attempted to locomote during the four weeks prior to crawling is presented as well. The range for the total over sessions was between 7 and 15, with one infant showing as many as 6 different

Table 10.3. Number of different modes of locomoting during 4 week prior to crawling

Infant	Week				No of Stages	Age at First Crawl (days)
	4	3	2	1		
P.C.	3	3	3	1	10	310
A.T.	2	3	1	1	7	286
M.H.	3	3	4	2	12	317
C.D.	2	2	4	1	9	281
A.C.	1	6	3	2	12	294
B.C.	3	2	4	4	13	249
A.G.	1	3	5	1	10	210
E.L.	4	3	3	3	13	243
T.C.	4	5	3	3	15	209
E.C.	2	5	3	1	11	261
K.M.	1	2	3	2	8	301
L.D.	3	2	5	1	11	252
R.A.	4	2	4	1	11	237
S.W.	4	3	2	3	12	273
E.U.	1	1	3	4	9	247

Source: After Goldfield, 1993.

ways of locomoting at one observation. In order to examine whether this variability was related to the appearance of stable forms of locomotion (i.e., stages) a correlation was computed between number of different ways of locomoting and age of acquisition of first crawl. Infants who showed the highest variability in ways of locomoting were also likely to be the earliest to crawl, suggesting, perhaps, that variability is associated with actively exploring ways to achieve a particular task, rather than with error relative to an ideal postural form.

According to Gesell and Ames, the stages evident in prone locomotion at different ages are ordered sequentially because of a principle of reciprocal interweaving: an alternation between periods of predominant symmetry and asymmetry of posture. By contrast, it is hypothesized here that these stages reflect particular combinations of the three functional capabilities of orienting, propulsion and steering (see Table 10.4.). So, for example, during rocking, the infant is able to orient the body to the support surface in order to maintain balance, but is unable to either propel the body forward or steer the body along the support surface.

A scalogram analysis was performed on the data organized according to the stage sequence above. Watson and Fischer have noted that because the usual error-counting procedures in the scalogram treat deletion sequences as error, they may grossly overestimate the occurrence of error. Therefore, following the procedure of Watson and Fischer (1977), a model of acquisition and deletion called "first-in-first-out" (Coombs & Smith, 1973) was adopted

Table 10.4. Interaction of three capabilities generating stages of locomotor behavior

Stage	Orienting	Propulsion	Steering
Pivot	No	No	Yes
Low creep	No	Yes	Yes
Rock	Yes	No	No
High creep	Yes	Yes	No
Crawl	Yes	Yes	Yes

Source: After Goldfield, 1993.

here. According to this model, each behavior is first acquired in the predicted sequence, and then drops out one by one in the same sequence. Two other patterns were also considered part of the acquisition–deletion sequence, rather than as error: the alternating pattern highlighted by Gesell (+ − + −, or − + − +), and the appearance of a stage at a later point, even though it was absent previously (− + − −, − − + −). Quite a few of the infants in this study exhibited a particular behavior at only one observation, and such data accounts for the latter pattern (see Table 10.5).

A procedure for scalogram analysis was used to compute a coefficient of reproducibility, CR, a measure of whether the sequence constitutes a scale. The sequence of six stages generated by the model in Table 10.2 was scalable. Thus, the stages observed here may reflect *unique combinations of capabilities whose*

Table 10.5. Distribution of observed stage patterns

Pattern				Frequency
−	−	−	−	12
+	−	−	−	13
+	+	−	−	8
+	+	+	−	3
+	+	+	+	0
−	+	+	+	4
−	−	+	+	1
−	−	−	+	5
−	+	−	−	13
−	−	+	−	6
+	−	+	−	11
−	+	−	+	3
−	+	+	−	5
+	−	+	+	1
+	−	−	+	3
+	+	−	+	12

Source: After Goldfield, 1993.

organization into an action system for locomoting results from specific constraints on the infant's active attempts to kick, reach, and maintain orientation to the surface of support.

Consider the case of locomotion. In his observations of prone locomotion, Gesell (1939, 1946; Gesell & Ames, 1940) proposed that, because the muscles are arranged in bilateral pairs, asymmetries in posture might serve the compensatory function of shifting posture from symmetry to an "eccentric" position. The two influences of biomechanical symmetry and behavioral asymmetry, he argued, were responsible for the alternating periods of symmetry and asymmetry observed in stages preceding crawling. However, because Gesell's emphasis on *posture* did not consider how specific postural constraints imposed by other developing capabilities might influence *the development of new movement patterns*, he left unanswered the question of how lateral asymmetry actually contributed to developmental change in locomotor capability.

Might Gesell's observation of alternating periods of symmetry and asymmetry reflect a competitive process between different functions? Prior to crawling, infants use both hands to support the body as the legs attempt to propel it forward (transport). In order to actually move forward along the support surface, though, one hand must be free to reach ahead to something which affords approach. Thus, in a sense, these two functional capabilities of the hands compete with each other when the infant tries to perform both at the same time: if he tries to reach he falls, and if he uses both hands for support he does not get anywhere.

The hands by themselves, in other words, are articulatory resources (Reed, 1988a) whose functional possibilities must be selected as the infant tries to perform certain tasks. Lateral asymmetry in the use of the hands may resolve this competition for resources by providing a means for division of labor between the hands: instead of performing the functions of support and transport *at the same time*, reaching out with one hand is temporally sequenced with the other to maintain support (with the legs, an adequate tripod stance). The temporal alternation between support (stance) and transport that we refer to as crawling may result from this selection of the use of one hand for reaching and the other to catch the fall precipitated by reaching. The need for stability may dictate the particular pattern that emerges.

To examine the possible functional significance of lateral asymmetry for selecting the functions of the hands, Goldfield (1989) observed each of the 15 infants in a condition in which they were encouraged by the mother to approach an object while seated on the floor. The overall hand preference of an infant was used to classify each as either right- or left-handed. A second coder, blind to this classification, scored the hand upon which the infant landed as he or she fell forward and landed onto the hands. If hand preference determined the sequencing of the hands in performing support and transport, then there should

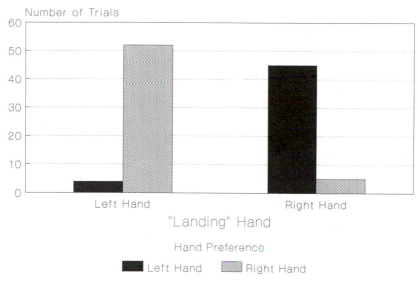

Figure 10.4. Number of trials during which infants fall from upright onto the right or left hand as a function of hand preference. (From Goldfield, 1989. Copyright © 1989 by the American Psychological Association. Reprinted by permission.)

be a close association between the hand which lands first on the support surface and the infant's preferred hand for reaching.

Figure 10.4 presents the number of trials on which infants fell onto their preferred or non-preferred hand (they never landed on both hands simultaneously). There was a strongly significant association between the infant's preferred hand for reaching and the order of hand contact with the support surface during falling onto the hands. Infants with a right-hand preference landed first significantly more often on their left (non-preferred) hand, and infants with a left-hand preference landed significantly more often on their right (non-preferred hand). Thus, in falling from upright into a crawl posture, infants appear to be landing in a way that leaves their preferred hand free to reach ahead of them as they begin to crawl.

A study by Kamm & Thelen (1989) supports this interpretation of these data. Each of five seated infants, on their first attempt at assuming a quadrupedal position, first rotated their sitting posture to face an object at a distance by pushing against the floor. They then leaned forward onto one hand, and either supported themselves or fell onto their abdomen because of the force of the fall. Three of the infants used the right hand for support significantly more than the left hand, and while the other two subjects showed no asymmetries in support hand use, they refused reaches on the left side for a number of weeks. Thus, there is a general postural anticipation of movement as infants prepare to locomote, and it appears that the orienting of the head and hand to one side is a fundamental part of this postural anticipation.

In the neuroscience tradition, lateral asymmetries in brain organization are used to explain both postural asymmetries and the timing of movement: behavioral asymmetries simply reflect asymmetries in the commands to the muscles. So, for example, Ramsay (1979) links right-hand preference for both reaching and tapping during infancy to left hemisphere specialization for speech. If, by contrast, we assume that the nervous system does not control, but only complements the forces generated by the limbs, how might we understand the role of lateral asymmetries in brain organization for the development of hand use in tasks such as reaching and quadrupedal locomotion?

If the muscles are abstractly like springs (see above), then one consequence of the influence of hemispheric asymmetry may be to differentially "tune" the elastic potential of the muscles on the left and right sides of the body. If so, then we would expect to observe a difference in the relative velocities of the right and left hands as infants alternate the use of the hands to perform the same act (i.e., reaching). Goldfield (1989) explored the possibility of asymmetries in the velocity of the hands during the first observations of infant crawling. The infant's preferred hand took less time to break contact with the support surface and then land again than did the non-preferred hand. Thus, as the infant first begins to fall in order to locomote, it appears as if the hands alternate support and transport because one hand gets to the support surface first. As the other hand lags behind the first during the fall forward, it is placed slightly ahead on the surface of support and the infant begins to crawl.

EXPLORING THE DYNAMICS OF THE BODY AS A CONSEQUENCE OF THE CHANGING POSTURAL MATRIX

Moving via locomotion and maintaining posture are functions which may sometimes compete with each other, and in so doing change dynamics. The function of posture is to achieve stability, the state in which uncontrolled movements of the perception and action systems are minimized (Riccio & Stoffregen, 1988, 1991). By contrast, locomotion has two functions: (1) mobility, getting an animal from one place to another, and (2) exploration, discovering sources of needed environmental support and paths to them (E. J. Gibson & Schmuckler, 1989). A task for the developing infant who is learning to locomote, then, is to learn to relax postural stability (i.e., exploit instability) in certain ways in order to become mobile, but without losing control entirely. This may involve the use of perceptual information in order to regulate the competition between postural control and movement.

Gibson and Schmuckler (1989) suggest that learning to locomote may involve the perceptual differentiation of peripheral and central radial optical flow for postural stability and locomotion, respectively:

Central radial flow is of prime utility for steering around obstacles and keeping on course during locomotion. Economical use of information in the array might be optimized by attention to such information for steering, whereas peripheral flow of smaller magnitudes, specifying staggers or wavering, would be left to control postural adjustments for staying upright. (p. 17)

One of the earliest opportunities infants have for exploring the perceptual consequences of mobility (central radial flow) for postural stability (peripheral flow) is during their early attempts at crawling. There is a period just prior to crawling when most infants will rock back and forth while on all fours without making any progression along the support surface (Goldfield, 1989). During the infant's first opportunities at rocking, the variability of its period is quite low, i.e., the oscillation is stable. However, over a period of days, period variability increases, and the infant eventually falls forward onto the ground. Concomitant with the increase in variability, one observes that the hands shift in their position on the support surface. How might we explain this transition? One possibility is that the infant is exploring central radial flow, largely to the exclusion of peripheral flow, because of the usefulness of this information for guiding independent mobility. The shift in position of the hands introduces instability into the oscillation, but the infant's attention to central flow allows the system to become posturally unstable. This postural instability may result in a transition to a new locomotor pattern: crawling.

FROM STANDING TO FIRST STEPS

What is the relationship between learning to stand and learning to walk? Woollacott and Sveistrup (1992) suggest that transitional periods in acquisition of standing and walking reflect alternate freezing and release of degrees of freedom (df) at certain joints. They characterize learning by three phases: (1) inability to control excessive df, which pushes infants outside the limits of postural stability (cf. McCollum & Leen, 1989), (2) reduction of df to simplify control, and (3) controlled release of df. Woollacott and Sveistrup find support for their model in changes of coordination during the transition to independent stance and walking between 7 and 14 months.

During pull to stand (at around 9 months), the components of limb movement occur separately and in different combinations. There is late onset latency and high variability of activation of hamstring (H) and trunk extensor (TE) muscles. As the infant gains experience in standing while locomoting via independent cruising (walking while holding on) at around 10 months, reduction of df begins. With the emergence of independent stance at 11 months, df are reduced to 1 by constraining sway to the ankle joint via increase in stiffness at the hip and knee. (The ankle may be chosen as a joint to control postural sway because it exhibits the slowest oscillations). When the infant begins to walk independently at around 13 months, there is once again evidence of multiple df at the hip and knee, but these are now controlled in the service of the task. The consequence of releasing df in a controlled way is that movement becomes both precise and rich via motor equivalence (Fentress, 1989; Woollacott & Sveistrup, 1992).

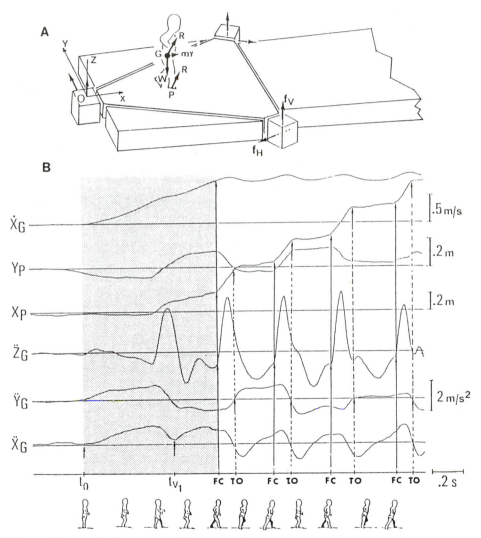

Figure 10.5. (A) The force plate and measures of the experimental parameters. (B) Sequence of steps of a child showing (1) the transient phase between upright posture and steady-state gait (in grey), (2) several steps at steady-state velocity. X_P is displacement of the center of pressure along the antero-posterior axis; $\dot{X}_G$ is the instantaneous velocity of the center of gravity along the antero-posterior axis. The double integrated terms X, Y, and Z give the acceleration at the center of gravity along the three axes. (From Bril & Breniere, 1991. Copyright © 1991 by North-Holland Press. Reprinted by permission.)

Another approach to the question of the relation between stance and the first steps is a study by Breniere, Bril, and Fontaine (1989). They offer evidence for the claim I make in Chapter 7 that controlled movement may emerge as a consequence of a competition between gravitational and muscular forces. During a transitional phase from upright stance to steady-state locomotion between 15 to 18 months, stable posture is upset when the infant allows the body to fall forward in order to initiate walking. Breniere and colleagues addressed two questions about this transitional phase: (1) Does the falling forward which initiates gait anticipate the characteristics of gait itself (i.e., steady state velocity)? And (2) is steady-state velocity achieved by the end of the first step, as in adults?

To address the first question, Breniere and colleagues used force plate data to examine displacement of the center of gravity during the period preceding the first step, what they refer to as instant t_{x_0} (see Fig. 10.5). In both children and adults, movement from a stable upright stance in order to initiate the first step occurs by falling forward. However, in adults, there is also a backward shift in the center of foot pressure before falling forward into the first step. This is considered evidence of anticipation of the upcoming first step and gait initiation. In the children participating in this study, there was no systematic shift of the center of foot pressure toward the heels. The children also differed from adults in the length of time it takes to reach steady-state velocity: adults reach steady-state at the end of the first step, but children require two to three steps to do so. Taken together, these data indicate that relatively new walkers do not use posture to anticipate gait as adults do.

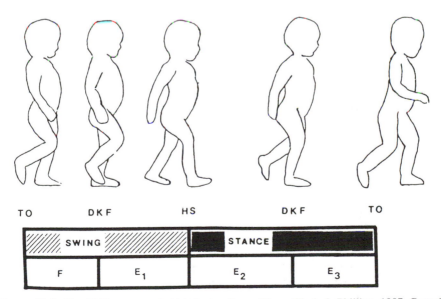

Figure 10.6. The Philippson cycle in infant walkers. (From Clark & Phillips, 1987. Copyright © 1987 by the Helen Dweight Reid Educational Foundation. Reprinted by permission.)

Once infant walkers reach steady-state velocity, their step-cycle organization is virtually identical to that of mature walkers. Clark and Phillips (1987) filmed infants who had been walking for between 3 and 10 months in order to examine whether their step cycle fit the familiar adult Philippson cycle. The Philippson cycle consists of four phases: (see Fig. 10.6): the swing phase (from toe-off to heel-strike) is divided into f and E1 phases. The F phase begins at toe-off and ends as knee extension begins during swing. The E1 phase begins at knee extension and ends at heel-strike. The stance phase (from heel-strike to toe-off) consists of E2 and E3 phases (Clark & Phillips, 1987).

Infants exhibited all four Philippson cycle phases in relatively the same proportion as that of mature walkers. Moreover, the infant walkers adjusted to differences in walking speed in the same way as adults, i.e., by shortening the duration of E3 (beginning with maximum knee flexion and ending with toe-off) during which force is applied. And finally, infants appear to have discovered how to exploit the dynamics of the swinging limb, because the swing phase (especially F) changes little with increases in speed.

From a dynamic perspective, the characteristics of the step cycle discovered by infant walkers involves the tapping of energy:

> The step cycle is a self-maintaining limit-cycle oscillator that taps energy during the E3 phase of the cycle and dissipates it throughout the remaining phases. ... The organization (i.e., the form) we see in the step cycle is one that emerges from the flow of energy—energy put in during the E3 phase. In this interpretation, the Philipsson step cycle is not specified by the central nervous system, but rather arises in accord with the physical law that governs biological systems. (Clark & Phillips, 1987, p. 432)

THE AFFORDANCES FOR LOCOMOTION

Adolph, Eppler, and Gibson (1993) have extended the Gibsonian taxonomy of affordances (see Chapter 3) to the ecological niche of the young infant learning to locomote. They distinguish several of the environmental properties which infants must discriminate in order to locomote effectively on a variety of support surfaces. In order to afford locomoting, a surface must be sturdy, sufficiently extended, free of barriers and obstacles, rigid, frictional, and relatively flat. Eleanor Gibson, of course, pioneered the use of the visual cliff apparatus to study how infants learn the relarionship between the properties of surfaces and their capabilities for locomotion (E. J. Gibson & Walk, 1960; Walk & Gibson, 1961). More recent work by Gibson and her students has systematically explored the locomotor behavior of infants when confronted with surfaces that vary in the above properties.

E. J. Gibson et al. (1987) examined the significance of rigid and deforming surfaces, which vary in the stability afforded for locomotion, on the behavior of crawling versus walking infants. When presented with a rigid plywood surface, which afforded crawling or walking, or a compliant waterbed, which only afforded crawling, the behavior of crawlers was distinctive from that of walkers. Walkers hesitated in crossing, performed more evasive activities, and haptically and visually explored more before traversing the waterbed by means of crawling. Moreover, in forced choice tasks, they preferred the rigid surface. By contrast, crawlers hardly hesitated in traversing either surface. Thus, crawlers, who have an effective and stable tripod for support, do not hesitate or explore the surface, because any surface will do. Walkers, on the other hand, who require a surface which will sustain balance for a style of locomotion using two points of contact with the ground, and promotes forward sway, explore more deliberately and select a more stable form of locomoting when crossing the waterbed.

What about surface friction? As is evident from viewing the classic film of McGraw in which one of a pair of twins (Johnny) is given enriched experience on slippery surfaces, there is a difference in behavior when descending as compared to ascending. On steep slopes, the adventurous infant would venture down the slope more slowly than when ascending, often losing the resistance of friction and sliding head first, to the gasps of undergraduate viewers in the audience. Adolph, Gibson and Eppler (1988) further investigated the behavior of 11- to 19-month-olds on differently textured 35-degree slopes (smooth, carpeted, slatted, and 3 by 3 stairs). The slopes rose to the four corners of a square central platform, and a child could choose any of the slopes to ascend or descend. Prior to attempting ascent, the children typically walked around the apparatus, visually exploring each slope. Similarly, they moved around the platform in a way that facilitated visual exploration prior to descent. Overall, the stairs, which offered the most support for traversal, were used most often for ascent and descent. This supports Adolph et al.'s claim that during exploration, these children were looking for information about the friction afforded by the surfaces.

Adolph, Eppler, and Gibson (1993) and Adolph and Eppler (1992) then pursued the question of the nature of the constraints of the developing body that might contribute to differences in the way crawlers (8.5 months old) versus walkers (14 months old) ascended and descended slopes varying in inclination (10, 20, 30, and 40 degrees) (see Fig. 10.7). All of the children attempted to ascend the slopes, even the steepest one, with little hesitation. By contrast, crawlers and walkers performed very differently when descending. Walkers hesitated longer, used haptic exploration before descending, and on the steepest slopes slid down without mishap. Crawlers, however, plunged down headfirst with little hesitation or haptic exploration, requiring recue by the experimenter. This suggests that the older infants are actively exploring the surfaces for information relevant to locomotion. But what is the nature of that information?

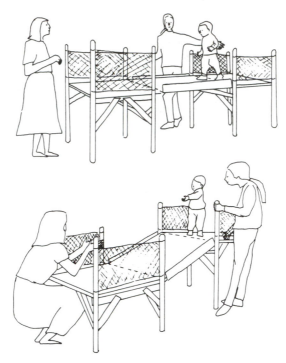

Figure 10.7. Walkway with adjustable slope. Top view: warm-up on flat walkway. Platforms at each end (71 cm high) allow walkway to be completely horizontal. Parent stands at far end of walkway while experimenter follows alongside child. Bottom view: descending trial. Platform at each end (71 and 39 cm) allow walkway to slant at 20 degrees. Parent beckons to child from far end of walkway while experimenter follows alongside. From Adolph, Eppler, & Gibson, 1993. Copyright © 1993 by the Society for Research in Child Development. Reprinted by permission.)

    While scaling the properties of the environment to dimensions of the body has proved to be an effective means of measuring the affordances for climbing (stairs) in adults (Warren, 1984), this is not the case for similar studies with infants. Ulrich, Thelen, and Niles (1990) failed to find a relationship between riser height for stairclimbing and body dimensions of infants. Adolph et al. (1993) suggest that the reason for this finding may be that body dimensions are only useful to describe affordance boundaries when between subject variability contributes to differences in size and mass rather than postural control, coordination, or muscle strength as in infants.
    In a break from the tradition of distinguishing infants solely on the basis of whether or not they have locomotor experience (see, e.g., Campos, Bertenthal, & Kermoian, 1992; discussed in Chapter 12), Adolph and Eppler (1992) have attempted to quantify the affordance boundaries for crawling versus walking by using the psychophysical technique of "staircasing": increments in the degree of slope is modified to suit each subject, and most

trials are presented near threshold. By increasing the slope until subjects fail or refuse to climb, it is possible to compute a ratio of failures to refusals as an index of affordance boundaries.

Another approach is suggested by the recent work with adults by Warren and Kay (1995). A motion analysis system records the displacement of markers placed at the joints of adults walking on a treadmill. As subjects walk, a large back-projection screen is used to present a computer-generated image of an optical flowfield specifying forward motion through a "corridor" (depicted by an appropriate stream of points). Because the computer display allows precise control over the composition of the flowfield, it is possible to introduce systematic optical perturbations in the flow, such as a lateral sway, and observe whether there are systematic changes in the dynamics of the markers during walking. Preliminary results indicate that sway influences certain aspects of the dynamics, but not others. Adult locomotion is a stable dynamic system, not easily perturbed. When there is greater instability, as in new walkers, the same kind of perturbation may be more disruptive. Stability, then, may be the key to affordance boundaries.

CHAPTER 11

THE PERFORMATORY ACTION SYSTEM: MANUAL ACTIVITY

Increase in size and a shift in diet appear to be two of the major factors involved in the evolution of prehensility in the primates. ... With increase in body size a critical point is reached where a potentially unstable system is produced and lateral displacement of the axis of gravity will lead to overbalancing. Without some compensatory trick such as prehensility, large animals would find it extremely difficult to move about among slender, leaf- and fruit-bearing branches and keep their balance.

Napier, 1980, pp. 92–93

In John Napier's lovely book entitled *Hands*, the structure and function of the human hand is placed within the context of primate evolution. In the evolution of primates, we see how a change in habitat from living among low shrubs on the forest floor to living in trees where food was more plentiful may have resulted in modification of the structure of the hand, most notably, into a hand with an opposable thumb (see Fig. 11.1). As Napier notes, in the epigraph at the head of this chapter, size seemed to have played an important role in the evolution of prehensility. There may also have been concomitant changes in the central nervous system that capitalized on the opening up of a new range of possibilities for action (e.g., holding a fruit in one hand while opening it with the other, reaching out rapidly to catch a branch during a precipitous fall). One possibility, for example, is that neural circuits relating Broca's region and prefrontal cortex became more highly specialized for control of co-articulation of the muscles of the hand and fingers as well as the vocal tract (Greenfield, 1991; Simonds & Scheibel, 1989). The processes discussed in Chapter 4 by which the brain is able to adapt to the structure of the body may have been involved during such evolutionary transformations of the hand (Purves, 1988).

A consequence of this phylogenetic transformation of primate morphology is that the human hand at birth is capable of "becoming" a variety of special-purpose devices for grasping, pounding, gesturing, and using a very wide array of objects as tools (see Fig. 11.2). This is captured nicely by Bruner

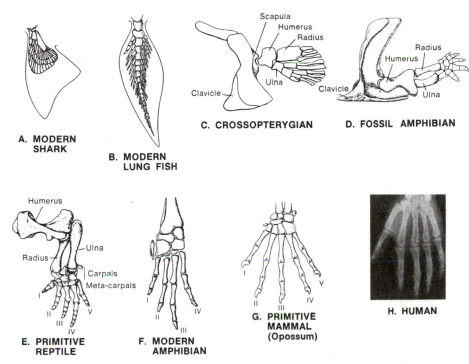

Figure 11.1. Evolution of the bony structure of the forelimbs. (From Shepherd, 1988. Copyright © 1988 by Oxford University Press, Inc. Reprinted by permission.)

(1971), who notes that the morphological change in the hand from monkey to human has tended toward despecialization:

> The hand is freed from its locomotor function, from its brachiating function, and from such specialized requirements as were answered by claws and by exotic forms of finger pads. Becoming more despecialized in function means becoming more varied in the functions that can be fulfilled. (p. 246)

At the same time, there is an ontogenetic change in the size of the hand as a consequence of growth and in the nature of the objects with which the infant comes into contact. A challenge for the developing infant is to discover the potentialities of the hand for acting under morphological and task constraints. In this Chapter, I discuss the process by which exploration by infants of the actions of the arm and hand in different task contexts may allow them to discover how to transform the hand into particular special-purpose devices. Throughout the chapter, I make use of Gibson's distinction between the performatory and exploratory functions of action systems. Keeping in mind the distinction between state, parameter, and graph dynamics, I begin by considering the functions of the hand and the special-purpose devices that accomplish these functions.

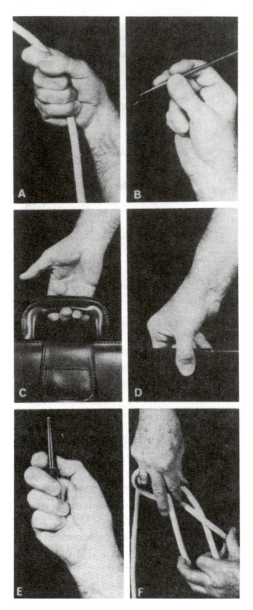

Figure 11.2. The hand becomes a variety of special-purpose devices. (From Shepherd, 1988. Copyright © 1988 by Oxford University Press, Inc. Reprinted by permission.)

CLASSIFYING THE FUNCTIONS OF THE HAND

Napier (1980) distinguishes two classes of movement of the hand, prehensile and non-prehensile:

> Prehensile movements are those in which an object, fixed or free, is held by gripping or pinching action between the digits and the palm. Non-prehensile movements of the whole hand include pushing, lifting, tapping and punching movements of the fingers. (p. 74)

Table 11.1. Functions of the hand as a
task-specific device

Function	Special-purpose device
Passive	Carrier, scooper, pusher
Percussive	Tapper, clapper, pounder
Expressive	Pointer, communicator
Exploratory	Groomer, toucher
Prehensile	Reacher, grasper

Source: After Wallace, Weeks, and Kelso, 1990.

A widely held functional taxonomy for prehensile movements of precision and power grips, respectively, is based upon the possible postural configurations that result from opposition between the thumb and the terminal pads of one or all of the other digits. The precison grip is made between the terminal digit pad of the opposed thumb and the pads of the fingertips, and the power grip between the surface of the fingers and the palm with the thumb acting as a "buttress" (Napier, 1980).

Elliott and Connolly (1984) propose a classification of movement patterns of the hands based upon which parts of the hand cooperate with each other. In simple synergies, all movements of the digits are the same, for example, the pinch is used when small objects are held between the pulp surfaces of the opposed thumb and index finger. Reciprocal synergies involve combinations of movements in which each of the participating fingers shows a different movement, for example, flexion of the fingers with adduction of the thumb while turning screwing a small freely turning nut (the twiddle). The final type of movement pattern is sequential, with the movement of the fingers pausing so they can be repositioned with respect to the surfaces of the object being manipulated.

Wallace, Weeks, and Kelso (1990) have organized non-prehensile movements into a group of functions for which there are a variety of instantiations, which I here refer to as special-purpose devices (see Table 11.1). From the standpoint of the theory of action systems proposed in this book, I consider the prehensile and non-prehensile functions as special-purpose devices. The advantage of conceptualizing such functions in dynamic terms, rather than just offering them as a taxonomy is that it becomes possible to examine how such functions are assembled, and how changing intentions and tasks allow the actor to switch between one function and another.

THE COOPERATION OF SUBSYSTEMS IN MANUAL ACTIVITY

The nervous subsystem. Different methodologies have been used to examine the possible roles of different brain areas, pathways, and circuits for

planning and executing manual activity. One of the most widely cited of these
is the use of lesion studies with monkeys to draw parallels to developmental
changes observed in that species and in human infancy. For example, the
studies of Kuypers (1962) and Lawrence and Hopkins (1976) show that there
is an association between development of the pyramidal tract and the onset of
independent hand and finger movements in monkeys. Researchers of human
infant reaching have interpreted these studies to mean that brain growth makes
possible specific changes in observable behavior (see, e.g., Hofsten, 1989;
Lockman & Ashmead, 1983). Similarly, the extensive studies of Diamond on
lesions to the prefrontal cortex of the monkey (see Diamond, 1991, for a
review), are related to the planning of complex manual acts (Hofsten, 1989).

Another methodology is to use neural networks to model the adaptive
control of human infant arm movements (e.g., Bullock & Grossberg, 1988,
1990; Gaudiano & Grossberg, 1992; Grossberg & Kuperstein, 1989; Kuperstein, 1988). Grossberg and his colleagues have drawn upon the observations
of Piaget on the the primary circular reaction to examine what parts of the brain
might enable an "infant robot" to learn to reach for objects that it sees. For
example, Grossberg and Kuperstein (1989) showed that the eye movement
system can use visual error signals to correct movement parameters via
cerebellar learning. Gaudiano and Grossberg (1992) propose that learning via
circular reactions is accomplished by associative learning from parietal cortex
to motor cortex.

A third methodology has been to examine correlations between structural
and functional changes in the brain and behavioral development. A case in
point is the assumption that the transition between early reflexive behavior
(e.g., the palmar reflex grasp) and later active exploratory use of the hands
reflects the development of cortical functioning (e.g., McGraw, 1941a,b, 1945).
Another example is the use of lateral preferences in hand use to make
inferences about the status of the functioning of the left hemisphere of the brain
(e.g., Liederman, 1988; Ramsay, 1983).

The musculotendon and link-segment subsystems. This chapter
highlights two ways in which developmental changes in the musculotendon
and link-segment system may influence dynamics: through control of muscle
properties (e.g., equilibrium point), and through changes in the size and
strength of the body. In Chapter 2, I discussed Bernstein's view that peripheral
biomechanics (reactive inertial, centripetal, and Coriolis torques) play a role in
giving form to temporal patterns of of multijoint rhythmic limb movements.
This has been demonstrated in simulation studies discussed by Saltzman
(1992). In his simulations, limit-cycle oscillators were defined for the shoulder
and elbow joints, respectively, and the elbow rest angle was systematically
varied while all other parameters were held constant. When plotted on an
angle–angle (Lissajous) plot, this simple parameter manipulation resulted in a

rich array of patterns. Moreover, there was an interval-ratio entrainment of the joints indicating that, even without explicit attempts to couple these oscillators, their limit-cycles were coupled through the reactive torques of the arm's intrinsic biomechanics (Saltzman, 1992). Saltzman interprets these findings as follows:

> These simulation data suggest a possible role for static equilibrium configuration (i.e., rest configuration) in multijoint rhythmic tasks may be the harnessing of pattern-forming properties (modal dynamics) that are intrinsic to selected regions of the workspace. . . . This formative power may be exploited at the highest levels of skill acquisition, when and if it fosters the growth of modal patterns that are compatible with the constraints and goals of an intended task. (p. 245)

A study by Thelen and her colleagues, discussed below, suggests that this interaction between the peripheral musculature and temporal patterning is involved in the acquisition of reaching by infants. The nervous systems of infants who initially attempt to secure an object by wildly flailing the arms may gradually adjust the parameter for equilibrium setting and, in so doing, transform a limit-cycle oscillation into a discrete reach.

While it is evident that the arm and hand undergo rapid growth during infancy, there has been little research on the question of the effect of limb growth on the development of manual activity. An apparent challenge for the developing nervous system is to be able to recalibrate control parameters for reaching as the arm lengthens and the span of the hand grasp increases. The demonstration that cortical maps of monkeys shift their boundaries following experimental removal of a portion of a finger suggests the possibility that growth-related recalibration may employ a similar mechanism (Kaas, 1991) (see Fig. 11.3). There are two phenomena, reviewed below, which suggest that visual experience during the active use of the arms and hands makes such recalibration possible: the oft-noted observation of the prolonged gazing at the hands by infants just prior to the onset of visually guided reaching (see, e.g., Piaget, 1952), and the classic findings by Held and colleagues on the significance of self-produced action for development of visually guided limb placement (e.g., Held & Bauer, 1966). But there is also other evidence which suggests that proprioception may also play a critical role in learning to use the hands.

One of the techniques for understanding the nature of cooperation between the brain and growing arms and hands in the control of manual activity is to formulate equations of motion to quantify the dynamics of the interconnected segments of the arm and hand (see below). To do so, however, requires anthropometric measures. Schneider and Zernicke (1992) used measurements from 70 infants to formulate linear regression equations. These equations, can be used to predict limb parameters for the equations of motion.

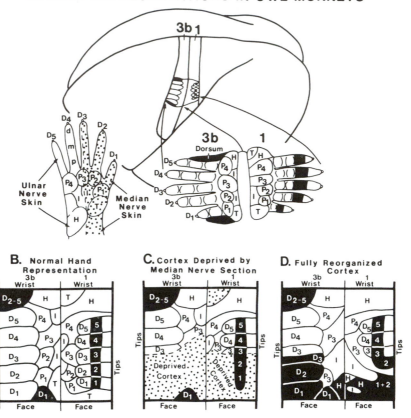

A. HAND REPRESENTATIONS IN OWL MONKEYS

Figure 11.3. The reorganization of the hand representations in Areas 3B and 1 of somatosensory cortex of monkeys after section of the median nerve. (A) The location and normal somatotopic organization of the two hand representations are indicated on a dorsolateral view of the owl monkey brain. The two representations are basically mirror images of each other, adjoined at the 3b/1 border; the major difference is in the representation of dorsal digit and hand surfaces (black). The median nerve subserves the glabrous skin of the medial hand, while the ulnar nerve innervates the dorsal and glabrous surfaces of the lateral hand. The rest of the hand is subserved by the radial nerve. Digits and palmar pads are numbered in order, insular (I), hypothenar (H), thenar (T) pads, and distal (d), middle (m), and proximal (p) phalanges are indicated. (B) The normal hand representations are schematically portrayed in more detail. (C). The cortex normally devoted to the median nerve is marked by dots (the deprived cortex). The organization of hand representations after complete reactivation following median nerve section. Much of the deprived cortex is activated by stimulation of the dorsal hand and digit surfaces (black). In addition, palmar pads innervated by the ulnar nerve have increased their cortical representation. The ulnar and radial nerves do not grow into the anesthetic skin. (From Kaas, Merzenich, & Killackey, 1983. Copyright © 1983 by Annual Reviews, Inc. Reprinted by permission.)

CONSTRAINTS ON MANUAL ACTIVITY

State-specific influences on manual activity. Several studies have demonstrated that there are specific state-related postures and movements of the hand during the first weeks of life (Fogel & Hannan, 1985; Legerstee, Corter, & Kienapple, 1990; Trevarthen, 1977). For example, Fogel and Hannan (1985) found that between 9 and 15 weeks, infants were more likely to point before or after mouthing, spread their fingers when looking away from mother, and curl their fingers during vocalizations.

In Chapter 1, I discussed Wolff's definition of states as the possible configurations of collective variables. Other investigators equate states with arousal, but that is not the same as state as a collective variable. Instead, arousal is a continuous variable, a control parameter. Arousal may drive the collective variable, here the degrees of freedom (df) of the musculotendon and link segments variables of the hand, into different stable configurations, but arousal itself is not a state. For example, because the CURL gesture precedes or follows all other hand actions, it may be a neutral or rest state during low arousal. In the context of the mother present and engaging the baby (Legerstee et al., 1990), a state of moderate arousal, shifts of attention to and away from the mother are accompanied by a POINT. During POINT, the df assemble into a gesture in which the index finger is extended, while the others remain curled. By contrast, when the baby is looking away from the mother, the hand changes from CURL to SPREAD (fingers extended). Here, there is still a moderate level of arousal, but when that increases, the fingers CLOSE into a fist.

One way to think about the relation between arousal and specific configurations of the hand is with respect to an example from von Holst and Saint Paul discussed by Kelso and Schoner (1987). Von Holst and Saint Paul found that when they applied electrical stimulation to an electrode in a fixed position in the brainstem of a domestic fowl, the behavior of the bird progressed through a predictable series of behaviors: looking about, standing up, walking, crouching, flying away). Kelso and Schoner interpret the behaviors as collective variables being driven by changes in stimulus strength or electrode depth. From a developmental standpoint the idea that arousal may drive collective variables like the df of the hand into different postures is appealing. Developmental changes in the differentiation of those behaviors may be interpreted as differential influences of tuning and gating of the control parameters (an idea I return to later in this chapter).

Competing goals. Different control parameters may attempt to influence the df of the hand as a consequence of the goals of a particular action system, such as appetition or basic orienting. For example, in Chapter 9, I suggested that during an organismic drive state of hunger, spontaneous rhythmic movements of the mouth are coupled to flexions of the arm that bring the hand to the mouth for feeding. Blass et al. (1989) describe this coupling as follows:

> One possible mechanism for engaging hand–mouth coordination, therefore, is that there is a threshold for mouthing expressed in frequency, intensity, or duration, that must be achieved before the hands are brought to the mouth. Stated differently, the hand may be recruited to the mouth through activation of the oral motor system and not directly by the sensory qualities of the stimulus that activated this system. (p. 970)

Similarly, in Chapter 10, I suggested that when an object affords approach for the prone infant, the hands are used cooperatively as part of the locomotor action system. While prone, where the hand is placed relative to the shoulder may introduce postural instability, and propel the body forward. In the next section, I extend the idea that competing influences on the hands influence their actions by examining how head turning (the basic orienting system) promotes extension of the arm via the asymmetric tonic neck response (ATNR).

The ATNR. We saw in Casaer's studies of neonatal posture in Chapter 8 that mouthing tends to bring limbs toward the mouth via *flexion*. My emphasis here is on the way in which objects in the visual field may activate head turning, and in so doing may set the parameters of the arm and hand for *extension* in the direction of the object. Consider an observation by Bullinger (1981). Infants as young as 3 days old who have their head supported while they are seated upright are able to orient toward a visual target placed at eye level and track moving objects with head rotations. However, it may take up to 15 s for the head, initially turned to one side, to stabilize in a new position: there is a sudden acceleration toward the target, an oscillation, and then a stabilization into a new position on the other side oriented toward the object. Amiel-Tison (1985) reports a similar finding with respect to head control and reaching. When the head of the newborn is supported by an adult, reaching becomes more accurately directed toward a target.

These observations of the influence of head orientation on manual activity are highly suggestive of changing patterns of equilibrium point control. In Chapter 4, muscle was described as mechanically analogous to a spring, with the consequence that movement could be conceived of as a series of equilibrium points between opposing spring like forces. As described by Mussa-Ivaldi and Bizzi (1989):

> The muscle is characterized by a set of integrable functions between length and tension at steady state. Neural input selects a particular function (length–tension curve) out of this set. Then for any given value of muscle activation, the position at which the length dependent forces due to opposing muscles are equal defines an equilibrium position and a stiffness at a joint. (p. 776)

The arm may exhibit point-attractor dynamics, with the equation of motion for arm movement including a parameter for equilibrium position, influenced by the ATNR (see below for a further discussion of this point). As the object moves across the visual field, there may be a slow resetting of equilibrium position, and the head is moved in a ballistic fashion until it achieves that position (equifinality, see Chapter 2). At the same time that the head position is changing, there is an extension of the arm in the direction of head orientation. Here, the hand may be enslaved to the function of orienting by the eye–head system, but only temporarily. As soon as the infant habituates to the object or person, oral movements may bring the hand back to the mouth. This switching of "masters" attests to the soft assembly of special-purpose devices when activated under the constraints of different functions.

The body midline. Another postural constraint on reaching is the body midline. Provine and Westerman (1979) examined the development of the ability of a group of 9 to 20-week-olds to extend one hand across the body midline to touch an object while the other hand was restrained beneath a blanket wrapped around the body. The object was presented either at body midline, in front of the ipsilateral shoulder, or in front of the contralateral shoulder. While even the youngest infants touched the objects when it was ipsilateral to the free hand, it was not until 15 weeks that most infants crossed the midline to touch the object when it was in a contralateral position. Provine and Westerman propose that this developmental change might reflect the formation of "commisural neural circuits that integrate and coordinate activity on the two sides of the body" (p. 441). Another, dynamic, explanation might be that it is more difficult to maintain balance when lifting the arm across the center of the body (especially with the other arm restrained out of view).

THE RELATION BETWEEN REACHING AND GRASPING

Two components. Jeannerod (1984) has identified two components of adult prehension; consistent with the idea that there are different coordinative structures for reaching and grasping. A reaching or *transportation* component moves the arm and hand within a body-centered space, while a *manipulation* component makes contact with and conforms to the properties of objects (see Table 11.2). Both of these performatory components appear also to serve exploratory functions: transportation permits infants to prepare for encounters with objects by "pointing their feelers toward them" (Hofsten, 1982), while manipulation sustains the perception–action cycle. How are these components related to each other developmentally?

The transport component. There are several studies which demonstrate that infant reaches during the first year consist of a sequencing of movement

Table 11.2. Development of transport and manipulation functions of the hands

	Transport	Manipulation
Direction	Newborns exhibit arm extensions toward visually perceived objects	
Distance	There are more frequent arm movements toward objects that are within reach than those beyond reach; by five months, the extent of an arm movement is adjusted to object distance	Between 5 and 7 months, infants begin to align fingers around an object as the hand approaches it
Size	Infants use two hands for larger objects	Infants vary the distance between thumb and finger to match the size of a graspable object
Orientation	Five-month-olds rotate the hand while keeping the digits in position to make a grasping movement only after contacting the rod. Nine-month-olds rotate their hands on the basis of visual information during the approach phase of the reach	

units, and of a roughly straight trajectory also seen in the single transport component of adult reaches (Fetters & Todd, 1987; Hofsten & Lindhagen, 1979; Hofsten, 1991; Mathew & Cook, 1990). In the first such study, Hofsten and Lindhagen (1979) used velocity profiles to divide movement into units consisting of one acceleration and one deceleration. He found that the earliest successful reaches at 15 to 18 weeks consisted of several of these units. Fetters and Todd (1987) further examined the "unit" question by comparing the inflection points of speed (slowing down) with curvature peaks. They report the same coupling of speed and curvature seen in adults.

Consistent with an earlier study by Mathew and Cook (1990), Hofsten (1991) has found developmental changes in the structure of reaching movements between 19 and 31 weeks, suggesting that infant reaching is controlled by equilibrium position, and that this control improves with age. Hofsten reports that there was one unit that moved the hand a longer distance than others, what he calls a transport unit (cf. Jeannerod, 1984). Over repeated observations every 3 weeks, Hofsten found that (1) by 31 weeks, most reaches begin with the transport unit, (2) the transport unit increases in duration and covers a larger proportion of the approach (while remaining units changed little), (3) there was a decreasing number of units in a reach, with 58 percent of reaches having just two units by 31 weeks (as in adults), and (4) there was a straightening of reach trajectories.

The manipulation component. A classic cross-sectional study of the relation between reach and grasp was conducted in 1931 by H.M. Halverson, a colleague of Gesell at Yale. Halverson (1931,1932, 1937) did careful cinematographic analyses of infants between 16 and 52 weeks of age when presented with a 1-inch cube. Among the variables examined in the study were how long the infant initially looked at the cube before reaching, descriptions of the trajectory, hand orientation and thumb position during approach, types of grasp, and methods of lifting the cube. In other words, Halverson presaged many of the contemporary kinematic analyses on manual activity. There are convergent findings pointing to a transition at 28 weeks in the way that the hand is controlled during its approach to the cube. Halverson (1931) finds:

1. Heightened duration of looking at the cube before reaching at 28 weeks, as compared with other ages.
2. A decrease in the number of changes of direction of the hand during approach to the object.
3. A change from circuitous to straight-line trajectories.
4. Rotation of the hand prior to making contact with the cube more prominent beginning at 28 weeks.
5. Up until 28 weeks, infants raise their hands relatively high in reaching for the cube; this diminishes between 28 and 52 weeks.
6. Instead of directing the entire hand towards the cube, the infant begins to point the hand so that the index and medius fingers pass over the cube.

As we shall see below, these changes are suggestive of anticipatory control of reaching as a function of the visually perceived properties of the object to be grasped.

This early study by Halverson is most often cited for its classification of types of grasp in a particular order of acquisition during the period from 16 to 52 weeks. The most notable features of the transitions in these grasp types are in the increasing use of the thumb rather than the palm for taking hold of the cube, and a change in the manner of approach (e.g., the orientation of the fingers). Halverson concludes from the apparent progression in the use of these different types of grasp that they reflect growth-related change in the size of the hand and in its perceptual capabilities.

In a more recent study of infant grasp, Newell, Scully, McDonald, and Baillargeon (1989) question Halverson's conclusion about the progression of types of grasp because that study only used a 1-inch cube. They propose that with different task constraints, a different set of grip configurations would be evident (see Fig. 11.4). When they systematically manipulated object size, Newell et al. found that even infants as young as 4 months could differentiate grip configurations (by using the fingertips) as a function of object properties. However, while at 4 months, infants require haptic information to adjust grip (i.e., they shape the hand only after object contact), between 4 and 8 months, they shape the hand prior to contact.

Newell et al. emphasize in their data the change in grip configuration with age. It is interesting to note that Halverson (1931) seemed to also recognize the

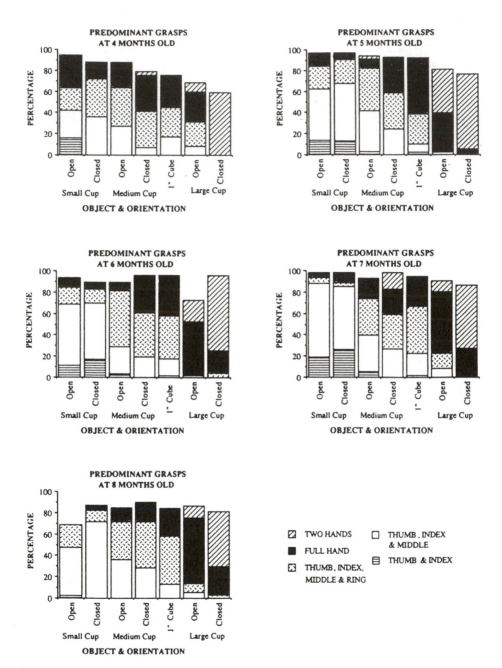

Figure 11.4. Percentage of the five predominant grip configurations as a function of age and object properties (T = thumb, I = index finger, M = middle finger, and R = ring finger). (From Newell, Scully, McDonald, & Baillargeon, 1989. Copyright © 1989 by John Wiley and Sons, Inc. Reprinted by permission.)

changing role of perceptual information for regulating a characteristic of grip, namely, force:

> Young infants from birth to 6 months exhibit a grasp of a force entirely disproportionate with the pressure necessary to hold and lift the seized object. . . . As the age of the infant increases, the force of the grip diminishes, until at 52 weeks he takes the cube with the fingertips in a manner which suggests the presence of some appreciation of the amount of pressure required to lift and hold the cube. (pp. 258–259)

The idea that infants become better able to anticipate the force required for acting upon an object based solely on visual perceptual information is supported by a series of studies by Mounoud and his colleagues (Mounoud, 1973; Mounoud & Hauert, 1982). Infants were repeatedly handed an object, which was then replaced by one that was identical in appearance, but much lighter in weight. If the infant was using visual information to anticipate the mass of the object, then the arm should suddenly rise when the object is grasped and lifted. This anticipatory response is not seen until about 9 months. I return to the question of the role of vision in anticipatory guidance of the hand after considering the earliest reaches.

FROM PRE-REACHING TO VISUALLY GUIDED REACHING

Is the earliest reaching reflexive? As in locomotion, there has been a longstanding controversy over the role of early reflexes for later voluntary activity in grasping and reaching Twitchell (1965, 1970) suggests that the idea that voluntary grasping emerges from a primitive reflex is an over-simplification, since it is possible to distinguish different types of early grasps, and because avoidance is also part of the learning that takes place. McGraw (1941b) makes a similar observation, noting the distinction between grasping that is part of the suspension-grasp reflex and grasping that is a visually elicited response to objects.

Twitchell (1965, 1970) identifies three kinds of reflexive responses of the arm and hand in the first four months: the neonatal traction response, the grasp reflex (2 to 8 weeks), and the instinctive grasp reaction (20 to 44 weeks). The neonatal traction response is a flexor synergy of the upper limb elicited by stretching the shoulder flexor and adductor muscles. Contact with the palm is not the adequate stimulus. Instead, finger flexion occurs as part of the synergistic flexion at all the joints during shoulder flexion. In the grasp reflex, contact stimulation of the palm causes all the fingers to flex. Initially, the grasp reflex remains synergically linked to the traction response, but gradually becomes differentiated from it. Then, between 16 and 20 weeks, there is a "fractionation" of the grasp reflex, with the possibility of isolated flexion of each of the fingers.

What distinguishes the instinctive orientation response from the other two is an active orientation of the hand as a function of where it is stimulated, beginning at about 16 weeks. Initially, stimulation of the radial part of the hand leads to supination, and then gradually, ulnar stimulation leads to pronation. About four weeks later, contact stimulation of the hand leads to directional orienting and to palpating movement, eventuating in adjusting to the object with the finger closing around it. At the same time (between 12 and 20 weeks), one begins to see an avoidance reaction develop to an object when the infant is irritable.

Pre-reaching. In early work on precursors to visually guided reaching, White, Castle, and Held (1964) (discussed further below) argued that during the earliest reaches by 2-month-olds, the grasp reflex keeps the hand in a fisted position, precluding the use of visual information to regulate the opening of the hand to objects. However, in a study by Bower (1972) with 2-week-olds, it was found that hand span was appropriately accommodated when an object was present. While Ruff and Halton (1978) failed to replicate these findings, DiFranco, Muir, and Dodwell (1978) further examined the question and found some full-arm raises with hands shaped to fit the target, what Trevarthen (1974) subsequently called "pre-reaches."

One of the methodological problems with the earlier studies was the use of a single camera and static objects. Hofsten (1982) remedied these problems by using two cameras for a three-dimensional analysis of newborn arm and hand movements when presented with a slow and irregularly moving object. Hofsten was first able to show that failure to replicate Bower was probably due to a confounding of general level of motor activity. In a second experiment, he measured the accuracy of aim of the hand toward the object, with the idea that aiming would occur only if there was eye–hand coordination. When neonates visually fixated the object, their movements were aimed closer to the object (although rarely hitting it) than when they were not fixating it. Head orientation included active looking, and was not simply a passive consequence of the ATNR, since the aim of contralateral reaches was significantly better than ipsilateral ones. The hand slows down as it reaches the object, and opens in preparation to contact in about half of reaches during visual fixation.

Hofsten concludes that early coordination of reach and grasp reflects the early functioning of the basic orienting system:

> Manipulation of objects in the surrounding is not the sole function of the hand. The arm and hand also constitute an important information gathering system. The function of neonate reaching seems to be attentional rather than manipulative. When the neonate looks at an object and reaches out for it, both the reaching and the looking are parts of the same orienting response toward the object. (p. 460)

Of course, Hofsten may be only partly correct. In at least half of the reaches, manipulation/grasping is anticipated by the neonate. This may be a manipulative function in addition to, rather than instead of, an orienting function.

On the view of task dynamics that infants may assemble a "virtual arm" for a particular task (see below), how might basic orienting be involved in reaching and grasping? Consider the different postural constraints on adults imposed during two performatory tasks: lifting and aiming. In lifting an object that is relatively heavy, the shoulder, trunk, and perhaps leg muscles must be recruited to assist arm flexion. By contrast, when performing a movement of the hand that requires high precision, such as aiming the hand toward a target (e.g., Asatryan & Feldman, 1965), shoulder and trunk muscles must act as "fixers" so that the body can serve as a stable platform (Greene, 1982).

An implication of such postural constraints is that observed developmental changes in transport and manipulation may reflect a process of differentiation of control of certain muscle groups, or *selection* (see Chapter 6). Greene (1982) suggests that this process of selection in skill acquisition may involve three components:

1. Create basic synergies by channeling excitation to all of a set of functionally related muscles while not exceeding the limits of such a set (e.g., a synergy of trunk and arm muscles for transport of the arm) (here called assembly; see Chapter 7).
2. Split individual joints away from the basic synergy and control them separately (e.g., fingers for grasping).
3. Inhibit unwanted components of motion either by inhibiting particular muscles or fixating trunk and limb for stability.

In other words, pre-reaching may reflect the assembly of a task-specific device for reaching, but one that is only an approximate solution, with exploratory and performatory activity not yet differentiated in the perception–action cycle. As infants have the opportunity to hold objects in the hand, grasping begins to take on a new function: active orientation to the properties of things that afford grasping. The grasp as a differentiated part of a reach–grasp system develops only later. In the next sections, I consider how this differentiation may come about. It is only when vision is used *in parallel* to both guide the hand to the target and prepare the hand to grasp the object that such differentiation can occur .

Visually guided reaching. Following upon the observations of Piaget that were so influential in the 1960s, White et al. (1964) conducted a longitudinal study of the development of visually guided reaching in a group of 34 infants reared in an institution (due to "inadequate family conditions"). The rationale for this and later studies by White was to identify a group of infants with whom it would be possible to perform a study of visual enrichment, and so explore the role of vision in reaching.

White et al. (1964) first documented a normative longitudinal sequence of eye–hand coordination between 2 and 6 months. They propose that initially, the dominance of postural reflexes and immature vision prevent the infant from looking at the hands at midline. Beginning at around 2 months, the ATNR "drops out," releasing the arms from their asymmetric posture. The consequence is that the hands begin to explore each other at midline, but there is little visual regard of the hands. At the same time, infants begin active swiping at a seen object, but with fisted hands. By 3 months, when the eyes can converge upon objects within reach, infants begin to spend considerable amounts of time looking at their hands at midline. Swiping is replaced by a prehensory response in which the hand is raised close to a stationary object, followed by a series of alternating glances from object to hand and back. Between 3 and 4 months, grasping is still not yet oriented to the object, but remains centered on tactual exploration between the hands. It is not until between 4 and 5 months that alternating visual glances "become coordinated with the slow moving of the hand directly to the object which is fumbled at and slowly grasped" (p. 360).

In subsequent work, White (1969) used an enrichment paradigm (cf. Bertenthal & Campos, 1987) to identify the ways in which two components in the normative sequence—tactual interplay of hands and swiping—were influenced by different kinds of visual experience. Enrichment consisted of particular conditions of extra handling, increased mobility, introduction of colorful mobiles, attachment of colorful, graspable pacifiers to the side rails of the crib, and placing patterned mitts on the hands. Each of these had specific effects, most notably, the earlier onset of swiping and mature visually guided reaching in the pacifier condition.

More recent work on visually guided reaching has focused on the ability of infants to use vision to anticipate the trajectories of moving objects. As discussed earlier, during pre-reaching, newborns get close to a moving object, but rarely touch it. By 18 weeks, they use visual information about the trajectory of a moving object to begin reaching for an object before it actually comes within reach of their hand. Hofsten and Lindhagen (1979) and Hofsten (1980, 1983) analyzed three-dimensional reach trajectories and found that reaches were aimed at the point where the hand will in the future reach the object, a "predictive strategy." Even with a fast-moving object (60 cm/s), aiming is accurate and there is little timing error.

Hofsten and Ronnqvist (1988) were interested in the developing coordination between reach and grasp. They examined the distance between thumb and index finger and between index finger and target during reaching by infants between 5 and 13 months of age for different-sized wooden spheres. The spheres were mounted in such a way that each could be moved around a vertical axis. The timing of the closing of the hand in relation to the encounter with the sphere changed significantly between 5 and 13 months. The younger infants closed the hand only after contacting the sphere. The 9-month-olds started closing the hand before contact, but the 13-month-olds did so significantly earlier in the reach. In order to examine whether reach and grasp are part of an integrated activity, Hofsten and Ronnqvist examined whether closing the hand interrupted the velocity of the hand (as measured by the curvature of approach). The 13-month-olds were less likely to interrupt the approach when the hand started to close than were the other two age groups.

Orienting the hand to the properties of the object. Earlier, I reviewed the studies of visually elicited ballistic reaches, and concluded that even very young infants appear sensitive to the direction of objects. More recent research has centered upon the adjustment of the hand to object distance, size, and orientation (see Bushnell & Boudreau, 1991, 1993, for reviews) . There appear to be systematic developmental changes during the first year in the properties of objects used to orient the hand during reaching. Object distance does not influence reaching until around 3 months, while infants do not adjust hand shape to object orientation until about 4 months. For example, when small rods were presented either vertically or horizontally to a group of 5-month-olds, they adjusted orientation of their hands as they contacted the rod. By contrast, 9-month-olds made hand orientations prior to actual contact. This suggests that infants initially use visual information to constrain degrees of freedom at the shoulder and elbow (for extension), and only later can simultaneously constrain together shoulder, elbow, and wrist (see Fig. 11.5).

The onset and decline of visually guided reaching. A curious trend in reaching concerns the changing roles of visual information (Bushnell, 1985). We have just seen that at birth, ballistic reaches are visually elicited, but vision is not used to correct trajectories that deviate from a direct path to a target. Visually guided reaching emerges at about 4 months, undergoes a period of intense practice, and then declines at about 9 months to be replaced by an "integrated sequence" that is quickly, accurately, and smoothly executed. What is the difference between pre-reaching and visually guided reaching? In the former errors are not informative, since the infant is not looking at the hand as it approaches the target. However, with visually guided reaching, they can adjust the relation between the seen target and the trajectory of the hand. Thus, visually elicited pre-reaching may decline in favor of visually guided reaching because it leads them to be more successful. Bushnell suggests that there is a shift in control during the transition from pre-reaching to reaching: pre-reaching is based upon a matching of the sight of the target with proprioceptive information, while reaching involves matching sight of the target with sight of the hand.

	OBJECT SUBSTITUTION	1 INCH CUBE	VARYING OBJECT PROPERTIES
NEWBORN		PRIMITIVE GRASP REFLEX	
1 MONTH			
2 MONTHS			
3 MONTHS			
4 MONTHS		POWER GRIP SQUEEZE	ADJUST NUMBER OF DIGITS USED TO GRASP AS A FUNCTION OF OBJECT SIZE, ONLY AFTER OBJECT CONTACT
5 MONTHS			
6 MONTHS	NO REACTION TO SUBSTITUTION OF LIGHT OBJECT FOR IDENTICALLY APPEARING HEAVY ONE		
7 MONTHS			
8 MONTHS		SUPERIOR PALM GRASP	
9 MONTHS	ARM SUDDENLY RISES DUE TO VISUAL ANTICIPATION		SHAPE HAND PRIOR TO OBJECT CONTACT ON THE BASIS OF ANTICIPATORY VISUAL INFORMATION
10 MONTHS			
11 MONTHS			
12 MONTHS		SUPERIOR FOREFINGER PRECURSOR GRASP	

Figure 11.5. Some trends in grasp during the first year for three different tasks: substituting a light object for a heavy one, presentation of a 1-inch cube, and presentation of objects of different size.

But if visually guided reaching is successful, why does it decline at around 9 months? Bushnell (1985) suggests that reaching becomes overlearned:

> the infant now knows so well how to get the seen hand to the seen target in any given location that he or she need not constantly monitor the gap between them to glean and make use of its information. (p. 149)

Bushnell characterizes "knowing" in terms of Bruner's ideas of automatization of the skill, release of attention required in guiding the behavior, and embedding the behavior as a component itself in a higher-order act (see, e.g., Bruner, 1973a). Others have argued that the emergence of knowing during this period may reflect the ability to "activate hypotheses" (Zelazo, 1979). In the sections below, I consider a dynamic alternative, namely that the transition from ballistic pre-reaching to visually guided reaching involves (1) an initial assembly of the degrees of freedom of the arm into a mass-spring system as a control structure (2) an exploration of the spring-like properties of the system, and (3) visual tuning of the stiffness and damping parameters of the system.

The significance of proprioception for reaching. While Bushnell (1985) has emphasized vision in both pre-reaching and reaching, other researchers have raised the question of whether vision is as important for the earliest reaches as Bushnell and others have suggested. In a departure from earlier paradigms, such as prism displacement studies (e.g., Lasky, 1977; McDonnell, 1975), Clifton and Ashmead and their colleagues (e.g., Ashmead, McCarty, Lucas, & Belvedere, 1993; Clifton, Muir, Ashmead, & Clarkson, 1993; Perris & Clifton, 1988) have shed light on the role of vision in early reaching by testing infants in the dark. Clifton et al. repeatedly presented objects in full lighting or glowing ojects in the dark to infants between 6 and 25 weeks of age. Even though infants could not see their hand or arm in the dark, infants first contacted the object in both conditions at around 12 weeks. This suggests that proprioceptive information guided these early reaches.

Ashmead et al. (1993) examined the role of vision in reaching by distinguishing the point at which during a reach perceptual information about locations of the target and the hand are incorporated. In a particularly clever variation of the darkened room procedure, the initiation of reaching by the infant triggered a burglar alarm which, on some trials, switched the illumination from one toy to another identical one placed adjacently. This effectively appeared as though the toy suddenly moved laterally. A motion analysis system was used to analyze whether adjustments to the apparent target movement occurred during a particular reach segment. It is important to note that the apparent movement occurred relatively late in the reach, likely during the second reach segment of the hand's trajectory to the target. Five-month-olds showed no adjustment for target switches, and 9-month-olds adjusted to target displacements only on those trials when they were wearing a visible marker on their hands. Because the adjustment occurred at the end of a segment, Ashmead et al. conclude that it is only the approach phase, the latter portion of a reach, that is under strong visual guidance. The early transport phase is apparently quite well aimed without the sight of the hand.

A DYNAMIC APPROACH TO REACH AND GRASP

Action units. Kinematic analyses such as those done by Hofsten and Fetters have identified control parameters, e.g., equilibrium points, which may change developmentally. However, these studies do not explain the assembly of the coordinated pattern of reaching in the first place, nor how changes in a control parameter might influence coordination. What is the nature of the control structure underlying the coordination of reach and grasp?

In line with the motor-action controversy discussed in Chapter 1, I suggest here that the unit of interest for examining the nature of the control structure underlying reaching movements is an *action unit*, the coordinative structure or special-purpose device (Saltzman & Kelso, 1987). Thus, while a movement unit (see Fetters & Todd, 1987) is defined by a kinematic trajectory, an action unit is defined as an invariant relationship among components of a complex system. Action units have three properties: (1) they are defined abstractly in a functional, task-specific manner, (2) they operate autonomously, i.e., the equations describing them are not explicit functions of an independent time variable, and (3) they are defined in the language of dynamics, not kinematics. This last point is critical for seeing how one can move from the kinematic data of Hofsten and Fetters to address the nature of the control regime underlying observed developmental changes in reaching. Control regimes:

> are defined by task-specific relationships among the system's dynamic parameters (e.g., stiffness, damping), and these relationships are specified according to the abstract functional demands of the performed skill. These control regimes serve to convert an effector system into the appropriate task-demanded special purpose device. Furthermore, a given dynamic regime generates motions that are characteristic of a particular skill and underlies the system's ability to compensate spontaneously for unpredicted disturbances. (Saltzman & Kelso, 1987, p. 86)

While Hofsten does not specify the nature of the control system underlying movement units, he does suggest that the answer lies with identifying brain structures involved in planning reaches. For example, in a commentary on several studies which used a dynamic systems approach to study the development of action, Hofsten (1989) turns to changes in the developing brain as an explanation for both the execution and planning of motor acts. He cites the work of Diamond (1988; and see Goldman-Rakic, Issaroff, Schwartz, & Bugbee, 1983) on the role of the prefrontal cortex in planning and Kuypers (e.g., Kuypers, 1982, 1985) on the role of the pyramidal pathways for the development of fine motor skills such as articulated finger movements. However, while it is clear that the brain plays a fundamental role in reaching, attributing an observed behavioral change to a particular brain system does not tell us anything about the nature of the control structure that the brain participates in (see, Goldfield, 1990; Beek & Bingham, 1991, and Chapter 1 of this book for a further discussion of this controversy).

A dynamic approach offers an immediate advantage to addressing the role of the brain in the organization and control of reaching and other action: the description of the control structure at the scale of observable behavior can be worked down to brain subsystems because the abstract nature of dynamics allows for scale independence (see Chapter 5) (Beek & Bingham, 1991; Haken, 1983; Schoner & Kelso, 1988). Let us, then, turn to some specific developmental data on reaching to see how a task-dynamic approach (developed with adult data) can address the question of the nature of the underlying control structure.

Thelen and her collaborators (e.g., Thelen et al., 1993; Zernicke & Schneider, 1993) have conducted an extensive longitudinal analysis of the dynamics of reaching in young infants. One of the most striking findings in this work is that some infants begin to reach by wildly flailing the arms, and only gradually come to perform the smooth reaching trajectories characteristic of the mature reach. Other infants hardly move at all prior to initiating a reach. There are two fundamental questions in this work: (1) what underlies the transition from the earliest arm flailing or small body movements to smooth reaches, and

Table 11.3. Individual styles in learning to reach

Infant	Context for Learning to Reach	Task in Learning to Reach	How Achieved (Torque Modulation)
Gabriel (reach onset at 15 weeks)	High velocity "flapping" via shoulder flexions and extensions of both arms in mirror-like movements	Control (damp out) energetic movements by stiffening limbs (i.e., use muscle co-activation and reduce velocity)	Use muscle torques at shoulder to counteract motion-dependent torques
Nathan (reach onset at 12 weeks)	Large and fast spontaneous movements of both arms, with greater magnitude of left	Control energetic movements by stiffening limbs	Use muscle torques, largely at elbow, to counteract both motion-dependent and gravitational torques
Justin (reach onset at 12 weeks)	Mostly unilateral, smaller, and less frequent movements	Scale up reach velocity and force	Control muscle torques at shoulder while increasing velocity and force
Hannah (reach onset at 22 weeks)	Small and slow movements; almost entirely unilateral	Scale up reach velocity and force	Gradually increase velocity via muscle torques at shoulder working primarily against gravity

Source: After Thelen et al., 1993.

(2) what characterizes the individual styles in reaching? Thelen et al. offer intriguing insights into each of these questions.

Thelen and her colleagues, adopting a Bernsteinian perspective use intersegmental dynamics (see Chapter 4) as a tool for investigating the developmental transition in reaching in four infants. Table 11.3 summarizes the characteristic reaches of these infants, and demonstrates that there appear to be two distinctive styles: "flappers" and "watchers." The former need to damp out their enthusiastic limb oscillations in order to reach the target, while the latter must scale up their initially quiescent limb activity. Zernicke and Schneider (1993) address the question of transition from flailing to reaching by focusing on one infant, Nathan, destined to become as famous in motor development annals as McGraw's Johnny and Jimmy. Recall, first, that Bernstein's work implies that skilled movements are those that capitalize on reactive forces, what Zernicke and Schneider call motion-dependent torques. They offer evidence that Nathan's development of precisely coordinated reaches were related to a more effective use of motion-dependent torques. Between 5 and 22 weeks, Nathan primarily used flexor muscle torques at both shoulder and elbow to counteract gravitational extensor torque (see Fig. 11.6). However, by 51 weeks,

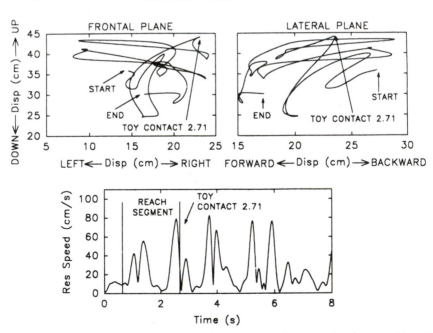

Figure 11.6. Exemplar trial for Nathan's left hand at reach onset showing transition from spontaneous to goal-oriented reaching movement. Top panels: 8-s hand path in the frontal and lateral planes. Bottom panel: Resultant speed for the same segment. (From Thelen et al., 1993. Copyright © 1993 by the Society for Research in Child Development. Reprinted by permission.)

Nathan was able to reduce motion-dependent torques and use them to complement the muscle torques. Thus, like other instances of the acquisition of skill, the development of reaching involves being able to capitalize on reactive forces in order to complement the activity of the muscles.

The flapping in Nathan's initial intentions to reach seem to not be characteristic of all young infants. Thelen et al. (1993) report that in contrast to infants with high energy early movements such as Nathan and Gabriel, there are those infants, like Hannah and Justin, who were more quiet (see Fig. 11.7). Their task in learning to reach was not to damp out oscillations of the arms, but rather to provide additional muscle power to lift their arms against gravity. A fascinating and, perhaps, revelatory characteristic of the reaches of the flappers versus the watchers is that the former most often reached with both hands, while the latter used only one. Thelen et al. propose that whether or not bilateral coupling emerges in reaching is dependent upon the "excitation" of the system, but do not elaborate on this notion.

What is required to assemble the multiple segments into a special-purpose device for reaching? The action-system approach offered in this book would first turn to the basic orienting system and the control of body posture. When

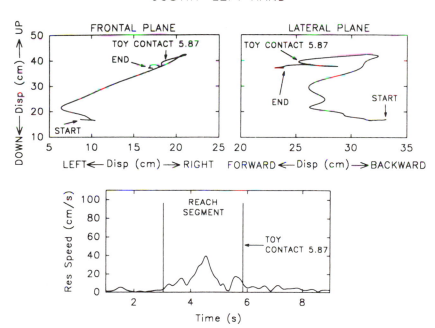

Figure 11.7. Exemplar trial for Justin's left hand at reach onset showing reach segment emerging from small movements. Top panels: 8-s hand path in the frontal and lateral planes. Bottom panel: Resultant speed for the same segment. (From Thelen et al., 1993. Copyright © 1993 by the Society for Research in Child Development. Reprinted by permission.)

the seated infant first attempts to reach, he or she may be unable to use the trunk as a stable postural base to counteract the forces generated by the arms as they extend out toward an object. The wild flailing may be a consequence of this postural instability. According to this view, as infants become capable of independent sitting, their reaching should improve. A test of this hypothesis would be to examine the dynamics of reaching as a function of whether the infant is capable of independent sitting.

Another possibility follows from work done by Saltzman (1992) on the formative role of the biomechanical properties of the arm in shaping a limb's observable movement patterns. Saltzman examined simulations of the oscillation of a two-jointed arm (e.g., what the arm would do when polishing a car or mixing spaghetti sauce in a bowl). The virtual arm consisted of thin

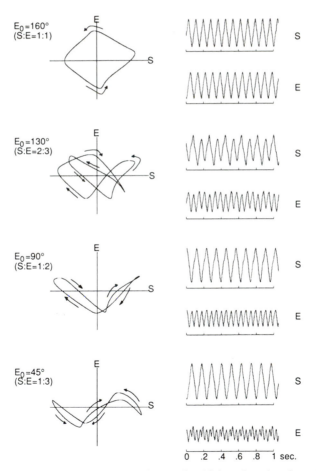

Figure 11.8. Lissajous (left column) and time series (right column) trajectories for simulated two-joint arm. S = shoulder, E = elbow, E_0 = elbow rest angle. The figure shows the steady-state movement patterns for trials at different settings for elbow rest angle. (From Saltzman, 1992. Copyright © 1992 by Elsevier Science Publishers. Reprinted by permission.)

rods with length and mass, and had limit-cycle controllers at each joint. When all other parameters were held constant and elbow rest angle was systematically varied, Lissajous diagrams revealed that certain stable patterns spontaneously emerged at certain elbow rest angles (see Fig. 11.8). What is so special about elbow rest angle? Changing the elbow rest angle apparently changed the natural frequencies of the segments so that they became "close enough" to integer ratios of each other that they began to entrain each other at exactly that ratio. These data are, thus, a dynamic interpretation of Bernsteinian insight that increasing skill is characterized by better use of the reactive forces of a limb in order to shape the temporal structure of movement patterns.

As applied to infant manual activity, the initial oscillatory motion of the limbs followed by a gradual straightening of the trajectory into a discrete reach might reflect the processes of assembly and tuning. Spontaneous activity may result in the assembly of a task-specific device for reaching, but with elbow rest angle continuing to freely vary. During a period of active exploration, infants may systematically explore the rest angle and the parameters may settle at a value that effectively transforms the activity into a system with point-attractor dynamics. A test of this hypothesis would involve measurement of the elbow rest angle during the period of active exploration to determine whether it changes in a systematic fashion.

Perceptual learning. The developmental changes in the role of vision for reaching were discussed above. I suggest here that the observed changes in the role of visual information in reaching might be related to the changing patterns of connectivity in control networks coupled to the articulators in task space. Recall that in Chapters 2 and 4, and earlier in this chapter, there was a discussion of how connectionist networks coupled to articulatory dynamics were being used in simulation studies to account for learning by model (and robot) arms. Such networks may be useful for understanding the transition from pre-reaching to visually guided reaching to skilled reaching in human infants.

Jordan (1990) has developed a hybrid network consisting of two subnetworks: a motor program (which I would prefer to call an activation network, given some of the connotations of motor program discussed in Chapter 1) and a forward model, as well as a task space. The motor program generates torques which cause the arm to follow a desired (virtual) trajectory. The forward model is a "learned internal mapping that allows the system to predict the results it expects to obtain, given the state of the environment and the output of the motor program" (p. 798). The task space is a space in which environmental specifications of tasks are provided for the learner. By virtue of the architecture of the two subnetworks, learning by the forward model during an exploratory phase is propagated backward to the motor program, which changes its connection weights accordingly. This back propagation through the forward model allows the motor program subnetwork to generate new torques.

How might a control regime consisting of two subnetworks, one for generating activations and the other for adapting predictions to observed consequences, account for an initial visual elicitation of reaching, visually guided reaching, and skilled reaching? Pre-reaching may reflect the output of virtual trajectories by the motor program subnetwork without benefit of the back propagated learning by the forward model. The onset of visually guided reaching would reflect a new connectivity between the two subnetworks. During visually guided reaches, the forward model would change the weights of the motor program and, hence, relate virtual trajectories to real world outcomes. Once the motor program has changed the weights for all possible trajectories, it could again operate without benefit of the forward model. This would have several consequences: skilled reaches would be as fast as the early ballistic pre-reaches, but now would be errorless because of prior learning.

OBJECT EXPLORATION, AGE, AND AFFORDANCES

On the view that the infant's exploratory behavior is related in functional ways to properties of objects and surfaces (see Chapter 3), one would predict that the particular ways in which infants explore objects with the hands should differ as they encounter objects varying in size, shape, texture, etc. In Chapter 9, I discussed how the mouth is used to explore the properties of objects, and that the way infants suck is influenced by properties of the nipple. In this section I examine changes in the development of exploratory use of the hands and in the way that the quality of exploration is adapted to particular object properties.

Rochat (1989) has examined age-related changes in exploration of objects. When an object is placed in the hand of infants as young as two months of age, it is simply held in the same way that it was placed there. If the object is moved, both hands are typically used for transporting the object to the mouth. Indeed, Rochat asserts that "bimanual coordination is initially linked to the oral system and is later reorganized in relation to vision when behaviors such as fingering emerge" (p. 882).

By 4 months, both hands are increasingly involved in exploring and manipulating objects. The most notable developmental change is fingering involving the use of both hands: one hand holds the object while the other one scans it with the tip of the fingers. Here, the most sensitive parts of one hand actively explore the surfaces of the object while the other hand supports it. Rochat proposes that fingering is linked to vision. He finds that infants are more likely to be looking at the object while fingering it, and that fingering decreases significantly when infants are placed in the dark. Ruff (1984) provides evidence that fingering activity becomes increasingly specific during the first year for exploration of object properties. When she systematically manipulated presentation of objects to 6-, 9-, and 12-month-olds according to object texture, shape, and surface pattern, Ruff found that infants used more fingering for textured objects.

Palmer (1989) also studied a group of 6-, 9-, and 12-month-olds in order to examine the specificity of actions used for exploration relative to the properties of weight, size, texture rigidity, and sound, and relative to the nature of the surface of a table top. Infants wave light objects more than heavy ones; pick up, release, and bang small objects more than large ones; squeeze furry objects but mouth smooth ones; mouth and squeeze squishy objects more than hard ones; and wave and mouth sounding objects, but bang and finger silent ones. When babies sit at a table with a hard table top they are more likely to bang bells against it than against a soft table top; and with a soft table top, they more quickly bring the bells to their mouth.

Once infants begin to use two hands, there is considerable flexibility in the ways in which it is possible to combine performatory and exploratory activities into a coordinated routine. This flexibility may arise because one hand becomes increasingly dedicated to exploration, while the other hand holds or orients the object to facilitate exploration. In other words, the onset of a stable hand preference seems to facilitate the differentiation of functions for the hands.

THE SERIAL ORDER PROBLEM

Serial ordering and laterality. Serial ordering in manual activity, such as tapping does not appear until later in the first year. The reason for this late appearance has been attributed to the development of left hemisphere functioning (Ramsay, 1979, 1984, 1985; Young, Lock, & Service, 1985). Ramsay (1979) reports that both 15- and 22-month-old groups prefer to use their right hand for tapping (hitting a xylophone with one hand or striking together a stick held in each hand. Young et al. (1985) coded frequency of left and right hand use by 8- to 15-month-olds as they picked up objects and made gestures to adults. Infants preferred to use their right hand for offering objects and pointing. Perhaps the most striking demonstration of the emergence of a new capability for serial ordering is the report by Ramsay (1984) that infants demonstrate a strong unimanual right hand preference (hand of initial toy contact) *during the same week* that they begin to use duplicated syllable babbling (e.g., dadada).

Serial ordering in object manipulation. Combining objects by placing one on top of or inside another is a hallmark of performatory skill acquisition during later infancy. An example is actions by which nesting cups are combined. When children between 11 and 36 months are given the opportunity to combine nesting cups, they typically use one of three strategies (Greenfield, Nelson, & Saltzman, 1972). In order of acquisition, these are: pairing (a single active objects acts on a stationary one), pot (multiple active objects act on a stationary one), and subassembly (two objects are combined into a pair, which is then carried as a single unit in the next combination) (see Fig. 11.9).

Greenfield (1991) considers the developmental changes observed in nesting as a marker of a more general capacity for hierarchical ordering, extending to tool use and grammar. An example of tool use is the process by which infants learn to use a spoon (Connolly & Dalgleish, 1989). Learning to use the spoon, in Greenfield's view, is a special case of object combination "programs." When the infant puts the spoon in the dish or in the mouth, this is

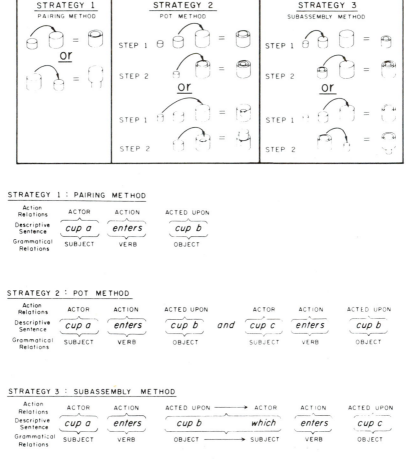

Figure 11.9. Three strategies for combining nesting cups. (From Greenfield, 1991. Copyright © 1991 by Cambridge University Press, Inc. Reprinted by permission.)

"pairing;" when the spoon is brought to the mouth with one hand while food is brought to the mouth with the other, the mouth serves as a "pot" for food and spoon. Finally, as the infant puts food on the spoon, and then puts the food-filled spoon in the mouth, this is evidence of subassembly.

The basis for the development of hierarchical organization in the domains of object combination, tool use, and grammar, according to Greenfield (1991) is the development of neural circuits between specific brain regions. She cites evidence that between 12 and 15 months, developing input structures in the left orofacial motor area receive input from the neighboring Broca's region, and that between 24 and 36 months, Broca's region begins to receive input from the anterior prefrontal area.

While these areas of the brain may indeed be contributing to the development of serial ordering in object combination and tool-use tasks and in grammatical production, identifying these brain areas does not explain the process by which serial ordering is made possible. An examination of the relational properties of the objects being combined, in addition to the increasing complexity of the ordering *per se* makes it clear that the process underlying serial ordering must include a specification of the task space in functional terms in addition to a description of the brain areas involved. For example, Connolly and Dalgleish (1989) observe that holding the spoon, loading food onto it, transporting the loaded spoon from dish to mouth while maintaining an anti-spill orientation, and emptying food from spoon to mouth are the components to be ordered. In other words, the development of serial ordering seems dependent upon the ability to use perceptual information about the relation between body (e.g., mouth, hand) and environmental properties (food, spoon, dish) to create a sequence of activities. An emphasis on the function of the spoon for eating widens the composition of the components involved in serial ordering to include the properties of the food, bowl and spoon, in addition to the articulators of the mouth and hand and the circuits of the brain.

A second shortcoming of Greenfield's grammar of action model is that it ignores the learning that occurs between the acquisition of strategies. In the original Greenfield et al. (1972) paper, infants at a particular age showed a mix of strategies, suggesting trial-and-error learning. Infants may be learning to explore the affordances of the cups in nesting, or the spoon in eating.

An implication of this critique is that a functional and dynamic account of serial ordering might better reflect the control problem faced by the infant. In an earlier section, I described Saltzman and Kelso's (1987) task-dynamic model for discrete reaching: the task space is modeled as a two-dimensional point attractor. Saltzman and Kelso (1987) also present a simulation of a cup to mouth task in which the goal is to move a cup of liquid from table top to mouth while maintaining a horizontal cup orientation that prevents spillage during movement. Here, the task space is more complex than in discrete reaching.

A second organizational level in a dynamic control system proposed by Saltzman and Munhall for speech (referred to as intergestural control) may be applied more generally to other articulators. The key to such application is identifying the gestural primitives involved. I propose here that for manual tasks, the gestural primitives can be identified with respect to the transport and grasp components, the orientation capabilities of each of the segments of the arm, and the opening and closing of the hand and mouth.

CHAPTER 12

THE EXPRESSIVE ACTION SYSTEM

My first child was born December 27th, 1839, and I at once commenced to make notes on the first dawn of the various expressions which he exhibited, for I felt convinced, even at this early period, that the most complex and fine shades of expression must all have had a gradual and natural origin.

Darwin, 1958, p. 131

The methodological problems confronting the construction of a comprehensive taxonomy of basic expressions and basic emotions increases exponentially when one considers that even the various patterns of cry vocalization are only one component of a much larger collective variable. ... The large number of potentially independent degrees of freedom involved in vigorous crying could in principle generate an almost infinite number of combinations. ... In fact, however, only a limited number of low dimensional ensembles are actually observed.

Wolff, 1993, p. 192

The study of expressive acts has a long history deeply embedded in biological theories concerned with affect and the emotions, such as evolution and psychoanalysis (Izard, 1977). These views tend to treat expressive acts as an innately endowed means for communicating affective states. For example, in the first epigraph above, Charles Darwin wasted little time in observing his newborn son in order to seek evidence for a theory of the natural origins of emotions. Darwin believed that emotional expressions were widespread in the animal kingdom and innate in humans because they served the communicative function of specifying internal states to others, which has significant adaptive value (Zajonc, 1985; Zajonc, Murphy, & Inglehart, 1989). More recently, a distinction has been made between the social-regulatory and communicative functions of expression (Charlesworth, 1982). People smile for different reasons—when they are happy or pleased or when they wish to express their pleasure to others. The study of the communicative function, e.g., what the smile signifies to others, is typically the domain of psychologists. By contrast, observing and describing the social conditions under which smiling occurs and the immediate effect on the observer is of greater interest to ethologists (Charlesworth, 1982).

The communicative function of expression seems obvious when the focus of study is the face alone. A smile communicates our experience of positive affect, while crying communicates that we are upset. However, when we include facial expressions as part of a larger system of basic orienting and perceptual exploration, it becomes evident that expression is used for communication but also serves a regulatory function (Charlesworth, 1982). For example, infant crying often occurs with the head and eyes averted, or with the head turning from side to side (and indeed the gesture for "no" consists of cycles of left–right, right–left head turns).

In the second epigraph at the head of this chapter, Wolff, a scientist who has adopted an ethological approach to describing infant behavior, underlines the importance of treating facial expressions as part of a more macroscopic set of subsystems. This chapter further explores the subsystems contributing to emotional expression and how control structures assembled for expressive action (e.g., the relation between brows and mouth in smiling) are nested within basic orienting (head turning). A central theme is that the earliest expressive acts emerge from the components of the subsystems, and that the gradual differentiation of the emotions occurs in the context of learning in a social context. The embedding of expressive acts in a social context makes adult caregivers part of the regulatory system, and may be the basis for the later differentiation of energy regulation (e.g., turn-taking) for communicative acts.

In examining the evidence that expressive acts are made possible by control structures whose functions include both energy regulation (e.g., thermoregulation, regulation of autonomic arousal) and communication, I first consider endogenous smiles and cry vocalizations, the earliest expressive acts. Then, I examine how infants may use expressive acts for regulating energy expenditure: gaze averting to regulate autonomic arousal (Brazelton, Koslowski, & Main, 1974), and facial expression, crying and postural adjustments for thermoregulation (Woodson, 1983; Zajonc et al., 1989). Next, I attempt to specify how social influences may transform these early expressive acts into more differentiated forms. Given a nascent visual–haptic mapping evident in neonatal imitation (Meltzoff & Moore, 1977), perceptual exploration of faces during early social interaction may make possible differentiation of visual–haptic correspondences of the facial musculature, not unlike the way visual exploration of objects is involved in differentiated use of the fingers. Participation in later social routines (e.g., games) may provide a context for assembling coupled control structures (Hodapp et al., 1984; Hodapp & Goldfield, 1985).

THE COMPONENTS OF THE EXPRESSIVE ACTION SYSTEM

Facial articulators and coordinative structures. The human face is a complex collection of articulators which act cooperatively during expression. Studies describing which areas of the face are used to perform discrete facial expressions are consistent with the claim that the facial musculature is organized into coordinative structures even early in infancy (Fogel & Hannan, 1985). Oster (1978; Oster & Ekman, 1980) adapted the Facial Action Coding System of Ekman and Friesen (1976) to measure facial movements of infants. This coding system identifies action units (AUs), discrete, visible actions of muscle groups, defined on the basis of functional anatomy.

Though facial movements of very young infants often appear random and uncoordinated, Oster and Ekman (1980) were able to identify distinct muscle group movements in both premature and full-term infants. One example is the action (AU9) that raises the upper lip, deepens the nasolabial fold, and elevates the nostril wings. AU9 may be seen as a component of a pre-cry grimace or in an infant who has just tasted a sour lemon-glycerine swab. These distinct muscle groups do not combine in random ways. Consider the act of smiling, made possible by the action of the zygomaticus major muscle (AU12) which raises the corners of the mouth obliquely upward. Frowning (lowering and drawing together the brows) rarely occurs with zygomatic action.

Table 12.1. The smile as an assembly of action units

Region	Action Unit	Action	Combinations
Brow-forehead	AU 1,2	Independent actions of frontalis, which can separately raise inner and outer corners of brows	AU1+2 (brows raised at both ends and slightly arched) AU 1+4 (oblique brows raised and drawn together in the middle) AU 2+4 (brows raised at their outer ends, but lowered and drawn together in the middle) AU 1+2+4 (brows evenly raised, flattened, and knit)
	AU4 (knit brow)	Combined actions of procerus and depressor supercilii (which lowers brows) and corrugator (which draws brows together and downward)	
Eyelids	AU 6,7	Contraction of muscles around eyes (which raise and straighten lower lids)	
Mouth	AU 12 (smile)	Zygomaticus produces upturned mouth corners	AU 4 precedes AU 12; AU 6,7 + AU 12 (smooth brow and contraction of orbicularis oculi which further raises cheek)

Moreover, these distinct muscle group movements are temporally patterned in a way that is suggestive of serial ordering via activation scores, as discussed in Chapter 9. Consider the relation between eyebrow and mouth in smiling. Oster (1978) used the FACS to score the smiles of two infants during social play in the first year. She found that the social smile (AU12) was very often accompanied by a precise onset and offset of brow movement. Smiling is preceded by a 3–20 second period of intensely knit brows, accompanied by visual fixation of the parent's face (see Table 12.1). At the onset of the smile, there is a relaxation of the brows. Thus, smiling is not just a movement of the mouth, but a temporally patterned cooperative assembly of mouth and brow.

Embedding of expression in basic orienting. The expressive action system consists of articulatory components of the face (notably, the muscles controlling the brows, eyes, and mouth) whose organization is initially embedded within the activities of the basic orienting system. When used for expressive behavior during the first three months of life, the basic orienting system acts cooperatively with the autonomic nervous system to regulate the perceptual organs. Arousal, either intrinsic or extrinsic, appears to act as a continuously scaled control parameter (Thelen, 1989) which directs exploration of the perceptual organs, especially the eye–head system. For example, in young mammals, arousal appears to drive the organization of the orienting system into one of two stable states: approach or withdrawal (Schneirla, 1959, 1965; Turkewitz & Kenny, 1982). Schneirla (1959) hypothesized that intensity of stimulation determines the direction of reaction relative to a source, with low intensities tending to evoke approach reactions, and high intensities withdrawal reactions. Like Gibson, Schnierla proposes that what changes with development is the influence of learning via perceptual exploration.

Consider, for example, the approach–withdrawal pattern evident in the earliest patterns of looking and gaze aversion during early social interaction (Brazelton et al., 1974; Stern, 1974). Brazelton et al. (1974) report a stark contrast between the kind of interaction evident in mother–infant dyads and the behavior of very young infants toward inanimate objects. With an object out of reach, the 1-month-old infant stares for long periods, with the tongue jerked out towards it and then withdrawn, the body in a tense, sitting posture, the arms and legs flexed and the fingers and toes aimed at the object is brought within reach, the mouth opens, the neck arches forward, the arms swipe, and the legs kick. The intent prolonged state of attention is finally disrupted by turning away from the object. Here, then, it seems that the affordances of the object for grasping with the mouth, hands, and feet orient the infant to the approach the object and prepare a variety of potential action systems for exploration and action. But the affective arousal concomitant with sustained visual exploration results in an abrupt transition to withdrawal: the eye–head system orients away.

By contrast, when the infant interacts socially with an adult, the bistable approach–withdrawal pattern of basic orienting is regulated during visual exploration of the facial expression of the partner. Mother and baby exhibit a smooth cycling of approach and withdrawal for an extended period of time. Here, it seems that facial expression is information-specific to the level of the control parameter driving the social interaction between the bistable states of approach and withdrawal. That the infant uses the mother's facial expression as information for regulating approach and withdrawal is evident in studies which experimentally perturb the dynamics of the facial articulators of the mother by having her present a "still face." Rather than the smooth cycling usually apparent, the infant turns away from the mother's face and begins to stare at his hands, and his body movements become abrupt and incoordinated.

The initial approach–withdrawal behavior of the newborn may reflect a bistable state at the level of state dynamics, with the behavior of the caregiver (or the optical properties of an object at a distance) and the infant's internal regulatory system acting as joint control parameters which regulate the infant's level of arousal. Conceived of as a bistable dynamic system, an optimum level of arousal would maintain the infant in an approach state (i.e., oriented toward the mother or inanimate object). As arousal is scaled upward, there is an abrupt and spontaneous shift from approach to avoidance (turning away) (see Fig. 12.1). With increased capability for perceptual exploration, the kinds of events

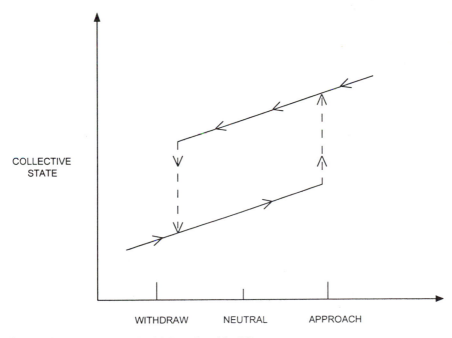

Figure 12.1. Approach and withdrawal as bistable states.

that elicit approach behavior change, along the lines of the theory of affordances discussed in Chapter 3.

During the first year, the coordinative structures evident from birth may become organized in new ways with the basic orienting system, as the infant gains greater control of independent movement of the head and upper torso against the effects of gravity. Michel, Camras, and Sullivan (1992), for example, examined the relationship between brow movements and up–down head movements in 5- and 7-month-olds. Using the FACS, they coded the co-occurrence of a variety of facial muscle group movements as a function of actions of orienting postures when presented with toys in different positions within the visual space. They found that raised brow movements significantly co-occurred with head-up and/or eyes-up movements for both ages. The facial expression of "interest," which includes raised eyebrows, therefore, appears to be part of a larger coordinative structure involving the use of the eye–head system to explore the environment.

TRANSITION FROM ENDOGENOUS TO SOCIAL SMILES

Endogenous smiles. Early observations by Wolff (1959, 1963) as well as more recent work by Emde and colleagues (e.g., Emde & Koenig, 1969; Emde, Gaensbauer, & Harmon, 1976) demonstrated that the first smiles of full-term infants were spontaneous, or of endogenous origin (i.e., not related to known exteroceptive events). Endogenous smiling has been commonly observed in state 2 sleep (in association with rapid eye movements), but rarely in sleep state 1, and almost never during wakefulness. Endogenous smiling also occurs while the neonate is drowsy in the transition from waking to sleep, but never in the transition from sleep to waking. These smiles occur in close temporal contiguity with eyelid drooping and closure, leading Wolff to propose that these smiles are spontaneous discharges.

These spontaneous discharges may, themselves, be concomitants of the enhanced fluctuations of neuromotor activity during the transition from the out of phase organization characteristic of state 2 to the stable one of state 1 (cf. the work of Haken et al., 1985, discussed in Chapter 2). The reason why discharges may not occur during wakefulness or sleep state 1 is that these are more stable states, and so are not accompanied by the enhanced fluctuations that may be the source of spontaneous discharges. During the transition from state 2 to state 1, such critical fluctuations do occur, and so one would expect endogenous smiles.

This interpretation of endogenous smiles as an emergent outcome of enhanced fluctuations during state transitions is supported by two findings reported by Wolff (1987). He presented neonates in sleep states 1 and 2 or when drowsy with acoustically complex sounds at low intensity. He found that mouthing was elicited in the transition from waking to sleep, but not from sleep to waking. Since sleep state 2 is defined by a collection of rhythms which includes out-of-phase respiratory movements of the chest and abdomen, the findings are consistent with the proposal that the state 2 to state 1 transition is one in which enhanced fluctuations "emit" spontaneous motor discharges.

Wakeful smiling. Although endogenous smiles rarely occur during wakefulness, Wolff (1987) reports that by the end of the second week, infants begin to smile regularly when they are alert inactive. In contrast, visual events (e.g., a silent nodding head, smiling face, two-dimensional face) were visually explored, but produced no smile. By five weeks, all of the infants in Wolff's sample smiled reliably to the human voice, and also began to smile at the visual events alone. These findings raise three questions of interest. (1) What is the relation between endogenous and wakeful smiling? (2) Why are wakeful smiles elicited earlier by the human voice than by visual events? (3) Why do infants smile to events that serve no obvious social function? I will return to these questions below, after considering the opposite pole of emotional expression, crying and avoidant behavior.

CRYING

The components of cries. The human cry is a complex acoustic signal because it is produced via the cooperation of a number of subsystems: the subglottal respiratory system, the laryngeal sound source, and the vocal and nasal tracts (Golub & Corwin, 1985). It is widely believed that the durations of the units within the cry sequence and the time intervals between cry units are dependent upon the state of the infant's respiratory system (Stark, 1989). Sound production, though, is dependent upon laryngeal events. Truby and Lind (1965) distinguish three aspects of sound produced at the larynx. During phonation, the vocal folds vibrate at an F_0 range of approximately 250–700 Hz; hyperphonation results from a "falsetto"-like vibration with an F_0 range of 1000–2000 Hz; and dysphonation is a consequence of turbulence noise. The vocal tract introduces into the sound output several spectral peaks or formants, whose position depends upon the shape of the vocal tract.

Other components of cries. Wolff (1987) reports an intriguing observation concerning the relation between the respiratory pattern of crying and the flexion and extension of the limbs. He notes a phase correlation between the discrete movements of the arms or legs and the onset of the expiratory cry sound about 40 percent of the time at 2 weeks after birth. This apparent synchronization is more likely to occur during cry than fussing. During the second and third month, however, this relationship declines. Why should this relationship hold during crying in the first two months? One possibility is that limb movement and respiration are part of a coordinative structure, relating perhaps to escape or avoidance of noxious stimulation.

The functions of cries. In addition to describing its organizational characteristics, the cry can be characterized by its function in both regulation and communication. Cries occur during periods of thermal stress (Woodson, 1983). As ambient temperature drops, the basic orienting system acts to change posture, flexing the limbs and torso, so that surface area of the skin is reduced, and heat loss is decreased. Crying, as part of the basic orienting system serves a complementary function: it is the culmination of increasing activity of the effectors of the body in order to generate heat (Bruck, 1978). Crying also serves to regulate heat gain by eliciting warming physical contact with the body of an adult (Phillips, 1974).

FROM EARLY BEHAVIORAL STATES TO DIFFERENTIATED EMOTIONS

Classic accounts of how emotions arise out of the infant's interaction with the social and physical environment (e.g., Bridges, 1932; Werner, 1948) appreciated that emotional expression was a product of a variety of neural, visceral, glandular, and behavioral components, but failed to go beyond a descriptive theory. More recent organizational accounts have attempted to specify how arousal is related to organizational change in behavior by means of "tension release" mechanisms which require the assumption of a schema as a control structure which mediates input and output (e.g., Cicchetti & Pogge-Hesse, 1980; Sroufe, 1979; Sroufe & Waters, 1976). However, such a control structure fails to specify how the threshold boundaries that exist for transitions between emotional expressions determine the particular organization of behaviors observed. For example, it is postulated that endogenous smiles occur when the level of neurological excitation (presumably subcortical) rises above and then falls below some postulated threshold. This is really no different than earlier hydrodynamic models of the brain that postulate the appearance of certain forms of behavior when there is excess energy in a system (e.g., Freud, 1905) or ego theories which postulate an ego evolving out of early need states (e.g., Spitz, 1965).

Beyond psychodynamics. How might the action systems account offered here help to move beyond the various models that are heir to psychodynamics? In this section, I address three questions which, I believe, must be addressed by any theory of expressive acts. (1) What is the origin of the "primary emotions"? (2) What is the source for the thresholds at which an emotion seems to abruptly change? (3) How do the emotions become "blended" during infant development? The theory of expressive acts is based upon the distinction between state, parameter, and graph dynamics. Recalling the distinction made in Chapter 1, each level is distinguished by the time scale at which component variables change. Changes in the variables which constitute the graph dynamic level occur at the longest time scale, and those at the state dynamics level at the shortest time scale. The facial expressions of an infant, according to this scheme, are a collection of variables at the state dynamic level, while the longer-time-scale changes in the spontaneous appearance of different facial expressions occur at the graph dynamic level.

The proposal of the existence of "primary emotions" is consistent with other developmental theories of the emotions (Ekman, Friesen, & Ellsworth, 1972; Izard & Malatesta, 1987; Fox & Davidson, 1984), but the means for establishing these primary emotions presented here is based specifically upon the process of pattern formation evident in complex biological systems, rather than upon an assumption of innateness (see Chapter 5). Emotions may be considered as "emergent," rather than preformed. For example, I discussed above the apparent biphasic nature of the earliest expressive behavior. The biphasic nature of the first emotional expressions observed in infants may reflect the way that the nervous system "condenses out" dynamic patterns. This is supported by research on changes in brain activity during the emergence of expressive acts in young infants (Fox & Davidson, 1985; Rothbart, Taylor, & Tucker, 1989), which suggests that the cerebral cortex may be described by a state space that is differentiated along an axis of approach and withdrawal.

Let us, then, turn to the question of thresholds. In a dynamic systems account the relationship between thresholds at which bifurcations between states occur is well established for both physical and biological systems (see, e.g., Haken, 1983). The thresholds are evident in the layout of basins of attraction in parameter space. With respect to expressive acts, parameter space substitutes for the internal schema which acts as a "set point" for determining when a smile occurs. A dynamic account postulates bifurcation thresholds evident in parameter space. And, rather than requiring that the schema becomes elaborated with development, developmental changes in the thresholds for state transitions are seen as a differentiation of parameter space.

The third question concerns the apparent "blending" of emotional expressions seen during infancy (Fox & Davidson, 1984). Emotional blending is attributed by Fox and Davidson to increased functional integrity of the commissural system which allows for greater sharing of influences between the cerebral hemispheres. In the dynamic account offered here, blending may occur in a manner akin to the gestural score model of Saltzman and Munhall (1989), discussed in Part II. If each of the coordinative structures evident at birth were considered as a gestural primitive, then what may change with development is the blending of activation influences on these coordinative structures.

PERCEPTION–ACTION COUPLING IN THE EXPRESSIVE ACTION SYSTEM

Neonatal imitation. Whether or not neonates are able to produce the same gesture they have just observed an adult perform is a question that has received much attention, since this behavior may be indicative of the first instances of perception–action coupling (see Chapter 3). In the prototypic experimental paradigm, a repeated measures design is used to expose infants to several gestures by an adult. Videotapes of the infant's behavior before, during, and after exposure are used to identify the probability that an infant behavior follows the same adult behavior. Since the initial report of neonatal imitation (Meltzoff & Moore, 1977), a substantial amount of evidence has accumulated which demonstrates that newborns are capable of imitating a variety of perceived gestures, including mouth opening, tongue protrusion, lip protrusion, head movement, and hand movement (Field, Woodson, Greenberg, & Cohen, 1982; Fontaine, 1984; Vinter, 1986). The failures to replicate this phenomenon (e.g., Hayes & Watson, 1981; McKenzie & Over, 1983) have been shown to be due to design problems (Meltzoff & Moore, 1989).

Meltzoff, Kuhl, and Moore (1991) propose that imitation by neonates is made possible by a process of active intermodal mapping (AIM): establishing an equivalence between body transformations they see and body transformations that they feel themselves make. The equivalence is initially only an approximate one among newborns, because there is some temporal delay between the seen act and the produced one, and because the infants modify their expressive acts over successive efforts. At first, newborns produce reduced approximations of the adult model, e.g., small tongue movements inside the oral cavity. Gradually, they more accurately match the adult's display. Meltzoff et al. (1991) suggest that infant use proprioceptive information from their own movements to modify the form of the activity over time.

More recently, Kuhl and Meltzoff (1982, 1984, 1988) have attempted to identify the basis for the mapping between the sight of a person's mouth movements and the information contained in the corresponding acoustic signal. The results of these studies support the view that there is a direct mapping between the perception of speech and the properties (e.g., timing) of the articulators that produced that speech (cf. Liberman & Mattingly, 1989, 1991). For example, infants presented with the vowel /a/ looked longer at a face producing /a/, and those who heard /i/ looked longer at a face producing that vowel. This finding has also been replicated with consonant–vowel syllables such as *lulu* and *mama*. Kuhl and Meltzoff then used synthetic spectral information to explore the nature of the "intermodal invariant" linking sight of the articulators and speech sound. While adults are able to perceive a relation between pure tones ranging between 750 and 4000 Hz and vowels presented visually (/a/ or /i/), infants did not show the same effect. Thus, it is still not clear what information supports the perception–action coupling of infant mouth and ear.

In a third line of research, Kuhl and Meltzoff (1982, 1988) have examined vocal imitation. Kuhl and Meltzoff (1988) gave infants the opportunity to listen to speech sounds presented via tape recorder. They found that infants listening to speech were more likely to produce speech than infants listening to pure tones. Moreover, analysis of the first and second formants produced by the infants indicate that when they heard /a/, their vocalizations had fewer first and second formants than when they heard /i/. This suggests that the infants were imitating phonetic distinctions in the speech signal.

What, then, might be the basis for the coupling of perceiving and acting by infants even as early as the first days of life. One possible answer follows from an ecological account of the relation between information and dynamics (see, e.g., Kugler & Turvey, 1987; Warren, 1990): information is an alternative description of dynamics. The ongoing dynamics of the articulators, whether observed visually in someone else's expressive acts or felt haptically in one's own expressive acts, uniquely specify the same information. This information may be described relative to both state and parameter spaces. In state space, there is information specific to the attractors towards which all movement trajectories tend, while in parameter space, there is information which specifies a landscape of basins created by different values of the parameters of the system.

Spontaneously moving the articulators (e.g., the mouth) to perform some coordinated act (e.g., opening) or, equivalently, perceiving that same act reveals attractor dynamics and parameterizations which are potentially available to be detected by the perceptual organs. The attractors put the actor/perceiver into the basin of attraction for a class of activity (e.g., moving the mouth), and then exploration of the attractor dynamics make it possible to better approximate a stable or optimal form of the act. So, when neonates begin to imitate an observed act, they may do so on the basis of a perceived stable attractor for coordinated mouth movements. As they explore the consequences of their own activity, they may systematically vary available parameters (e.g., optical flow variables in the adult model) so that they come to better approximated that form.

SOCIAL REGULATION

Early social regulation and attractor dynamics. One implication of the competence observed in neonatal imitation is that infant expressive acts may be best understood in a social context. We saw in Chapter 11 that there is evidence of pre-reaching and expressive manual abilities in the first months of life. The work of Trevarthen and his colleagues places these activities in the context of what he calls "intersubjective engagement." Trevarthen argues that expressive manual abilities reflect a functional readiness for communication with other humans. The basis for this competence is a cortical representation of "external reality and the people in it," an idea akin to the just-discussed claim of active intermodal mapping. In Trevarthen's research, though, as well as in related work (e.g., Brazelton et al., 1974; Stern, Spieker, & MacKain, 1982; Tronick, Als, Adamson, Wise, & Brazelton, 1978), the intermodal mapping between infant and adult is a more extended temporal sequence of events than in the Meltzoff, Moore, and Kuhl studies. This extended temporal sequence is seen as the framework for prosodic (melodic) and pragmatic (turn-taking) components of communication. It is both an ontogenetic adaptation for production and perception of the young infant and an anticipation of later competence.

The precise nature of the temporal mesh between neonate and adult during vocalizations and eye-to-eye contact remains controversial. Some of the early work on the timing of social interaction suggested that newborns have a high degree of temporal synchrony in movement of parts of their bodies, and moreover, that newborn movement were synchronized with the speech rhythms of an adult (Condon & Sander, 1974). Condon and Sander used microanalysis of film (manual back-and-forth viewing) to analyze the timing of infant movements relative to adult speech. They concluded that because neonatal movements occurred within 1/30 s of the phoneme boundaries of recorded and live adult speech, it implied a high degree of coordination between the two.

Subsequent work has both criticized the methodology used and has found it difficult to achieve acceptable reliability using the "back-and-forth" viewing procedure (Dowd & Tronick, 1986; McDowall, 1978; Rosenfeld, 1981). For example, Dowd and Tronick used a 3–D motion analysis system to record the timing of movement of a group of infants at 2 and 10 weeks. They examined movement of the infant's wrists relative to adult speech. According to lag-sequential analyses of the data, there was no evidence of interdependence between right and left arm movements, or between arm movements and speech events. Dowd and Tronick emphasize the issue of whether infants at 2 and 10 weeks are capable of detecting phoneme boundaries and changing direction of movement of body segments at these boundaries. However, they suggest that synchronization in the timing of social interaction may develop later during infancy. A consideration of attractor dynamics may provide some insight into why this is so.

While neonates may be capable of generating the attractor dynamics of a single perceived event (e.g., mouth opening) during neonatal imitation, infants may not be able to begin to perceive or produce the kinds of serial dynamics (Saltzman & Munhall, 1989) required for ongoing social interaction and communication until they are at least 12 weeks old. Moreover, the development of serial dynamics for communication probably extends throughout the entire infancy period. Let us first consider the developing ability to perceive the dynamics of biological motion. Bertenthal, Proffit, & Cutting (1984) presented 3- and 5-month-old infants with dynamic point-light displays of human walkers. Using an habituation procedure, they found that the infants discriminated between upright and inverted moving walkers, but not between upright and inverted static displays. Using a different paradigm (forced-choice preferential looking), Fox and McDaniel (1982) found that 4- and 6-month-olds preferred a point-light display of the profile of a human running in place to a display consisting of the same number of point-lights moving randomly. However, 2-month-olds showed no such preference. One implication of these two studies is that infants are not capable of picking up information about the dynamics of temporally extended biological motion until they are 12 weeks old.

How, then, might a dynamic account describe an adult and infant participating in early social interaction. Adults are not only capable of discriminating a variety of biological motions in moving point-light displays (Cutting & Proffitt, 1981), but also of maintaining coordination with other people (walking and talking together, playing music, dancing). Schmidt, Carello, and Turvey (1990) were able to characterize adults watching each other's oscillating leg and maintaining a common tempo as a situation in which the control structure for coordination (an attractor) occurs over two nervous systems and is linked by perception. This control structure exhibited the same properties of phasing as that for coordination in a single individual: there are two distinct modes, alternate and symmetric, and the alternate mode is less stable (evident by an abrupt transition to the symmetric mode at high frequencies). Thus, an adult engaging in social interaction with infants is capable of using visual perception to pick up information about the dynamics of a shared control structure. But, as we have just seen, infants do not initially have this same capability: it only develops gradually.

In Chapter 7, I proposed a model of the assembly and tuning of control structures for action systems. For an attractor to emerge as a control structure, conditions (e.g., intentional constraints) must be established which allow the control structure to emerge. The control structure must then be tuned by parameterizing its functionally relevant properties to accomplish a given task in a changing environment. The assembly and tuning of control structures, therefore, is inherently based upon the dynamic properties of the relation between body and environment. Extant models of social regulation propose that adults initially act as a kind of "scaffold," adjusting behavior and "props" at or just ahead of the infant's current level of skill; infants are apprentices and adults are the experts that help them to learn their trade (Bruner, 1981, 1983; Hodapp & Goldfield, 1985; Kaye, 1982; Rogoff, 1990; Rogoff, Ellis, &

Gardner, 1984; Winter & Goldfield, 1991). What follows is an outline of a preliminary attempt to place these ideas about social regulation in the context of a shared dynamic control structure.

The dynamics of apprenticeship. Thus far in discussing dynamic systems, I have largely made reference to a class of attractors (described by equations of motion) that are autonomous: autonomous equations contain no terms in which time is involved explicitly. By contrast, when I discussed in Chapter 7 the process by which infants learned to kick while suspended in order to bounce, I adopted an equation of motion which was nonautonomous, one with a forcing function that included time on the right-hand side of the equation. The essential idea about a nonautonomous system is that the time variable affects, but is unaffected by, the rest of the system variables (Beek, Turvey, & Schmidt, 1992). Here, I suggest that the apprentice-learner or scaffolded relation evident in early social interaction may be modeled by a coupling between systems which gradually change their frame of reference. Shared actions are initially nonautonomous, with the mother entirely assuming control of the shared system. Actions become autonomous as infants play independently with toys, and gradually can shift between being autonomous or nonautonomous as infants become part of a reciprocal relationship with another person.

The kinds of behaviors characteristic of adults during social interaction may be construed as the assembly and tuning of nonautonomous attractors so they become autonomous. First, adults use activities such as postural adjustments to constrain the infant's activities so they fall within the basin of attraction of the nonautonomous attractor. Adults may then use low-dimensional information specific to the infant's coordinative abilities to guide these activities to the minimum of the potential function of the control structure. As the infant becomes able to assume greater control over the control structure, the time variable in the forcing function gradually becomes incorporated into the infant's own activities until the point at which their coordinated actions become autonomous.

Let us consider the transfer of control in mother–infant games to see how the assembly–tuning model might work during social interactions (see Fig. 12.2). To do so, I summarize a case study of games played between one mother–infant dyad, as reported by Trevarthen and Hubley (1978) (and see Eckerman, 1993). These observations illustrate the importance of rhythmical repetitions for sustaining the temporal organization of a game: the mother assembles an attractor via rhythmical repetition, and then varies the parameters of the component trajectories, allowing the infant to explore the attractor dynamics of the trajectories. For example, during "games of the person" at 25 weeks that characterize "secondary intersubjectivity," the mother moves her head in-and-out and makes exaggerated facial expressions, such as opening the

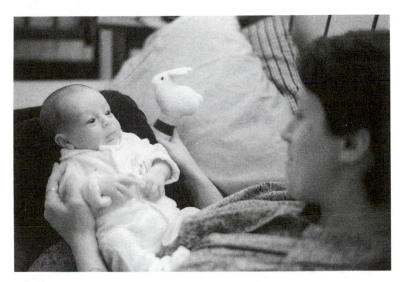

Figure 12.2. Facial expression of a 3-month-old during social interaction with a parent.

mouth widely three or four times in succession. She then puts her finger in her mouth to make a "pop" or wiggle her nose. Between 25 and 28 weeks, games shift their focus to objects animated by the mother. As was the case for the way she moved her face, the mother moves the object in repeated cycles, and then introduces variations, such as making the toy swoop towards the child's face or fly from side to side above her head.

This kind of game anticipates the appearance of these same kinds of actions on objects that the baby performs on her own, what Piaget referred to as "secondary circular reactions," between 28 and 32 weeks. The baby shakes and repeatedly bangs objects she is holding. Here, as the infant assumes control in creating an attractor, the role of the mother shifts: she now moves her head in the same rhythm as the object, and introduces sound patterns, such as "bang, bang, bang" that map onto the temporal organization of the toy's movement. At 34 weeks, the infant is more apt to explore the properties of different objects by using the same shaking and banging motion, and thus also takes control over the tuning phase. The mother releases control of both assembly and tuning, and takes the role of observer or assistant, occasionally changing the arrangement of the toys.

Trevarthen and Hubley (1978) note an interesting prelude to reciprocal control over games with toys. The infant and her mother banged hands on the table in alternation, and while looking at the mother, the infant grinned at the effect they produced. Here, a facial expression may be information which specifies that the mother's rhythmical actions are optimally timed to fit with those of the infant. The beginnings of a new kind of reciprocity in play also occurs at a time when the infant becomes adept at two-handed play—

repeatedly exchanging objects between her hands. This suggests the possibility that shared control over a toy in a game at around 8 months may be related to the development of the ability to control two autonomous systems at the same time, whether they are one's own hands or include the articulators of another person.

THE FUNCTIONAL SIGNIFICANCE OF FEAR

Fear and locomotion. During the infancy period, the experience of fear may serve a specific function related to locomotion: it may keep the infant from a precipitous fall upon approaching a drop-off from the support surface. A series of studies by Bertenthal and Campos has demonstrated that the development of fear of heights as measured by behavior on the visual cliff is functionally related to locomotor experience. Early work by Campos (1976) demonstrated that infant heartrate decelerates during attentiveness and accelerates during periods of wariness or fear. When very young infants are placed on the visual cliff, there is a deceleration of heartrate between a baseline period and descent over the shallow side, but an acceleration of heartrate when they are lowered over the deep side (see Fig. 12.3). Subsequent studies have used this heartrate change as the major dependent measure of fearfulness. Bertenthal and Campos (1984) pretested a group of 7.3-month-old infants for

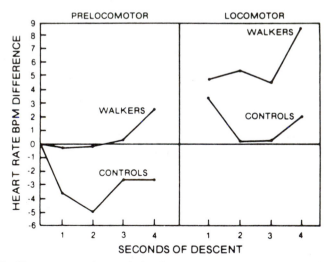

Figure 12.3. Heart-rate reactions to being lowered toward the deep side of the visual cliff in infants with at least 40 hours of artificial ("walker") locomotor experience compared to age- and sex-matched controls. Left panel shows data from infants tested when unable to move without assistance. Right panel shows data from infants tested 5 days after beginning to crawl spontaneously. (From Bertenthal & Campos, 1987. Copyright © 1987 by the Society for Research in Child Development. Reprinted by permission.)

locomotor skill in order to assign infants to either a prelocomotor or locomotor group. The prelocomotor infants showed no heartrate change as they were lowered onto either the deep or shallow side. The locomotor infants, by contrast, showed a significant acceleratory response as they were lowered onto the deep side, but no cardiac change when lowered onto the shallow side.

In order to determine whether the difference between the groups was due to age of onset of crawling or crawling experience, Bertenthal, Campos, and Barrett (1984) assigned infants to groups in a way that would distinguish age of onset of crawling from locomotor experience. Half of the infants were tested after 11 days of locomotor experience and half after 41 days' experience, using the dependent measure of whether or not infants would crawl across the deep or shallow side of the visual cliff. The infants were further divided into groups based upon age of onset. Sixty to 80 percent of the infants with 41 days of locomotor experience avoided the deep side of the visual cliff, but only 30 to 50 percent with 11 days' experience avoided the deep side. Performance did not vary as a function of age of onset of crawling.

Another paradigm used to test the relation between locomotor experience and fear on the visual cliff is to give prelocomotor infants enriched experience, by placing them periodically in infant walkers. Here again, the dependent measure was heartrate change. Infants given enriched experience with locomotion showed significantly greater heartrate acceleration on the deep side than did age-matched controls. Prelocomotor control infants with no locomotor experience were the only group to show heart-rate deceleration (indicating attentiveness or interest) when lowered onto the deep side of the cliff. A complementary source of evidence for a relation between locomotor experience and fear on the visual cliff comes from a case study of an orthopedically handicapped infant (Bertenthal & Campos, 1987). The infant was born with two congenitally dislocated hips, effectively preventing locomotor experience until the cast was removed between 8 and 9 months. When tested on the Bayley scales, the infant was otherwise normal. The infant was tested on the visual cliff once a month between 6 and 10 months. It was only after the locomotor experience of crawling following removal of the cast that the infant showed an increased acceleratory response on the deep side and a decreased deceleratory response on the shallow side of the visual cliff.

Bertenthal and Campos (1989) offer a systems analysis of performance on the visual cliff which treats fear of heights as an emergent phenomenon that is based upon changes in several components, including visual–vestibular coordination, visual attention, social referencing, and goal orientation. Let us consider each of these in turn. In Chapter 8, I reviewed some of the studies which demonstrate that infants show postural compensations to vestibular disorientation soon after birth (e.g., the Moro response). However, they do not respond as vigorously to visual information specifying self-motion until 7 to 9 months (Bertenthal & Bai, 1989; Butterworth & Hicks, 1977; Lee & Lishman,

1975). Bertenthal and Campos (1989) suggest from their review of these data that between 7 and 9 months, infants are functionally prepared to use correlated visual–vestibular information for locomotion.

The component of visually attending to the relation between egomotion and the changing layout of surfaces and objects in the environment (proprioceptive, exproprioceptive and exteroceptive frames of reference, Lee & Young, 1986) also contributes to the emerging relation between fear and locomotion. Once infants become independently mobile, the relation between the body and environment is constantly changing. In order to be able to orient oneself to the the environment, it is necessary to attend to the changes that result from self-motion and those that are not under the infant's control. In other words, as a consequence of becoming independently mobile, *infants become oriented toward what events they can control and what events are independent of their control*. It has been well-documented that infants are more fearful of events that are not under their own control than those that are (Gunnar, 1980). This suggests that controllability is a fundamental issue in the relation between fear and locomotion.

The emergence of a relation between independent locomotion, control over events, and arousal of fear suggests the possibility that infants may become increasingly likely to use perceptual information to determine the relative costs and benefits of particular goal-directed acts. This is supported by the finding that the social signal of an adult to the locomotor infant on the visual cliff (social referencing) contributes to whether or not the infant crosses (Klinnert, 1984). Another way of thinking about perceptual information concerning the costs and benefits of certain goals is in terms of affordances. In Chapter 3, I discussed the work of Warren (1984) and others which shows that adult perception of information specific to performing goal-directed tasks is scaled to the requirements of the actor's body in performing the task (e.g., stair-climbing). But how are these perceptual boundaries learned in the first place?

I propose here that affective arousal may be instrumental in the learning of affordances. One example is the way that fear emerges during the course of gaining perceptual control over locomotion. During the earliest performance of locomotor activity, when infants do not locomote independently, perceptual consequences of the act are not under sufficient control of the actor. When acts are not well correlated with perceptual consequences, the arousal concomitant of the perceptual boundaries may be very high and experienced as fear. With increased experience, the perception–action correlation increases, and arousal decreases. What may remain in affective experience (and, abstractly, in parameter space) as a consequence of learning is a boundary which specifies the range of energy costs (measured by arousal) for performing the act relative to an intended goal.

Part IV
Conclusion

CHAPTER 13

CONCLUSIONS AND DIRECTIONS

In this book, I have presented a tapestry of ideas whose colors and textures derive from disciplines often outside the purview of scientists interested in human development: dynamic systems, developmental biology, and ecological psychology. These ideas were used as the foundation for a theory of the assembly and tuning of action systems during infancy. Earlier developmentalists, especially Piaget, recognized the importance of a theory of behavioral development with strong ties to physics and biology (see, e.g., his *Biology and knowledge*, 1971). Owing to training in biology at the beginning of this century, Piaget incorporated fundamental concepts from Darwin into his theory of behavioral development. As a young malacologist, Piaget studied variation in shell patterns. Later, when he applied biology to behavior, Piaget proposed that infant learning was based upon repetition of an action that led to an initial random event (i.e., a circular reaction).

There have been unprecedented advances in developmental biology that have cast new light on the implications of biology for behavioral development. The most recent work on morphogenesis suggests that the Darwinian selection process may not act upon random variation, but rather upon inherent order (Kauffman, 1993). For example, shell coloration patterns result from a travelling "wave" of pigment-secreting activity in reaction–diffusion processes (Meinhardt & Klingler, 1987). Similarly, the radial and spiral cleavage patterns evident during embryogenesis apparently are a consequence of the natural harmonic modes which arise on a sphere (Goodwin & Trainor, 1980). Like other forms of morphogenesis, the observable actions of infants may also exhibit inherent order. A consequence for behavioral development of a selection process which acts upon the products of self-organizing systems rather than random variation is that the development of sensorimotor skills may be more highly constrained than Piaget believed. The development of skills may be based on specialized perception–action systems already adapted in certain ways for particular tasks, and prepared for guidance by social routines.

In the theory of assembly and tuning, I offered the view that high-dimensional movement trajectories are constrained into low-dimensional action patterns in much the same way that pattern emerges in other complex biophysical systems. The constraints on emergent forms include properties of both actor and environment, such as the architecture of the nervous system, the masses and lengths of the limbs, the material properties of environmental surfaces, and a range of forces acting on the body (gravitational, Coriolis, etc.). Assembly is a process that establishes a temporary relation among the subsystem components according to the laws of dynamics, transforming the the the components into a task-specific action system such as a kicker, walker or shaker. Once assembled, the parameters of this dynamic system are tuned to adapt the action pattern to particular conditions. We saw in infant bouncing, for example, that kicking results from the assembly of a mass-spring system, and the system is tuned by "locking onto" the natural resonance of the physical spring.

NEW QUESTIONS

While writing the book and considering the origins of action systems, the nature of each of the action systems, and the emergence of new forms, I found that new questions were raised at each turn. For example, I approached the origins question by adopting the view that nature uses a small set of solutions for similar problems. The processes of morphogenesis and selection in embryogenesis (e.g., sheets of epithelial cells) were applied to the development of action. How well might these processes fit other developmental domains, such as cognition? I argued for a common informational array as a way to relate basic orienting to locomotion. Is basic orienting the foundation for all action systems, or are there special linkages among some of the action systems? It has been argued that language is "special" (e.g., Liberman & Mattingly, 1989). If so, how is it related to the other action systems? I proposed that new forms of action emerge as a consequence of changes in both the biological and social constraints on state dynamics. What specific aspects of behavioral change does the caregiver use to change the environment so that new learning opportunities arise? A brief consideration of these new questions may provide directions for future research into perception–action systems.

Nature uses a small set of solutions for many similar problems. A fundamental question addressed in this book is how, during ontogeny, infants learn to use the body to perform task-specific functions. I have argued that the answer to this question is embedded in the evolutionary history of the process by which biological systems have harnessed physical energy to perform work. Particular action modes—orienting to the environment, eating, locomoting, manipulating, and expressing emotions—evolved in the human species because of the availability of particular resources throughout our species history. But while some of these modes are well adapted in humans to provide survival at birth, each also has considerable capacity for adaptation during ontogeny. As the developing infant enters new habitats during ontogeny (i.e., new opportunities for learning), action systems within a particular mode are assembled from the complex array of extant system components.

Like other complex biological systems, human action systems are capable of becoming a variety of task-specific biophysical devices for doing work: levers, pulleys, springs, and clocks all "self-assemble" according to principles of dynamics. This harnessing of energy to perform work has occurred throughout the evolution of multicellular animals in the context of the availability of particular resources, physical laws of scaling, and the historical contingency of already available parts. During ontogeny, the many elements of the nervous, circulatory, musculotendon and link segment systems assemble into devices that do work according to the constraints of body morphology and size, the physical constraints of the forces acting upon and generated by the body, and the social constraints of caregivers. The assembled devices are capable of generating bounded families of actions (attractors). These attractor dynamics only generate *potential* ways for satisfying particular intentions. The performance of acts that are *useful* in particular task-specific contexts require a tuning of these attractor dynamics. This is where the perceptual systems become crucial. In the evolution of multicellularity, animals competed for available resources. Via selection, those assemblies of components that cooperated so that they were well adapted to detect new energy sources (cf. *Dictyostelium*) were better able to compete and were more likely to survive and reproduce. Similarly, during ontogeny, selective processes active during the perceptual exploration of bodily dynamics within a structured surround (e.g., via competition and cooperation in neural networks) may be more likely to form bounded energy flows in neuromuscular cooperativity. We saw possible models for this both in Edelman's competitive networks and Kauffman's Boolean networks.

An implication of the claim that the ontogeny of action systems follows the same principles of morphogenesis and selection as do other branches of biology is that the present approach may provide a linkage between developmental studies and cognitive science. At present, cognitive science is largely dominated by a computational approach which begins with the elements of connectionist networks as a *fait accompli*, and focuses on how connectivity changes, witness the elegant volume, *The computational brain* by Churchland and Sejnowski (1992). There have, however, been new developments in computation which address the question of the origins of these network elements. For example, a flurry of work on connectionist networks has focused on ways to allow neural network architecture to evolve adaptively, including creating new nodes (Fahlman & Labiere, 1990) and internode connections (Bodenhausen & Waibel, 1991). So-called artificial life, or a-life, is another foray by computer scientists into questions of development. Holland's genetic algorithms (Holland, 1992) attempt to parallel the origins of life by means of creating the pre-biotic conditions from which life may have spontaneously emerged. And by modeling biological self-replication via a computer program, after a period of about one billion instructions executed by the system, Ray (1992) has observed the emergence of "creatures" with specific adaptations. Genetic algorithms and kindred approaches hold the promise of developmental research which grows network architectures in order to test hypotheses about the ontogeny of action. But unless we simultaneously consider the relation between network architecture and the intrinsic dynamics of the body, such approaches will fall short of the mark.

Another implication of the theory of action systems is that dynamics exhibits intentionality. Recent work in the application of dynamic systems to adult action has developed a theory of intentional dynamics (e.g., Kugler, Shaw et al., 1989/1990; Kugler, Shaw, & Kinsella-Shaw, in press; Shaw & Kinsella-Shaw, 1988). These ideas may have particular relevance for understanding the origins of intentionality in infant action, and how intentionality changes during the infancy period. In traditional approaches to cognitive development, the transition from action to cognition is based upon the presumed onset of a mental representation and symbolic functioning (see, e.g., Adams, 1984; Fischer, 1980; Kagan, Kearsley, & Zelazo, 1978; Piaget, 1954). A challenge to the action systems theory presented here is to understand both the origins of cognition, and its role in the control of action. One way to address this challenge is by considering the dynamics of intentionality.

Following the reasoning of Weir (1985), Kugler et al. (1989/1990) adopt a philosophical view called teleological determinism which assumes that goals (future states) somehow act causally backward in time in order to guide systems down goal paths. This is possible because perceptual information may be shown to flow temporally backward relative to the temporally forward flow of action paths. To further examine this point, let us reconsider teleology with reference to the distinction between teleomatic and teleonomic, as Shaw and Kinsella-Shaw do, following Mayr (1976, 1982):

> Natural systems that have intentions have the capability to select goals. If they also have the realistic means to attain those goals, then they are said to be causally teleomatic—that is, proceeding by physical law. ... On the other hand, teleonomic implies that the physical causal basis for goal-directed behavior is not sufficient; there must be something more. In addition, there must be a *rule* that initializes the causal laws governing the teleomatic process. (Shaw & Kinsella-Shaw, 1988, p. 161)

I have proposed in this book that action systems are both teleomatically driven by the infant's own states (affective, motivational, organismic, etc.) and teleonomically directed by the social scaffolds assembled by adults during games. Cognition, then, must be considered as mutually assembled by infant and adult.

Action systems are regulated by a common informational array, and all action systems are differentiated forms of basic orienting. Following Gibson, I described the environment of the developing infant as a both a densely nested informational array and as a resource for differentiated functions. An implication of beginning the story of the development of action systems within a common informational array, is that each of the action systems becomes differentiated within this array. As an action system, basic orienting makes use of fundamental invariants—the horizon boundary, surfaces, edges—as well as characteristics of optical flow specifying sway. For example, locomotion is a differentiated form of orienting in the sense that it is a kind of controlled loss of orientation. We saw in the infant's first steps that infants allow themselves to fall forward, and hence to allow the optic array to flow at a certain rate, in order to escape the stasis of bipedal standing.

The relationship among the other action systems remains more difficult to establish, and more research is needed. This is especially true for the performatory and expressive use of the mouth and hands. For example, it is commonly believed that manual gestures are fundamentally related to the semantic underpinnings of communication and to the serial ordering of speech for purposes of communication. Converging lines of evidence for this claim include the link between hemispheric specialization for serially ordered behavior in both performatory and communicative modes, and the concomitance of left hemisphere dominance and laterality of the hands (see, e.g., Studdert-Kennedy, 1991). The story for the relation between speech and action may be a special one.

The understanding of how action systems produce speech, using articulators that are available for other actions (e.g., appetitive behavior, vegetative respiration, cry vocalizations) is a major challenge for any developmental theory (see volume by Ferguson, Menn, & Stoel-Gammon, 1992). There are some promising ideas from work which has attempted to simulate the underlying gestural dynamics that may make possible co-articulated and serially ordered speech.

In Chapter 2, I noted how the work of von Holst anticipated some of the present concerns of research in dynamic systems. Another biologist whose work anticipated dynamic approaches to the study of coordination was Paul Weiss. Among his many contributions was the idea that behavior was the outcome of activity within a hierarchy of functional levels (Weiss, 1941). Weiss is, perhaps, best known for his demonstration of central activation of muscle groups as evidence of a hierarchy of control. He conducted a series of experiments on salamander locomotion which reversed the orientation of the front limbs so they pointed backward rather than forward. For animals so treated, the muscles performed the same contraction and relaxation, but because the orientation was reversed, the direction of motion was backward.

Weiss used an innovative means of analyzing the contribution of particular muscles over time in the execution of a movement: he composed what he called myochronograms or "scores" (alluding to the temporal entry and exit of particular instruments in a piece of music). He used these scores to examine the timing of central activation of particular muscles in various contexts. For example, he compared the scores of normal and surgically reversed salamanders during retreat from a noxious stimulus. In both animals, the activation score is the same, but the operated animal's efforts to retreat from the noxious stimulus results in approach

Weiss astutely notes that the repertoire of fixed and discrete scores is not due to rigidly established neural connections. Rather, a score is based upon "definite dynamic properties (time parameters; chemical affinities; or the like) of the central agents" (1941, p. 261). This is a critical point, and I will return to it shortly with reference to recent work by Saltzman and Munhall (1989) and Jordan (1989) examining the dynamics of activation scores.

In many ways, Weiss's introduction in the 1930s of chronological scores to describe salamander locomotion anticipates the contemporary use of kinematic data to infer the functions underlying coordination and control of movement. Weiss assumed that it was possible to directly translate observed movement into presumed patterns of muscle activation by slow-motion "picture analysis." This approach, of course, neglects all of the mechanical influences on the limbs, as noted by Bernstein (1967). Moreover, there are at least three additional problems of the assumption that a central score reflects muscle activation following from Bernstein's work. First, a score based on muscle activation implies that each participating muscle is activated individually, and thus it is not clear on what basis different combinations of muscle activation are selected. Second, such a score requires a very large number of control signals to produce even simple movements. And finally, it ignores contextual dependency: different muscles can produce the same movements.

The task-dynamic model of Saltzman and his colleagues (e.g., Browman & Goldstein, 1987, 1990; Saltzman & Kelso, 1987; Saltzman & Munhall, 1989) offers a way of preserving Weiss's important insight about blended influences on control structures as the basis for coordination and regulation of movement that is in keeping with Bernstein. The task-dynamic model generates blending influences on coordinative structures, functional collections of variables. In a task-dynamic approach, a coordinative structure may be described abstractly in different "spaces." In a task space which describes the functional relation between actor and environment, a coordinative structure is a task-specific control regime with particular attractor dynamics, such as a mass-spring system.

The study of activation influences on coordinative structures is a new area of research and is best documented for adult speech. In the task space for speech, the abstract function for the control regime is called a gesture, "a family of functionally equivalent articulatory movement patterns that are actively controlled with reference to a given speech-relevant goal (e.g., a bilabial closure)" (Saltzman & Munhall, 1989, p. 334). Thus, gestures are not the articulatory movements themselves, but rather the functions underlying the observed movements. Once a control regime for the task is identified, the parameters for the gesture must be set. For vocal tract variables, the three parameters are rest position, stiffness, and damping: rest position determines the tract variable position toward which the system moves, stiffness determines the duration of tract variable motions associated with the gesture, and damping ratio determines behavior on approach to the rest position (e.g., overshoot) (Browman & Goldstein, 1990).

For each gesture defined at the task-dynamic level, there is another level of parameterization of the parameters. These parameter settings operate at a longer time span defined by the "temporal interval during which a gestural unit actively shapes movements of the articulators" (Saltzman & Munhall, 1989, p. 342). This temporal patterning of gestural activity is accomplished by a gestural score that "represents the activation of gestural primitives over time across parallel tract-variable output channels" (Saltzman & Munhall, 1989, p. 342). The gestural score is, thus, the temporal intervals operating for each gesture.

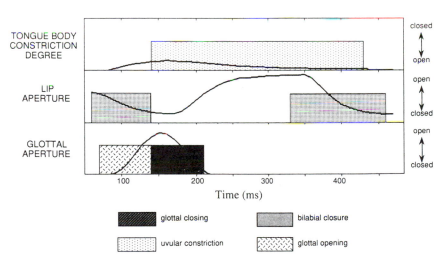

Figure 13.1. Gestural score used to synthesize the sequence /pʌb/. Filled boxes denote intervals of gestural activation. Box heights are uniformly either 0 (no activation) or 1 (full activation). The waveform lines denote tract-variable trajectories generated during the simulation. (From Saltzman & Munhall, 1989. Copyright © 1989 by Lawrence Erlbaum Associates, Inc. Reprinted by permission.)

During speech, several gestures simultaneously "compete" for control of the tract variables with which they are associated (see Fig. 13.1). When a given gesture's activation is maximal, it exerts maximal influence on the articulatory components. Here, then, is how blending is achieved: the activations of several gestures overlap in time within and/or across tract variables.

While the earliest actions of infants may be captured by simple control regimes, such as a mass-spring system, an explanation of serial order requires a model that "can be used to define a time-invariant dynamic system with an intrinsic time scale that spans the performance of a given output sequence" (Saltzman & Munhall, 1989, p. 357). For example, infant kicking can be modeled by a simple mass-spring system (Thelen, Skala, & Kelso, 1987), but *how do we model the control structure underlying a child running toward a ball, kicking it, and jumping up and down with glee?* The task-dynamic approach (see, e.g., Saltzman & Kelso, 1987; Saltzman & Munhall, 1989) provides a potential meeting ground between dynamic models of the earliest actions of infants and connectionist models of the serial ordering characteristic of the behavior of older infants and young children. What are connectionist models?

> Connectionist models are simplified, stripped-down versions of real neural networks similar to models in physics such as models of ferromagnetism that replace iron with a lattice of spins interacting with their nearest neighbor. This type of model is successful if it falls into the same equivalence class as the physical system; that is, if some qualitative phenomena (such as phase transitions) are the same for both the real system and the model system. (Sejnowski, 1986, p.388)

Connectionist models are important for understanding the development of action systems because they begin to deal with the problem of serial order, i.e., how sequences of actions are controlled.

Saltzman and Munhall (1989) propose a hybrid dynamic system which incorporates the highly parallel organization of neural networks with task dynamics in order to account for more complex kinds of postures and movements than those successfully modeled by point and periodic attractors (e.g., reaching). In this model of serial dynamics, attractors (the layout of activation nodes in a neural network) at an *intergestural level* influence the setting of parameters of the inherent dynamics of the articulators at the *interarticulator level* (See Fig. 13.2). These cooperativities at the inter-articulator level self-organize as a consequence of their intrinsic dynamics and are maintained by the attractor dynamics of the connectionist network:

> Contextually-conditioned variability across different utterances results from the manner in which the influences of gestural units associated with these utterances are gated and blended into ongoing processes of articulatory control and coordination. The activation coordinate of each unit can be interpreted as the

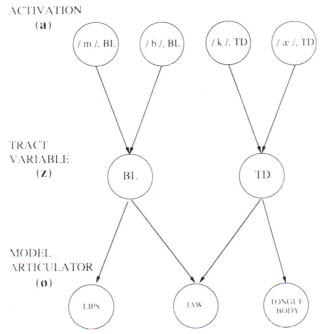

Figure 13.2. Example of the "anatomical" connectivity pattern between the intergestural level and interarticulator level. The intergestural level consists of gestural activation variables, and the interarticulatory level consists of tract and model articulatory variables. (From Saltzman & Munhall, 1989. Copyright © 1989 by Lawrence Erlbaum Associates, Inc. Reprinted by permission.)

> strength with which the associated gesture "attempts" to shape vocal-tract movements at any given point in time. (Saltzman & Munhall, 1989, p. 335)

An important challenge for the present theory, then, is to extend the study of action systems so that we may truly have an understanding of the contribution of influences at multiple levels using the same dynamic principles.

Growth-related bodily changes as well as social supports influence the competition and cooperation of subsystem components and, hence, open opportunities for the emergence of new forms. While early scientists such as Arnold Gesell may have overestimated the significance of maturation for the development of behavior, growth of bodily subsystems clearly must play an important role in the emergence of new forms. Similarly, there is a long history of attempts to chronicle the way in which changes in the environment elicit new forms of behavior. Neither maturation, nor environmental influences alone, however, can account for both the stability and flexibility of the rich array of behaviors reviewed in the third Part of this book. Piaget's interactionist approach, which posited an underlying structure in behavior, seemed an attractive solution to these two extremes. But Piaget placed the burden of development on the infant alone, without support from the caregiver. More recent research on the role of the caregiver in skill acquisition (Bruner, 1983, Hodapp & Goldfield, 1985; Winter & Goldfield, 1991; Rogoff, 1990) has demonstrated that adults change the organization of their behaviors as well as the structure of the environment to sustain the infant's interest in the activity, and to direct attention to the critical information required to learn the task.

The solution to the problem of emergence of action systems offered in this book rests with the way in which entry into new environmental (especially social) niches as well as growth of bodily systems creates new opportunities for action. This is the beginning of an extension of the ideas of Vygotsky to the development of action systems. Vygotsky's analysis of learning was based upon the view that the adult created learning opportunities that were somewhat in advance of the child's learning. I suggest there that biological growth may also open new opportunities for developmental change. Consider, for example, the relation between bodily growth and the introduction of solid foods. The nursing mother will often continue to breastfeed her baby while introducing solid foods into the diet, and gradually wean the infant off the breast. There are a number of motivations for the mother to create this new niche for the infant's learning to eat solids: changing infant nutritional needs (i.e., milk no longer sustains the infant), the painful consequences of the emergence of teeth for sucking on the nipple, and increased freedom for the mother. As infants eat a wider variety of solid foods, milk becomes more of a nutritional supplement than a mainstay of the diet. Infants, as a result, must become more skilled in using both the hands and eating implements in order to get solid food. It is, thus, a change in the availability of resources, both intrinsic and social, that may create the conditions for the emergence of new eating skills.

Once the conditions for the emergence of a new skill become extant, there may be a change in the parameters governing the state dynamics underlying the skill. Consider, for example, the role of the caregiver in providing postural support for infants learning to walk. In none of the traditional accounts of locomotor development is the role of the caregiver ever mentioned. However, it is clear that adult efforts at assisting the infant in maintaining balance and strengthening the muscles may change task parameters. In African cultures which provide enriched opportunities for exercising the leg muscles, infants locomote earlier than age-matched American babies. Such exercise gives infants enhanced opportunities to map the haptic experience of the soles of the feet onto the movement of the legs, and hence tune the dynamic parameters of the system. But how can we relate the dynamics of infant and caregiver?

In the chapters of Part III, the emergence of order in action systems was presented, in large part, relative to constraints that reduce the dimensionality of a collection of microscopic components, or *holonomic constraints*. Holonomic constraints are expressed functionally as a relation among coordinates, and do not materially alter the system (e.g., a ball rolling down an inclined plane is holonomically constrained because its motion follows the laws of mechanics) (Kugler et al., 1989/1990). By contrast, *non-holonomic constraints* require some mechanism in order to sustain a relationship evident as macroscopic order among microscopic components (e.g., the output of a computer program is non-holonomically constrained by its program).

The treatment of the development of action systems in Part III of the book imply that the holonomic intentions of an adult caregiver may initially have the status of being non-holonomic for the infant, but gradually become holonomic. For example, neonatal sucking activity is evident during sleep, regardless of time since last feeding (Wolff, 1987), but can also be elicited by placement of a nipple in the infant's mouth during feeding. From the frame of reference of the infant's action systems, being fed by another person is a non-holonomic intention because feeding may be on a "schedule" that is not strictly related to the physiological cycles of hunger of the neonate.

Stated in dynamic terms, a caregiver may be thought of as "an operator that selects the goal, seeks anticipatory, goal-relevant information, initiates the action, and sustains it to completion down the goal-path" (Kugler et al., 1989/1990, p. 28). The non-holonomic activities of the caregiver may be thought of as creating a layout of singular points (attractors) at which choices (change of direction, speeding up, slowing down) may be made by the neonate. At these singular points, "there is insufficient information in the field to define uniquely the future path" (Kugler et al., 1989/1990, p. 26). Between these points on the goal path, though, the neonate's acts are holonomically constrained by the attractor dynamics of its own central nervous system. It should be emphasized that the particular layout of attractors is temporary, in that it changes according to the task. While it is evident that infants gradually become active participants in social inter-actions, it is not at all obvious how this process occurs. From the standpoint of intentional dynamics, the question may be framed as how the infant learns to become an intentional operator.

The process of learning to become an intentional operator has been addressed by Shaw, Repperger, Kadar, and Sim (1992). They offer a mathematical description of an intentional operator that selects two kinds of goal parameters, target and manner, that serve as the boundary conditions on perception–action cycles. A target is a kinematically specified family of goal paths in space-time (Shaw et al., 1992). Target parameters denote time, distance, and direction to contact a target. Manner involves the selection of kinetic criteria for performing an act (how much of resources will be expended). Manner parameters denote the impulse, work, and torque forces to move the system to the target in a specified time. In other words, learning to be an intentional operator involves learning to direct the interplay of the system parameters.

Consider the "intentional spring" task used by Shaw et al. (1992) to study how an adult subject learns to imitate the way an instructor stretches a given spring that moves with one degree of freedom. The task is a haptic one, since the learner is blindfolded and wears earplugs. There are three phases. First, the task goal is established by allowing the learner to experience his or her arm being pulled through the motion to be learned. The learner is also directed to attend to the manner and target of the instructor's pulling (i.e., noting the frequency of oscillation and target length to which the spring is brought to rest by the instructor at the end of each pull). Second, the learner is instructed to gradually assume control of the spring, while the instructor relinquishes control. If the learner's performance differs from a criterion, the instructor resumes control. Finally, the task is completed when the instructor's intentions are assimilated by the learner (there are no longer corrections made). Shaw et al. provide a mathematical model to describe the learner's progress in assimilating the instructor's intention (the details of which are outside the purview of this chapter).

These three phases of "absorbing extrinsic influences into the intrinsic autonomy of a system" in the Shaw et al. task are also evident in the learning of skills in the context of early games. To illustrate this point, I will discuss some research I conducted on early games with Robert Hodapp (Hodapp et al., 1984; Hodapp & Goldfield, 1985; and see Winter & Goldfield, 1991). We analyzed the behaviors of 17 mother–infant pairs during monthly visits from 8 to 16 months as they played the games of "roll the ball" and "hide and seek". During the earliest phases of learning, the mother (instructor) established the goals of the task by moving the infant passively through it. This effectively got the infant interested in the task. So, for example, in roll the ball, the mother initially rolled the ball to the infant, waited briefly, then rolled it back to herself. In peek-a-boo, the mother initially did both the hiding and uncovering. Next, in roll the ball, mothers were observed to create a target by holding out her hand to receive the ball, and encouraging the infant to act (i.e., establish a manner for utilizing resources). Once the infant began to roll the ball on their own, mother's immediately stopped requesting the ball or holding out a hand to encourage returning it. Soon, the infant initiated the game by holding out the ball.

CLINICAL DIRECTIONS

The remaining sections offer directions for the application to clinical populations of some of the ideas presented in this book. One clinical direction is in the domain of populations suffering from delays and disorders in what is traditionally called motor development. There is a tradition in the study of atypical patterns of motor development to clinically distinguish infants on the basis of a deficit in a particular area of the brain (e.g., cerebellar ataxia).

However, in the approach taken in this book, the coordination and control of action is studied in the context of an ensemble of subsystems, including the neural subsystem, each with its own developmental rate. New behavioral functions emerge from interactions among the ensemble of subsystems. From this perspective, a central problem in understanding atypical development is identifying how particular characteristics of one or more subsystems are responsible for the delayed emergence or disorders of particular forms of behavior.

I consider two issues in the application of the developmental theory of action systems to clinical populations, first, the issue of assessment of motor function, with special reference to the neonatal period. At present, both neonatal neurological examinations (e.g., Prechtl, 1977) and behavioral assessments (e.g., Brazelton, 1973) rely heavily on clinical evaluation of reflexes and tonus (e.g., reactions to passive movements), to the exclusion of measures of the temporal organization of action systems. These examinations may, thus, be determining only a narrow range of functioning of action systems. By incorporating measures of the dynamics of action in a variety of action systems (e.g., sucking in the appetitive mode, reaching for or shaking and banging objects in the performatory mode, kicking in the locomotor mode, crying in the expressive mode), it should be possible to devise new assessment procedures for determining neuromotor status.

A related issue concerns the diagnosis of "motor" disorders resulting from insults to the central and peripheral nervous systems. The current approach to diagnosis, by medical practitioners and physical and occupational therapists alike, places an emphasis on the symptoms which characterize the disorder. So, for example, cerebral palsy is characterized by hypertonia and hemisyndromes, while the emphasis in Down syndrome is placed on hypotonia (see, e.g., Connor, Williamson, & Siepp, 1978). I would argue that Down syndrome and cerebral palsy may be characterized with reference to disorders of coordination and control in a variety of action systems. As we have seen in this book, coordination is a description of how the free variables of action systems are assembled into ensembles, and control identifies the values assigned to that ensemble (e.g., values for stiffness and damping). For example, if CNS insults disrupt the mechanism for setting equilibrium positions (see Chapter 11), then cerebral palsy may be understood with reference to equilibrium position control. Cerebral palsy may reflect a persistent asymmetry in control of length and stiffness of particular collections of muscles. Measurement of attractor dynamics in cerebral palsy might reveal "imbalances" in the competition among attractors in the assembly of an action system (e.g., for locomotion) (see Chapter 10).

Assessment: An emphasis on reflexes. The contemporary assessment of neuromotor functioning during infancy reflects a longstanding tradition of distinguishing between subcortical and higher cortical functioning in the central nervous system. This tradition has been evident at least since the 1930s, for example, in Myrtle McGraw's reliance on Conel's (1929) masterwork, *The postnatal development of the human cerebral cortex*, to explain the developmental changes she observed in locomotor behavior. Because subcortical nuclei are well developed at a time when reflexive behaviors are evident, McGraw concluded that the earliest reflexes evident in newborns were indicators of a dominance of subcortical functioning. The progressive voluntary control of movement, and the decline of reflexive functioning were taken by McGraw as evidence that higher cortical centers came to gradually inhibit the activity of the subcortical nuclei.

This tradition of highlighting the early function of the reflexes and their later decline has continued in the extensive development of neurological assessments in Europe, e.g., Prechtl's neurological examination (1977; original, 1964), the method of Saint-Anne Dargassies (1983), and Amiel-Tison's neurological examination (1979, 1985) as well as in assessment tools developed in this country, such as the early work of Paine (1960), Brazelton's neonatal behavioral assessment (1973), Korner's procedures for assessing preterm babies (Korner & Thom, 1990), and the associated primitive reflex profiles developed by Capute and his colleagues (Capute et al., 1982). One reason for the continued belief that infant reflexes come to be inhibited by higher centers is the comparison made in classical neurology between healthy infants and pathological adults. It is often cited that lesions of the adult cortex may release the appearance of infantile motor patterns (Paulson & Gottlieb, 1968). However, as noted by Prechtl (1981), the highly invariant nature of these pathological reflexes is never seen in the healthy infant.

Despite the difference between the normal transition from reflexive to voluntary functioning during infant development, and recovery from adult pathology, the reflex–voluntary dichotomy continues to be adhered to in clinical research. For example, Capute et al. (1982) longitudinally examined the presence of three reflexes, the asymmetrical tonic neck reflex (ATNR), the tonic labyrinthine supine (TLS) and the Moro at regular intervals during the first year. Both the ATNR and TLS are present at 2 weeks, peak by 2 months, and then smoothly decline. By 9 months these reflexes can only be elicited in 25 percent of infants tested. All infants continue to show the Moro reflex at two weeks, but it also declines, being present in about 15 percent of infants at 9 months. Capute et al. report that these reflexes begin to diminish as rolling and independent sitting develop, suggesting that the diminution of these reflexes is related to the appearance of specific volitional motor activity.

Beyond reflexes. The temporal coincidence of the decline of reflexes and the onset of volitional motor activity does not necessarily imply that reflexes come under specific and permanent inhibition from higher cortical centers. Broadening the consideration of action repertoire of the newborn to include spontaneous action reveals a variety of possible mechanisms by which early patterns change during development (see, e.g., Prechtl, 1981). In line with the action systems perspective of this book, I would argue for a model of developmental transitions in which a function that is evident at a particular period in development emerges from the particular combination of components that are extant, e.g., a particular set of neural network connections, or a particular coupling of articulators. Rather than starting the analysis of action systems from reflexive functioning, I have in this book highlighted the attractor dynamics of spontaneous activities of the infant which become evident in the domains of appetitive, performatory, locomotor and other functions. Postural attitudes attributed to primitive reflexes take on new meaning when considered in light of these spontaneous activities. Postural reflexes, I would argue, reflect the process of parameterization of tunable dynamic systems. During sucking, for example, there is a concomitant postural change: strong flexion in the arms and fingers, and strengthening of the palmar grasp. This reflects the active tuning of particular muscle groups associated with particular attractor dynamics (Saltzman & Kelso, 1987).

In Chapter 11, I introduced the idea that the relation between sucking and posture reveals the functioning of a control system within an organized assembly of components. Here, I elaborate upon that idea as a way of promoting a broadening of assessment of infant activity in neurological assessments to include the dynamics of spontaneous activity. Rather than assessing reflexes or muscle tonus *per se*, neurological examinations ought to take advantage of newly emerging technologies for examining the dynamics of spontaneous acts, including motion analysis of limb trajectories (e.g., Thelen & Ulrich, 1991), analysis of the acoustics of cry (e.g., Lester, 1985) and of the phase coupling among coupled respiratory and sucking rhythms during behavioral state transitions (Curzi-Dascalova & Plassart, 1978).

Towards a neonatal neurological assessment based upon the dynamics of spontaneous activity. While such an assessment is not presently in use, its components are suggested by some of the ideas presented in this book. First, the assessment should consider spontaneous activity within each of the action systems. Table 13.1 presents the action systems to be assessed, the attractor that is characteristic of that action system, and some of the variables which identify the status of coordination and control of action at particular periods in development. The appetitive system is particularly well-suited to neonatal assessment, since it is one of the earliest coordinated systems evident in behavior, and I will use it to illustrate the possibilities of neurological evaluation based upon dynamics. Second, the study of temporal organization makes it possible to directly examine how changes in behavior occurring at one time scale may influence the organization of behavior at a second time scale.

Table 13.1. Towards an assessment of attractor dynamics as a potential clinical tool

Action system	Assessment of Attractor Dynamics
Locomotor	Phase-plane analysis of cooperation of limb segments; analysis of stability by measuring relaxation time following experimental perturbation
Appetitive	Analysis of stability of non-nutritive and nutritive sucking by measuring influence of behaviuoral state on sucking; examination of superposition of sucking rhythm on respiration
Performatory	Analysis of developmental changes in equilibrium point control of arm and hand during unimanual and bimanual reaching

For example, sleep–wake cycles span a time scale of minutes and hours, while respiratory or sucking rhythms occur at a much shorter time scale (tenths of a second). Coordination at multiple time scales implies that changes evident in respiration over several sleep-state cycles may influence the organizational stability of respiration within a particular sleep state. Disruptions in coordination may be predictive of persistent brain injury. For example, inconsistencies in the distribution of behavioral states predicts risk for developmental problems such as Sudden Infant Death Syndrome (Thoman, Denenberg, Sievel, Zeidner, & Becker, 1981).

There is evidence that oral and respiratory rhythms are disordered in high-risk infants, especially those born prematurely. The temporal parameters of neonatal non-nutritive sucking (NNS) discriminate between healthy infants and those with perinatal distress (Wolff, 1968; Eishima, 1991). Temporal patterns of sucking are disorganized in infants with intraventricular hemorrhage and asphyxia (Braun & Palmer, 1986), and after high forceps delivery (Kron, Stein, & Goddard, 1966). On the view that a fundamental character of behavior is its tendency to maintain itself in a stable state, despite mild perturbation, stability may be a useful measure of neurological damage. The conditions under which behavior remains in a stable state may reveal much about the ability of the nervous system to recover from early insult.

Consider the stability of respiration. Following a dynamic systems methodology (Kelso et al., 1992), the first step in evaluation of stability is to identify a collective variable. In respiration, a collective variable is the phase between movements of the chest and abdomen. When neonates are in a state of active sleep, chest and abdomen are most often out of phase, and there is higher respiratory frequency. However, when in quiet sleep, chest and abdomen are in phase, with slower breathing (Curzi-Dascalova & Plassart, 1978). The collective variable may be abstractly represented as a ball situated in a potential landscape consisting of hills, valleys, plateaus, etc. (see Fig. 13.3).

Behavioral state may be envisioned as influencing the shape of that potential by changing the values of parameters which define it. The current

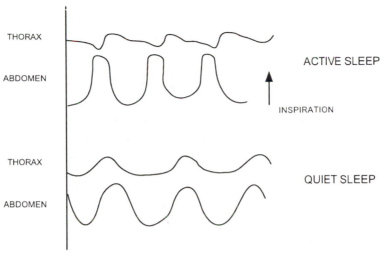

Figure 13.3. Phase of the thorax and abdomen in active sleep (out of phase) and quiet sleep (in phase).

value of the system's parameter set is represented as the location of the ball on the surface. A valley represents the minimum where the ball is at equilibrium, with the ball moving downhill whenever it can. As parameters change, the dynamics of observed behavior (e.g., respiratory phase) change. The minimum becomes increasingly shallow and, at a critical point, it becomes completely flat. Beyond the critical point, the original minimum vanishes. In general terms, the stability of a system can be measured empirically by local relaxation time, the duration of the transient between two stable states. As the minimum flattens out, relaxation time increases and then, at the transition, decreases sharply to a small value corresponding to the other stable state (called critical slowing down). The flattening of the potential is seen as an enhancement of fluctuations. These two features, critical slowing down, and enhancement of fluctuations, represent evidence that the transition between states is due to a loss of stability.

Because the longer time scale distribution of behavioral states encompasses the temporal course of phase transition in movement of the chest and abdomen, continuous changes in behavioral state may be one influence on the scaling of parameters. This scaling may occur as follows. During active sleep, there is increased variability in the respiratory cycle, and at the same time, there is higher respiratory frequency. As fluctuations increase, the high respiratory frequency may amplify these fluctuations to a critical value, and a respiratory phase transition may occur. As fluctuations (measured by SD of chest movements) are scaled up by higher respiratory frequency during active sleep, there is a transition from out-of-phase to in-phase respiration.

A TAXONOMY OF DISORDERS OF ACTION SYSTEMS: BEYOND SYMPTOMS

Developmental neurology. In contemporary developmental neurology, the attempt to understand the consequences of brain injury under the rubric of the cerebral palsies is tied to the specifics of anatomical and functional brain development (Wigglesworth, 1984). However, attempting to isolate particular functional regions and associate them with specific behavioral deficits is problematic (Goldfield, 1990), since, as is evident in Chapter 4, the CNS is a massively parallel distributed control system. Even if one were able to identify the precise location of brain lesions, there may be marked discrepancies between the presence of lesions and the development of behavior. This is because the brain is a highly complex adaptive system that may recover from the effects of early damage by exploiting other areas of the brain that are not yet committed to specific functions (St. James-Roberts, 1979).

An alternative approach to understanding the effects of early brain injury is to treat the brain as a dynamic system with certain organizational principles. For example, an overarching organizational scheme in this book is to describe dynamics of action systems at three levels: state, parameter, and graph dynamics. From a dynamic perspective, then, it may be of some heuristic value to use these levels to define three different kinds of developmental disorders of action that may result from brain injury: (1) disorders of state dynamics (coordination), evident in extremes of stability in behavioral rhythms such as respiration (e.g., following intraventricular hemorrhage associated with extreme prematurity), (2) disorders of parameter dynamics, evident in the setting of parameters during learning, and (3) disorders of graph dynamics, evident in the assembly of subcomponent processes into new skills. In this alternative approach, rather than using behavioral symptoms to identify a particular kind of disorder, disordered behavior is treated as a reflection of underlying dynamics at one or more of these three levels (see Table 13.2).

Disorders of state dynamics. One example of how state dynamics may be a sensitive measure of the developmental problems in coordination is a study by Heriza (1991). She examined spontaneous kicking movements in three groups of infants: low-risk preterm infants born without medical complications, high-risk preterm infants born with documented intraventricular hemorrhage (IVH), and full-term healthy infants. All were videotaped at birth, and again at 40 weeks postgestational age (PGA). The kicking of all of the infants exhibited the characteristic action pattern attributed to a limit-cycle attractor (see Fig. 13.4). However, the preterm infants showed decreased movement amplitude and peak velocity, and more extended at at all joints. Two of the high-risk preterms showed disorganization in kicking: the ankle was out

Table 13.2. A taxonomy of disorders based upon state, parameter, and graph dynamics

Type of Dynamics	Disorder	Variables of Coordination and Control
State	High-risk birth associated with prematurity	Variability of temporal pattern (e.g., of sucking); degree of coupling (e.g., between sucking and respiration)
Parameter	Cerebral palsy	Imbalances in equilibrium-point control in different muscle groups
Graph	Motor retardation (e.g., Down syndrome)	Delay in development of 0.5 phase lag in locomotor stepping; delay in postural control (basic orienting)

of phase with the knee and hip in one infant (see Fig. 13.4(*a*)), and the hip was out of phase with the knee and ankle in the other (see Fig. 13.4(*b*)).

Another illustration of the sensitivity of state dynamics for detecting problems in coordination of action systems is a study of Down syndrome (DS) by Ulrich, Ulrich, and Collier (1992). They longitudinally tested a group of DS infants to examine the organization of alternating stepping on a treadmill. DS infants, like normals, are able to produce alternating steps on the treadmill, but they do so significantly later than normal infants (13 months rather than 6 months). Thus, like normal infants, the basic pattern for locomotion is well in

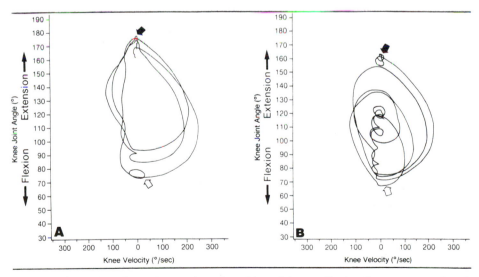

Figure 13.4. Typical phase-plane trajectories of knee joint amplitude of movement and peak velocity of preterm infant at 40 weeks (A) and full-term infant (B). The filled arrow indicates the beginning of the kick flexion movement; the open arrow indicates peak flexion. (From Heriza, 1988. Copyright © 1988 by The American Physical Therapy Society. Reprinted by permission.)

place before actual walking begins, but the entire process is delayed. While Thelen and Ulrich attribute such delays to "rate limiters" (Soll, 1979), more work needs to be done to specify the graph dynamic processes which control the timing of these rate limiting factors (see below).

Disorders of parameter dynamics. In order to perform a particular skill, an action system must be parameterized, and as the learning of a task proceeds, the parameters must be constantly updated. Such parameterization allows the actor to adapt to changing sensorimotor mappings (Saltzman & Munhall, 1992). Studies by Fetters and her colleagues (Tronick et al., 1991) suggest that some preterm infants may exhibit disorders of parameterization. One measure of parameterization is the setting of equilibrium position of the muscles, evident in changes in the length of the action units discussed in Chapter 11. Fetters found that preterm infant reaches decreased, as did those of full-term infants, but that the preterms still had a greater number of action units in their reaches as compared to full term infants. She also found that, like the full-term infants, the straightness ratio increased, but unlike the full-term infants, the proportion of the reach consisting of the first action unit was unchanged from 7 to 12 months. So, unlike normal full-term infants these preterm infants, though healthy in other ways, did not increase the length of the first unit.

Disorders of graph dynamics. Graph dynamics refers to processes that influence the changes in a system's architecture (i.e., the size, composition and connectivity of the set of equations used to represent the system; Saltzman & Munhall, 1992). Graph dynamic disorders, therefore, are disorders of action systems which may result from (1) a slowing down in the assembly of components into new skills (size), or (2) aberrant composition or connectivity of the components. The slowing down of the assembly of components is traditionally referred to as motor retardation. In the normal process of the assembly of skills, there is some suggestion that the degrees of freedom of component subsystems must change their timing so that they can reorganize and become part of a new ensemble. The slowing down of assembly that may underlie observed delays in the achievement of "motor milestones" may result because one or more of the components being assembled is unable to rapidly enough change its timing.

An example of the role of timing of a component of postural control and overall motor retardation may be seen in the timing of muscle activation in Down syndrome infants. Shumway-Cook and Woollacott (1985a,b), for example, measured leg muscle EMG and responses on a platform which caused sudden anterior–posterior sway in Down syndrome infants. Onset latencies of muscle activation were slower in the Down syndrome infants, who were also delayed in their overall motor development. Thus, because of a slower muscle activation time, the overall growth of postural control may be delayed.

Another type of graph dynamic disorder is the absence of a normal coupling of components (i.e., a disorder of connectivity). One example of a disorder of connectivity is a study by Dreier, Wolff, Cross, & Cochran (1979) on the coupling of neonatal non-nutritive sucking (NNS) and respiration. A group of normal full-term newborns was compared with preterm infants examined at 34, 40, and 46 weeks of conceptional age. The full-term infants showed a shortening of breath intervals in the middle of sucking bursts and a lengthening of the breath interval spanning the end of sucking bursts. Thus, sucking resulted in a speeding up of respiration during bursts, and a slowing down of respiration during pauses, as would be predicted for a nonlinear coupling between the two rhythms. By contrast, preterm infants with low obstetric optimality ratings showed significantly less change of breath duration during NNS than preterm infants with high optimality scores. Moreover, the coupling between NNS and respiration differentiated between infants with low and high optimality scores on obstetric assessment, even when neurological examination was not discriminating. It remains to be seen whether these early graph dynamic disorders are related to the later acquisition of skills.

References

Abend, W., Bizzi, E., & Morasso, P. (1982). Human arm trajectory formation. *Brain*, **105**, 331–348.

Abraham, R., & Shaw, C. (1987). Dynamics: A visual introduction. In F.E. Yates (Ed.), *Self-organizing systems. The emergence of order* (pp. 543–597). New York: Plenum.

Adams, J.A. (1984). Learning of movement sequences. *Psychological Bulletin*, **96**, 3–28.

Adolph, K., & Eppler, M. (1992). Actual versus perceived possibilities for toddlers' locomotion over slopes: A psychophysical procedure. Poster presented at the International Conference on Infant Studies, May 1992, Miami Beach, FL.

Adolph, K.E., Gibson, E.J., & Eppler, M.A. (1988). Toddlers' exploration of non-horizontal surfaces. Poster presented at the meeting of the International Society for Ecological Psychology, October 1988, Storrs, CT.

Adolph, K., Eppler, M., & Gibson, E.J. (1993). Crawling versus walking infants' perception of affordances for locomotion over sloping surfaces. *Child Development*, **64**, 1158–1174.

Alberts, J.R., & Cramer, C.P. (1988). Ecology and experience: Sources of means and meaning of developmental change. In E.M. Blass (Ed.), *Handbook of behavioral neurobiology* (Vol. 9, pp. 1–62). New York: Plenum.

Alexander, R.M. (1989). *Dynamics of dinosaurs and other extinct giants*. New York: Columbia University Press.

Alexander, R.M., & Bennet-Clark, H.C. (1977). Storage of elastic strain energy in muscle and other tissue. *Nature*, **265**, 114–117.

Amiel-Tison, C. (1979). Birth injury as a cause of brain dysfunction in full-term newborns. In R. Korobkin & C. Guilleminault (Eds.), *Advances in perinatal neurology* (pp. 57–83). New York: SP Medical and Scientific Books.

Amiel-Tison, C. (1985). Pediatric contribution to the present knowledge on the neurobehavioral status of infants at birth. In J. Mehler & R. Fox (Eds.), *Neonate cognition* (pp. 365–380).

Anokhin, P.K. (1935). *Problems of center and periphery in the physiology of nervous activity.* Gorki: Gosizdat.

Anokhin, P.K. (1940). Problems of localization from the point of view of systematic ideas on nervous functions. *Neurolog. i Psikhiat.*, 9.

Anokhin, P.K. (1974). *Biology and neurophysiology of conditioned reflex and its role in adaptive behavior.* Oxford: Pergamon.

Arbib, M. (1987). A view of brain theory. In F. Yates (Ed.), *Self-organizing systems: The emergence of order* (pp. 279–312). New York: Plenum.

Ardran, G.M., Kemp, F.H., & Lind, J. (1958). A cineradiographic study of breast feeding. *British Journal of Radiology*, **31**, 156–162.

Arshavsky, Y.I., & Orlovsky, G.N. (1985). Role of the cerebellum in the control of rhythmic movements. In S. Grillner, G. Stein, G. Douglas, H. Forssberg, & R. Herman (Eds.), *Neurobiology of vertebrate locomotion* (pp. 677–689). Stockholm: Wenner-Gren.

Arutyunyan, G., Gurfinkel, V., & Mirsky, M. (1969). Investigation of aiming at a target. *Biophysics*, **13**, 536–538.

Asatryan, D.G., & Feldman, A.G. (1965). Functional tuning of the nervous system with control of movement or maintenance of a steady posture— I. Mechano-graphic analysis of the work of the joint on execution of a postural task. *Biophysics*, **10**, 925–935.

Ashby, W.R. (1960). *Design for a brain* (2nd ed.). New York: Wiley.

Ashmead, D.H., McCarty, M.E., Lucas, L.S., & Belvedere, M.C. (1993). Visual guidance in infants' reaching toward suddenly displaced targets. *Child Development*, **64**, 1111–1127.

Baer, K.E., von (1828). *On the developmental history of animals: Observation and reflection* (in German). Konigsberg: Borntrager.

Beek, P.J. (1989) Timing and phase locking in cascade juggling. *Ecological Psychology*, **1**, 55–96.

Beek, P.J., & Bingham, G.P. (1991). Task-specific dynamics and the study of perception and action: A reaction to von Hifsten (1989). *Ecological Psychology*, **3**, 35–54.

Beek, P.J., & Meijer, O.G. (1988). On the nature of the motor- action controversy. In O. Meijer & K. Roth (Eds.). *Complex movement behavior: The motor–action controversy* (pp. 157–185).

Amsterdam: Elsevier.

Beek, P.J., Turvey, M.T., & Schmidt, R.C. (1992). Autonomous and nonautonomous dynamics of coordinated rhythmic movements. *Ecological Psychology*, **4**, 65–95.

Beek, W. (1990). Synergetics and self-organization: A response. In H.T. Whiting, O.G. Meijer, & P.C. van Wierengen (Eds.), *The natural-physical approach to movement control* (pp. 37–56). Amsterdam: VU University Press.

Beer, G., de (1958). *Embryos and ancestors* (3rd ed.). Oxford: Clarendon Press.

Bekoff, A. (1981). Embryonic development of the neural circuitry underlying motor coordination. In M. Cowan (Ed.), *Studies in developmental neurobiology* (pp. 134–170). New York: Oxford University Press.

Belen'kii, V., Gurfinkel, V., & Pal'tsev, Y. (1967). Elements of control of voluntary movements. *Biophysics*, **12,** 135–141.

Berkinblit, M.B., Feldman, A.G., & Fukson, O.I. (1986). Adaptability of innate motor patterns and motor control mechanisms. *Behavioral and Brain Sciences*, **9**, 585–599.

Bernstein, N. (1967). *The coordination and regulation of movements*. Oxford: Pergamon.

Bernstein, N. (1984). Biodynamics of locomotion. In H.T.A. Whiting (Ed.), *Human motor actions: Bernstein reassessed* (pp. 171–222). Amsterdam: North Holland.

Bertenthal, B.I., & Bai, D.L. (1989). Infants' sensitivity to optical flow for controlling posture. *Developmental Psychology*, **25**, 936–945.

Bertenthal, B.I., & Campos, J.J. (1984). A re-examination of fear and its determinants on the visual cliff. *Psychophysiology*, **21**, 413–417.

Bertenthal, B.I., & Campos, J.J. (1987). New directions in the study of early experience, *Child Development*, **58**, 560–567.

Bertenthal, B.I., Campos, J.J., & Barrett, K.C. (1984). Self- produced locomotion: An organizer of emotional, cognitive, and social development in infancy. In R. Emde & R. Harmon (Eds.), *Continuities and discontinuities in development* (pp. 175–210). New York: Plenum.

Bertenthal, B.I., Proffit, D.R., & Cutting, J.E. (1984). Infant sensitivity to figural coherence in biochemical motions. *Journal of Experimental Child Psychology*, **37**, 213–230.

Bingham, G.P. (1988). Task-specific devices and the perceptual bottleneck. *Human Movement Science*, **7**, 225–264.

Bingham, G.P., Schmidt, R., Turvey, M., & Rosenblum, L. (1991). Task dynamics and resource dynamics in the assembly of a coordinated rhythmic activity. *Journal of Experimental Psychology: Human Perception and Performance*, **17**, 359–381.

Bizzi, E., Accorno, N., Chapple, W., & Hogan, N. (1982). Arm trajectory formation in monkeys. *Experimental Brain Research*, **46**, 139–143.

Bizzi, E., Hogan, N., Mussa-Ivaldi, F., & Giszter, S.

(1992). Does the nervous system use equilibrium-point control to guide single and multiple joint movements? *Behavioral and Brain Sciences*, **15**, 603–613.

Blass, E.M., Fillion, T.J., Rochat, P., Hoffmeyer, L.B., & Metzger, M.A. (1989). Sensorimotor and motivational determinants of hand–mouth coordination in 1–3 day-old human infants. *Developmental Psychology*, **25**, 963–975.

Bobath, K. (1980). A neurophysiological basis for the treatment of cerebral palsy. *Clinics in Developmental Medicine* (No. 75). Philadelphia: Lippincott.

Bodenhausen, U., & Waibel, A. (1991). The Tempo 2 algorithm: Adjusting time-delays by supervised learning. In R. Lippman, J. Moody, & D. Touretzky (Eds.), *Advances in neural information processing systems III*. San Mateo, CA: Morgan Kaufmann.

Bonner, J.T. (1974). *On development*. Cambridge, MA: Harvard University Press.

Bonner, J.T. (1988). *The evolution of complexity*. Princeton: Princeton University Press.

Bosma, J.F. (1967). Human oral function. In J.F. Bosma (Ed.), *Oral sensation and perception* (pp. 98–110). Springfield, IL: Thomas.

Bosma, J.F. (1986). *Anatomy of the infant head*. Baltimore: Johns Hopkins University Press.

Bosma, J.F., Hepburn, L.G., Josell, S.D., & Baker, K. (1990). Ultrasound demonstration of tongue motions during suckle feeding. *Developmental Medicine and Child Neurology*, **32**, 223–229.

Bower, T.G.R. (1972). Object perception in infants. *Perception*, **1**, 10–12.

Boylls, C., & Greene, P. (1984). Introduction: Bernstein's significance today. In H. Whiting (Ed.), *Human motor actions: Bernstein reassessed*. Advances in Psychology, Vol. 17 (pp. xix–xxix). Amsterdam: North-Holland.

Brake, S.C. (1991) New information about early feeding and motivation: Techniques for recording sucking in rats. In H. Shair, G. Barr & M. Hofer (Eds.), *Developmental psychobiology* (pp. 32–46). New York: Oxford University Press.

Brake, S.C., Shair, H., & Hofer, M.A. (1988). Exploiting the nursing niche: The infant's sucking and feeding in the context of mother-infant interaction. In E. Blass (Ed.), *Handbook of behavioral neurobiology* (pp. 347–388). New York: Plenum.

Brakke, K.E., & Savage-Rumbaugh, E.S. (1991). Early postural behavior in *Pan*: Influences on development. *Infant Behavior and Development*, **14**, 265–288.

Braun, M.A., & Palmer, M.M. (1986). A pilot study of oral-motor dysfunction in "at-risk" infants. *Physical Occupational Therapy in Pediatrics*, **5**, 13–25.

Brazelton, T.B. (1973). The neonatal behavioral assessment scale. *Clinics in Developmental Medicine, No. 50*, London: Heinemann.

Brazelton,T.B., Koslowski, B., & Main, M. (1974).

The origins of reciprocity: The early mother–infant interaction. In M. Lewis & L. Rosenblum (Eds.), *The effect of the infant on its caregiver* (pp. 49–75). New York: Wiley.

Breniere, Y., Bril, B., & Fontaine, R. (1989). Analysis of the transitions from upright stance to steady state locomotion in children with under 200 days of autonomous walking. *Journal of Motor Behavior*, **21**, 20–37.

Bridges, K. (1932). Emotional development in early infancy. *Child Development*, **3**, 324–341.

Bril, B., & Breniere, Y. (1991). Timing invariances in toddlers' gait. In J. Fagard & P.H. Wolff (Eds.), *The development of timing control and temporal organization in coordinated action* (pp. 119–133). Amsterdam: North-Holland.

Brooks, D.R., & Wiley, E.O. (1986). *Evolution as entropy.* Chicago: University of Chicago Press.

Brooks, V. (1986). *The neural basis of motor control.* New York: Oxford University Press.

Browman, C.P., & Goldstein, L. (1987). Tiers in articulatory phonology with some implications for casual speech. *Haskins Laboratories Status Report on Speech Research, SR-92*, 1–30.

Browman, C.P., & Goldstein, L. (1990). Gestural specification using dynamically defined articulatory structures. *Journal of Phonetics*, **18**, 299–320.

Brown, T.G. (1914). On the nature of the fundamental activity of the nervous system; together with an analysis of the conditioning of rhythmic activity in progression, and a theory of evolution of function in the nervous system. *Journal of Physiology*, **48**, 18–46.

Bruck, K. (1978). Thermoregulation: Control mechanisms and neural processes. In J. Sinclair (Ed.), *Temperature regulation and energy metabolism in the newborn.* New York: Grune & Stratton.

Bruner, J.S. (1971). The growth and structure of skill. In K.J. Connolly (Ed.), *Motor skills in infancy* (pp. 245–269). New York: Academic Press.

Bruner, J.S. (1973a). Organization of early skilled action. *Child Development*, **44**, 1–11.

Bruner, J. (1973b). *Beyond the information given.* New York: Norton.

Bruner, J.S. (1981). Intention in the structure of action and interaction. In L.P. Lipsitt (Ed.), *Advances in infancy research* (Vol. 1). Norwood, NJ: Ablex.

Bruner, J.S. (1983). *Child's talk: Learning to use language.* New York: Norton.

Buka, S.L., & Lipsitt, L.P. (1991). Newborn sucking behavior and its relation to grasping. *Infant Behavior and Development*, **14**, 59–67.

Bullinger, A. (1981). Cognitive elaboration of sensorimotor behaviour. In G. Butterworth (Ed.), *Infancy and epistemology: An evaluation of Piaget's theory* (pp. 179–199). Brighton: Harvester.

Bullock, D., & Grossberg, S. (1988). Neural dynamics of planned arm movements: Emergent invariants and speed-accuracy properties during trajectory formation. *Psychological Review*, **95**, 49–90.

Bullock, D., & Grossberg, S. (1990). Motor skill development and neural networks for position code invariance under speed and compliance conditions. In H. Bloch & B. Bertenthal (Eds.), *Sensory-motor organizations and development in infancy and early childhood* (pp. 1–22). Amsterdam: Kluwer.

Burke, P.M. (1977). Swallowing and the organization of sucking in the human newborn. *Child Development*, **48**, 523–531.

Burton, G., & Turvey, M.T. (1990). Perceiving the length of rods that are held but not wielded. *Ecological Psychology*, **2**, 325–366.

Bushnell, E. (1985). The decline of visually guided reaching during infancy. *Infant Behavior and Development*, **8**, 139–155.

Bushnell, E.W., & Boudreau, J.P. (1991). The development of haptic perception during infancy. In M. Heller & W. Schiff (eds.), *The psychology of touch* (pp. 139–161). Hillsdale, NJ: Erlbaum.

Bushnell, E.W., & Boudreau, J.P. (1993). Motor development and the mind: The potential role of motor abilities as a determinant of aspects of perceptual development, *Child Development*, **64**, 1005–1021.

Buss, L. (1987). *The evolution of individuality.* Princeton: Princeton University Press.

Butterworth, G., & Hicks, L. (1977). Visual proprioception and postural stability in infancy: A developmental study, *Perception*, **6**, 255–262.

Calder, W.A. (1984). *Size, function, and life history.* Cambridge, MA: Harvard Press.

Camhi, J.M. (1984). *Neuroethology: Nerve cells and the natural behavior of animals.* Sunderland, MA: Sinauer.

Campos, J.J. (1976). Heart rate: A sensitive tool for the study of emotional development. In L.P. Lipsitt (Ed.), *Developmental psychobiology: The significance of infancy* (pp. 1–34). Hillsdale, NJ: Erlbaum.

Campos, J.J., Bertenthal, B.I. & Kermoian, R. (1992). Early experience and emotional development: The emergence of wariness of heights. *Psychological Science*, **3**, 61–64.

Capute, A.J. (1979). Identifying cerebral palsy in infancy through the study of primitive reflex profiles. *Pediatric Annuals*, **8**, 34–42.

Capute, A.J., Shapiro, B.K., Accardo, P.J., Wachtel, R.C., Ross, A., & Palmer, F.B. (1982). Motor functions: Associated primitive reflex profiles. *Developmental Medicine and Child Neurology*, **24**, 662–669.

Carew, T.J., & Ghez, C. (1985). Muscles and muscle receptors. In E. Kandel & J. Schwartz (Eds.), *Principles of neural science* (pp. 443–456). New York: Elsevier.

Carmichael, L. (1970). Onset and early development of behavior. In P. Mussen (Ed.), *Carmichael's manual of child psychology* (pp. 447–563). New York: Wiley.

Casaer, P. (1979). *Postural behavior in newborn infants. Clinics in developmental medicine, No. 72.* London: Heinemann.

Cavagna, G.A., Heglund, N.C., & Taylor, C.R. (1977). Mechanical work in terrestrial locomotion: Two basic mechanisms for minimizing energy expenditure. *American Journal of Physiology,* **233**, R243–R261.

Chandler, L.S., Andrews, M.S., & Swanson, M.W. (1980). *Movement assessment of infants: A manual.* Rolling Bay, WA: Rolling Bay Press.

Changeux, J.P. (1985). Remarks on the complexity of the nervous system and its ontogenesis. In J. Mehler & R. Fox (Eds.), *Neonate cognition* (pp. 263–284). Hillsdale, NJ: Erlbaum.

Charlesworth, W.R. (1982). An ethological approach to research on facial expressions. In C.E. Izard (Ed.), *Measuring emotions in infants and children* (pp. 317–334). Cambrdige: Cambridge University Press.

Churchland, P.M. (1989). *A neurocomputational perspective.* Cambridge, MA: MIT Press.

Churchland, P.S. (1986). *Neurophilosophy: Toward a unified science of the mind/brain.* Cambridge, MA: MIT Press.

Churchland, P.S., & Sejnowski, T. (1992). *The computational brain.* Cambridge, MA: MIT Press.

Cicchetti, D., & Pogge-Hesse, P. (1980). The relation between emotion and cognition in infant development. In M. Lamb & L. Sherrod (Eds.), *Infant social cognition* (pp. 205–272). Hillsdale, NJ: Erlbaum.

Clark, J.E., & Phillips, S.J. (1987). The step cycle organization of infant walkers. *Journal of Motor Behavior,* **19**, 421–433.

Clifton, R.K., Muir, D.W., Ashmead, D.H., & Clarkson, M.G. (1993). Is visually guided reaching in early infancy a myth? *Child Development,* **64**, 1099–1110.

Coghill, G.E. (1929). *Anatomy and the problem of behavior.* Cambridge: Cambridge University Press.

Collett, T.S. & Land, M.F. (1975). Visual control of flight behavior in the hoverfly *Syritta pipiens. Journal of Comparative Physiology,* **99**, 1–66.

Condon, W., & Sander, L. (1974). Neonate movement is synchronized with adult speech: Interactional participation in language acquisition, *Science,* **183**, 99–101.

Conel, J.L. (1929). *The postnatal development of the human cerebral cortex.* Cambridge, MA: Harvard Press.

Connolly, K., & Dalgleish, M. (1989). The emergence of a tool- using skill in infancy. *Developmental Psychology,* **25**, 894–912.

Connor, F.P., Williamson, G.G., & Siepp, J.M. (1978). *Program guide for infants and toddlers with neuromotor and other developmental disabilities.* New York: Teachers College Press.

Coombs, C.H., & Smith, J.E. (1973). On the detection of structure in attitudes and developmental processes. *Psychological Review,* **80**, 337–351.

Coons, S. & Guilleminault, C. (1982). Development of sleep–wake patterns and non-rapid eye movement sleep stages during the first six months of life in normal infants. *Pediatrics,* **69**, 763–798.

Coons, S. & Guilleminault, C. (1984). Development of consolidated sleep and wakeful periods in relation to the day/night cycle in infancy. *Developmental Medicine and Child Neurology,* **26**, 169–176.

Corlett, E., & Mahaveda, K. (1970). A relationship between a freely chosen working pace and energy consumption. *Ergonomics,* **13**, 517–524.

Coryell, J.F., & Michel, G.F. (1978). How supine postural preferences of infants can contribute toward the development of handedness. *Infant Behavior and Development,* **1**, 245–257.

Cowan, W.M, Fawcett, J.W., O'Leary, D.M., & Stanfield, B.B. (1984). Regressive events in neurogenesis. *Science,* **225**, 1258–1265.

Crook, C.K. (1979). The organization and control of infant sucking. *Advances in Child Development and Behavior,* **14**, 209–253.

Crook, C.K., & Lipsitt, L.P. (1976). Neonatal nutritive sucking: Effects of taste stimulation upon sucking rhythms and heart rate. *Child Development,* **47**, 539–542.

Crowell, D.H. (1967). Motor development. In Y. Brackbill (Ed.), *Infancy and early childhood: A handbook and guide to human development.* New York: Free Press.

Curzi-Dascalova, L. (1982). Phase relationships between thoracic and abdominal respiratory movement during sleep in 31–38 weeks CA normal infants. Comparison with full-term (39–41 weeks) newborns. *Neuropediatrics,* **13**, 15–20.

Curzi-Dascalova, L., & Plassart, E. (1978). Respiratory and motor events in sleeping infants: their correlation with thoracico-abdominal respiratory relationships. *Early Human Development,* **2**, 39–50.

Cutting, J.E., & Proffitt, D.R. (1981). Gait perception as an example of how we may perceive events. In H. Pick & R. Walk (Eds.), *Perception and perceptual development,* Vol. 2 (pp. 249–273). New York: Plenum.

Darwin, C. (1958). *Autobiography 1809–1882* (N. Barlow, Ed.). New York: Norton.

Davis, W.E. (1986). Development of coordination and control in the mentally handicapped. In H. Whiting & M. Wade (Eds.), *Themes in motor development* (pp. 148–157). Dordrecht: Martinus Nijhoff.

Dean, J. (1990). The neuroethology of perception and action. In O. Neuman & W. Prinz (Eds.), *Relationships between perception and action* (pp. 81–131). Berlin: Springer-Verlag.

De Casper, A.J., & Fifer, W.P. (1980). Of human bonding: Newborns prefer their mothers' voices. *Science*, **208**, 1174–1176.

deVries, J.I., Visser, G.H., & Prechtl, H.F.R. (1982). The emergence of fetal behaviour. I. Qualitative aspects. *Early Human Development*, **7**, 301–322.

Diamond, A. (1988). Abilities and neural mechanisms underlying AB performance. *Child Development*, **59**, 523–527.

Diamond, A. (1991). Frontal lobe involvement in cognitive changes during the first year of life. In K.R. Gibson & A.C. Petersen (Eds.), *Brain maturation and cognitive development*. New York: Aldine de Gruyter.

DiFranco, D., Muir, D.W., & Dodwell, P.C. (1978). Reaching in very young infants. *Perception*, **7**, 385–392.

Dittrichova, J., Brichacek, V., Paul, K., & Tautermannova, M. (1982). The structure of infant behavior: An analysis of sleep and waking in the first months of life. In W. Hartup (Ed.), *Review of child development research*, Vol. 6 (pp. 73–100). Chicago: University of Chicago Press.

Dowd, J.M., & Tronick, E.Z. (1986). Temporal coordination of arm movements in early infancy: Do infants move in synchrony with adult speech? *Child Development*, **57**, 762–776.

Drachman, D.B., & Coulombre, A.J. (1962). Experimental clubfoot and arthrogryopsis multiplex congenita. *Lancet*, 523–526.

Dreier, T., Wolff, P.H., Cross, E.E., & Cochran, W.D. (1979). Patterns of breath intervals during non-nutritive sucking in full term and "at risk" preterm infants with normal neurological examinations. *Early Human Development*, **3**, 187–199.

Dyer, B.D., & Obar, R. (Eds.) (1985). *The origins of eukaryotic cells*. New York: Van Nostrand Reinhold.

Easter, S., Purves, D., Rakic, P., & Spitzer, N. (1985). The changing view of neural specificity. *Science*, **230**, 507–511.

Eckerman, C.O. (1993). Toddlers' achievement of coordinated action with conspecifics: A dynamic systems perspective. In L.B. Smith & E. Thelen (Eds.), *A dynamic systems approach to development: Applications* (pp. 333–357). Cambridge MA: MIT Press.

Edelman, G. (1987). *Neural Darwinism: The theory of neuronal group selection*. New York: Basic Books.

Edelman, G. (1988). *Topobiology: An introduction to molecular embryology*. New York: Basic Books.

Eishima, K. (1991). The analysis of sucking behaviour in newborn infants. *Early Human Development*, **27**, 163–173.

Effgen, S.K. (1982). Integration of the plantar grasp reflex as an indicator of ambulation potential in developmentally disabled infants. *Physical*

Therapy, **62**, 433–435.

Ekman, P., & Friesen, W.V. (1976). Measuring facial movement. *Environmental Psychology and Nonverbal Behavior*, **1**, 56–75.

Ekman, P., Friesen, W.V., & Ellsworth, P. (1972). *Emotion in the human face: Guidelines for research and an integration of findings*. Elmsford, NY: Pergamon.

Elliot, J.M., & Connolly, K.J. (1984). A classification of manipulative hand movements. *Developmental Medicine and Child Neurology*, **26**, 283–296.

Emde, R.N., & Koenig, K.(1969). Neonatal smiling and rapid eye movement states. *Journal of the American Academy of Child Psychiatry*, **11**, 177–200.

Emde, R.N., Gaensbauer, T.J., & Harmon, R.J. (1976). *Emotional expression in infancy*. Psychological Issues Monograph **37**. New York: International Universities Press.

Enoka, R.M. (1988). *Neuromechanical basis of kinesiology*. Champaign, IL: Human Kinetics.

Erenberg, A., Smith, W., Nowak, A., & Franken, E. (1986). Evaluation of sucking in the breast-fed infant by ultrasonography. *Pediatric Research*, **20**, 409a.

Eshkol, N., & Wachman, A. (1958). *Movement notation*. London: Weidenfeld & Nicolson.

Fahlman, S.E., & Labiere, C. (1990). The cascade-correlation learning architecture. In D.S. Touretzky (Ed.), *Advances in neural information processing systems*, II (pp. 524–532). San Mateo, CA: Morgan Kaufmann.

Farmer, J.D. (1990). A rosetta stone for connectionism. *Physica, D*, **42**, 153–187.

Farmer, J.D., & Belin, A. (in press). Artificial life: the coming evolution. *Proceedings in honor of Murray Gell-Mann's 60th birthday*. Cambridge: Cambridge University Press.

Fel'dman, A.G. (1986). Once more on the equilibrium-point hypothesis (λ model) for motor control. *Journal of Motor Behavior*, **18**, 17–54.

Fentress, J.C. (1984). The development of coordination. *Journal of Motor Behavior*, **16**, 99–134.

Fentress, J.C. (1989). Developmental roots of behavioral order: Systemic approaches to the examination of core developmental issues. In M.R. Gunnar & E. Thelen (Eds.), *Systems and development. The Minnesota Symposia on Child Psychology*, Vol. 22 (pp. 35–76). Hillsdale, NJ: Erlbaum.

Fentress, J.C. (1990). Animal and human models of coordination development. In C. Bard, M. Fleury & L. Hay (Eds.), *Development of eye–hand coordination across the life-span* (pp. 3–25). Columbia, SC: University of South Carolina Press.

Fentress, J.C., & McLeod, P.J. (1986). Motor patterns in development. In E. Blass (Ed.), *Developmental processes in psychobiology and neurobiology*. New York: Plenum Press.

Ferguson, C., Menn, L., & Stoel-Gammon, C.

(1992). *Phonological development: Models, research and implications.* Timonium, MD: York.

Fetters, L., & Todd, J. (1987). Quantitative assessment of infant reaching movements. *Journal of Motor Behavior,* **19**, 147–166.

Field, J., Muir, D., Pilon, R., Sinclair, M., & Dodwell, P. (1980). Infants' orientation to lateral sounds from birth to three months. *Child Development,* **51**, 295–298.

Field, T.M., Woodson, R., Greenberg, R., & Cohen, D. (1982). Discrimination and imitation of facial expression by neonates. *Science,* **218**, 179–181.

Fifer, W.P., & Moon, C. (1988). Auditory experiences in the fetus. In W.P. Smotherman & S.R. Robinson (Eds.), *Behavior of the fetus* (pp. 175–188). Caldwell, NJ:Telford.

Finkel, L.H., Reeke, G.N., Jr., & Edelman, G.M. (1988). A population approach to the neural basis of perceptual categorization. In L. Nadel, L. Cooper, & P. Culicover (Eds.), *Computational models of cognition and perception.* Cambridge, MA: MIT Press.

Fischer, K.W. (1980). A theory of cognitive development: The control and construction of hierarchies of skills. *Psychological Review,* **87**, 477–531.

Flanagan, J.R., Ostry, D.J., & Feldman, A.G. (1990). Control of human jaw and multi-joint arm movements. In G. Hammond (Ed.), *Cerebral control of speech and limb movements.* Amsterdam: Elsevier.

Fogel, A., & Hannan, T.E. (1985). Manual actions of nine-to fifteen-week-old human infants during face-to-face interaction with their mothers. *Child Development,* **56**, 1271–1279.

Fontaine, R. (1984). Initiative skills between birth and six months. *Infant Behavior and Development.* **7**, 323–333.

Forssberg, H., Stokes, V., & Hirschfeld, H. (1992). Basic mechanisms of human locomotor development. In M. Gunnar & C. Nelson (Eds.), *Developmental behavioral neuroscience. Minnesota symposia on child psychology,* Vol. 24. Hillsdale, NJ: Erlbaum.

Fowler, C., & Turvey, M.T. (1978). Skill acquisition: An event approach with special reference to searching for the optimum of a function of several variables. In G. Stelmach (Ed.), *Information processing in motor control and learning.* New York: Academic Press.

Fox, N.A., & Davidson, R.J. (1984). Hemispheric substrates of affect: A developmental model. In N.A. Fox & R.J. Davidson (Eds.), *The psychobiology of affective development* (pp. 353–381). Hillsdale, NJ:Erlbaum.

Fox, R., & McDaniel, C. (1982). The perception of biological motion by human infants. *Science,* **218**, 486–487.

Frankel, G.S., & Gunn, D.L. (1940). *The orientation of animals.* New York: Oxford University Press.

Freeman, W.J. (1991). The physiology of perception. *Scientific American,* **264**, 78–85.

Freud, S. (1905). Three essays on the theory of sexuality. In A. Strachey (Ed.), *Standard Edition,* Vol. 7 (pp. 135–243). London: Hogarth.

Gallistel, C.R. (1980). *The organization of action: A new synthesis.* Hillsdale, NJ: Erlbaum.

Garcia-Rill, E. (1986). The basal ganglia and the locomotor regions. *Brain Research Reviews,* **11**, 47–63.

Gardner, H. (1983). *Frames of mind: The theory of multiple intelligences.* New York: Basic Books.

Garfinkel, A. (1987). The slime mold *Dictyostelium* as a model of self-organization in social systems. In F. E. Yates (Ed.), *Self-organizing systems: The emergence of order* (pp. 181- 212). New York: Plenum.

Garstang, W. (1922). The theory of recapitualtion: A critical restatement of the biogenetic law. *Journal of the Linnaean Society of London, Zoology,* **35**, 81–101.

Gaudiano, P., & Grossberg, S. (1992). Adaptive vector integration to endpoint: Self-organizing neural circuits for control of planned movement trajectories. *Human Movement Science,* **11**, 141–155.

Gelfand, I., Gurfinkel, V., Fomin, S., & Tsetlin, M. (Eds.). (1971). *Models of the structural-functional organization of certain biological systems.* Cambridge, MA: MIT Press.

Geschwind, N., & Levitsky, W. (1968). Human brain: Left–right asymmetrics in temporal speech region. *Science,* **161**, 186–187.

Gesell, A. (1939). Reciprocal interweaving in neuromotor development. *Journal of Comparative Neurology,* **70**, 161–180.

Gesell, A. (1946). The ontogenesis of infant behavior. In L. Carmichael (Ed.), *Manual of child psychology* (pp. 295–331). New York: Wiley.

Gesell, A., & Ames, L. (1940). The ontogenetic organization of prone behavior in human infancy. *Journal of Genetic Psychology,* **56**, 247–263.

Gesell, A., & Ames, L.B. (1950). tonic-neck reflex and symmetro-tonic behavior. *journal of Pediatrics,* **36**, 165–178.

Gesell, A., & Ilg, F. (1937). *Feeding behavior of infants.* Philadelphia: Lippincott.

Ghez, C. (1985). Introduction to the motor systems. In E.R. Kandel & J.H. Schwartz (Eds.), *Principles of neural science* (2nd ed.) (pp. 430–441). Amsterdam: Elsevier.

Ghiselin, M. (1969). *The triumph of the Darwinian method.* Berkeley: University of California Press.

Ghiselin, M. (1981). Categories, life, and thinking. *Behavioral and Brain Sciences,* **4**, 269–313.

Gibson, E.J. (1969). *Principles of perceptual learning and development.* New York: Appleton-Century-Crofts.

Gibson, E.J. (1982). The concept of affordances in

development: The renascence of functionalism. In W.A. Collins (Ed.), *The concept of development. The Minnesota Symposia on Child Psychology* (pp. 55–81). Hillsdale, NJ:Erlbaum.

Gibson, E.J. (1988). Exploratory behavior in the development of perceiving, acting, and the acquiring of knowledge. *Annual Review of Psychology, 39*, 1–41.

Gibson, E.J. (1991). *An odyssey in learning and perception.* Cambridge, MA: MIT Press.

Gibson, E.J., & Schmuckler, M.A. (1989). Going somewhere: An ecological and experimental approach to the development of mobility. *Ecological Psychology, 1*, 3–25.

Gibson, E.J., & Walk, R.D. (1960). The "visual cliff". *Scientific American, 202*, 64–71.

Gibson, E.J., & Walker, A.S. (1984). Development of knowledge of visual-tactual affordances of substance. *Child Development, 55*, 453–460.

Gibson, E.J., Riccio, G., Schmuckler, M.A., Stoffregen, T.A., Rosenberg, D., & Taormina, J. (1987). Detection of the traversability of surfaces by crawling and walking infants. *Journal of Experimental Psychology: Human Perception and Performance, 13*, 533–544.

Gibson, J.J. (1950). *The perception of the visual world.* Boston: Houghton-Mifflin.

Gibson, J.J. (1966). *The senses considered as perceptual systems.* Boston: Houghton-Mifflin.

Gibson, J.J. (1967). The mouth as an organ for laying hold on the environment. In J.F. Bosma (Ed.), *Oral sensation and perception* (pp. 111–136). Springfield, IL: Thomas.

Gibson, J.J. (1977). The theory of affordances. In R. Shaw and J. Bransford (Eds.), *Perceiving, acting, and knowing* (pp. 67–82). Hillsdale, NJ: Erlbaum.

Gibson, J.J. (1979). *The ecological approach to visual perception.* Boston: Houghton-Mifflin.

Gilbert, S.F. (1988). *Developmental biology.* Sunderland, MA: Sinauer.

Glansdorff, P., & Prigogine, I. (1971). *Thermodynamics of structure, stability, and fluctuations.* Chichester: Wiley.

Glass, L., & Mackey, M.C. (1988). *From clocks to chaos: The rhythms of life.* Princeton: Princeton University Press.

Gleick, J. (1989). *Chaos.* New York: Penguin.

Golani, I., & Fentress, J. (1985). Early ontogeny of face grooming in mice. *Developmental Psychobiology, 18*, 529–544.

Goldberger, A.L., Rigney, D.R., & West, B.J. (1990). Chaos and fractals in human physiology. *Scientific American, February*, 43–49.

Goldfield, E.C. (1983). The ecological approach to perceiving as a foundation for understanding the development of knowing during infancy. *Developmental Review, 3*, 371–404.

Goldfield, E.C. (1989). Transition from rocking to crawling: Postural constraints on infant movement. *Developmental Psychology, 25*, 913–919.

Goldfield, E.C. (1990). Early perceptual-motor development: A dynamical systems perspective. In H. Bloch & B. Bertenthal (Eds.), *Sensorymotor organizations and development in infancy and early childhood.* Dordrecht: Kluwer.

Goldfield, E.C. (1993). Dynamic systems in development: Action systems. In E. Thelen & L. Smith (Eds.), *Dynamic systems in development: applications.* Cambridge, MA: MIT Press.

Goldfield, E.C., & Dickerson, D.J. (1981). Keeping track of locations during movement in 8 to 10-month-old infants. *Journal of Experimental Child Psychology, 32*, 48–64.

Goldfield, E.C., & Shaw, R. (1984). Affordances and infant learning: A reply to Horowitz. *Developmental Review, 4*, 126–135.

Goldfield, E.C., Kay, B., & Warren, W. (1993). Infant bouncing: The assembly and tuning of an action system. *Child Development., 64*, 1128–1142.

Goldman, M.D., Pagani, M., Trang, H.T., Praud, J.P., Sartene, R., & Gaultier, P. (1993). Asynchronous chest wall movements during non-rapid eye movement and rapid eye movement sleep in children with bronchopulmonary dysplasia. *Annual Review of Respiratory Diseases, 147*, 1175–1184.

Goldman-Rakic, P.S. (1988). Changing concepts of cortical connectivity: Parallel distributed cortical networks. In P. Rakic & W. Singer (Eds.), *Neurobiology of cortex* (pp. 177–202). New York: Wiley.

Goldman-Rakic, P.S., Isseroff, A., Schwartz, M.L., & Bugbee, N.M. (1983). The neurobiology of cognitive development. In M. Haith & J. Campos (Eds.), *Handbook of child psychology,* vol. 2 (pp. 281–344). New York: Wiley.

Golub, H.L., & Corwin, M.J. (1985). A physioacoustic model of the infant cry. In B.M. Lester & C.F. Boukydis (Eds.), *Infant crying: Theoretical and research perspectives* (pp. 59–82). New York: Plenum.

Goodkin, F. (1980). The development of mature patterns of head- eye coordination in the human infant. *Early Human Development, 4*, 373–386.

Goodwin, B.C., & Trainor, L.E. (1980). A field description of the cleavage process in embryogenesis. *Journal of Theoretical Biology, 85*, 757.

Goslow, G.E., Jr. (1985). Neural control of locomotion. In M. Hildebrand, D. Bramble, K. Liem, & D. Wake (Eds.), *Functional vertebrate morphology* (pp. 338–377). Cambridge, MA: Belknap/Harvard.

Gottlieb, G. (1981). Roles of early experience in species- specific perceptual development. In R. Aslin, J.R. Alberts, & M.R. Petersen (Eds.), *Development of perception* (Vol.1, pp. 5–44). San Diego: Academic Press.

Gottlieb, G. (1983). The psychobiological approach to developmental issues. In M. Haith & J. Campos (Eds.), *Handbook of child psychology* (pp. 1–26). New York: Wiley.

Gottlieb, G. (1987). The developmental basis of evolutionary change. *Journal of Comparative Psychology*, **101**, 262–271.

Gould, S.J. (1977). *Ontogeny and phylogeny*. Cambridge, MA: Belknap/Harvard.

Gould, S.J. (1980). Is a new and general theory of evolution emerging? *Paleobiology*, **6**, 119–130.

Gowitzke, B.A., & Milner, M. (1988). *Scientific bases of human movement* (3rd ed.). Baltimore: Williams & Wilkins.

Greene, P.H. (1982). Why is it easy to control your arms? *Journal of Motor Behavior*, **14**, 260–286.

Greenfield, P.M. (1991). Language, tools, and brain: The ontogeny and phylogeny of hierarchically organized sequential behavior. *Behavioral and Brain Sciences*, **14**, 531–551.

Greenfield, P.M., Nelson, K., & Saltzman, E. (1972). The development of rulebound strategies for manipulating seriated nesting cups: A parallel between action and grammar. *Cognitive Psychology*, **3**, 291–310.

Gregg, C.L., Haffner, M.E., & Korner, A.F. (1976). The relative efficacy of vestibular-proprioceptive stimulation and the upright position in enhancing visual pursuit in neonates. *Child Development*, **47**, 309–314.

Grillner, S. (1985). Neurobiological bases of rhythmic motor acts in vertebrates. *Science*, **228**, 143–149.

Grossberg, S., & Kuperstein, M. (1989). *Neural dynamics of sensory-motor control: Expanded edition*. Elmsford, NY: Pergamon.

Gunnar, M. (1980). Control, warning signals, and distress in infancy. *Developmental Psychology*, **16**, 281–289.

Haken, H. (1983). *Synergetics, an introduction: Non-equilibrium phase transitions and self-organization in physics, chemistry, and biology* (3rd ed.). Berlin: Springer.

Haken, H., Kelso, J.A.S., & Bunz, H. (1985). A theoretical model of phase transition in human hand movements. *Biological Cybernetics*, **51**, 347–356.

Hall, W.G. (1975). Weaning and growth of artificially reared rats. *Science*, **190**, 1313–1315.

Hall, W.G., & Oppenheim, R.W. (1987). Developmental psychobiology: Prenatal, perinatal, and early postnatal aspects of behavioral development. *Annual Review of Psychology*, **38**, 91–128.

Hall, W.G., & Williams, C.L. (1983). Sucking isn't feeding, or is it? A search for developmental continuities. *Advances in the study of behavior*, Vol. 13 (pp. 219–254). New York: Academic Press.

Halverson, H.M. (1931). An experimental study of prehension in infants by means of systematic cinema records. *Genetic Psychology Monographs*, **10**, 107–283.

Halverson, H.M. (1932). A further study of grasping. *Journal of Genetic Psychology*, **7**, 34–63.

Halverson, H.M. (1937). Studies of grasping responses of early infancy: I, II, III. *Journal of Genetic Psychology*, **51**, 371–449.

Hamburger, V., Wenger, E., & Oppenheim, R. (1966). Motility in the chick embryo in the absence of senspry input. *Journal of Experimental Zoology*, **162**, 133–160.

Hartbourne, R., Giuliani, C., & MacNeela, J. (1987). Kinematic and electromyographic analysis of the development of sitting posture in infants. *Developmental Medicine and Child Neurology*, **29**, 31–32.

Hayes, L.A., & Watson, J.S. (1981). Neonatal imitation: Fact or artifact? *Developmental Psychology*, **17**, 655–660.

Held, R., & Bauer, J.A. (1966). Visually guided reaching in infant monkeys after restricted rearing. *Science*, **155**, 718–720.

Heriza, C.B. (1988). Organization of leg movements in preterm infants. *Physical Therapy*, **68**, 1340–1346.

Heriza, C.B. (1991). Implications of a dynamical systems approach to understanding infant kicking behavior. *Physical Therapy*, **71**, 222–235.

Hildebrand, M. (1985). Walking and running. In M. Hildebrand, D.M. Bramble, K.F. Liem, & D.B. Wake (Eds.), *Functional vertebrate morphology* (pp. 38–57). Cambridge, MA: Harvard/Belknap.

Hodapp, R., & Goldfield, E.C. (1985). Self versus other regulation in the infancy period. *Developmental Review*, **5**, 274–288.

Hodapp, R., Goldfield, E.C., & Boyatzis, C. (1984). The use and effectiveness of maternal scaffolding in mother-infant games. *Child Development*, **55**, 772–781.

Hofer, M.A. (1981). *The roots of human behavior: An introduction to the psychobiology of early development*. New York: Freeman.

Hofer, M. (1988). On the nature and function of prenatal behavior. In W. Smotherman & S. Robinson (Eds.), *Behavior of the fetus* (pp. 3–18). Caldwell, NJ: Telford.

Hofsten, C. von (1980). Predictive reaching for moving objects by human infants. *Journal of Experimental Child Psychology*, **30**, 369–382.

Hofsten, C. von (1982). Eye–hand coordination in the newborn. *Developmental Psychology*, **18**, 450–461.

Hofsten, C. von, (1983). Catching skills in infancy. *Journal of Experimental Psychology: Human Perception and Performance*, **9**, 75–85.

Hofsten, C von. (1989). Motor development as the development of systems: Comments on the special section. *Developmental Psychology*, **25**, 950–953.

Hofsten, C. von (1991). Structuring of early reaching movements: A longitudinal study. *Journal of Motor Behavior*, **23**, 280–292.

Hofsten, C. von, & Lindhagen, K. (1979). Observations on the development of reaching for moving objects. *Journal of Experimental Child Psychology*, **28**, 158–173.

Hofsten, C. von, & Ronnqvist, L. (1988). Preparation for grasping an object: A developmental study. *Journal of Experimental Psychology: Human Perception and Performance*, **14**, 610–621.

Holland, J.H. (1992). Genetic algorithms. *Scientific American*, **267**, 66–73.

Hollerbach, J.M., Moore, S.P., & Atkeson, C. (1987). Workspace effect in arm movement kinematics derived by joint interpolation. In G. Gantchev, B. Dimitrov, & P. Gatev (Eds.), *Motor control* (pp. 197–208). New York: Plenum.

Holt, K.G., Hamill, J., & Andres, R. (1990). The force-driven harmonic oscillator as a model for human locomotion. *Human Movement Science*, **9**, 55–68.

Hopfield, J., & Tank, D. (1985). "Neural" computation of decisions in optimization problems. *Biological Cybernetics*, **52**, 141–152.

Hoyt, D., & Taylor, C.R. (1981). Gait and the energetics of locomotion in horses. *Nature*, **292**, 239–240.

Hurov, J.R. (1991). Rethinking primate locomotion: What can we learn from development? *Journal of Motor Behavior*, **23**, 211–218.

Huxley, A.F. (1974). Muscular contraction. *Journal of Physiology*, **243**, 1–43.

Iberall, A.S., & Soodak, H. (1987). A physics for complex systems. In F.E. Yates (Ed.), *Self-organizing systems: The emergence of order* (pp.499–520). New York: Plenum.

Izard, C.E. (1977). *Human emotions*. New York: Appleton-Century- Crofts.

Izard, C.E., & Malatesta, C.Z. (1987). Perspectives on emotional development I: Differential emotions theory of early emotional development. In J. Osofsky (Ed.), *Handbook of infant development*, Vol. 2 (pp. 494–554). New York: Wiley.

Jacob, F. (1982). *The possible and the actual*. Seattle: University of Washington Press.

Jeannerod, M. (1984). The timing of natural prehension movements. *Journal of Motor Behavior*, **16**, 235–254.

Jeka, J., & Kelso, J.A.S. (1989). The dynamic pattern approach to coordinated behavior. A tutorial review. In S.A. Wallace (Ed.), *Perspectives on the coordination of movement* (pp. 3–45). Amsterdam: Elsevier Science Publications.

Johnston, T. (1981). Contrasting approaches to a theory of learning. *Behavioral and Brain Sciences*, **4**, 125–173.

Johnston, T., & Turvey, M.T. (1980). A sketch of an ecological metatheory for theories of learning. In G. Bower (Ed.), *The psychology of learning and motivation* (pp. 147–205). New York: Academic Press.

Jordan, M.I. (1986). An introduction to linear algebra in parallel distributed processing. In D.E. Rumelhart & J.L. McClelland (Eds.), *Parallel distributed processing*, Vol. 2 (pp. 365–421). Cambridge, MA: MIT Press.

Jordan, M.I. (1989). Serial order: A parallel distributed processing approach. In J. Elman & D. Rumelhart (Eds.), *Advances in connectionist theory: Speech*. Hillsdale, NJ: Erlbaum.

Jordan, M.I. (1990). Motor learning and the degrees of freedom problem. In M. Jeannerod (Ed.), *Attention and performance XIII: Motor representation and control* (pp. 796–836). Hillsdale, NJ: Erlbaum.

Jordan, M.I., & Rosenbaum, D.A. (1989). Action. In M. Posner (Ed.), *Foundations of cognitive science* (pp. 727–767). Cambridge, MA: MIT Press.

Jordan, M.I., & Rumelhart, D. (1992). Forward models: supervised learning with a distal teacher. *Cognitive Science*, **16**, 307–354.

Jordan, D., & Smith, P. (1977). *Non-linear ordinary differential equations*. Oxford: Oxford University Press.

Jouen, F. (1984). Visual-vestibular interactions in infancy. *Infant Behavior and Development*, **7**, 135–145.

Jouen, F. (1988). Visual-proprioceptive control of posture in newborn infants. In B. Amblard, A. Berthoz, & F. Clarac (Eds.), *Posture and gait: Development, adaptation and modulation* (pp. 13–22). Amsterdam: Elsevier.

Jouen, F. (1990). Early visual-vestibular interactions and postural development. In H. Bloch & B. I. Berthenthal (Eds.), *Sensory-motor organizations and development in infancy and early childhood* (pp. 199–215). Dordrecht: Kluwer.

Jurgens, H., Peitgen, H., & Saupe, D. (1990). The language of fractals. *Scientific American*, **263**, 60–67.

Kaas, J.H. (1987). The organization of neocortex in mammals: Implications for theories of brain function. *Annual Review of Psychology*, **38**, 129–151.

Kaas, J.H. (1991). Plasticity of sensory and motor maps in adult mammals. *Annual Review of Neuroscience*, **14**, 137–167.

Kaas, J.H., Merzenich, M.M., & Killackey, H.P. (1983). The reorganization of somatosensory cortex following peripheral nerve damage in adult and developing animals. *Annual Review of Neuroscience*, **6**, 325–356. Palo Alto: Annual Reviews.

Kagan, J., Kearsley, R.B., & Zelazo, P.R. (1978). *Infancy: Its place in human development*. Cambridge, MA: Harvard University Press.

Kalaska, J.F., & Crammond, D.J. (1992). Cerebral cortical mechanisms of reaching movements. *Science*, **255**, 1517–1523.

Kamm, K., & Thelen, E. (1989). Sitting to quadruped: A developmental profile. Presented at the Society for Research in Child Development, April 1989, Kansas City.

Karch, D., Rothe, R., Jurisch, R., Heldt-Hildebrandt, R., Lubbesmeier, A., & Lemburg, P. (1982).

Behavioral changes and bioelectric brain maturation of preterm and fullterm newborn infants: a polygraphic study. *Developmental Medicine and Child Neurology*, **24**, 30–47.

Kauffman, S.A. (1989). Principles of adaptation in complex systems. In D. Stein (Ed.), *Lectures in the sciences of complexity* (pp. 619–712). New York: Addison-Wesley.

Kauffman, S.A. (1990). Requirements for evolvability in complex systems: Orderly dynamics and frozen components. In W. Zurek (Ed.), *SFI Studies in the sciences of complexity* (pp. 151–192). New York: Addison-Wesley.

Kauffman, S.A. (1991). Antichaos and adaptation. *Scientific American*, **264**, 78–84.

Kauffman, S.A. (1992). The sciences of complexity and "origins of order." In J. Mittenthal, & A. Baskin (Eds.), *Principles of organization in organisms. SFI Studies in the Sciences of Complexity* (pp. 303–319). New York: Addison-Wesley.

Kauffman, S.A. (1993). *The origins of order*. New York: Oxford University Press.

Kauffman, S.A., & Johnsen, S. (1991). Co-evolution to the edge of chaos: coupled fitness landscapes, poised states, and co-evolutionary avalanches. In C. Langton, C. Taylor, J. Farmer, & S. Rasmussen (Eds.), *Artificial life II, SFI studies in the sciences of complexity*. New York: Addison-Wesley.

Kauffman, S.A., Shymko, R., & Trabert, K. (1978). Control of sequential compartment formation if *Drosophila. Science*, **199**, 259.

Kay, B.A. (1988). The dimensionality of movement trajectories and the degrees of freedom problem: A tutorial. *Human Movement Science*, **7**, 343–364.

Kay, B.A., Kelso, J.A.S., Saltzman, E.L., & Schoner, G. (1987). Space-time behavior of single and bimanual rhythmical movements: Data and limit cycle model. *Journal of Experimental Psychology: Human Perception and Performance*, **13**, 178–192.

Kay, B.A., Saltzman, E., & Kelso, J.A.S. (1991). Steady-state and perturbed rhythmical movements: A dynamical analysis. *Journal of Experimental Psychology: Human Perception and Performance*, **17**, 183–197.

Kaye, K. (1977). Toward the origin of dialogue. In H.R. Schaffer (Ed.), *Studies in mother–infant interaction*. New York: Academic Press.

Kaye, K. (1982). *The mental and social life of babies*. Chicago: University of Chicago Press.

Kaye, K., & Wells, A.J. (1980). Mother's jiggling and the burst-pause pattern of neonatal feeding. *infant Behavior and Development*, **3**, 29–46.

Kelso, J.A.S. (1981). Contrasting perspectives on order and regulation in movement. In J. Long & A. Baddeley (Eds.), *Attention and Performance IX* (pp. 437–457). Hillsdale, NJ: Erlbaum.

Kelso, J.A.S. (1984). Phase transitions and critical behavior in human bimanual coordination.

American Journal of Physiology: Regulatory, Integrative and Comparative, **246**, R1000–R1004.

Kelso, J.A.S., & Kay, B.A. (1987). Information and control: A macroscopic analysis of perception–action coupling. In H. Heuer & A. Sanders (Eds.), *Perspectives on perception and action* (pp. 3–32). Hillsdale, NJ: Erlbaum.

Kelso, J.A.S., & Saltzman, E.L. (1982). Motor control: Which themes do we orchestrate? *The Behavioral and Brain Sciences*, **5**, 554–557.

Kelso, J.A.S., & Scholz, J.P. (1985). Cooperative phenomena in biological motion. In H. Haken (Ed.), *Synergetics of complex systems in physics, chemistry, and biology*. Berlin: Springer-Verlag.

Kelso, J.A.S., & Schoner, G.S. (1987). Toward a physical (synergetic) theory of biological coordination. *Springer Proceedings in Physics*, **19**, 224–237.

Kelso, J.A.S., & Tuller, B. (1981). Toward a theory of apractic syndromes. *Brain and Language*, **12**, 224–245.

Kelso, J.A.S., & Tuller, B. (1985). A dynamical basis for action systems. In M. Gazzaniga (Ed.), *Handbook of cognitive neuroscience*. New York: Plenum.

Kelso, J.A.S., Southard, D., & Goodman, D. (1979). On the nature of human interlimb coordination. *Science*, **203**, 1029–1031.

Kelso, J.A.S., Tuller, B., Vatikiotis-Bateson, E., & Fowler, C. (1984). Functionally specific articulatory cooperation following jaw perturbations during speech: Evidence for coordinative structures. *Journal of Experimental Psychology: Human Perception and Performance*, **10**, 812–832.

Kelso, J.A.S., Scholz, J.P., & Schoner, G. (1986). Non-equilibrium phase transitions in coordinated biological motion: Critical fluctuations. *Physics Letters A*, **118**, 279–284.

Kelso, J.A.S., Ding, M., & Schoner, G. (1992). Dynamic pattern formation: A primer. In J. Mittenthal & A. Baskin (Eds.), *The principles of organization in organisms*. New York: Addison-Wesley.

Kelso, J.A.S., Ding, M., & Schoner, G. (1993). Dynamic pattern formation: A primer. In L. Smith & E. Thelen (Eds.), *A dynamic systems approach to development* (pp. 13–50). Cambridge, MA: MIT Press.

Kent, R.D. (1992). The biology of phonological development. In C. Ferguson, L. Menn, & C. Stoel-Gammon (Eds.), *Phonological development: Models, research, implications* (pp. 65–90). Timonium, MD: York.

Kent, R.D., Mitchell, P.R., & Sancier, M. (1991). Evidence and role of rhythmic organization in early vocal development in human infants. In J. Fagard & P.H. Wolff (Eds.), *The development of timing control and temporal organization in coordinated action* (pp. 135–149). Amsterdam:

Elsevier.

Kimura, T., Okada, M., & Ishida, H. (1979). Kinesiological characteristics of primate walking: Its significance in human walking. In M. Morbeck, H. Preuschoft, & N. Gomberg (Eds.), *Environment, behavior, and morphology: Dynamic interactions in primates* (pp. 297–311). New York: Gustav Fischer.

Klinnert, M. (1984). The regulation of infant behavior by material facial expression. *Infant Behavior and Dvelopment*, 7, 447–465.

Koopmans-van Beinum, F.J., & van der Stelt, J.M. (1986). Early stages in the development of speech movements. In B. Lindblom & R. Zetterstrom (Eds.), *Precursors of early speech* (pp. 37–50). New York: Stockton Press.

Korner, A., & Thom, V. (1990). *Neurobehavioral assessment of the preterm infant.* New York: Macmillan.

Krantz, W., Gleason, K., & Caine, N. (1988). Patterned ground. *Scientific American*, **261**, 68–76.

Kron, R.E., Stein, M., & Goddard, K.E. (1966). Newborn sucking behavior affected by obstetric sedation. *Pediatrics*, **37**, 1012–1016.

Kugler, P.N., & Turvey, M.T. (1987). *Information, natural law, and the self-assembly of rhythmic movement.* Hillsdale, NJ: Erlbaum.

Kugler, P.N., & Turvey, M.T. (1988). Self-organization, flow fields, and information. *Human Movement Science*, 7, 97–129.

Kugler, P.N., Kelso, J.A.S., & Turvey, M.T. (1980). On the concept of coordinative structures as dissipative structures: I. Theoretical lines of convergence. In G. Stelmach & J. Requin (Eds.), *Tutorials in motor behavior* (pp. 3–47). Amsterdam: North-Holland.

Kugler, P.N., Kelso, J.A.S., & Turvey, M.T. (1982). On the control and coordination of naturally developing systems. In J.A.S. Kelso & J. Clark (Eds.), *The development of movement control and coordination* (pp. 5–78). New York: Wiley.

Kugler, P.N., Shaw, R.E., Vincente, K.J., & Kinsella-Shaw, J. (1989/1990). Inquiry into intentional systems I: Issues in ecological physics. Report No.30. Research Group on Mind and Brain, Perspectives in Theoretical Psychology and the Philosophy of Mind. University of Bielefeld.

Kugler, P.N., Shaw, R.E., & Kinsella-Shaw, J. (in press). The role of attractors in intentional systems. In D.S. Palermo & R.R. Hoffman (Eds.), *Cognition and the symbolic processes*, Vol. 3: *Applied and ecological perspectives.* Hillsdale, NJ: Erlbaum.

Kuhl, P.K., & Meltzoff, A.N. (1982). The bimodal perception of speech in infancy. *Science*, **218**, 1138–1141.

Kuhl, P.K., & Meltzoff, A.N. (1984). The intermodal representation of speech in infants. *Infant Behavior and Development*, 7, 361–381.

Kuhl, P.K., & Meltzoff, A.N. (1988). Speech as an intermodal object of perception. In A. Yonas (Ed.), *Perceptual development in infancy: The Minnesota Symposia on Child Psychology* (Vol. 20, pp. 235–266). Hillside, NJ: Erlbaum.

Kuperstein, M. (1988). Neural model of adaptive eye-hand coordination for single postures. *Science*, **239**, 1308–1311.

Kupfermann, I., & Weiss, K.R. (1978). The command neuron concept. *Behavioral and Brain Sciences*, **1**, 3–39.

Kuypers, H.G.M. (1962). Corticospinal connections: Postnatal development in rhesus monkey. *Science*, **138**, 678–680.

Kuypers, H.G.M. (1982). A new look at the organization of the motor system. In H. Kuypers & G. Martin (Eds.), *Process in brain research*, Vol. 57 (pp. 381–397). Amsterdam: Elsevier.

Langlois, A., Baken, R.J., & Wilder, C.N. (1980). Pre-speech respiratory behavior during the first year of life. In T. Murray & J. Murray (Eds.), *Infant communication: Cry and early speech* (pp. 56–84). Houston: College Hill Press.

Langreder, W. (1949). Über Foetalreflexe und deren intrauterine Bedeutung. *Zeitschrift Fur Geburtshilfe und Gyakologie*, **131**, 237–245.

Laskey, R.E. (1977). the effect of visual feedback of the hand on the reaching and retrieval behavior of young infants. *Child Development*, **48**, 112–117.

Lawrence, D.G., & Hopkins, D.A. (1976). The development of motor control in the rhesus monkey: Evidence concerning the role of corticomotor-neuronal connections. *Brain*, **99**, 235–254.

Lee, D.N. (1974). Visual information during locomotion. In R.B. McLeod & H.L. Pick (Eds.), *Perception: Essays in honor of James J. Gibson.* New York: Cornell University Press.

Lee, D.N. (1978). The functions of vision. In H.L. Pick & E. Saltzman (Eds.), *Modes of perceiving and processing information.* Hillsdale, NJ: Erlbaum.

Lee, D.N. (1980). The optic flow field: The foundation of vision. *Philosophical transactions of the Royal Society of London*, *B290*, 169–179.

Lee, D.N. (1990). Getting around with light or sound. In R. Warren & A. Wertheim (Eds.), *Perception and control of self- motion.* Hillsdale, NJ: Erlbaum.

Lee, D.N. & Lishman, J.R. (1975). Visual proprioceptive control of stance. *Journal of Human Movement Studies*, **1**, 87–95.

Lee, D.N., & Young, D.S. (1986). Gearing action to the environment. *Experimental Brain Research*, **15**, 217–230.

Legerstee, M., Corter, C., & Kienapple, K. (1990). Hand, arm, and facial actions of young infants to a social and nonsocial stimulus. *Child Development*, **61**, 774–784.

Lehrman, D.S., & Rosenblatt, J.S. (1971). The study of behavioral development. In H. Moltz (Ed.),

The ontogeny of vertebrate behavior. New York: Academic Press.

Lenard, H.G., von Bernuth, H., & Prechtl, H.F.R. (1968). Reflexes and their relationships to behavioral state in the newborn. *Acta Paediatrica Scandinavica*, **3**, 177–185.

Lester, B.M. (1985). Introduction: There's more to crying than meets the ear. In B.M. Lester & C.F.Z. Boukydis (Eds.), *Infant crying: Theoretical and research perspectives* (pp. 1–27). New York: Plenum.

Liberman, A.M., & Mattingly, I.M. (1989). The motor theory of speech perception revised. *Cognition*, **21**, 1–36.

Liberman, A.M., & Mattingly, I.M. (1991). A specialization for speech perception. *Science*, **243**, 489–494.

Lieberman, P. (1985). The physiology of cry and speech in relation to linguistic behavior. In B.M. Lester & C.F.Z. Boukydis (Eds.), *Infant crying: Theoretical and research perspectives* (pp. 29–57). New York: Plenum.

Liederman, J. (1983). Mechanisms underlying instability in the development of hand preference. In G. Young, S.J. Segalowitz, C.M. Corter, & S.E. Trehub (Eds.), *Manual specializations and the developing brain* (pp. 71–92). New York: Academic Press.

Liederman, J., & Kinsbourne, M. (1980). The mechanism of neonatal rightward turning bias: A sensory or motor asymmetry? *Infant Behavior and Development*, **3**, 223–238.

Lipsitt, L.P., Reilly, B.M., Butcher, M.J., & Greenwood, M.M. (1976). The stability and interrelationships of newborn sucking and heart rate. *Developmental Psychobiology*, **9**, 305–310.

Lockman, J.J., & Ashmead, D.H. (1983). Asynchronies in the development of manual behavior. In L. Lipsitt (Ed.), *Advances in infancy research* (pp. 114–36). Norwood, NJ: Ablex.

Lombardo, T. (1987). *The reciprocity of perceiver and environment: The evolution of James J. Gibson's ecological psychology.* Hillsdale, NJ: Erlbaum.

Lovejoy, C.O. (1988). Evolution of human walking. *Scientific American*, **261**, 118–125.

Luria, A.R. (1980). *Higher cortical functions in man.* New York: Basic Books.

Magnus, R. (1925). Animal posture (The Croonian Lecture). *Proceedings of the Royal Society of London*, **98**, 339–352.

Mandelbrot, B. (1982). *The fractal geometry of nature.* San Francisco: Freeman.

Margulis, L. (1981). *Symbiosis in cell evolution.* San Francisco: Freeman.

Margulis, L., & Sagan, D. (1986). *Origins of sex: Three billion years of genetic recombination.* New Haven: Yale University Press.

Marsden, C., Merton, P., & Morton, H. (1981). Human postural responses. *Brain*, **104**, 513–534.

Marsden, C., Merton, P., & Morton, H. (1983).

Rapid postural reactions to mechanical displacement of the hand in man. *Advances in Neurology*, **39**, 645–659.

Mathew, A., & Cook, M. (1990). The control of reaching movements by young infants. *Child Development*, **61**, 1238–1257.

Mayr, E. (1976). *Evolution and the diversity of life.* Cambridge: Harvard University Press.

Mayr, E. (1982). *The growth of biological thought.* Cambridge, MA: Belknap/Harvard.

McCollum, G., & Leen, T.K. (1989). Form and exploration of mechanical stability limits in erect stance. *Journal of Motor Behavior*, **21**, 225–244.

McDonnell, P.M. (1975). The development of visually guided reaching. *Perception and Psychophysics*, **18**, 181–185.

McDonnell, P.M. (1979). Patterns of eye-hand coordination in the first year of life. *Canadian Journal of Psychology*, **33**, 253–267.

McDonnell, P.M., & Corkum, V.L. (1991). The role of reflexes in the patterning of limb movements in the first six months of life. In J. Fagard & P.H. Wolff (Eds.), *The development of timing control and temporal organization in coordinated action* (pp. 151–174). Amsterdam: North-Holland.

McDowall, J. (1978). Interactional synchrony: A reappraisal. *Journal of Personality and Social Psychology*, **36**, 963–975.

McGraw, M.B. (1941a). Development of neuromuscular mechanisms as reflected in the crawling and creeping behavior of the human infant. *Journal of Genetic Psychology*, **58**, 83–11.

McGraw, M.B. (1941b). Neural maturation as exemplified in the reaching-prehensile behavior of the human infant. *Journal of Psychology*, **11**, 127–141.

McGraw, M.B. (1945). *Neuromuscular maturation of the human infant.* New York: Hafner.

McIntyre, J. (1988). Reflexes and the equilibrium point control model. *Society for Neuroscience Abstracts*, **14**, 951.

McIntyre, J., & Bizzi, E. (1992). Servo hypotheses for the biological control of movement. *Journal of Motor Behavior*, **25**, 193–202.

McKenzie, B., & Over, R. (1983). Young infants fail to imitate facial and manual gestures. *Infant Behavior and Development*, **6**, 85–95.

McMahon, T.A. (1984). *Muscles, reflexes, and locomotion.* Princeton: Princeton University Press.

Meinhardt, H. (1984). Models for pattern formation during development of higher organisms. In G. Malacinski (Ed.), *Pattern formation* (pp. 47–71). New York: Macmillan.

Meinhardt, H., & Klinger, M. (1987). A model for pattern formation on the shells of molluscs. *Journal of Theoretical Biology*, **126**, 63.

Melton, D.A. (1991). Pattern formation during animal development. *Science*, **252**, 234–241.

Meltzoff, A.N., & Borton, R.W. (1979). Intermodal matching by human neonates. *Nature*, **282**,

403–404.

Meltzoff, A.N., & Moore, M.K. (1977). Imitation of facial and manual gestures by human neonates. *Science*, **198**, 75–78.

Meltzoff, A.N., & Moore, M.K. (1989). Imitation in newborn infants: Exploring the range of gestures imitated and the underlying mechanisms. *Developmental Psychology*, **25**, 954–962.

Meltzoff, A.N., Kuhl, P., & Moore, M.K. (1991). Perception, representation, and the control of action in newborns and young infants: Toward a new synthesis. In M. Weiss & P. Zelazo (Eds.), *Newborn attention: Biological constraints and the influence of experience* (pp. 377–411). Norwood, NJ: Ablex.

Mendelson, M.J. (1979). Oculomotor activity and non-nutritive sucking are coordinated at birth. *Infant Behavior and Development*, **2**, 341–353.

Mendelson, M.J., & Haith, M.M. (1975). The relation between non- nutritive sucking and visual information processing in the human newborn. *Child Development*, **46**, 1025–1029.

Merzenich, M.M., Kaas, J.H., Wall, J.T., Nelson, R.J., Sur, M., & Felleman, D.J. (1983). Topographic reorganization of somatosensory cortical areas 3b and 1 in adult monkeys following restricted deafferentation. *Neuroscience, 8*, 33–55.

Michaels, C., & Carello, C. (1981). *Direct perception*. Englewood Cliffs, NJ: Prentice Hall.

Michel, G.F. (1981). Right-handedness: A consequence of infant supine head-orientation preference. *Science*, **212**, 685–687.

Michel, G.F. (1987). Self-generated experience and the development of lateralized neurobehavioral organization in infants. In J.S. Rosenblatt, C.G. Beer, M.C. Busnel, & P.C. Slater (Eds.), *Advances in the study of behavior*, vol 17 (pp. 61–83). New York: Academic Press.

Michel, G.F., Camras, L.A., & Sullivan, J. (1992). Infant interest expressions as coordinative motor structures. *Infant Behavior and Development*, **15**, 347–358.

Miller, D.B. (1988). Development of instinctive behavior: An epigenetic and ecological approach. In E.M. Blass (Ed.), *Handbook of behavioral neurobiology* (Vol. 9, pp. 415–444). New York: Plenum.

Mjolsness, E., Sharp, D., & Reinitz, J. (1991). A connectionist model of development. *Journal of Theoretical Biology*, **152** , 429–453.

Moltz, H. (1971). The ontogeny of maternal behavior in some selected mammalian species. In H. Moltz (Ed.), *The ontogeny of vertebrate behavior* (pp. 263–313). New York: Academic Press.

Moore-Ede, M. Sulzman, F., & Fuller, C. (1982). *The clocks that time us*. Cambridge, MA: Harvard University Press.

Morasso, P. (1981). Spatial control of arm movements. *Experimental Brain Research, 42*, 223–227.

Morgane, P.J., & Jacobs, M.S. (1972). Comparative anatomy of the cetacean nervous system. In R.J. Harrison (Ed.), *Functionalanatomy of marine mammals* (pp. 117–244). New York: Academic Press.

Mori, S., Matsuyama, K., Takakusaki, K., & Kanaya, T. (1988). The behaviour of lateral vestibular neurons during walk, trot, and gallop in acute precollicular decerebrate cats. *Progress in Brain Research*, **76**, 211–220.

Morowitz, H.J. (1978). *Foundations of bioenergetics*. New York: Academic Press.

Mounoud, P. (1973). Les conservations physiques chez le bébé. *Bulletin de Psychologie*, **27**, 722–728.

Mounoud, P., & Hauert, C. (1982). Development of sensorimotor organization in young children: Grasping and lifting objects. In G. Forman (Ed.), *Action and thought* (pp. 3–34). New York: Academic Press.

Mpitsos, G.J., Creech, H.C., Cohan, C.S., & Mendelson, M. (1988). Variability and chaos: neurointegrative principles in self-organization of motor patterns. In J.A.S. Kelso, A. Mandell, & J. Shlesinger (Eds.), *Dynamic patterns in complex systems* (pp. 162–190). Singapore: World Scientific.

Muller, S., Plesser, T., & Hess, B. (1985). The structure of the core of the spiral wave in the Belousov–Zhabotinskii reaction. *Science*, **230**, 661–663.

Murray, J.D. (1988). How the leopard gets its spots. *Scientific American*, **261**, 80–88.

Murray, J.D. (1989). *Mathematical Biology*. New York: Springer- Verlag.

Mussa-Ivaldi, F.A., & Bizzi, E. (1989). Geometrical and mechanical issues in movement planning and control. In M. Posner (Ed.), *Foundations of cognitive science* (pp. 769–792). Cambridge, MA: MIT Press.

Napier, J. (1980). *Hands*. New York: Pantheon.

Nashner, L.M., & McCollum, G. (1985). The organization of human postural movements: A formal basis and experimental synthesis. *Behavioral and Brain Sciences*, **8**, 135–172.

Nashner, L.M., & Woollacott, M. (1979). the organization of rapid postural adjustments of standing humans: An experimental-conceptual model. In R.E. Talbot & D.R. Humphrey (Eds.), *Posture and Movement*. New York: Raven.

Nelson, T.R. (1992). Biological organization and adaptation: Fractal structure and scaling similarities. In J. Mittenthal & A. Baskin (Eds.), *Principles of organization in organisms*. Boston: Addison-Wesley.

Newell, K.M., Kugler, P.N., van Emmerik, R.E., & McDonald, P.V. (1989). Search strategies and the acquisition of coordination. In S.A. Wallace (Ed.), *Perspectives on the coordination of movement* (pp. 85–122). Amsterdam: Elsevier.

Newell, K.M., Scully, D.M., McDonald, P.V., & Baillargeon, R. (1989). Task constraints and infant grip configurations. *Developmental Psy-*

chobiology, **22**, 817–832.

Newman, S.A. (1992). Generic physical mechanisms of morphogenesis and pattern formation as determinants in the evolution of multicellular organization. In J. Mittenthal & A. Baskin (Eds.), *Principles of organization in organisms* (pp. 241–267). New York: Addison-Wesley.

Nijhuis, J.G., Martin, C.B., & Prechtl, H.F.R. (1984). Behavioral states of the human fetus. In H.F.R. Prechtl (Ed.), *Continuity of neural functions from prenatal to postnatal life* (pp. 65–78). Philadelphia: Lippincott.

Nowakowski, R.S. (1987). Basic concepts of CNS development. *Child Development*, **58**, 568–595.

Ogata, K. (1970). *Modern control engineering*. Englewood Cliffs, NJ: Prentice-Hall.

Oppenheim, R.W. (1981). Ontogenetic adaptations and retrogressive processes in the development of the nervous system and behavior: A neuroembryological perspective. In K. Connolly & H. Prechtl (Eds.), *Maturation and development* (pp. 73–109). Philadelphia: Heinemann.

Oppenheim, R.W., & Haverkamp, L. (1986). Early development of behavior and the nervous system. In E.M. Blass (Ed.), *Handbook of behavioral neurobiology* (Vol. 8, pp. 1–33). New York: Plenum.

Oppenheim, R.W., Pittman, R., Gray, M., & Maderdrut, J. (1978). Embryonic behavior, hatching, and neuromuscular development in the chick following a transient reduction of spontaneous motility and sensory input by neuromuscular blocking agents. *Journal of Comparative Neurology*, **179**, 619–640.

Oster, G., & Alberch, P. (1982). Evolution and bifurcation of developmental programs. *Evolution*, **36**, 444–459.

Oster, H. (1978). Facial expressions and affect development. In M. Lewis & L. Rosenblum (Eds.), *Development of affect* (pp. 43–75). New York: Plenum.

Oster, H., & Ekman, P. (1980). Facial behavior in child development. In A. Collins (Ed.), *Minnesota symposia on child psychology* (pp. 231–276). Hillsdale, NJ Erlbaum.

Paine, R.S. (1960). Neurologic examination of infants and children. *Pediatric Clinics of North America*, **7**, 471.

Palmer, C. (1989). The discriminating nature of infants' exploratory actions. *Developmental psychology*, **25**, 885–893.

Parmelee, A.H.,Jr., Wenner, W.H., Akiyama, Y., Schultz, M., & Stern, E. (1967). Sleep states in premature infants. *Developmental Medicine and Child Neurology*, **9**, 70–77.

Paulson, G., & Gottlieb, G. (1968). Developmental reflexes: The reappearance of fetal and neonatal reflexes in aged patients. *Brain*, **91**, 37–52.

Peiper, A. (1963). *Cerebral function in infancy and childhood*. New York: Consultants Bureau

Pellionisz, A., & Llinas, R. (1979). Brain modeling by tensor network theory and computer simulation. The cerebellum: Distributed processor for predictive coordination. *Neuroscience*, **4**, 321–348.

Pellionisz, A., & Llinas, R. (1985). Tensor network theory of the metaorganization of functional geometries in the central nervous system. *Neuroscience*, **16**, 245–273.

Pennycuick, C.J. (1975). Mechanics of flight. In D.S. Farner & J.R. King (Eds.), *Avian biology* (Vol. 5, pp. 5–17). New York: Academic Press.

Perris, E., & Clifton, R. (1988). Reaching in the dark toward sound as a measure of auditory localization in infants. *Infant Behavior and Development*, **11**, 473–491.

Phillips, C. (1974). Neonatal heat loss in heated cribs vs. mothers' arms. *Child and Family*, **4**, 307–314.

Piaget, J. (1952). *The origins of intelligence in children*. New York: Norton.

Piaget, J. (1954). *The construction of reality in the child*. New York: Basic Books.

Piaget, J. (1971). *Biology and knowledge*. Chicago: University of Chicago Press.

Pick, H.L., Jr. (1989). Motor development: The control of action. *Developmental Psychology*, **25**, 867–870.

Pick, H.L., Jr. (1990). Issues in the development of mobility. In H. Bloch & B.I. Bertenthal (Eds.), *Sensory-motor organizations and development in infancy and early childhood*. Dordrecht: Kluwer.

Pick, H.L., Jr., & Saltzman, E. (Eds.). (1978). *Modes of perceiving and processing information*. Hillsdale, NJ: Erlbaum.

Prechtl, H.F.R. (1958). The directed head turning response and allied movements of the human baby. *Behaviour*, **13**, 212.

Prechtl, H.F.R. (1972). Patterns of reflex behavior related to sleep in the human infant. In C.D. Clemente, D.P. Purpura, & F.E. Meyer (Eds.), *Sleep and the maturing nervous system* (pp. 287–301). New York: Academic Press.

Prechtl, H.F.R. (1974). The behavioural states of the newborn (a review). *Brain Research*, **76**, 1304–1311.

Prechtl, H.F.R. (1977). *The neurological examination of the full- term newborn infant* (2nd ed.). Philadelphia: Lippincott.

Prechtl, H.F.R. (1981). The study of neural development as a perspective on clinical problems. In K. Connolly & H. Prechtl (Eds.), *Maturation and development: Biological and psychological perspectives. Clinics in developmental medicine. Nos. 77/78* (pp. 198–215). Philadelphia: Lippincott.

Prechtl, H.F.R., & Beintema, D.J. (1964). *The neurological examination of the full-term newborn infant. Clinics in developmental medicine, No. 12*. London: Heinemann.

Prechtl, H.F.R., & O'Brien, M.J. (1982). Behavioral states of the full-term newborn: The emergence of a concept. In P. Stratton (Ed.), *Psychobiology of the human newborn* (pp. 53–73). New York: Wiley.

Prechtl, H.F.R., Vlach, V., Lenard, H.G., & Grant, D.K. (1967). Exteroceptive and tendon reflexes in various behavioral states in the newborn infant. *Biology of the Neonate*, **11**, 159–175.

Prechtl, H.F.R., Fargel, J.W., Weinmann, H.M., & Bakker, H.H. (1979). Postures motility and respiration of low-risk preterm infants. *Developmental Medicine and Child Neurology*, **21**, 3–27.

Preyer, W. (1885). *Specielle Physiologie des Embryo*. Leipzig: Grieben.

Prigogine, I. (1980). *From being to becoming*. San Francisco: Freeman.

Prigogine, I., & Stengers, I. (1984). *Order out of chaos: Man's new dialogue with nature*. New York: Bantam.

Provine, R.R. (1988). On the uniqueness of embryos and the difference it makes. In W. Smotherman & S. Robinson (Eds.), *Behavior of the fetus* (pp. 35–46). Caldwell, NJ: Telford.

Provine, R.R., & Westerman, J.A. (1979). Crossing the midline: Limits on eye–hand behavior. *Child Development*, **50**, 437–441.

Purves, D. (1988). *Body and brain*. Cambridge, MA: Harvard Press.

Radinsky, L.B. (1987). *The evolution of vertebrate design*. Chicago: University of Chicago Press.

Raibert, M.H. (1986a). *Legged robots that balance*. Cambridge, MA: MIT Press.

Raibert, M.H. (1986b). Symmetry in running. *Science*, **231**, 1292– 1294.

Raibert, M.H., & Sutherland, I.E. (1983). Machines that walk. *Scientific American*, , 44–53.

Ralston, H.J. (1976). Energetics of human walking. In R.M. Herman, S. Grillner, P. Stein, & D. Stuart (Eds.), *Neural control of locomotion* (pp. 77–98). New York: Plenum.

Ramsay, D.S. (1979). Manual preference for tapping in infants. *Developmental Psychology*, **15**, 437–442.

Ramsay, D.S. (1984). Onset of duplicated syllable babbling and unimanual handedness in infancy: Evidence for developmental change in hemispheric specialization? *Developmental Psychology*, **21**, 64–71.

Ramsay, D.S. (1985). Fluctuations in unimanual hand preference in infants following the onset of duplicated syllable babbling. *Developmental Psychology*, **21**, 318–324.

Ray, T.S. (1992). Evolution and optimization of digital organisms. Paper presented to symposium on computational ecology, September 1992, Yale University.

Reed, E.S. (1982). An outline of a theory of action systems. *Journal of Motor Behavior*, **14**, 98–134.

Reed, E.S. (1985). An ecological approach to the evolution of behavior. In T. Johnston & A. Pietrewicz (Eds.), *Issues in the ecological study of learning* (pp. 357–383). Hillsdale, NJ: Erlbaum.

Reed, E.S. (1988a). Changing theories of postural development. In M. Woollacott & A. Shumway-Cook (Eds.), *The development of posture and gait across the lifespan* (pp.3–24). Columbia, SC:University of South Carolina Press.

Reed, E.S. (1988b). Applying the theory of action systems to the study of motor skills. In O. G. Meijer & K. Roth (Eds.), *Complex movement behavior: The motor-action controversy* (pp. 45–86). Amsterdam: Elsevier.

Reed, E.S. (1989). Neural regulation of adaptive behavior: An essay review of Neural Darwinism by Gerald M. Edelman. *Ecological Psychology*, **1**, 97–117.

Reed, E.S., & Jones, R. (1982). Introduction to Part 4. In E. Reed & R. Jones (Eds.), *Reasons for realism: Selected Essays of James J. Gibson*. Hillsdale, NJ: Erlbaum.

Reppert, S.M., & Weaver, D.R. (1988). Maternal transduction of light-dark information for the fetus. In W. P. Smotherman & S.R. Robinson (Eds.), *Behavior of the fetus* (pp. 119–139). Caldwell, NJ: Telford.

Riccio, G.E., & Stoffregen, T.A. (1988). Affordances as constraints on the control of stance. *Human Movement Science*, **7**, 265–300.

Riccio, G.E., & Stoffregen, T.A. (1991). An ecological theory of motion sickness and postural instability. *Ecological Psychology*, **3**, 195–240.

Roberton, M.A. (1982). Describing "stages" within and across motor tasks. In J.A.S. Kelso & J.E. Clark (Eds.), *The development of movement control and coordination* (pp. 293–307). New York: Wiley.

Robertson, S.S. (1988). Mechanism and function of cyclicity in spontaneous movement. In W.P. Smotherman & S.R. Robinson (Eds.), *Behavior of the fetus* (pp. 77–94). Caldwell, NJ: Telford.

Robertson, S.S., Cohen, A.H., & Mayer-Kress, G. (1993). Behavioral chaos: Beyond the metaphor. In L. Smith & E. Thelen (Eds.), *A dynamic systems approach to development* (pp. 119–150). Cambridge, MA: MIT Press.

Rochat, P. (1987). Mouthing and grasping in neonates: Evidence for early detection of what hard or soft substances afford for action. *Infant Behavior and Development*, **10**, 435–449.

Rochat, P. (1989). Object manipulation and exploration in 2 to 5-month-old infants. *Developmental Psychology*, **25**, 871–884.

Rochat, P., Blass, E.M., & Hoffmeyer, L.B. (1988). Oropharyngeal control of hand–mouth coordination in newborn infants. *Developmental Psychology*, **24**, 459–463.

Roffwarg, H.P., Muzio, J.N., & Dement, W.C. (1966). Ontogenetic development of the human sleep-dream cycle. *Science*, **152**, 604–619.

Rogoff, B. (1990). *Apprenticeship in thinking*. New York: Oxford University Press.

Rogoff, B., Ellis, S., & Gardner, W. (1984).

Adjustment of adult–child instruction according to child's age and task. *Developmental Psychology*, **20**, 193–199.

Rollinson, J., & Martin, R.D. (1981). Comparative aspects of primate locomotion with special reference to arboreal cercopithecines. *Symposium of the Zoological Society*, **48**, 377–427.

Rosen, G.D., & Galaburda, A.M. (1985). Development of language: A question of asymmetry and deviation. In J. Mehler & R. Fox (eds.), Neonate cognition. Hillsdale, NJ: Erlbaum.

Rosenbaum, D.A. (1991). *Human motor control*. San Diego: Academic Press.

Rosenblatt, J.S., & Lehrman, D.S. (1963). Maternal behavior of the laboratory rat. In H.L. Rheingold (Ed.), *Maternal behavior in mammals* (pp. 8–57). New York: Wiley.

Rosenfeld, H. (1981). Whither interactional synchrony? In K. Bloom (Ed.), *Prospective issues in infancy research* (pp. 71–97). Hillsdale, NJ: Erlbaum.

Rothbart, M.K., Taylor, S.B., & Tucker, D.M. (1989). Right-sided facial asymmetry in infant emotional expression. *Neuropsychologia*, **27**, 675–687.

Ruff, H.A. (1984). Infants' manipulative exploration of objects: Effects of age and object characteristics. *Developmental Psychology*, **20**, 9–20.

Ruff, H.A., & Halton, A. (1978). Is there directed reaching in the neonate? *Developmental Psychology*, **14**, 425–426.

Runeson, S. (1977). On the possibility of "smart" perceptual mechanisms. *Scandinavian Journal of Psychology*, **18**, 172–179.

Saint-Anne Dargassies, S. (1982). Developmental neurology from the fetus to the infant: Some French works. In W. Hartup (Ed.), *Review of Child Development Research* (pp. 45–72). Chicago: University of Chicago Press.

St. James-Roberts, I. (1979). Neurological plasticity, recovery from brain insult, and child development. In H. Reese & L. Lipsitt (Eds.), *Advances in child development and behavior* (pp. 254–319). New York: Academic Press.

Salk, L. (1962) Mother's heartbeat as an imprinting stimulus. *Transactions of the New York Academy of Sciences*, **24**, 753–763.

Saltzman, E.L. (1979). Levels of sensorimotor representation. *Journal of Mathematical Psychology*, **20**, 91–163.

Saltzman, E.L. (1992). Biomechanical and haptic factors in the temporal patterning of limb and speech activity. *Human Movement Science*, **11**, 239–251.

Saltzman, E.L., & Kelso, J.A.S. (1987). Skilled actions: A task–dynamic approach. *Psychological Review*, **94**, 84–106.

Saltzman, E.L., & Munhall, K. (1989). A dynamical approach to gestural patterning in speech production. *Ecological Psychology*, **1**, 333–382.

Saltzman, E.L., & Munhall, K. (1992). Skill acquisition and development: The roles of state-,

parameter-, and graph- dynamics. *Journal of Motor Behavior*, **24**, 49–57.

Schaap, P. (1986). Regulation of size and pattern in the cellular slime molds. *Differentiation*, **33**, 1–16.

Scherzer, A., & Tscharnuter, I. (1982). *Early diagnosis and therapy in cerebral palsy*. New York: Marcel Dekker.

Schindler, J.M. (1990). Basic developmental genetics and early embryonic development: What's all the excitement about? *Journal of NIH Research*, **2**, 49–55.

Schmidt, R.A. (1988). Motor and action perspectives on motor behavior. In O.G. Meijer & K. Roth (Eds.), *Complex movement behavior: The motor–action controversy* (pp. 3–44). Amsterdam: Elsevier.

Schmidt, R.C., & Turvey, M.T. (1989). Absolute coordination: An ecological perspective. In S.A. Wallace (Ed.), *Perspectives on the coordination of movement* (pp. 124–156). Amsterdam: Elsevier.

Schmidt, R.C., Carello, C., & Turvey, M.T. (1990). Phase transitions and critical fluctuations in the visual coordination of rhythmic movements between people. *Journal of Experimental Psychology: Human Perception and Performance*, **16**, 227–247.

Schmidt, R.C., Beek, P.J., Treffner, P.J., & Turvey, M.T. (1991). Dynamical substructure of coordinated rhythmic movements. *Journal of Experimental Psychology: Human Perception and Performance*, **17**, 635–651.

Schmidt, R.C., Treffner, P.J., Shaw, B.K., & Turvey, M.T. (1992). Dynamical aspects of learning an interlimb rhythmic movement pattern. *Journal of Motor Behavior*, **24**, 67–83.

Schneider, K., & Zernicke, R.F. (1992). Mass, center of mass, and moment of inertia estimates for infant limb segments. *Journal of Biomechanics*, **25**, 145–148.

Schneider, K., Zernicke, R., Ulrich, B., Jensen, J., & Thelen, E. (1990). Understanding movement control in infants through the analysis of limb intersegmental dynamics. *Journal of Motor Behavior*, **22**, 493–520.

Schneirla, T.C. (1959). An evolutionary and developmental theory of biphasic processes underlying approach and withdrawal. In M.R. Jones (Ed.), *Nebraska Symposium on Motivation* (Vol. 7, pp. 1–42). Lincoln: University of Nebraska Press.

Schneirla, T.C. (1965). Aspects of stimulation and organization in approach/withdrawal processes underlying vertebrate behavioral development. In D.S. Lehrman, R. Hinde, & E. Shaw (Eds.), *Advances in the Study of Behavior* (Vol. 1, pp. 1–71).

Schone, H. (1984). *Spatial orientation*. Princeton, NJ: Princeton University Press.

Schoner, G., & Kelso, J.A.S. (1988). Dynamic patterns of biological coordination: Theoretical strategy and new results. In J.A.S. Kelso, A.J. Mandell, & M.F. Shlesinger (Eds.), *Dynamic patterns in complex systems* (pp. 77–102). Singapore: World Scientific.

Schulte, F. (1974). The neurological development of the neonate. In J.A. Davis & J. Dobbing (Eds.), *Scientific foundations of pediatrics* (pp. 587–615). Philadelphia: Saunders.

Sejnowski, T. (1986). Open questions about computation in cerebral cortex. In J. McClelland, D. Rumelhart and the PDP Research group (Eds.), *Parallel distributed processing: Explorations in the microstructure of cognition* (pp. 372–389). Cambridge, MA: MIT Press.

Shaw, R.E., & Kinsella-Shaw, J. (1988). Ecological mechanics: A physical geometry for intentional constraints. *Human Movement Science*, 7, 155–200.

Shaw, R.E., & Turvey, M.T. (1981). Coalitions as models for ecosystems: A realist perspective on perceptual organization. In M. Kubovy & J. Pomerantz (Eds.), *Perceptual organization*. Hillsdale, NJ: Erlbaum.

Shaw, R.E., Turvey, M.T., & Mace, W.M. (1982). Ecological psychology: The consequence of a commitment to realism. In W. Weimer and D. Palermo (Eds.), *Cognition and the symbolic processes II*. Hillsdale, NJ: Erlbaum.

Shaw, R.E., Repperger, D.W., Kadar, E., & Sim, M. (1992). The intentional spring: A strategy for modeling systems that learn to perform intentional acts. *Journal of Motor Behavior*, 24, 3–28.

Shepherd, G., & Koch, C. (1990). Introduction to synaptic circuits. In G. Shepherd (Ed.), *The synaptic organization of the brain* (3rd Ed.) (pp. 3–31). New York: Oxford University Press.

Sheperd, G.M. (1988). *neurobiology* (2nd ed.). New York: Oxford University Press.

Sheppard, J.J., & Mysak, E.D. (1984). Ontogeny of infantile oral reflexes and emerging chewing. *Child Development*, 55, 831–843.

Sherrington, C.S. (1947). *The integrative action of the nervous system*. New Haven: Yale University Press (1st ed. 1906).

Shik, M.L., Severin, F.V., & Orlovsky, G.N. (1966). Control of walking and running by means of electrical stimulation of the mid brain. *Biofizika*, 11, 659–666.

Shipman, P., Walker, A., & Bichell, D. (1985). *The human skeleton*. Cambridge, MA: Harvard Press.

Shumway-Cook, A. (1988). Equilibrium deficits in children. In M. Woollacott & A. Shumway-Cook (Eds.), *The development of posture and gait across the lifespan* (pp.229–251). Columbia SC: University of South Carolina Press.

Shumway-Cook, A., & Woollacott, M.H. (1985a). Dynamics of postural control in the child with Down's syndrome. *Physical Therapy*, 65, 1315–1322.

Shumway-Cook, A., & Woollacott, M.H. (1985b).

The growth of stability: Postural control from a developmental perspective. *Journal of Motor Behavior*, 17, 131–147.

Simonds, R.J., & Scheibel, A.B. (1989). The postnatal development of the motor speech area. A preliminary study. *Brain and Language*, 37, 42–58.

Skarda, C.A., & Freeman, W.J. (1987). How brains make chaos in order to make sense of the world. *Behavioral and Brain Sciences*, 10, 161–195.

Smith, L., & Thelen, E. (Eds.). (1993). *A dynamic systems approach to development: Applications*. Cambridge, MA: MIT Press.

Smotherman, W.P., & Robinson, S.R. (1988). *Behavior of the fetus*. Caldwell, NJ: Telford.

Soechting, J.F., & Lacquaniti, F. (1981). Invariant characteristics of a pointing movement in man. *Journal of Neuroscience*, 1, 710–720.

Soll, D.R. (1979). timers in developmental systems. *Science*, 203, 841–849.

Solomon, H.Y., Turvey, M.T., & Burton, G. (1989). Gravitational and muscular variables in perceiving rod extent by wielding. *Ecological Psychology*, 1, 265–300.

Sommerhoff, G. (1969). The abstract characteristics of living systems. In F. Emery (Ed.), *Systems thinking*. Baltimore: Penguin.

Spitz, R. (1965). *The first year of life. A psychoanalytical study of normal and deviant development of object relations*. New York: International Universities Press.

Sporns, O., & Edelman, G.M. (1993). Solving Bernstein's problem: A proposal for the development of coordinated movement by selection. *Child Development*, 64, 960–981.

Squire, J.M. (1985). Molecular mechanisms in muscular contraction. In E. Evarts, S. Wise, & D. Bousfield (Eds.), *The motor system in neurobiology* (pp. 7–16). Amsterdam: Elsevier.

Sroufe, L.A. (1979). Socioemotional development. In J. Osofsky (Ed.), *Handbook of infant development* (pp. 462–516). New York: Wiley.

Sroufe, L.A., & Waters, E. (1976). The ontogenesis of smiling and laughter: A perspective on the organization of development in infancy. *Psychological Review*, 83, 173–189.

Stark, R.E. (1989). Temporal patterning of cry and non-cry sounds in the first eight months of life. *First Language*, 9, 107–136.

Stelmach, G., & Requin, J. (Eds.) (1980). *Tutorials in motor behavior*. Amsterdam: North-Holland.

Stent, G.S. (1987). Neural circuits for generating rhythmic movements. In F.E. Yates (Ed.), *Self-organizing systems: The emergence of order* (pp. 245–263). New York: Plenum.

Steriade, M., Jones, E., & Llinas, R. (1990). *Thalamic oscillations and signalling*. New York: Wiley.

Stern, D. (1974). Mother and infant at play: The dyadic interaction involving facial, vocal, and gaze behaviors. In M. Lewis & L. Rosenblum (Eds.), *The effect of the infant on its caregiver* (pp. 187–213). New York: Wiley.

Stern, D.N., Spieker, S., & MacKain, K. (1982). Intonation contours as signals in maternal speech to pre-linguistic infants. *Developmental Psychology*, **18**, 727–735.

Stevens, P.S. (1974). *Patterns in nature*. Boston: Little, Brown.

Stevenson, M.B., Roach, M.A., ver Hoave, J.N., & Leavitt, L.A. (1990). Rhythms in the dialogue of infant feeding: Preterm and term infants. *Infant Behavior and Development*, **13**, 51–70.

Stoffregen, T.A., & Riccio, G.E. (1988). An ecological theory of orientation and the vestibular system. *Psychological Review*, **95**, 3–14.

Stratton, P. (1982). Significance of the psychobiology of the human newborn. In P. Stratton (Ed.), *Psychobiology of the human newborn* (pp. 1–16). New York: Wiley.

Studdert-Kennedy, M. (1991). Language development from an evolutionary perspective. In N. Krasnegor, D. Rumbaugh, R. Schiefelbusch & M. Studdert-Kennedy (Eds.), *Biological and behavioral determinants of language development* (pp. 5–28). Hillsdale, NJ: Erlbaum.

Sutherland, D.H., Olshen, R., Cooper, L., & Woo, S.L. (1980). The development of mature gait. *The Journal of Bone and Joint Surgery*, **62A**, 336–353.

Swenson, R., & Turvey, M.T. (1991). Thermodynamic reasons for perception–action cycles. *Ecological Psychology*, **3**, 317–348.

Taylor, C.R., & Heglund, N.C. (1982). Energetics and mechanics of terrestrial locomotion. *Annual Review of Physiology*, **44**, 97–107.

Thatcher, R.W. (1991). Are rhythms of human cerebral development "traveling waves"? *Behavioral and Brain Sciences*, **15**, 666–678.

Thelen, E. (1983). Learning to walk is still an "old" problem: A reply to Zelazo. *Journal of Motor Behavior*, **15**, 139–161.

Thelen, E. (1989). Self-organization in developmental processes: Can systems approaches work? In M. Gunnar & E. Thelen (Eds.), *Systems and development. The Minnesota Symposia on Child Psychology* (pp. 77–117). Hillsdale, NJ: Erlbaum.

Thelen, E. (1990). Coupling perception and action in the development of skill: A dynamic approach. In H. Bloch & B. Bertenthal (Eds.), *Sensory-motor organizations and development in infancy and early childhood* (pp. 39–56). Dordrecht: Kluwer.

Thelen, E., & Fisher, D.M. (1982). Newborn stepping: An explanation for the "disappearing" reflex. *Developmental Psychology*, **18**, 760–775.

Thelen, E., & Ulrich, B. (1991). Hidden skills. *Monographs of the Society for Research in Child Development*, **56** (No. 1, Serial No. 223). Chicago: University of Chicago Press.

Thelen, E., Fisher, D., Ridley-Johnson, R., & Griffin, N. (1982). The effects of body build and arousal on newborn infant stepping. *Developmental Psychobiology*, **15**, 447–453.

Thelen, E., Fisher, D.M., & Ridley-Johnson, R. (1984). The relationship between physical growth and a newborn reflex. *Infant Behavior and Development*, **7**, 479–493.

Thelen, E., Kelso, J.A.S., & Fogel, A. (1987). Self-organizing systems and infant motor development. *Developmental Review*, **7**, 39–65.

Thelen, E., Skala, K.D., & Kelso, J.A.S. (1987). The dynamic nature of early coordination: Evidence from bilateral leg movements in young infants. *Developmental Psychology*, **23**, 179–186.

Thoman, E. (1990). Sleeping and waking states in infants: A functional perspective. *Neuroscience and Biobehavioral Views*, **14**, 93–107.

Thoman, E.B., Denenberg, V.H., Sievel, J., Zeidner, L.P., & Becker, P. (1981). State organization in neonates: Developmental inconsistency indicates risk for developmental dysfunction. *Neuropediatrics*, **12**, 45–54.

Thomas, L. (1974). *Lives of a cell*. New York: Norton.

Thompson, D.W. (1917/1942). *On growth and form*. London: Cambridge University Press.

Thompson, J.M.T., & Stewart, H.B. (1986). *Nonlinear dynamics and chaos: Geometrical methods for engineers and scientists*. New York: Wiley.

Tomita, M. (1967). A study of the movement pattern of four limbs in walking. *J. Anthrop. Soc. Nippon*, **75**, 120–146 (In Japanese).

Trevarthen, C. (1974). The psychobiology of speech development. In E. Lenneberg (Ed.), *Language and brain: Developmental aspects. Neurosciences Research Program Bulletin*, **12**, 570–585.

Trevarthen, C. (1977). Descriptive analysis of infant communicative behavior. In H.R. Schaffer (Ed.), *Studies in mother-infant interaction* (pp. 227–270). London: Academic Press.

Trevarthen, C., & Hubley, P. (1978). Secondary intersubjectivity: Confidence, confiding, and acts of meaning in the first year. In A. Lock (Ed.), *Action, gesture, and symbol: The emergence of language* (pp. 183–229). London: Academic Press.

Tronick, E.Z., Als, H., Adamson, L., Wise, S., & Brazelton, T.B. (1978). The infant's response to entrapment between contradictory messages in face-to-face interaction. *Journal of the American Academy of Child Psychiatry*, **17**, 1–13.

Tronick, E.Z., Beeghly, M., Fetters, L., & Weinberg, M.K. (1991). New methodologies for evaluating residual brain damage in infants exposed to drugs of abuse: objective methods for describing movements, facial expressions, and communicative behavior. In M.M. Kilbey & K. Asghar (Eds.), *Methodological issues in controlled studies on effects of prenatal exposure to drug abuse* (Monograph Series No. 114, pp. 262–290). Rockville, MD: National Institute on Drug

Abuse.

Truby, H.M., & Lind, J. (1965). Cry sounds of the newborn infant. In J. Lind (Ed.), *Newborn infant cry. Acta Paediatrica Scandinavica*, **163** (supp.).

Tuller, B., Turvey, M.T., & Fitch, H. (1982). The Bernstein perspective: II. The concept of muscle linkage or coordinative structure. In J.A.S. Kelso (Ed.), *Human motor behavior: An introduction* (pp. 253–270). Hillsdale, NJ: Erlbaum.

Turing, A.M. (1952). The chemical basis of morphogenesis. *Philosophical Transactions of the Royal Society of London, B237*, 37–72.

Turkewitz, G. (1977). The development of lateral differentiation in the human infant. *Annals of the New York Academy of Sciences*, **299**, 309–318.

Turkewitz, G. (1980). Mechanisms of a neonatal rightward turning bias: A reply to Liederman & Kinsbourne. *Infant Behavior and Development*, **3**, 239–244.

Turkewitz, G. (1988). A prenatal source for the development of hemispheric specialization. In D.L. Molfese & S.J. Segalowitz (Eds.), *Brain lateralization in children: Developmental implications* (pp. 73–82). New York: Guilford.

Turkewitz, G., & Kenny, P.A. (1982). Limitations on input as a basis for neural organization and perceptual development: A preliminary theoretical statement. *Developmental Psychobiology*, **15**, 357–368.

Turkewitz, G., Gordon, E.W., & Birch, H.G. (1965). Head turning in the human neonate: Effect of prandial condition and lateral preference. *Journal of Comparative and Physiological Psychology*, **59**, 189–192.

Turvey, M.T. (1977). Preliminaries to a theory of action with reference to vision. In R. Shaw & J. Bransford (Eds.), *Perceiving, acting, and knowing* (pp. 211–265). Hillsdale, NJ: Erlbaum.

Turvey, M.T. (1988). Simplicity from complexity: Archetypal action regimes and smart perceptual mechanisms as execution-driven phenomena. In J.A.S. Kelso, A.J. Mandell & M.F. Shlesinger (Eds.), *Dynamic patterns in complex systems* pp. 327–347). Singapore: World Scientific.

Turvey, M.T. (1990). Coordination. *American Psychologist*, **45**, 938–953.

Turvey, M.T., & Fitzpatrick, P. (1993). Commentary: Development of perception–action systems and general principles of pattern formation. *Child Development*, **64**, 1175–1190.

Turvey, M.T., & Shaw, R.E. (1978). The primacy of perceiving: An ecological reformulation of perception as a point of departure for understanding memory. In L.G. Nilsson (Ed.), *Perspectives on memory research: Essays in honor of Uppsala University's 500th anniversary* (pp. 167–222). Hillsdale, NJ: Erlbaum.

Turvey, M.T., Shaw, R.E., & Mace, W.M. (1978). Issues in the theory of action: Degrees of freedom, coordinative structures and coalitions. In J. Requin (Ed.), *Attention and performance VII* (pp. 557–595). Hillsdale, NJ: Erlbaum.

Turvey, M.T., Shaw, R.E., Reed, E.S., & Mace, W.M. (1981). Ecological laws of perceiving and acting: In reply to Fodor and Pylyshyn (1981). *Cognition*, **9**, 237–304.

Turvey, M.T., Fitch, H., & Tuller, B. (1982). The Bernstein perspective: I. The problems of degrees of freedom and context-conditioned variability. In J.A.S. Kelso (Ed.), *Human motor behavior: An introduction* (pp. 239–252). Hillsdale, NJ: Erlbaum.

Turvey, M.T., Rosenblum, L.D., Kugler, P.N., & Schmidt, R.C. (1986). Fluctuations and phase symmetry in coordinated rhythmic movements. *Journal of Experimental Psychology: Human Perception and Performance*, **12**, 564–583.

Turvey, M.T., Schmidt, R.C., Rosenblum, L.D., & Kugler, P.N. (1988). On the time allometry of coordinated rhythmic movements. *Journal of Theoretical Biology*, **130**, 285–325.

Turvey, M.T., Saltzman, E.L., & Schmidt, R.C. (1991). Dynamics and task specific coordinations. In N.I. Badler, B.A. Barsky, & D. Seltzer (Eds.), *Mechanics, control, and animation of articulated figures*. Cambridge, MA: MIT Press.

Twitchell, T. (1965). The automatic grasping response of infants. *Neuropsychologia*, **3**, 247–259.

Twitchell, T. (1970). Reflex mechanisms and the development of prehension. In K.J. Connolly (Ed.), *Mechanisms of motor skill development* (pp. 25–38). New York: Academic Press.

Ulrich, B.D. (1989). Development of stepping patterns in human infants: A dynamical systems perspective. *Journal of Motor Behavior*, **21**, 392–408.

Ulrich, B.D., Thelen, E., & Niles, D. (1990). Perceptual determinants of action: Stair-climbing choices of infants and toddlers. In J.E. Clark & J. Humphrey (Eds.), *Advances in Motor Development Research* (Vol. 3). New York: AMS Publishers.

Ulrich, B.D., Ulrich, D.A., & Collier, D.H. (1992). Alternating stepping patterns: Hidden abilities of 11–month-old infants with Down Syndrome. *Developmental Medicine and Child Neurology*, **34**, 233–239.

van der Pol (1926). On relaxation oscillations. *Philosophical Magazine*, **2**, 978–992.

Van Essen, D.C. (1982). Neuromuscular synapse elimination: Structural, functional, and mechanistic aspects. In N.C. Spizer (ed.), *Neuronal development*, pp. 33–371. New York: Plenum Press.

Van Vliet, M.A.T., Martin, Jr., C.B., Nijhuis, J.G., & Prechtl, H.F.R. (1985). Behavioral states in the fetuses of nulliparous women. *Early Human Development*, **12**, 121–135.

Vaughn, C.L., Davis, B.L., & O'Connor, J.C. (1991). *Dynamics of human gait*. Champaign, IL: Human Kinetics Publishers.

Vermeij, G. (1987). *Evolution and escalation. An ecological history of life.* Princeton: Princeton University Press.

Vincent, J.P., Oster, G.F., & Gerhart, J.C. (1986). Kinematics of gray crescent formation in *Xenopus* eggs: The displacement of subcortical cytoplasm relative to the egg surface. *Developmental Biology, 113,* 484–500.

Vinter, A. (1986). The role of movement in eliciting early imitations. *Child Development,* **57,** 66–71.

Vlach, V., von Bernuth, H., & Prechtl, H.F.R. (1972). State dependency of exteroceptive skin reflexes in newborn infants. *Developmental Medicine and Child Neurology,* **11,** 353–362.

Vogel, S. (1988). *Life's devices: The physical world of animals and plants.* Princeton, NJ: Princeton University Press.

von der Malsburg, C., & Singer, W. (1988). Principles of cortical network organization. In P. Rakic & W. Singer (Eds.), *Neurobiology of neocortex* (pp. 69–99). New York: Wiley.

von Holst, E. (1973). On the nature of order in the central nervous system. In R. Martin (Ed. and Trans.), *The collected papers of Erich von Holst, Vol. 1: The behavioral physiology of animals and man* (pp. 3–32). Coral Gables, FL: University of Miami Press (original work published 1937).

von Holst, E., & Mittelstaedt, H. (1973). The reafference principle. In E. von Holst, *The behavioral physiology of animals and man: Selected papers of E. von Holst,* Vol. 1. R.D. Martin, Trans. Coral Gables: University of Miami Press.

Waldrop, M. (1992). *Complexity: The emerging science at the edge of order and chaos.* New York: Simon & Schuster.

Walk, R.D., & Gibson, E.J. 91961). A comparative and analytical study of visual depth perception. *Psychological Monographs,* **75,** whole serial number 519.

Wallace, S.A., Weeks, D.L., & Kelso, J.A.S. (1990). Temporal constraints in reaching and grasping behavior. *Human Movement Science,* **9,** 69–93.

Warren, W.H., Jr. (1984). Perceiving affordances: Visual guidance of stair climbing. *Journal of Experimental Psychology: Human Perception and Performance,* **10,** 683–703.

Warren, W.H., Jr. (1988a). Action modes and laws of control for the visual guidance of action. In O.G. Meijer & K. Roth (eds.), *Complex movement behavior: The motor–action controversy* (pp. 339–380). Amsterdam: Elsevier.

Warren, W.H., Jr. (1988b). Critical behavior in perception-action systems. In J.A.S. Kelso, A.J. Mandell, & M.F. Shlesinger (Eds.), *Dynamic patterns in complex systems* (pp. 370–386). Singapore: World Scientific.

Warren, W.H., Jr. (1990). The perception–action coupling. In H. Bloch & B. Bertenthal (Eds.), *Sensory-motor organization and development in infancy and early childhood* (pp. 23–38). Dordrecht: Kluwer.

Warren, W.H., Jr., & Kay, B.A. (1995). Visual control of posture during walking: functional specificity. *Journal of Experimental Psychology: Human Perception and Performance,* in press.

Warren, W.H., Jr., Morris, M., & Kalish, M. (1988). Perception of translational heading from optical flow. *Journal of Experimental Psychology: Human Perception and Performance,* **14,** 646–660.

Watson, M.W., & Fischer, K.W. (1977). A developmental sequence of agency use in late infancy. *Child Development,* **48,** 828–835.

Weir, M. (1985). *Goal-directed behavior.* New York: Gordon & Breach.

Weiss, P. (1941). Self-differentiation of the basic patterns of coordination. *Comparative Psychology Monographs, Vol. 17.*

Wells, K.F. (1971). *Kinesiology.* Philadelphia: Saunders.

Werner, H. (1948). *Comparative psychology of mental development.* New York: International Universities Press.

West, M.J., King, A.P., & Arberg, A.A. (1988). The inheritance of niches: The role of ecological legacies in ontogeny. In E.Blass (Ed.), *Handbook of behavioral neurobiology* (Vol. 9, pp. 41–62). New York: Plenum.

White, B.L. (1969). The initial coordination of sensorimotor schemas in human infants—Piaget's ideas and the role of experience. In D. Elkind & J.H. Flavel (Eds.), *Studies in cognitive development: Essays in honor of Jean Piaget* (pp. 237–256). New York: Oxford University Press.

White, B.L., Castle, P., & Held, R. (1964). Observations on the development of visually-directed reaching. *Child Development,* **35,** 349–364.

Whiting, H.T.A. (Ed.), (1984). *Human motor actions: Bernstein reassessed.* Amsterdam: North-Holland.

Wicken, J.S. (1987). *Evolution, thermodynamics, and information.* New York: Oxford University Press.

Wigglesworth, J. (1984). Brain development and its modification by adverse influences. In F. Stanley & E. Alberman (Eds.), *The epidemiology of cerebral palsies* (pp. 12–26). Philadelphia: Lippincott.

Wilson, D.M. (1980). Insect walking. In C.R. Gallistel (Ed.), *The organization of action* (pp. 115–135). Hillsdale, NJ: Erlbaum.

Winfree, A.T. (1988). *Biological clocks.* New York: Scientific American Books.

Wing, A.M., & Kristofferson, A.B. (1973). The timing of interresponse intervals. *Perception and Psychophysics, 13,* 455–460.

Winter, D.A. (1989). Biomechanics of normal and pathological gait: Implications for understanding human locomotor control. *Journal of Motor Behavior,* **21,** 337–355.

Winter, J.A., & Goldfield, E.C. (1991). Caregiver-child interaction in the development of self: The contributions of Vygotsky, Bruner, and Kaye to Mead's theory. *Symbolic Interaction*, **14**, 433–447.

Wolff, P.H. (1959). Observations on newborn infants. *Psychosomatic Medicine*, **21**, 110–118.

Wolff, P.H. (1963). Observations on the early development of smiling. In B. Foss (Ed.), *Determinants of infant behavior, Vol. 2*, London: Methuen.

Wolff, P.H. (1966). The causes, controls, and organization of behavior in the neonate. *Psychological Issues*, **5**, 1–99.

Wolff, P.H. (1968). The serial organization of sucking in the young infant. *Pediatrics*, **42**, 943–956.

Wolff, P.H. (1969). Motor development and holotelencephaly. In R.J. Robinson (Ed.), *Brain and early development* (pp. 139–162). London: Academic Press.

Wolff, P.H. (1972). The interaction of state and non-nutritive sucking. In J.F. Bosma (Ed.), *Third symposium on oral sensation and perception* (pp. 293–310). Springfield, IL: Thomas.

Wolff, P.H. (1973). Natural history of sucking patterns in infant goats: A comparative study. *Journal of Comparative and Physiological Psychology*, **84**, 252–257.

Wolff, P.H. (1987). *The development of behavioral states and the expression of emotions in early infancy*. Chicago: University of Chicago Press.

Wolff, P.H. (1991). Endogenous motor rhythms in young infants. In J. Fagard & P. Wolff (Eds.), *The development of timing control and temporal organization in coordinated action* (pp. 119–133). Amsterdam: North Holland.

Wolff, P.H. (1993a). Endogenous rhythms in young infants. In J. Fagard & P.H. Wolff (Eds.), *The development of timing control and temporal organization in coordinated action* (pp. 119–133). Amsterdam: North-Holland.

Wolff, P.H. (1993b). Behavioral and emotional states in infancy: A dynamic perspective. In E. Thelen & L. Smith (Eds.), *Dynamic systems in development: Applications*. Cambridge, MA: MIT Press.

Wolff, P.H., & White, B. (1965). Visual pursuit and attention in young infants. *Journal of the American Academy of Child Psychiatry*, **4**, 473–484.

Wolpert, L. (1978). Pattern formation in biological development. *Scientific American*, **239**, 154–164.

Woodson, R.H. (1983). Newborn behavior and the transition to extrauterine life. *Infant Behavior and Development*, **6**, 139–144.

Woollacott, M.H. (1990). Development of postural equilibrium during sitting and standing. In H. Bloch & B.I. Bertenthal (Eds.), *Sensory-motor organizations and development in infancy and early childhood* (pp. 217–230). Amsterdam: Kluwer.

Woollacott, M., & Sveistrup, H. (1992). Changes in the sequencing and timing of muscle response coordination associated with developmental transitions in balance abilities. *Human Movement Science*, **11**, 23–36.

Woollacott, M., Debu, B., & Mowatt, M. (1987). Neuromuscular control of posture in the infant and child: Is vision dominant? *Journal of Motor Behavior*, **19**, 167–186.

Woolridge, M.W. (1975). A quantitative analysis of short-term rhythmical behaviour in rodents. Unpublished doctoral thesis, Oxford University.

Wright, P., & Crow, R. (1982). Nutrition and feeding. In P. Stratton (Ed.), *Psychobiology of the human newborn* (pp. 339–364). New York: Wiley.

Yates, F.E. (1987). General introduction. In F.E. Yates (Ed.), *Self-organizing systems* (pp. 1–14). New York: Plenum.

Young, A.W., Lock, A.J., & Service, V. (1985). Infants' hand preferences for actions and gestures. *Developmental Neuropsychology*, **1**, 17–27.

Zajonc, R.B. (1985). Emotion and facial efference: A theory reclaimed. *Science*, **228**, 15–21.

Zajonc, R.B., Murphy, S.T., & Inglehart, M. (1989). Feeling and facial efference: Implications of the vascular theory of emotion. *Psychological Review*, **96**, 395–416.

Zelazo, P.R. (1979). Reactivity to perceptual-cognitive events: Application for infant assessment. In R. Kearsley & I. Sigel (Eds.), *Infants at risk: Assessment of cognitive functioning* (pp. 49–83). Hillsdale, NJ: Erlbaum.

Zelazo, P.R. (1983). The development of walking: New findings and old assumptions. *Journal of Motor Behavior*, **15**, 99–137.

Zelazo, P.R., Zelazo, N.A., & Kolb, S. (1972). Walking in the newborn. *Science*, **177**, 1058–1059.

Zernicke, R.F., & Schneider, K. (1993). Biomechanics and developmental neuromotor control. *Child Development*, **64**, 982–1004.

AUTHOR INDEX

SUBJECT INDEX